Sunrise at Abadan

Sunrise at Abadan

The British and Soviet Invasion of Iran, 1941

Richard A. Stewart

PRAEGER

New York
Westport, Connecticut
London

Library of Congress Cataloging-in-Publication Data

Stewart, Richard A. (Richard Anthony), 1950–
    Sunrise at Abadan : the British and Soviet invasion of Iran, 1941
/ Richard A. Stewart.
    p.   cm.
    Bibliography: p.
    Includes index.
    ISBN 0–275–92793–8 (alk. paper)
    1. World War, 1939–1945—Campaigns—Iran.   2. Great Britain—
Foreign relations—Iran.   3. Soviet Union—Foreign relations—Iran.
4. Iran—Foreign relations—Great Britain.   5. Iran—Foreign
relations—Soviet Union.   6. World War, 1939–1945—Influence.
I. Title.
D766.7.I7S74   1988
940.53′55—dc19   88–9720

Library of Congress Catalog Card Number: 88–9720
ISBN: 0–275–92793–8

First published in 1988

Praeger Publishers, One Madison Avenue, New York, NY 10010
An imprint of Greenwood Publishing Group, Inc.

Printed in the United States of America

The paper used in this book complies with the Permanent
Paper Standard issued by the National Information Standards
Organization (Z39.48—1984).

P

In order to keep this title in print and available to the academic community, this edition
was produced using digital reprint technology in a relatively short print run. This would
not have been attainable using traditional methods. Although the cover has been changed
from its original appearance, the text remains the same and all materials and methods
used still conform to the highest book-making standards.

Contents

Illustrations

PHOTOGRAPHS—*following page 218*

Abadan Refinery, Iran, from over the Shatt-al-Arab River

Rajputanas March into Abadan Refinery Following Its Capture

Axis Merchantman on Fire, Sunrise, August 25, 1941

Gen. A. P. Wavell, Commander in Chief, India, and Lt. Gen. E.
P. Quinan, General Officer Commanding, Iraq

Iranian Sloop *Babr* after Being Shelled by HMAS *Yarra*

Major Abdullah Massoud of Iranian Cavalry Discusses Cease-fire
Terms with British Officers

Iranian Troops near Zibiri Following Cease-fire

British Forces Enter Kermanshah, August 30, 1941

British and Soviet Forces Meet South of Kazvin, August 31,
1941

Maj. Gen. William Slim, Maj. Gen. Vasily Novikov, and Brig.
James Aizelwood at Banquet in Kazvin

Crown Prince Mohammed Reza Pahlavi at His Coronation
Ceremony, September 17, 1941

Preface and Acknowledgments

The incidents depicted in this book are all true and fully documented. In conducting the research, I relied on primary sources wherever it was possible to include archival data, interviews, firsthand accounts, diaries, and official histories. Although certain incidents required detailed footnoting, I have consolidated the sources where feasible. In the Notes chapter at the back of the book, sources are cited with full bibliographic reference only once. For subsequent citations of a source, the reader may find it convenient to cross-reference with the Bibliography.

Many people and institutions assisted in the preparation of this book. Foremost, I thank my wife Cora, without whose constant support this work would not have been possible. Secondly, I express particular appreciation to Mr. Hassan Soburi's invaluable translation efforts and his useful insight into Iranian culture.

I also wish to recognize the translation efforts of the following individuals: Mr. Roy Pinto, Mr. Terry Thompson, and Mr. Al Graham (Russian); Mrs. Nina Blodgett (French); and Mrs. Elizabeth Hudry (German). I thank the research assistance provided by the following institutions: U.S. National Archives (Mr. John Taylor); British Public Records Office; Library of Congress (Mr. Al Graham and Mr. Ibrahim Poorhadi); Imperial War Museum; British National Army Museum (Miss E. Talbot Rice); Hoover Institution, Stanford University; British Petroleum Company (Dr. R. W. Ferrier); Pentagon Library; U.S. Naval Academy Library; and Georgetown University Library.

The following individuals deserve recognition for providing assistance to the author: Gen. Sir Ouvry L. Roberts, Brig. Gen. P. R. MacNamara, Brig. Gen. Patrick M. Kent, Mr. Hassan Hatefi, Mr. Mansur Hatefi, Rev. William M. Miller, Rev. Hugo Muller and his son Dr. Joseph P. Cochrane, Col. J. M. Forster, Col. R. C. Jackman, Maj. Gerald H. van Loo, Maj. J. B.

Oliphant, Lt. Col. A. T. B. Craig, Col. C. P. A. Joynes, Col. P. B. Winstanley, Lt. Col. R. M. Maxwell, Lt. Col. V. O. F. Wildish, Lt. Col. T. M. Lowe, Mr. Basil Chambers, Mr. Fatola Samiy, Mr. Malcolm Karam, Dr. Wilson Lazar, Mr. Edwin Wright, Dr. Danesh Foroughi, Capt. P. B. Arthur, Maj. Anthony Beyts, Maj. H. N. Clemas, Mr. Mustaffah Biazar, Mr. Mohammed Vasiri, Maj. Peter J. Baldwin, USMC, Col. Gerald H. Turley, USMC (Ret.), and Lt. Col. Brendan M. Greeley, USMC (Ret.)

I also acknowledge the copyright stipulations granted by the U.K. Public Records Office to quote material from their archives.

Sunrise at Abadan

Introduction

The great importance of the Caucasus to the Revolution is not to be seen in its being a source of raw materials, fuels, and food, but rather its position between Europe and Asia, and especially between Russia and Turkey and the strategic crossroads which pass through it. The Entente is aware of this too. And since it today controls Constantinople, which is the key to the Black Sea, it also would like to secure the direct passage towards the East via Transcaucasia. In the final analysis, that is what it is all about: who will own the oil fields and the most important roads leading to the interior of Asia? The Entente or the Revolution?

JOSEPH STALIN
Pravda, November 30, 1920

As the first glimmer of dawn lit the misty horizon on the morning of August 25, 1941, the HMS *Shoreham* trained her forward gun battery on the Iranian warship *Palang,* which was moored peacefully at an Abadan pier. A moment later, a shell slammed into the *Palang,* the explosion engulfing the vessel in a ball of fire and smoke. As the listing warship settled into the river mud, British and Soviet armies stormed across Iran's borders—commencing perhaps the most dramatic and controversial untold episode of World War II.

Attacked without provocation, Iran suffered her own "Pearl Harbor" three months prior to the United States' more famous Day of Infamy. Before the incident ended, Iran's army was crushed, her monarch was overthrown, the beleaguered Red Army was saved from defeat, a German conquest of the Persian Gulf oil fields was thwarted, and the conditions were created for the opening showdown of the Cold War.

Sunrise at Abadan is intended as a scholarly rendition and analysis of these events and the attendant moral issues. In addition, the compelling political

1

and human drama of this episode requires some portrayal to understand its moral significance.

Few incidents of World War II relate more directly to the current crisis in the Persian Gulf region than those described in this book. *Sunrise at Abadan* explains how—more by accident than design—the Anglo–Soviet invasion drew the United States deeply and inextricably into the affairs of Iran. For those familiar with the dramatic events affecting Iran and the two super-powers in 1979–80—in particular, the popular Islamic revolution that over-threw the shah, and the resulting strategic instability that drew the United States and the Soviet Union near the point of military confrontation—the events detailed in *Sunrise at Abadan* will seem strikingly similar. For it portrays the overthrow by virtual revolution of an unpopular shah, the strategic standoff between the Soviet Union and Britain over Iran, and the attempts by a prominent and fanatic Moslem holy leader—the Grand Mufti of Jerusalem—to fan religious revolution throughout the Middle East.

But aside from these interesting parallels, the events portrayed in *Sunrise at Abadan* are vital because they raise an inevitable legal and moral question. Under what conditions can pressing strategic requirements justify un-provoked military aggression against a neutral state? To Soviet dictator Joseph Stalin such "bourgeois" moral issues were irrelevant. In pursuit of "socialist revolution," he observed international convention when it suited his purpose. Otherwise, a suitable legal pretext could always be manufac-tured to justify Soviet aggression. But to British Prime Minister Winston Chruchill, the legal and moral questions surrounding Britain's actions against Iran could not be so easily evaded. "I was not without anxiety about embarking on a Persian war," he admitted in his memoirs, "but the argu-ments for it were compulsive."[1]

Churchill viewed the issue as a simple choice: thwarting Nazi world conquest versus scrupulously observing international convention. When confronted with an identical dilemma in respect to the necessity of military action against neutral Norway in late 1939, Churchill (then first lord of the Admiralty) argued for strategic necessity over respect for neutrality. No action was taken against Norway, but his eloquent and persuasive argu-ments were later applied to the case of Iran.[2]

The prime minister knew that he would require at least the tacit approval of President Franklin D. Roosevelt before attacking Iran. Roosevelt could have invoked U.S. moral authority and economic power to avert the Allied invasion. But instead, his administration stood by passively, brushing aside desperate Iranian pleas until it was too late. Moreover, Roosevelt even secretly approved the plans against Iran—only to later publicly deny any knowledge of British intentions.

In the end, though, we must consider what might have happened had Britain and the Soviet Union not occupied Iran. Germany might have triumphed over the depleted Red Army, secured the vital Persian Gulf oil fields, outflanked the British position in North Africa, and linked up with the Japanese in India. The result for the Allies would have been disastrous.

"No final answer can be given to the question whether the invasion of Persia was justified," wrote the former British ambassador to Iran, Sir Reader W. Bullard, in his memoirs.[3] The complexities of the issues surrounding the episode make a final conclusion elusively perplexing. "Of all this history must be the judge," wrote Sir Winston Churchill, who believed that "the final tribunal is our own conscience."

> The effect of our action . . . upon world opinion and upon our own reputation must be considered. We have taken up arms in accordance with the principles of the Covenant of the League [of Nations] in order to aid victims of German aggression. No technical infringement of international law, so long as it is unaccompanied by inhumanity of any kind, can deprive us of the good wishes of neutral countries. No evil effect will be produced upon the greatest of all neutrals, the United States. We have reason to believe that they will handle the matter in the way most calculated to help us. And they are very resourceful.
>
> The final tribunal is our own conscience. We are fighting to reestablish the reign of law and to protect the liberties of small countries. Our defeat would mean an age of barbaric violence, and would be fatal, not only to ourselves, but to the independent life of every small country in Europe. Acting in the name of the Covenant, and as virtual mandatories of the League and all it stands for, we have a right, and indeed are bound in duty, to abrogate for a space some of the conventions of the very laws we seek to consolidate and reaffirm. Small nations must not tie our hands when we are fighting for their rights and freedom. The letter of the law must not in supreme emergency obstruct those who are charged with its protection and enforcement. It would not be right or rational that the aggressor Power should gain one set of advantages by tearing up all laws, and another set by sheltering behind the innate respect for law of its opponents. Humanity, rather than legality, must be our guide. Of all this history must be the judge. We now face events.[4]

1

Game for the Domination of the World

It should be a cardinal axiom of British policy that Her Majesty's Government will not acquiesce in any European power, and more especially Russia, overrunning Central and Southern Persia and so reaching the [Persian] Gulf, or acquiring naval facilities in the latter even without such territorial connections.

LORD GEORGE CURZON
Viceroy of India
Despatch to Colonial Office, 1899

For most of a century, Britain and Russia vigorously competed for control of Iran, the Persian Gulf, and ultimately India. Poet Rudyard Kipling dubbed their rivalry "The Great Game." Lord George Curzon more soberly described Persia (Iran), Central Asia, and Afghanistan as "the pieces of a chessboard upon which is being played out a game for the domination of the world."[1]

The stage for this game was set late in the eighteenth century when Imperial Russia began expanding southward, in search of a warm-water port, while the British Empire simultaneously advanced into the Persian Gulf. The long struggle reached its climax when the British and the Soviets jointly invaded Iran in 1941. During the period in between, a major conflict between the two powers was prevented only by the geographic buffer of Afghanistan and Iran (Persia).

The indomitable Afghans sustained their sovereignty by ferociously defeating foreign armies foolish enough to venture into their formidable mountain redoubts. But the more placid (if tempestuous) Persians were different. Their land—though mountainous and arid—was more accessible and bountiful than that of their Afghan neighbors. Persia was a land of extremes and stark contrasts, both physical and cultural. Forested moun-

Map 1.1
1907 Division of Persia

tains bordered bleak plateaus. Dazzling mosques and palaces abutted wretched hovels. The Persians were a people whose life was expressed in superlatives.

The once powerful Persian Empire had long since crumbled under succeeding waves of Arab, Mongol, and Tartar conquerors. What survived the ravages evinced but a pathetic image of Persia's former grandeur. Receding into a dark age, Persia was further smothered by a regressive religious creed—Shia Islam—and suppressed by a succession of weak and unenlightened monarchs. Sequestered in Tehran, the facile shahs professed sovereignty over disparate rebellious tribes.

Weakness invited invasion. In the early 1700s, Peter the Great dispatched an officer to search for an outlet to the warm waters of the Indian Ocean. Learning of the disorder in Persia—ruled, at the time, by the weak Qajar dynasty—the tsar dispatched an army in 1722 to conquer the territories to the south. His expedition occupied northern Persia, including the shores of the Caspian Sea. But his gains were forfeited by his successors after his death. A similar situation occurred 74 years later when Catherine the Great sent an army to conquer Persia. In 1796, in the midst of the campaign, the empress died and her son Paul abandoned the venture.[2]

Great Britain meanwhile established a presence in the Persian Gulf, where the East India Company had conducted trade for many years. In 1898, Britain—fearing that Napoleon's army in Egypt might threaten India through the Persian Gulf—concluded an agreement with Persia, offering arms and aid to the shah in return for support against a possible French appearance. Though the threat from Napoleon soon receded, the British were now active in the Persian court.

In the early 1800s, Russian armies advanced southward again, defeating the Persians and conquering the Caucasus. In 1828, Russia concluded the Treaty of Turkomanchai with Persia, establishing the current northwestern borders and granting to Russia naval control of the Caspian Sea. Russia continued to press into Cental Asia, where no definite boundries existed. A circular disseminated to Russia's embassies throughout Europe in 1864 announced her intentions to expand into and pacify the various tribal regions of Central Asia.

This development alarmed the British, who feared that Russian expansion into Persia and Afghanistan would threaten India. Foreign Secretary Lord John Russell sought a formal agreement with the tsar in order to stabilize the existing frontiers and ensure that "both Powers would respect the independence of the Persian monarchy; would be careful not to encroach on the territory of Persia; and would act in concert to support and strengthen the authority of the Shah."[3] In response, Moscow assured London that its actions in Central Asia were apart from its correct relations with Persia.

The following year—1865—Russian armies stormed Tashkent and approached the Afghan frontier. Russian troops also advanced along the shores of the Caspian Sea. In 1869, they reached the Atrek River which the Russian and Persian governments agreed to establish as a boundry.

Over the next several years, Russia nibbled away at Persian territory in Central Asia. The British, who had extensive commercial interests in the Persian Gulf, became increasingly worried by the steady Russian advance. "We should immediately oppose further encroachment on Persian territory," Britain's commander in chief in India, Napier of Magdala, urged in 1875. He contended that

> By increasing our diplomatic influence in Persia, we shall best be able to prevent that country from giving Russia cause for aggression, but should they be driven to war, the people of Persia, supported by a British contingent and aided by British arms, supplies, and officers, would render the task of conquering the country as

difficult and exhaustive as the conquest of the Spanish peninsula was to France.[4]

British officials were divided over the best course of action—most favoring diplomatic over military measures. A series of formal protests and complaints over various Russian actions followed. The irresolution of Britain's policy during this period permitted Imperial Russia to consolidate its holdings up to the present northwestern boundries with Iran and to gain ascendancy in the Persian court.

In 1878, Shah Nasir Al-Din paid a state visit to Tsar Alexander II in Moscow, where he was deeply impressed by the military bearing and prowess of the Tsar's Imperial Cossack Guard regiment. The tsar generously offered to form such a regiment in Persia for the shah. Nasir Al-Din accepted; and, in 1885, the Persian Cossacks were established in Tehran under the command of Russian officers. The Persian Cossack Division expanded rapidly and soon became the best armed, equipped, and disciplined unit in the Persian Army. Russian command of this unit enhanced that country's influence over Persian affairs.[5]

British interest in Persia heightened with the discovery of oil near the Persian Gulf. An Australian, William Knox D'Arcy, obtained a 60-year oil lease from the reigning shah of Persia in 1901. In 1907, D'Arcy's exploration company struck its first geyser near Masjid-i-Suleiman in Persia's Khuzistan province.

The timing of this strike proved fortuitous for the British. The Royal Navy had just begun converting its fleet from coal- to oil-burning ships, and the British had no oil reserves of their own. They could obtain oil from U.S. or Dutch sources, but only at premium prices. Therefore, at the behest of the Admiralty, the Burma Oil Company obtained the rights to the D'Arcy concession, and formed the Anglo-Persian Oil Company (APOC) in 1909. To ensure a dependable supply of cheap oil for the Royal Navy, His Majesty's government purchased a controlling interest in the APOC in 1914. Meanwhile, the oil fields at Masjid-i-Suleiman were connected by pipeline to the island of Abadan, on the Shatt-al-Arab River, where construction of a large refinery was begun.

The British were anxious to settle their differences with Russia over Persia. In 1907, the two governments concluded the Convention of St. Petersburg, which divided Persia into Russian and British spheres of influence. The Russian sphere included most of northern and central Iran, while the British sector encompassed the southeastern region, with a neutral zone in between.[6]

When World War I broke out in 1914, Britain and Russia jointly occupied Persia—Russia in the north, and Britain in the south. Russian and Turkish armies fought for control of northwestern Persia. The war brought famine, killing millions of Persians.[7]

Anglo–Russian collaboration during the war might have ended their long rivalry but for Russia's collapse in 1917. The tsar's armies in Persia disintegrated and fled northward. Small British forces briefly filled the vacuum left by the Russians. Suddenly dominating Persia, the British government in 1919 forced a treaty on the shah, giving Britain virtual control of the Persian government.

The unpopular accord was still unratified by the nationalistic Persian parliament—the Majlis—when Bolshevik forces pursuing remnants of the White Russian Army landed in the coastal province of Gilan on the Caspian Sea in 1920. The Red forces allied themselves with local rebels, and declared the Soviet Republic of Gilan. The Persian government (backed by the British) dispatched the Persian Cossacks to drive out the Bolsheviks. The Bolsheviks and their Gilani rebel allies routed the Persian expedition. The Persians—feeling betrayed—immediately dismissed their White Russian officers.

Command of the Persian Cossacks was given to an ambitious and nationalistic colonel named Reza Khan. Once just a private soldier, Reza Khan had risen steadily through the ranks by displaying exceptional courage and leadership in various tribal campaigns. Standing more than six feet tall, he towered over most of his countrymen. A bulbous nose protruded from between two piercing, almost hypnotic eyes. Rigid, disciplined, and possessing strong military bearing, he was no ordinary individual. Though poorly educated and practically illiterate, he had grown bitter watching the misery inflicted on his country by foreign powers and a corrupt, regressive government. Conspiring with Persian dissident intellectuals—principally, the journalist Sayyid Zia al-Din Tabatabai—he plotted a coup d'etat.

On the morning of February 21, 1921, Col. Reza Khan marched his troops into Tehran and overthrew the moribund government. The new government—headed by Sayyid Zia al-Din, with Reza Khan as minister of war—renounced the pending treaty with Britain, and concluded a separate treaty with the Soviet Union. Article 6 of the new treaty reserved the right for the Soviet government to intervene militarily in Persia, should Soviet territory be threatened by a third power on Persian soil. But the U.S.S.R. assured the Persians that this clause applied only to White Russian forces.[8]

British and Soviet troops withdrew from Persia, leaving Reza Khan free to consolidate power. Expanding the army, he vigorously crushed the rebellious mountain tribes, and brought all regions under central authority. Restoring security and national pride, his prestige soared. He ousted Seyyid Zia al-Din and became prime minister. In 1923, the last Qajar ruler—Ahmad Shah—left for exile in Europe. Riding a wave of popular support (particularly among the wealthy and influential classes), Reza Khan established a new dynasty, crowning himself shah-in-shah (king of kings) on April 25, 1926, and adopting the surname of Pahlavi.[9]

His overriding goal was to rid Persia of foreign domination through a rapid program of modernization and industrialization. To this end, he imposed iron discipline on his people. Assuming absolute power, he turned the Majlis into a virtual rubber-stamp organ for his decrees. He intimidated his officials, and dealt mercilessly with Persia's corrupt and lethargic bureaucracy.

To modernize Persia, he expanded education, created Tehran University, ordered citizens to adopt European clothing, banned the veil, and established a European-style justice system—stripping the powerful mullahs of their traditional judicial authority. Religious opposition reached a peak in 1935 during riots in the holy city of Meshed. The shah's army brutally crushed the religious demonstrators, effectively quelling religious dissent.

In the early 1920s, Reza Pahlavi imported a team of U.S. financial experts headed by Dr. Arthur C. Millspaugh to reorganize Persia's notoriously inefficient and corrupt financial system. The Persian leader aimed to place Persia's finances on a sound footing—thereby attracting U.S. investment and industry, and avoiding economic dependence on Britain and the Soviet Union. Millspaugh and his team initially enjoyed considerable success in organizing tax collections and increasing state revenues. They helped to create the Persian National Bank, and solicited U.S. interest in Persian oil exploration. At Millspaugh's urging, U.S. engineers were hired to survey the route and to commence construction of the shah's greatest undertaking—the trans-Iranian railroad. Americans also were imported to supervise highway construction and maintenance, to advise on agriculture, and to assist with the rug and tourist industries.[10]

But the shah soon grew disillusioned with the Americans, and Millspaugh's efforts at reform met opposition from the powerful and wealthy. His attempts to control financial corruption within the Persian Army particularly irritated Reza Pahlavi, who personally benefited from the graft of local military commanders. Millspaugh's constant demands for greater authority further annoyed the monarch. "There can't be two shahs in this country and I am going to be THE shah," Reza Pahlavi declared.[11] The Millspaugh mission also failed to attract the U.S. capital investment that the shah had wanted. The Sinclair Oil Company did obtain an oil concession in northern Persia in the early 1920s; but, shortly after beginning exploration, the Americans encountered so many difficulties from the Persians, the Russians, and the British that they unilaterally canceled the concession. Millspaugh, who found himself increasingly undercut by the shah, resigned in 1927. The other Americans followed as their contracts expired. From then until the eve of World War II, Iran's relations with the United States remained slight, and were even broken for two years following a minor diplomatic incident involving the arrest of the Iranian minister in Washington for drunken driving.[12]

With the departure of the Americans, the shah still needed the help of a modern industrial power to achieve his goals. Gradually, he turned to Germany. German financial advisors had been working in Persia as early as

1925. In 1928, the Persian government granted Junkers Airline a concession for air service within Persia. The next year, Persia concluded a most-favored-nation treaty with Germany. In 1930, Dr. Kurt Jungblatt, a German, was appointed director of the Persian National Bank.[13]

After Adolph Hitler ascended to power Germany in 1933, trade between the two countries rose dramatically. In 1935, Hitler's economic minister, Dr. Hjalmar Schacht, arrived in Tehran, where he negotiated a major trade agreement. In exchange for Persian exports of cotton, wood, barley, rice, leather, rugs, dried goods, caviar, silver, and gold, Germany supplied industrial equipment, various machinery, and motor vehicles. Hundreds of German technicians, advisors, teachers, professors, and merchants poured into Persia, where they filled key positions in government ministries and industries—including finance, mining, agriculture, medicine, and communications. German-built factories required technicians to maintain the equipment. The government radio station in Tehran, for example, was built and maintained by Telefunken. German managers ran ports, telephone exchanges, telegraph stations, hydroelectric plants, and railway stations. German professors taught in Tehran University, and headed the colleges of Agriculture and Veterinary Medicine.

German engineers took over construction of the trans-Iranian railway. A marvel of engineering—with 2,100 bridges and 224 tunnels—the 900-mile railroad stretched from Bander-i Shahpur on the Persian Gulf to Mianeh below the Soviet border. Its completion facilitated the flow of goods between the two countries.

Nazi propaganda played heavily on the alleged Aryan origins of the two peoples. Capitalizing on the sudden popularity of the term, the shah decreed in 1936 that henceforth all foreign nations would refer to his nation as "Iran"—a native term meaning "home of the Aryans." Nazi-donated books filled the Tehran library. When the leader of the Hitler Youth, Baldur Von Shirach, visited Tehran in December of 1937, an eager minister of education arranged an audience with the shah. The nazi envoy behaved so rudely, however, that the monarch cut the meeting short, and then tongue-lashed the hapless education minister for arranging the audience.[14] Though many of his subjects were impressed by German efficiency and Nazi ideology, Reza Pahlavi remained a nationalist, viewing Germany as just another foreign power.

The shah's accomplishments, however, cost him his popularity. His subjects chafed at his corrupt and heavy-handed rule. Dr. Millspaugh believed that "had it not been for the beginnings of large-scale looting by Reza Khan [Pahlavi] and his Army, popular confidence in the government, indispensable to national unity, might have been gradually created in the minds of the people."[15]

The shah's secret police inspired terror. Dissidents and opponents were imprisoned or forced into exile. Even those officials who were closest to him lived in mortal fear of his wrath. The ruler became increasingly remote from his people, surrounding himself with a coterie of syncophants who catered to his whims while cautiously hiding unpleasant truths.

He maintained power through his coveted military, which he indulged with a major portion of the nation's revenues and whose local excesses he conveniently ignored. In 1925, conscription was instituted, when the army numbered 40,000. By 1941, the army had swelled to 126,000, including 14 divisions and five independent brigades. Modern arms and tanks were provided by the Czech firm, Skoda. A mechanized brigade of tanks, armored cars, and heavy artillery was based in Tehran. An air force of 200 obsolete British biplanes—mostly Hinds and Audaxes—was created, along with a small navy of Italian-built sloops and gunboats for patrolling the Persian Gulf.[16]

The average conscript was an illiterate peasant youth from a rural village. His living conditions were harsh; his pay, miserably low; and his officers, often brutal in maintaining discipline. Nevertheless, most soldiers served the shah loyally.

Despite his own military background, the shah knew very little about modern warfare. His army therefore lacked the training, logistics, and transport required for sustained operations. To train his officer corps, he sent many officers to schools abroad, and imported a French military mission to instruct at the Iranian military academy. Although French instruction was immensely popular, the monarch dismissed the French mission in 1939 following a political dispute with France. The French advisors were told—rather pompously—that the Iranian Army no longer required advice on military matters.[17]

By this time, war clouds were gathering over Europe. The shah was determined to remain clear of any European conflict. But he remained dependent on the European powers to support his military. Although the shah operated his own machine-gun factory in Tehran, he remained dependent on Nazi Germany—which had annexed Czechoslovakia in 1937, and thereby acquired the Skoda firm—for many of his arms and munitions. He also relied on the Italians to maintain his navy and on the British to support his air force.

The shah hoped ultimately to strengthen Iran sufficiently to be free of foreign dependency. But by the late 1930s, he realized that this hope was far from being achieved. When President Franklin Roosevelt politely sought to reestablish U.S. relations with Iran in October 1938, the shah eagerly accepted.[18] Not only did Reza Pahlavi personally admire Roosevelt, but the looming likelihood of war in Europe meant that the shah must prepare to obtain support from outside Europe.

In modernizing his country, the shah had enjoyed two decades of relative peace and freedom from foreign pressure. Great Britain had been preoccupied with affairs in Europe, troubles in its colonies, and its own ailing economy. Britain's Ango-Iranian Oil Company (AIOC) was even pressured by the shah—through the League of Nations—into paying higher royalties to the Iranian government. Neither had the Soviet Union caused much trouble. Joseph Stalin devoted most of this period to consolidating his grip on power and to modernizing Soviet industry.

But Anglo–Soviet relations with Iran were about to change. The main reason was an event on August 23, 1939, that upset the balance of power in Europe. Nazi Germany and its chief adversary, Soviet Russia, concluded a ten-year nonaggression treaty, known widely as the Ribbentrop-Molotov Pact after its signatories.[19] Hitler and Stalin thus freed themselves to pursue easy territorial gains in Eastern Europe. Their greed for new territory and their ultimate designs on the same regions would soon affect Iran.

2

Helpless Pawn on a Slippery Chessboard

News of war in Europe hit Iran like a bombshell, as it did the rest of the world. The shah's tempestuous daughter, Princess Ashraf, was combing her hair before her mirror that morning in early September 1939, when she heard her twin brother, Crown Prince Mohammed Reza, exclaim from the garden, "Germany has invaded Poland!" Shocked, she—like her brother—realized that the war could bode only ill for Iran.[1]

Iran declared its neutrality on September 4, but the war's effects were felt immediately. Britain imposed a blockade of all German sea commerce, trapping five merchant ships of the Hanza Line in the Persian Gulf port of Bander-i Shahpur. Iran's economy depended heavily on continued trade with Germany. On September 6, the minister of finance informed the German minister in Tehran that the shah's government desired to maintain and even expand trade with Germany if the problem of transporting goods around the blockade could be solved. He urged Berlin to seek an agreement with the U.S.S.R. to permit transit of German goods through the Soviet Union, and to support Tehran's efforts at negotiating a similar treaty with Moscow for the export of Iranian products.[2]

Germany's attitude toward Iran at the start of the war was influenced by the political realities created by the German–Soviet nonaggression treaty of August 1939, the Ribbentrop-Molotov Pact. The pact temporarily resolved differences between Adolph Hitler and Joseph Stalin by defining respective spheres of influence in eastern Europe. The two nations divided Poland, while the Soviet Union imposed treaties on the Baltic States that virtually eliminated their independence.

Despite its extensive commercial ties to Germany, Iran fell outside the German sphere of influence. Therefore Hitler's goals with respect to Iran became, first of all, to minimize or eliminate British influence even if that increased Soviet influence; second, to increase German influence; and, third,

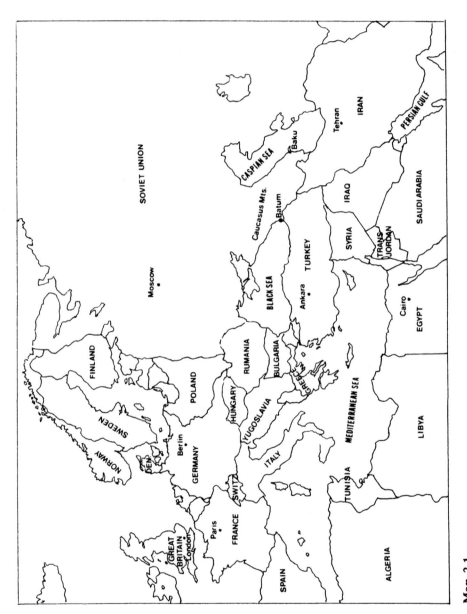

Map 2.1
Europe and the Middle East, 1940

to divert Stalin's attention away from Eastern Europe. The effect on Iran of this policy and of the preceding events were described by the U.S. chargé d'affaires, Cornelius Van Engert, to Washington on October 3, 1939.

> The Iranian Government views the Russo–German and Russo–Estonian treaties with the greatest alarm. For over a month, German and Soviet diplomacy has been bending every effort to undermine Iran's morale and weaken her will to resist blandishments and threats from Berlin and Moscow. The partition of Poland and the virtual loss of independence of the Baltic States have created fear that the Soviets will next turn their attention to the Black Sea and Caspian Sea and that crucial days lie ahead for Iran.[3]

On September 28, 1939, Germany concluded an agreement with the U.S.S.R., permitting German goods to pass via the Soviet Union to Iran. Tehran officially greeted this development, but some among the shah's advisors doubted the wisdom of continuing Iran's dependence on Germany. In early October, the shah convened his cabinet to discuss these concerns. Deputy Minister of Trade Vassighi urged the shah to move away from reliance on Germany, because he doubted whether Iran could depend on exclusive transport via the Soviet Union. Vassighi proposed instead seeking markets and sources of supply elsewhere, possibly with Italy and Japan. Foreign Minister Aalam backed this approach, doubting that Iran could rely on Soviet assurances. Aalam also feared Soviet intentions toward Iran, and cited recent Soviet pressure on the Baltic States and Finland. Finance Minister Bader disagreed with both men, and warned against irritating Germany by changing Iran's trade policy. Iran must continue trade with Berlin, he contended, until transit via the Soviet Union proved unworkable or Germany could no longer supply the goods urgently needed by Iran. The shah sided with Bader, and agreed that Iran must trade with Germany until it proved disadvantageous.

But Iranian attempts to negotiate a transit accord with Moscow were repeatedly stymied by the Soviets, who levied impossible demands such as the release of all Iranian communists from the shah's prisons and the exclusive use of Soviet oil in northern Iran. In late October, the frustrated Iranian monarch declared Irano–Soviet negotiations at an impasse.[4] Concerned by these developments, the German minister in Tehran warned Berlin on October 28, 1939, of the risks to Germany of Soviet pressure on Iran.

> Aside from the positive decision of the Shah on the economic policy to be continued by Iran [with Germany], it appears to be a very important point that doubts concerning Soviet Russia's attitude are entertained in the Iranian Cabinet. . . . Any possible aggressive

action by Russia against Iran will doubtless strengthen England's position in Iran and might possibly even drive Iran into the arms of our enemies, the Allies.[5]

Such had already happened to Iran's strategic neighbor, Turkey. Following fruitless Turkish diplomatic efforts in October 1939 to seek accommodation with Stalin, who kept insisting on revisions to the 1936 Montreux Convention governing control of the Turkish Straits, Turkish Foreign Minister Sukri Saracoglu returned from Moscow in frustration on October 17. He confided to U.S. Ambassador John MacMurray that the Soviets were "reverting to Tsarist Imperialism but were as yet unready to fight for their ambitions."[6] Two days later, Turkey concluded a defensive alliance with Britain and France, which excluded Turkey from joining in any Allied hostilities in event of war with the Soviet Union.[7] Despite this clause, Soviet Commissar for Foreign Affairs Vyacheslav Molotov denounced Turkey on October 31 for abandoning its "neutralism."[8]

Unlike the Turks, the shah of Iran eschewed any formal alliances because he was skeptical of their practical value. But he also chafed from mounting Soviet pressure as reports reached Tehran of fresh divisions in Soviet Turkestan.[9] Stalin decided to step up military pressure on both Turkey and Iran. On November 18, 1939, Molotov informed the German ambassador in Moscow, Count Von der Schulenberg, that the Red Army would soon begin reinforcing its forces in the Transcaucasus. He encouraged the Germans to use this information for "propaganda purposes."[10]

On September 30, 1939, the U.S.S.R. invaded Finland. In Tehran that evening, Iranian Finance Minister Rezaqoli Khosrovi confided to U.S. Chargé Engert that the Soviet invasion of Finland deeply disturbed his government. Khosrovi complained that the Soviets were coldly refusing all diplomatic overtures by Iran. He feared that Stalin had reached a secret agreement with Hitler, permitting Soviet domination of northern Iran. Khosrovi further prophesied that the Soviets might accuse Iran of being a base for a British invasion of the Soviet Union.[11]

The actions of the Soviet Union convinced the shah that he must act to counter its possible intentions against Iran. In January 1940, the Iranian Army began hastily constructing fortifications along its northern frontier, although the six Iranian divisions stationed along the Soviet border were too ill-equipped and understrength to counter any determined attacks.[12]

The shah had no real choice but to seek—covertly—military assistance from the Allies. In late January, the Iranian minister in London, Mohammed Moggadam, suggested to the Foreign Office that England and Iran form a secret alliance against the Soviet Union. The shah wanted to keep the arrangement confidential, lest it provoke the Soviets. In Tehran at the same time, Iranian Minister of War Mohammed Nakhjevan suggested to the British military attaché that "the time had come for Iran and Britain to coordinate . . . plans for war against Russia," and requested the urgent shipment of 60 modern bombers and first-line fighters.[13]

Though the British were not anxious to overcommit themselves in the Middle East, they were just as concerned as the shah over the looming Soviet threat to Iran and its strategic oil fields. Britain's war effort depended on the secure and continuous flow of oil from the Persian Gulf. When the Red Army invaded eastern Poland on September 17, Prime Minister Neville Chamberlain's cabinet had to decide whether or not to declare war on the Soviet Union. The British War Cabinet agreed not to extend the war to the Soviet Union, because they would not save Poland and they might then also be forced to divert forces to meet Soviet attacks in the Middle East.[14]

Allied fears of Soviet intentions in the Middle East were not baseless. British Military Intelligence began detecting Soviet troop concentrations north of Iran in September 1939. On October 6, the British Military Chiefs of Staff apprised the War Cabinet that the Soviets were reinforcing garrisons along the Iranian and Turkish borders with armored troops and aircraft.[15]

The War Office directed the Indian Army General Staff to develop a contingency plan to protect the oil fields. A plan was therefore conceived to dispatch an infantry brigade to the Iraqi port of Basra—in advance of a larger force—in preparation for occupying the Iranian oil fields. The British ruled out direct landings at the Iranian ports of Abadan and Bander-i Shapur, due to treacherous navigation and poor facilities.[16]

From Cairo, Egypt, in December 1939, Britain's Middle East Commander in Chief Gen. Sir Archibald P. Wavell presented the War Office with a comprehensive analysis of the Soviet threat to Iran, and recommended British counteractions. The stocky, ruddy-faced Wavell—a keen geostrategist who had served in the Transcaucasus and was fluent in Russian—theorized that, if the Soviets attacked Iran, they would deploy five or six divisions through Tabriz while simultaneously landing on the Caspian coast. Either or both forces would advance on Tehran, where Soviet bombers would be within striking range of the oil fields. If the Soviets continued to advance, Wavell believed that Iran's difficult road and railway network would limit the advancing forces.[17]

Asserting that Britain should react militarily to such an invasion in order to protect vital air bases in Turkey and Iraq, Wavell advocated deploying at least a division and fighter squadron to defend the Iranian oil fields and Basra, and expanding this force to three divisions if the Soviets advanced southward from Tehran. He recommended that the expeditionary force come from India, which had the available shipping and a secure route through the Persian Gulf. Wavell further suggested that, in response to a Soviet move, Anglo–French air forces based in Turkey and Iraq could strike the vulnerable Soviet oil-producing facilities in the Caucasus.

The British War Cabinet agreed with Wavell's views and, on December

19, issued a policy paper stating that—"at the first signs of Russian aggression against Iran"—British forces would provide "internal security and air defense of the Anglo–Iranian oil fields and the port of Basra." "It is of particular importance," they noted, "that a Russian advance should not be allowed to penetrate far enough to deny us the airbases we shall require in Iraq and Turkey in order to strike at the centers of Russian oil production in the Caucasus, the only objective in Russia open to effective air attack."[18]

On January 3, 1940, the British War Office ordered the Indian Army to prepare a division for possible deployment to the Anglo–Iranian oil fields. This initial force would be reinforced, if required, by two more divisions and mobile forces. The War Cabinet directed the Indian government on January 15 to plan for deployment of three divisions to defend the Iranian oil fields.[19]

At about this time, the Iranian government approached the British with a bid for military aid and a secret alliance. On February 7, the War Cabinet directed the Chiefs of Staff to study the Iranian proposals. They responded on February 23 that Britain could not spare any aircraft for Iran and that, even if the Soviets invaded, there might be no need to send forces into Iran unless Soviet air attacks developed. They recommended instead that Britain "preserve Iranian neutrality until such time as we need Iranian cooperation for offensive operations against Russia." "We see no reason," they concluded, "to coordinate plans with [Iran] in advance." The chiefs admitted that, if "we had to operate against the Russian oil fields in the near future, we should have to obtain the active assistance of Iran." But they feared that, in exchange, the shah "might at the time demand the assistance of a British force in the defense of northern Iran." "The future is still too uncertain," they contended, "to justify us mortgaging forces to help the Shah by embarking on coordinated war plans, as suggested by the Iranian Minister."[20]

The British War Cabinet accepted these opinions. But both the Foreign and Indian Offices decided on February 19 that a Soviet attack against either Iran or Afghanistan would constitute a casus belli for declaring war on the Soviet Union.[21]

Pressing ahead with plans to intervene in Iran, British staff officers from both the Middle East and India commands met in mid-March 1940 to coordinate a plan—code-named HERRING—to dispatch three divisions to Iran and Iraq. The conferees agreed that HERRING would include one imperial and two Indian divisions, supported by base and line-of-communications troops. The advance echelon of HERRING—the Fifth Indian Division—was code-named TROUT. The Middle East Command at Cairo agreed to maintain a separate brigade for emergency deployment to Iraq. The forces would be deployed from and logistically supported by India, but would be directed by General Wavell in Cairo.[22]

Following this conference, two British staff officers assigned to HERRING—Col. Frank W. Messervy and Capt. A. B. Wilson, Royal Navy—

surveyed the prospective area of operations, and submitted a draft operational plan on April 10, 1940. Assuming that either a Soviet invasion or a potentially hostile Iran might threaten the great Abadan oil refinery, their plan called for deploying Force TROUT (the Fifth Indian Division) to Basra prior to entering Iran. The division's Ninth Infantry Brigade would secure Abadan Island and the Shatt-al-Arab waterway in advance of the rest of the division. British gunboats, minesweepers, and tugs would support the operation while the Royal Air Force (RAF) provided air cover.

Their plan dismissed an opposed waterborne assault on Abadan as too risky because the island was defended by at least one Iranian infantry regiment. Instead, they selected the villages of Kasba and Khosroabad—farther down the Shatt-al-Arab—as the principal sites for night landing. The Royal Navy would block the Karun River and the Khor Musa Channel to prevent Iranian gunboats from interfering with the landings. At dawn following the assault, the RAF would bomb the Iranian naval vessels based at Khorramshahr.

In May, this plan was followed by a detailed study of the Abadan refinery and oil field region by Frank W. Lane, an official of the Anglo-Iranian Oil Company (AIOC). Lane's findings and recommendations were submitted to the British General Staff. He noted that the Khuzistan oil fields consisted of 35 producing wells and many miles of pipeline. The Abadan refinery— he pointed out—was particularly vulnerable to attack by aircraft, because its high pressure pipes carried highly inflammable fluids and gases. A bomb exploding on one of the refinery's plants might ignite a conflagration that could envelop the entire complex. Camouflage was of little use—he explained—because the power station, pumping stations, and major process units were too large.

Lane suggested that they place defenses against sabotage and air attack at key points, such as the producing wells, pumping stations, and refinery installations. He recommended that dummy systems be used to simulate flames and pipelines. Lane also called for emplacing sandbags and splinterproof walls in the refinery and at the pumping stations. But, he emphasized, only an extensive air defense system could adequately protect the refinery.

Lane theorized that a Soviet advance on the oil fields would be either down the Khorramabad road, along the trans-Iranian railway, or through Iraq. To counter this, he recommended deploying a Basra-based British expeditionary force to Abadan and Khorramshahr. The RAF would evacuate AIOC families while the Royal Navy was securing Khorramshahr. The British force would then advance through Ahvaz to establish a defensive line in the mountains to the north. Mechanized cavalry patrols would screen the exposed flanks.

The British initially viewed their plans in this theater as purely defensive. However, the War Cabinet soon found itself drawn into an offensive scheme against the Soviet Union. Submitting to strong public pressure to aid the gallant Finns in their struggle against the Soviets, French Premier Eduard Deladier initiated joint planning with the British to deploy a large expeditionary force of "volunteers" to Finland. The only route for moving and supplying such a force lay over the vital Narvik railway, which ran through neutral Norway and Sweden. Since their actions would violate Scandinavian neutrality anyway, the French and British General Staffs determined that the planned expedition should also occupy the northern Swedish iron ore mines—thus denying this vital war material to Nazi Germany.[23]

A grand Allied strategy rapidly evolved, which presupposed both violation of neutrality and armed conflict with the Soviet Union. Deladier therefore considered extending the strategy a step further to include denying Soviet oil supplies to Germany by bombing the oil fields in the Caucasus. On January 19, 1940, he directed his General Staff to study this proposal. The French General Staff submitted their response on February 22—noting that the Caucasus produced 80 percent of Soviet oil supplies. "Bombardment of the oil fields of Baku and Batum," they contended, "would considerably curtail Germany's supplies of fuel" and would also cripple the Soviet economy. Their plan envisioned employing 6–8 bomber groups based in Syria, Turkey, Iran, or Iraq.[24]

The British Chiefs of Staff apprised the War Cabinet on March 8 that "the French have a project for attacking the Caucasus from bases in Syria with longrange bombers drawn from Tunisia." The chiefs believed, however, that only a fraction of Germany's oil was coming from the U.S.S.R. because "Russian production is just sufficient to meet the requirements of [her] internal economy." They did agree that "a largescale interruption" of Soviet oil supplies would, in time, "paralyze the Russian military effort and disorganize Russian life." "The most vulnerable oil objectives in the Caucasus," they indicated, "are the refineries at Baku, Grozni and Batum. We are advised that a refinery, once effectively destroyed, could not be repaired under nine months at least." Therefore, "a plan for the attack of these installations is now being worked out by the air staff in the Middle East." Britain having only three long-range bomber squadrons in the Middle East, the chiefs noted the "possibility that Iran might be engaged as an ally on our side. In this event, we should presumably be able to make use of Tehran as an advanced aerodrome."[25]

The War Cabinet considered this proposal and, on March 12, agreed that it was not yet in Britain's interest to declare war on the Soviet Union. Adequate forces to meet both Italian and Soviet threats in the Middle East would not be available before late 1940. Since an imminent clash with the Soviet Union over Iran seemed unlikely, the British leaders declined to dispatch bombers to the Middle East.[26]

Nevertheless, the Soviets soon caught wind of the scheme. France's ambassador in Ankara, René Massigli, learned from Turkish Foreign Minister

Sukri Saracoglu on March 14 that the Soviets were worried about an Allied attack on Baku. Saracoglu confided that his ambassador in Moscow had learned the day before from U.S. Ambassador Laurence Steinhardt that the Soviets were seeking advice from U.S. engineers on how best to extinguish oil fires resulting from aerial bombardment. The U.S. technicians reportedly were not encouraging. The soil surrounding the oil fields was so thickly saturated—they told the Soviets—that perhaps months or years would be required to fully restore operation. Even worse, the local population would have to be evacuated at least 50 kilometers. Encouraged by Saracoglu's comments, Massigli outlined the proposed Allied plans against Baku, and ventured the fact that French and British bombers would have to cross either Turkish or Iranian territory. Saracoglu weighed his response carefully, replying, "Do you anticipate any objections on the part of Iran?" Inferring Turkish approval, Massigli hastily cabled Paris that "there would be no difficulties on the part of Turkey."[27]

The Allied Supreme War Council met on March 27 to reconsider its strategy against the Russo–German partnership. Because of Finland's collapse some days earlier, the Allied leaders agreed that they could no longer occupy the Swedish iron ore fields.[28] Although their plans were thwarted, their effort established an ethical precedent best summed up by then First Lord of the Admiralty Sir Winston S. Churchill: "Small nations must not tie our hands when we are fighting for their rights and freedom."[29] This would not be the last time the British faced the problem of forcibly occupying a vital railway through neutral territory to aid a beleaguered ally.

The new French premier, Paul Reynaud, remained eager to attack the Caucasus, and pressed the Allied Supreme War Council for an immediate decision. He argued that the entire Baku region could be destroyed, and the Soviet economy crippled decisively. But the British would agree only to study the matter further, and refused to stage bombers in Iraq or Syria.[30]

Nevertheless, aerial reconnaissance of the Caucasus commenced immediately. On March 30, an unmarked British Special Intelligence Service (SIS) reconnaissance aircraft flew through Iranian airspace and over Baku. Though spotted by the Soviets, it encountered no resistance, and returned safely with its air photos. Four days later, a second mission was run over Batum; it encountered Soviet antiaircraft fire, but completed the mission.[31]

Sensing Allied intentions, Molotov warned his countrymen—in a speech to the Supreme Soviet on March 29—of "extensive and suspicious activity" in the "Near East generally . . . mainly the colonial armies headed by [French] General Weygand." "We must exercise vigilance in regard to attempts to utilize the [Allied] troops for purposes hostile to the Soviet Union," he cautioned, threatening that "any such attempt would evoke on our part countermeasures against the aggressors." He further warned "our neighbors" not to become "tools of this aggressive policy against the USSR."[32]

Backing words with action, the Soviets began redeploying forces from the Finnish front in late March, transferring two corps headquarters and three infantry divisions to the Transcaucasus Military District. Other reinforcements—including even the Soviet General Staff artillery reserve—joined the trainloads of troops, tanks, cavalry, and artillery pouring into Baku and Tbilisi. Altogether, five infantry divisions, one tank division, a cavalry division, and two light tank regiments were added to the district's existing six mountain infantry divisions, two mountain cavalry divisions, and one light tank regiment. The Transcaucasus garrison expanded from an independent field army to an okrug—an army group with about 200,000 men and nearly 1,000 tanks.[33]

The Soviets constructed fortifications along the borders with Iran and Turkey while also creating an independent air defense organization in the Transcaucasus. Three aviation divisions and a separate air brigade were deployed to the district—swelling the number of military aircraft from only 40 before the war to nearly 500 in 1940.[34]

Across the Caspian Sea, meanwhile, the Central Asian Military District facing northeast Iran was simultaneously reinforced by the 28th Mechanized, 58th Infantry, and Fourth Cavalry Corps.[35] The large armor concentration in both districts, along with the strategic artillery reserve, indicated a strong offensive capability.

The French General Staff meanwhile completed its plan for bombing the Caucasus oil fields. A staff estimate on April 5 concluded that between 30 and 35 percent of the Batum refinery facilities would be destroyed within a six-day period. The plan called for six French bomber groups and three British bomber squadrons to attack the refineries and oil fields at Batum, Baku, Grozny, and Poti. Nearly 100 aircraft, carrying 70 tons of bombs, would be required.[36]

Eager to proceed with the plan, Premier Paul Reynaud summoned his Middle East commander, Gen. Maxime Weygand, to Paris for consultations. Weygand estimated that it would require at least three more months to prepare the forward airfields and assemble the necessary French and British bombers. Weygand left Paris on April 12 and flew directly to Cairo to confer with his British counterparts. Reaching Beirut on April 17, he cabled Paris that the operation would be ready by late June or early July.[37]

But just as the Allies began to rush toward certain collision with the Soviet Union, their plans were suddenly thwarted by a massive German offensive against France and the lowland countries. On the morning of May 10, 1940, German panzers rolled into Belgium while Nazi paratroops descended on the Netherlands. German armored spearheads plunged into France, and tore a massive hole that unraveled the Allied line.

In Tehran on May 10, U.S. Chargé de'Affaire Cornelius Van Engert alerted Washington that Soviet Ambassador Matvei Y. Filimonov was warning Iran not to become "a tool of Britain," following press reports of plans to bomb Baku and the reinforcement of Allied troops in the Middle

East. Perceiving German involvement in the Soviet threats, Engert contended that

> The Soviet Embassy and German Legation are apparently working in close collaboration in Iran. Both seem determined, although from different motives, to exploit fully all advantages the Russo–German understanding gives them. Germany has undoubtedly been inciting the Soviets to adopt a greater aggressive policy toward Iran . . . in the hope of weakening and perhaps eliminating British influence. Moscow seems to be tempted by the chance for easy spoils and easy diplomatic or military victories.[38]

Germany's minister in Tehran, Erwin C. Ettel, apprised Berlin on May 19 that "any weakening of England on the battlefields in the West will automatically harm the English position in Iran, thus also the position of the Anglo-Iranian Oil Company which is vital to the British Empire." Explaining that the Soviets were preparing to take advantage of Iran following England's defeat, he noted that the "Shah and . . . his government are, without a doubt, clearly aware of the dangers which threaten Iran from the Soviet Union." He concluded that, "in the event of a defeat of England, the position of the country in relation to the powerful neighbor from the north would be much more difficult owing to the end of English counterpressure."[39]

In Beirut that same day, British, French, and Turkish military leaders met to discuss joint strategy against the Axis. Allied defeats were unnerving the Turks. To stiffen Turkish resolve, the French offered two divisions from Syria if Germany or the Soviet Union should attack Turkey. The French and British raised the proposed offensive against the Caucasus a final time, but the Turks refused to support the operation for fear of Soviet retaliation. Even British offers to deploy forces to Mosul in northern Iraq failed to assure them. Allied plans against the Caucasus died.[40]

In France, meanwhile, the fast-moving German legions drove the British Expeditionary Force from the continent, and then turned and dispersed what remained of the French Army. Advancing German troops entered La Charité on the Loire River, capturing a special train carrying the secret papers of the French General Staff. Among the documents were the secret Allied plans to bomb the Caucasus oil fields—which intelligence experts hastily dispatched to Berlin.[41]

Despite the situation in France and the abandonment of the air offensive against the Soviet Union, the British General Staff continued preparations to intervene in Iran. But not all British officials were in agreement with this policy: One of the principal objectors was the minister in Iran, Sir Reader W. Bullard. Bullard—with many years of service in the Levant and Persia—cabled the Foreign Office on May 24, 1940, his view "that infringement of Iranian neutrality must not come from us, and that even if that neutrality is first infringed by Russia or by German activities, unless we can defend the oil fields with overwhelming force, our best card is strict respect for Iranian neutrality." However, his arguments failed to persuade Foreign Secretary Sir Anthony Eden, who responded five days later that he would "deal separately with the political questions" of Iranian neutrality.[42]

Forging ahead, the British contingency force staffs met in Bombay from June 21 to 24 to finalize their plans against Iran. Their major challenge was to devise a plan for securing the vulnerable Abadan refinery without damage. Agreeing that the best approach was a surprise coup de main, the conferees submitted several ideas for discussion. One proposed a surprise dawn attack by 2,000 men carried up the Shatt-al-Arab aboard either four destroyers or two cruisers. This was dismissed because the warships could be easily recognized approaching the jetties and then a machine gun could inflict heavy casualties on the tightly packed decks.[43]

A second proposal advocated loading the troops aboard merchant vessels and moving them upriver unobtrusively on the pretense of delivering stores. Disguised as Indian laborers, the soldiers would carry concealed weapons and, on mooring at the jetty, would overpower Iranian officials— then would fan out, led by AIOC guides, to seize key installations before Iranian troops could respond. The conferees agreed on this idea, and decided that a battalion of Indian soldiers would be employed. Their surprise attack would be supported by landing a second battalion south of Abadan at Khosroabad, which would then advance overland to reinforce the first. A third battalion would be kept in reserve for a landing at Kasba, if the first two attempts failed.

On June 29, Secretary of State for India Leopold Amery informed the War Cabinet that one division with base and line-of-communications troops were preparing for deployment to Iraq and Iran. The lead brigade including motor transport and horsedrawn artillery would be ready to embark by the end of July, to be followed by a second brigade in late September.[44]

Meanwhile, Joseph Stalin took advantage of the Allied collapse in France to exert his own territorial ambitions. In mid-June, Soviet forces occupied Lithuania, Latvia, and Estonia. Two weeks later, Stalin grabbed the eastern portion of Rumania. Then his attention turned toward Iran and Turkey.

In Tehran on July 2, Soviet Ambassador Matvei Filimonov outlined Stalin's intentions to his German counterpart, Erwin Ettel. The Soviet government planned to demand "secure transit rights" on Iranian railways and "free zones" in the Persian Gulf, the Soviet envoy explained. His government would also insist that all British influence be eliminated. Iran could retain its political independence, but no "third power" would be allowed a "position of political influence." Filimonov castigated the shah's policies, and stated that the Iranian masses would not "submit . . . forever" to their "miserable social conditions."[45]

Growing German hostility and increasing Nazi–Soviet colloboration in Iran infuriated the shah. Radio Berlin had even directly attacked the shah on several occasions. On June 15, the monarch sacked and imprisoned his pro-German prime minister, Dr. Matine-Daftary—replacing him with the more neutral Ali Mansur. To satisfy the British minister's complaints that the Iranian press was portraying a one-sided, pro-German view of the war, English-speaking personnel were assigned to the official Pars News Agency to translate Reuters dispatches.[46]

The Soviets heightened their pressure on Turkey and Iran. On June 25, Molotov met with the Italian ambassador, and castigated Turkey for "claiming that she is the sole mistress of the [Turkish] Straits," and accusing Turkey of "threatening the Soviet Union in the areas southeast of Batum."[47] Berlin actively encouraged these actions. On July 1, Nazi Foreign Minister Joachim von Ribbentrop directed his ambassador in Ankara, Franz von Papen, to "not attempt to exert influence on Turkish–Soviet relations with a view to improving them."[48]

In London that same day, the War Cabinet—alarmed by mounting Soviet pressure on Iran and Turkey, along with pro-Nazi unrest in Iraq and the defection of French forces in Syria—directed the deployment of British forces to stablize the Persian Gulf region. On July 3, the Chiefs of Staff proposed implementing Plan TROUT, thus deploying an Indian division to the Iranian oil fields.[49]

The Germans heightened the growing crisis between the Soviet Union, Turkey, Iran, and Britain on July 3 by publishing excerpts from the captured French General Staff documents, detailing the Allied plans to bomb the Caucasus oil fields. The Soviet press seized on the documents as proof of Turkish and Iranian complicity in the plan. The Turks issued an ineffectual denial while the Iranian press expressed surprise at the Soviet assertions, since Iran knew nothing of the plot.[50]

Capitalizing on the explosive revelations, Soviet Ambassador Filimonov levied secret demands on the Iranian government on July 7 that it relinquish control of Azerbaijan and the Caspian Sea coast, permit Soviet use of various airfields, and place all railways under Soviet control. So serious was the matter that the Iranians dared not admit having received the demands. The next day, U.S. Chargé Engert reported the rumors of Soviet demands and the Iranian suspicion that the Soviets were seeking a pretext to invade. On July 10, Prime Minister Ali Mansur anxiously asked German Minister Ettel if he knew the reason for the increasingly hostile Soviet attitude. Mansur denied receiving any demands, but the Germans obtained a text through their Luftwaffe attaché in Bulgaria.[51]

Ettel warned Berlin that the Iranians were particularly angry at the Germans, especially after a German radio broadcast on July 19 denouncing the shah and his government. Everyone in Iran assumed, the German envoy explained, "that Iran is faced with a common German–Russian front."[52]

From Moscow on July 11, German Ambassador Von der Schulenberg described Soviet relations with Iran and Turkey as "serious." The Iranians, he apprised Berlin, "believe that the [German] White Paper [on the French General Staff plans] has induced the Soviet Government to take action against Iran." "However," he added, "the Iranian ambassador here is too clever not to see that the documents in the White Book were only a pretext for the Soviet Government's conduct and that Moscow would simply have found another pretext if this one had not presented itself at the moment."[53]

The Soviets acted against Turkey as well—secretly demanding that Ankara cede bases in the Dardanelles and return the former Russian provinces of Kars and Ardahan. Turkish Prime Minister Refik Saydam bluntly refused the demands. On July 12, he appeared before the Turkish Grand National Assembly to denounce Soviet accusations of Turkish complicity; he declared that Turkey had not agreed to hostile action against the Soviet Union, but was now resolved to use force to protect her borders against attack. The lone foreign diplomat allowed in the chambers was the British ambassador. The Turks mobilized nearly 1 million men—calling Stalin's bluff, and displaying confidence in British military support.[54]

German Ambassador Franz Von Papen—aware that Moscow would shy away from a costly and hazardous military campaign against Turkey— suggested to Berlin on July 12 that attention be shifted to Iran, where "it would be different [from Turkey] if, for example, Soviet Russia wanted to exploit the situation to push forward to the sea in the direction of the Persian Gulf."[55]

The German military attaché in Tehran cabled Berlin on July 10 that everyone was expecting a Soviet invasion. Two days later, the Reich consul in Tabriz reported that the Iranian Army was conducting maneuvers south of Tabriz. The Iranians, he added, had called up reserves and dispatched troops toward Julfa on the Soviet border.[56] Von Ribbentrop instructed his minister in Tehran—Ettel—on July 15 that "German mediation in any Iranian–Soviet differences is out of the question."[57]

Two days later—on July 17—the British Foreign Office drafted a memorandum in which it concluded that Hitler and Stalin were allied against Britain and that Hitler hoped to check the Soviet Union's ambitions in Europe by encouraging a Soviet move toward the Persian Gulf. In India, meanwhile, the lead element of Force TROUT—the Ninth Indian Brigade—prepared for dispatch to Basra. A convoy of 19 ships including three troop transports was forming in Bombay harbor to embark the brigade.[58]

An Anglo–Soviet military confrontation over Iran seemed imminent. On August 1, Commissar for Foreign Affairs Molotov addressed the Supreme Soviet, and publicly warned that the U.S.S.R. was disturbed by the revelations of Allied plans against the Caucasus and the appearance of foreign aircraft over Baku and Batum. Terming these overflights "intolerable," he declared that "any repetition . . . could lead to nothing but complications in our relations with our neighbors." The U.S.S.R., he stated, was compelled to "intensify our vigilance on these southern Soviet frontiers."[59]

The next morning, the Turkish ambassador in Moscow told Sir Stafford Cripps that Molotov's address demonstrated that the Soviet "attitude to Turkey and Iran is not decided but there is a threatening situation left open [in case] the Soviet Government decided to act." Cripps warned London that "it is already very late, perhaps too late."[60]

Indeed it might have been too late, with British troops immediately bound for Iran. But that same day, the British War Cabinet met and agreed to divert the Fifth Indian Division from the Persian Gulf to North Africa. This was the result of an urgent cable from General Wavell in Cairo, who desperately needed the troops to face the Italians and who also feared that sending the division to Basra might provoke a Soviet invasion of Iran. He further contended that the Fifth Indian Division—with only two brigades and virtually no antiaircraft guns—was too weak to defend the Iranian oil fields. His views were supported by the viceroy of India, Lord Linlithgow, and the commander in chief, India, Gen. Sir Robert Cassels.[61]

Tensions over Iran quickly began to subside, for several reasons: Stalin feared that, if he invaded Iran, the British might retaliate against the Caucasus oil fields; and further, his efforts to coerce the shah into political concessions—the way he had succeeded with the Baltic States and Rumania—failed. Iran's stubborn monarch stood determined to face any challenge, while simultaneously seeking ways to avoid confrontation. As U.S. Chargé Engert explained on August 9, 1940:

> The Shah resents the role of a helpless pawn upon the slippery chessboard of power politics and is pathetically anxious to give the impression that he is following his own policy and not that of some great power; nor does he want Iran to become a protectorate either in form or in fact. And as he can be very stubborn when aroused he is credited with a recent instruction to his Foreign Minister that there must be no undue compliance with Soviet demands for he had the firm intention of holding the northern provinces at all costs. . . . The ultimate safety of Iran oddly enough is now considered closely linked with the British cause.[62]

Throughout the month of August, Britain's fate hung in the balance as the Luftwaffe bombarded England nightly and German invasion troops and barges gathered in France. From Moscow, Soviet leaders followed the developing situation with keen interest. The bombardment dragged on and on—day after day—but England seemed no nearer to collapse. In mid-August, the British ambassador in Moscow, Sir Stafford Cripps, reported that the continued British resistance was impressing the Soviets.[63] Western diplomats also detected simultaneously a softening in the Soviet attitude toward Iran and Turkey. On August 15, the U.S. chargé d'affaires in Moscow, Walter Thurston, reported that "the fact that rumors of pressure on Turkey have become somewhat less persistent recently may indicate that the Soviets have decided to defer an active move in this area."[64]

Confronted by Turkish and Iranian steadfastness backed by British strength, Stalin temporarily suspended Soviet pressure until Britain's fate could be determined. The Soviets also began detecting fresh German units along their western borders, for Hitler had directed his High Command on August 9 to implement AUFBAU OST (Buildup East). Twelve German divisions were ordered redeployed to Poland.[65]

With winter rapidly approaching and England still strongly in the war, Stalin decided to defer any move against Iran at least until spring. The winter respite afforded the Soviet General Staff an opportunity to more thoroughly study the Iranian theater of operations. Lt. Col. Sergei M. Shtemenko, a staff officer with the operations department of the General Staff, was assigned this task. His study focused on Iranian geography, industry, military targets, and probable invasion routes into Iran and Iraq.[66]

Meanwhile, as German aircraft losses over Britain mounted and the Royal Air Force remained perplexingly vigorous, Hitler's enthusiasm for invading the British Isles waned. On September 19, the discouraged Nazi leader halted the further assembly of his invasion fleet, and ordered the existing ships dispersed. He then shifted his focus eastward, where Soviet forces in eastern Rumania threatened German access to the vital Rumanian oil fields.[67]

Hitler determined that the Soviets needed to be distracted away from the Balkans. On September 26, Adm. Karl Raeder suggested to Hitler that Germany could avoid a clash with the Soviet Union over the Balkans if the Soviets could become bogged down fighting the British in the eastern Mediterranean. Hitler agreed that the Soviets should be encouraged to move south toward Iran and India.[68]

The Germans decided to invite the Soviets to join the three Axis Powers—Germany, Italy, and Japan—in dividing up the spoils expected from the collapse of Britain. On October 17, 1940, the Soviet government was invited to Berlin to discuss "delimitation of interests on a world-wide scale." Stalin agreed to send Molotov.[69]

British government officials learned of these impending discussions, and attempted to short-circuit Nazi plans by offering the Soviets a counterproposal of their own. On October 22, Ambassador Sir Stafford Cripps presented a proposed agreement to the Soviet Foreign Ministry—promising aid to the Soviet Union if it were attacked, and that Britain would not join any anti-Soviet alliance after the war and would recognize Soviet sovereignty over the occupied Baltic States. In return, the Soviets would have to treat Britain as benevolently as it did Germany and maintain a "benevolent neutrality" toward Iran and Turkey. Including a veiled threat, the

British further promised not to attack Soviet territory—in particular Baku and Batum—by way of Iran and Turkey. The Soviets curtly shelved the proposal.[70]

Discussions between Moscow and Berlin commenced on November 12. Ribbentrop assured Molotov that "England was beaten and it is only a question of time before she would finally admit her defeat." He relayed Hitler's view that the Soviet Union, Germany, Italy, and Japan must delineate their respective "spheres of influence . . . along very broad lines." Contending that Germany, Italy, and Japan were expanding in a southerly direction, he asked "whether Russia in the long run would not also turn to the south for the natural outlet to the sea." When Molotov asked which sea, Ribbentrop asked whether "in the long run, the most advantageous access to the open sea for Russia could not be found in the direction of the Persian Gulf and Arabian Sea." Molotov evaded a direct response, insisting that "precision was necessary" in defining the long-term "spheres of influence."[71]

During the next two days, Molotov conferred with Hitler personally. The Nazi leader professed the need for continued Nazi–Soviet friendship and collaboration. Molotov agreed that both countries should cooperate and avoid war with each other. But when discussion focused on such prickly questions as the Soviet control of Finland and the Dardanelles, tensions rose and agreement remained elusive. On November 14—the final night of Molotov's visit—a British air raid interrupted a banquet in Molotov's honor. While hiding in the bomb shelter, Ribbentrop again pressed Molotov—emphasizing that "the decisive question was whether the Soviet Union was prepared and in a position to cooperate . . . in the great liquidation of the British Empire." He then handed Molotov the draft of a proposed four-power pact between Germany, Italy, Japan, and the Soviet Union. An attached secret protocol proposed that "the Soviet Union declares that her territorial aspirations center south of the national territory of the Soviet Union in the direction of the Indian Ocean." Molotov remained inscrutable. Ribbentrop pressed him for a response "to the question of whether the Soviet Union was in principle sympathetic to the idea of obtaining an outlet to the Indian Ocean." The Soviet official evasively responded that, if the war with England was already won, then why was Hitler speaking of a "life and death struggle" against Britain? The next day Molotov returned to Moscow with the German proposal.[72]

The British—gleaning the substance of the Berlin discussions—publicly accused Germany of selling out Iran. The allegations so worried Iranian officials that, on November 14, Deputy Foreign Minister Djevad Amery indignantly confided to U.S. Chargé Engert that Molotov's meeting with Hitler supplied "fresh proof that Soviet policy was devoid of all moral foundations." Amery believed that Germany and the Soviet Union would use any means to attain their goals.[73]

Four days later, the German minister in Tehran, Erwin Ettel, warned

Berlin that "this [British] propaganda has succeeded in disturbing official Iranian circles and in exciting the Iranian merchants." Prime Minister Ali Mansur had already approached Ettel regarding the British accusations. The German minister feigned ignorance. But he warned Berlin that he required guidance for future such conversations. "A statement that Iran was not discussed on the occasion of Molotov's visit would suffice to bring about a tranquilizing effect," he suggested cynically.[74]

In Berlin that day, two Iranian diplomats beseeched the state secretary for foreign affairs, Ernst von Weizsacker, to explain the purpose of Molotov's visit. Weizsacker brushed aside the concerns of the director general of the Iranian Foreign Ministry, Sayah, and the minister in Berlin, Moussa Noury-Isfandiary, attributing the rumors to "English intrigues." Erwin Ettel followed a similar line in Tehran, and informed Weizsacker on November 23 that his assurances had "a calming effect" on the Iranian prime minister.[75]

Stalin meanwhile studied the proposed four-power pact and decided to accept, provided that Hitler would agree to certain stipulations relating to Finland and the Dardanelles. Molotov delivered the formal reply to Ambassador Von der Schulenberg on the evening of November 25, 1940. The Soviet government insisted that Germany withdraw its troops from Finland—"which belongs to the Soviet Union's sphere of influence"—and demanded the right to establish bases near the Dardanelles. The Soviet sphere of influence, as defined by Germany in the document, was acceptable in general terms, with the wording modified to read that "the area south of Batum and Baku [in the Transcaucasus] in the general direction of the Persian Gulf is recognized as the center of aspirations of the Soviet Union."[76]

Stalin summoned certain high Soviet officials two weeks later to inform them of his intended but highly secret policy. The chief of Soviet Military Intelligence, Lt. Gen. F. I. Golikov, returned from meeting with Stalin, and assembled his key staff officers amidst unusually high security measures— including armed guards on the doors to Golikov's office and a list of attendees that had to be personally signed. Golikov warned his staff that the information he was relaying was top secret. He stated that Germany would soon bring Britain to her knees, thus opening the way for the U.S.S.R. to occupy the British oil fields and strategic routes through the Middle East. He went on to describe Stalin's strategy, which included annulling the "temporary" Nazi–Soviet Pact when the moment was propitious. Golikov assured his staff that, in the meantime, a German attack on the Soviet Union was highly unlikely because Hitler and his generals were not "maniacs or lunatics" and "were not going to attempt suicide."[77]

The Soviet leaders could not have been more mistaken about Hitler and his generals. When informed of Stalin's counterproposal of November 25, the fuehrer was incensed. Soviet demands regarding Finland and the Dardanelles were completely unacceptable. War with the Soviet Union was now unavoidable. On December 18, 1940, the German High Command secretly issued Directive Number 21—Operation BARBAROSSA—which directed planning for the invasion of Russia.[78]

When, after some weeks, Stalin failed to receive an answer from Hitler to his response of November 25, Molotov told Ambassador Von der Schulenberg on January 19, 1941, that "the Soviet Government was counting on an early German reply." The German envoy assured him that there was no reason for concern. The delay, he explained, was due to the need for extensive discussions with the other Axis partners. Molotov accepted this explanation.[79]

The British, meanwhile, updated their plans for possible intervention in Iraq and Iran—redesignating Plan HERRING as SABINE based on the increased German threat to the Middle East. On February 21, 1941, Gen. Sir Claude Auchinleck, commander in chief, India, presented General Wavell with a fresh analysis. Auchinleck believed that Britain must plan for a possible Axis attack through Turkey or via the southern U.S.S.R. and the Caucasus to Iraq. In such an event, Soviet forces might also take advantage of the weak British situation, and advance from the Caucasus through Iran or Turkey. Auchinleck feared that pro-Axis elements in Iraq might also grab power, permitting Axis use of Iraqi air bases against the British.[80]

To counter Soviet or Axis attacks on Iran or Iraq, the Indian General Staff proposed deploying a force to Basra—a force that could secure the Shatt-al-Arab and the Iranian oil fields, and then advance north to occupy Baghdad and the vital areas in northern Iraq. At least three divisions plus mechanized forces would be required, and the operation would pose severe logistical problems. Auchinleck noted the serious shortage of shipping, and explained that it would take at least 13 days to move and establish a division at Basra. He proposed immediately forming a corps headquarters to initiate the necessary planning, while staging the lead division for rapid embarkation. He further suggested that his staff direct the force operations—subject to guidance from Wavell—and that the Middle East Command provide the necessary air support.

Meanwhile, the shah of Iran was studying defensive measures of his own. As the spring of 1941 approached, many in Iran feared a Soviet invasion encouraged by the Germans. The shah therefore directed his Supreme War Council to prepare a detailed plan of defense against a Soviet attack. Brig. Gen. Hassan Arfa considered Iran's vast northern frontier to be indefensible, and proposed that supplies be prepositioned and forces concentrated in the difficult mountain regions of central and southern Iran. If the Soviets attacked, he contended, the government could retreat to this redoubt—leaving behind a screen of light, mobile forces to delay the enemy advance by demolishing roads, bridges, and railways.[81]

Maj. Gen. Haji Ali Razmara disagreed, and proposed instead that the Iranian Army attempt to defend the entire northern border. The Soviets would then have to engage the army if they crossed the frontier. The War Council favored Razmara's approach because they feared admitting to the shah that they could not defend the northern regions. The shah accepted Razmara's plan—leading General Arfa to conclude that the king did not really believe Iran could resist a Soviet attack but, rather, hoped to discourage a Soviet advance by displaying a willingness to defend the border.

Fortifications were constructed along various approaches into northern Iran. TNT charges were placed in the narrow and strategic Daradiss Gorge, several miles south of the important border crossing at Julfa. The vital Shibli Pass was fortified with artillery positions connected by telephone. Entrenchments were dug along the road from the border city of Astara to Rasht.[82]

Still lacking an answer from Hitler on their counterproposal of November 25, 1940, the Soviets nevertheless proceeded with preparations to advance into Iran. In March, the Soviet General Staff completed its invasion study, advocating a multiprong advance from the Transcaucasus and Central Asia. The main axis ran from Julfa through Tabriz to Tehran, supported by secondary routes toward Rezeiyeh and along the Caspian coast. The Caspian port of Bander-i Pahlavi was considered a key target for an amphibious assault. Central Asian forces would advance through Gorgan to Tehran and from Ashkhabad to Meshed. The plan included optional routes of advance as far south as the Persian Gulf.[83]

The Soviets hoped Britain would not interfere with the invasion. Otherwise, the Red Army expected to engage British–Indian forces near Kermanshah and in northern Iraq. "Should the territory of Iran become a theater of war against the Soviet Union," the study stated, "then this [Revandus to Baghdad] axis of operational advance will become the most important because it constitutes the shortest route to Iraq. . . . The Revandus road will allow the British, in case of war against the Soviet Union, to bring troops by the shortest route from the . . . Persian Gulf or from the Mediterranean ports via the northeastern parts of Iran to the Transcaucasian border of the USSR."[84]

The Soviet planners were impressed—but not deterred—by the ruggedness and sheer immensity of Iran. "Nearly all roads of the [Iranian] theater of war lead through some kind of mountainous region or other," the study observed. "The main axis of advance [Julfa to Tehran] allows for the possibility of many bypassing operations which makes it possible to overcome defensive lines of the opponent," the planners believed. "Thus," they concluded, "the mountainous terrain of the Iranian theater of war constitutes no insurmountable natural obstacle."[85]

The Soviet General Staff commenced planning in March for the extensive command and staff exercises scheduled for the Transcaucasus and Central Asia Military Districts in May. In April, Colonel Shtemenko personally carried the completed exercise plans for the Transcaucasus/Central Asia to the deputy chief of the General Staff, Lt. Gen. Nicolay F. Vatutin, for approval. Vatutin concurred with the plans, and then informed Shtemenko that either he himself or the chief of the General Staff would personally direct the exercises.[86]

Meanwhile, the British remained determined to oppose either a Soviet or a German advance toward the Persian Gulf. On March 15, 1940, British staff officers from the Middle East Command and Indian General Staff convened in Cairo to finalize the details of Plan SABINE—the defense of Iraq and the Iranian oil fields. During the conference, General Wavell accepted most of General Auchinleck's suggestions for SABINE, and even arranged for Auchinleck to communicate directly with the War Office. Three Indian divisions (the Sixth, Eighth, and Tenth) were earmarked for SABINE. The British not only feared a possible Soviet attack, but were also anxious to get control of Iraq—where pro-German Arab sympathizers threatened the pro-British government. Worried that Indian troops might not reach Iraq in time if a pro-Axis coup occurred, the conferees decided to form a striking force from British forces in Palestine, which would be in addition to the forces earmarked for SABINE.[87]

But events were moving too swiftly for the British. During March and April 1941, German forces occupied Bulgaria, overran Yugoslavia, and invaded Greece. By May, both they and their Italian allies were firmly positioned in the eastern Mediterranean. With their Vichy allies controlling Syria, the alluring Iranian oil fields of the Persian Gulf were no longer completely beyond Hitler's grasp. Having decided to invade the Soviet Union as soon as his forces were ready, Adolph Hitler was no longer interested in encouraging a Soviet move into Iran. At this propitious moment, pro-Axis conspirators in Iraq were about to present Hitler with a golden opportunity to reach out for the oil fields of the Persian Gulf.

3
_____

The Arab Liberation Movement Is Our Natural Ally

In the early hours of April 2, 1941, a servant awakened Prince Abdullilah—the trim and youthful regent of Iraq—to warn that Iraqi soldiers were surrounding the royal palace. Realizing that a coup d'état was in process, the frightened prince scurried away from the Baghdad palace in his pajamas, and hid until daybreak.[1]

The next morning, a veiled visitor attired in a woman's chador sought entrance to the U.S. legation. Minister Paul Knabenshue was surprised to discover that his visitor was really the hapless Prince Abdullilah seeking refuge. Knabenshue summoned his official car, and concealed the regent under cushions in the backseat. With the Stars and Stripes flying from the hood, the minister and his wife anxiously passed through several checkpoints set up by the coup leaders to catch the prince. Once outside Baghdad, they raced across the desert to the Royal Air Force Station at Habbaniya—50 miles to the west—where the regent was whisked aboard a British aircraft and flown to safety aboard a British gunboat at Basra.

In Baghdad meanwhile, Iraqi rebels seized control of the government, and deposed the regent. The group was led by the pro-Nazi former Prime Minister Rashid Ali al Gailani. Rashid Ali had allied himself with four Iraqi colonels who together controlled the key military garrisons around Baghdad.

But the real power and inspiration behind the movement was the nefarious Haj Muhammad Amin al-Husseini, Grand Mufti of Jerusalem. Having escaped arrest in British-controlled Palestine for his fanatical anti-Zionist and anti-British agitation, al-Husseini obtained refuge in Iraq in 1939, where his visions of an independent pan-Arab empire found eager support. As described by British press attaché Freya Stark, the mufti was "a young-looking though white-haired, handsome man, wearing his turban like a halo, his eyes light blue and shining and a sort of radiance as of a just-

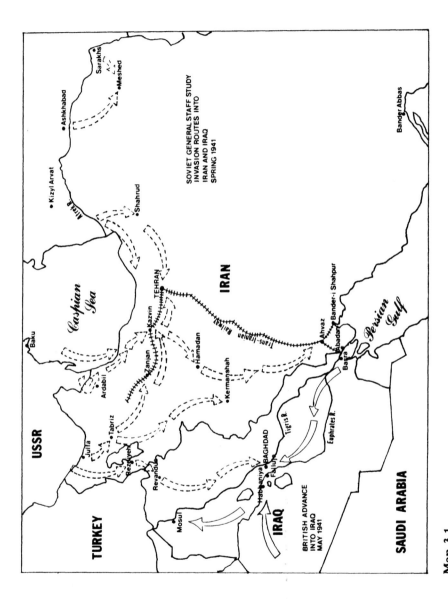

Map 3.1
British Advance into Iraq, May 1941; Soviet General Staff Study Invasion Routes into Iran and Iraq, Spring 1941

fallen Lucifer about him . . . sad and blackhaired, with venom in his glance."[2] The mufti advocated the use of terrorism to expel the British from the Middle East and to purge the Jews from Palestine.

At the time, Iraq was still allied with Britain, and had dutifully expelled the German legation when the war began. The Italian legation, however, was active in Baghdad, and served as a center of Axis intrigue. Further, the mufti had established secret communications with the former German minister to Iraq, Fritz Grobba, in Berlin.

The regent—Prince Abdullilah—was pro-British, and ruled Iraq in the stead of his nephew—the six-year-old king, Feisel II. The intrigues of the mufti, Rashid Ali, and the four colonels compelled Abdullilah in late March 1941 to take measures intended to head off a confrontation. Orders were issued to break up the power of the colonels by transferring them to remote garrisons. When this ploy became apparent, the conspirators acted against the regent.

After seizing power on April 2, the rebels named Rashid Ali as head of the new government. Rashid Ali realized that the Germans and Italians were still too distant from Iraq to offer effective assistance. He therefore sought diplomatic recognition from the British, to avoid military intervention. However, the newly arrived British ambassador, Sir Kinahan Cornwallis, remained cautiously aloof.

When news of the revolt reached London, Prime Minister Winston Churchill directed that the rebellion be quelled before the Iraqis could invite Nazi intervention, which would threaten the Anglo–Iranian oil fields. On April 8, the prime minister ordered the Indian government to dispatch a division immediately to Basra. Plan SABINE was implemented. General Auchinleck diverted the lead brigade of the Tenth Indian Division—destined for Malaya—to the southern Iraqi port of Basra, and promised Churchill five more brigades by June. Four days later—on April 12—the 20th Indian Brigade and the Tenth Indian Division staff left Karachi for Basra.[3]

This precipitate British action disturbed Gen. Archibald Wavell, the commander in chief of the Middle East. Wavell was skeptical of Churchill's "critical decision" to intervene in Iraq, and warned the British leader on April 10 that "I am fully committed in Cyrenaica and Greece, and can spare nothing for Iraq." The Chiefs of Staff nevertheless directed Wavell to immediately dispatch an expeditionary force from Palestine to reinforce the exposed RAF station at Habbaniya, outside Baghdad. Wavell countered by stating that the Palestine garrison was too weak to support such an operation.[4]

In Iraq, meanwhile, Ambassador Cornwallis caught Rashid Ali off guard on April 16 by announcing the imminent arrival of an Indian brigade at Basra. Cornwallis sought Iraqi permission for safe landing of the force— explaining that, because of the critical situation in Egypt, Britain was exercising its rights under the 1939 Anglo-Iraqi Treaty to pass troops through Iraq to Palestine. Rashid Ali reluctantly agreed, providing that the force would not exceed a mixed brigade and would quickly pass through Iraq. The Iraqi leader feared a premature confrontation, and believed that his four army divisions could deal—if necessary—with a small British force.[5]

The convoy transporting the 20th Indian Brigade entered the Shatt-al-Arab waterway at 2:30 A.M. on the morning of April 18. The HMAS *Yarra*—an Australian sloop mounting four-inch and three-inch guns—escorted the convoy. As she steamed slowly up the shadowy river, her crewmen anxiously scanned the dim Iraqi shoreline. As dawn broke, they sighted the massive oil refinery at Abadan, where curious crowds of Iranians and British were gathered along the Iranian bank of the river. British oil employees and their families waved handkerchiefs to signal their relief at the arrival of the British force. Four whitewashed Iranian warships that were lapping at anchor—their guns covered by canvas—rendered honors as the *Yarra* passed. The brigade landed unopposed at Basra, and quickly occupied key points around the city.[6]

In Baghdad, Iraqi leaders agreed to resist further British landings. Desperately short of war matériel, however, Rashid Ali urged the Italian minister to airlift rifles and ammunition—in turn, promising to place airfields at the disposal of the Axis.[7]

On April 20, Churchill ordered at least three more brigades to Basra; he directed Ambassador Cornwallis to explain to the Iraqis that the troops in Basra would not be moving on to Palestine, but would be establishing a major base. The British minister was not to "entangle himself by explanations."[8]

In Berlin, the Germans were also reacting to the British move into Iraq. On April 21, Foreign Minister Ribbentrop advised Hitler that Germany could provide immediate assistance to Iraq only by air. Deployment of Luftwaffe units to Iraq was "out of the question" for the moment, however, due to the excessive range. Ribbentrop also questioned whether the Iraqis had the will to resist the British.[9]

A week later—on April 27—Ribbentrop briefed Hitler that the Luftwaffe was studying direct intervention in Iraq while 600 tons of arms were being prepared for shipment to the rebels. The munitions had been intended for Iran, but they could hopefully be diverted upon reaching Turkey. The Vichy French in Syria were also being pressed to release arms to Iraq. The same day, Ribbentrop assured Rashid Ali that the Axis powers would "stand behind the present Iraq Government . . . in their struggle against England, and will do everything they possibly can."[10]

In Baghdad, British Ambassador Cornwallis bluntly told the Iraqi leaders on April 28 that 2,000 additional British troops would arrive at Basra the next day. Rashid Ali convened his Defense Council which agreed to militarily confront the British. Realizing that Iraq's forces near Basra were too weak, the council chose instead a more exposed target: the RAF air base at Habbaniya.[11]

During the night of April 29/30, Iraqi infantry and artillery began surrounding the almost indefensible air station. Protected only by a barbed wire fence and 14 blockhouses, the air station was backed against the Euphrates River and faced a high, dominating plateau. The garrison consisted of only 1,200 native levies—mostly Assyrians and Kurds—and a squadron of 18 RAF armored cars. Their largest weapons were mortars and machine guns. In addition, the flying school had some 1,000 instructors and students, but only 56 operational aircraft—all antiquated biplanes. About 400 men of the First King's Own Regiment had arrived by air on April 29— giving slight reinforcement.[12]

Shortly after dawn on April 30, an Iraqi envoy demanded that all British air activity cease. The air officer commanding refused, threatening reprisals if the Iraqis interfered with training flights. A tense standoff ensued, with the air station virtually being held hostage. The following day, the Habbaniya garrison received authorization to attack if the Iraqis failed to withdraw. More Iraqi troops and guns arrived on the plateau. Soon, two full Iraqi brigades and ten artillery batteries were deployed on the heights overlooking the airstrip. For the British garrison, an escape without heavy losses was all but impossible.

Shortly before dawn on May 2, the garrison received a radio message from Churchill; "Strike hard if you strike at all."[13] At sunrise, British aircraft swarmed over the plateau, the first bombs falling at precisely five o'clock. A minute later, Iraqi shells came crashing down on the station. The engagement ensued all morning. British aircraft landed amidst exploding shells, while bomb-fitters climbed all over the aircraft with fresh ammunition. By 10 A.M., Iraqi fire began to slacken as the bombing took its toll. But just as soon as it let up, the shelling would resume again. Miraculously, the air station suffered little damage. In Baghdad, Rashid Ali was shaken by the day's events; he appealed desperately to Berlin for immediate assistance—asking also that the former German minister, Fritz Grobba, be dispatched at once to Baghdad.[14]

In London, word of the fighting prompted Churchill to revert command of all British forces in Iraq to Wavell. He immediately ordered his Middle East chief to form a relief force in Palestine—the forces at Basra being too distant to render effective aid.[15]

Wavell angrily responded that "I have consistently warned you that no assistance could be given to Iraq under present circumstances. . . . My forces are stretched to the limit everywhere." Several hours later—after further consideration—he radioed London that he would improvise a mechanized brigade in Palestine, but only to impress the Iraqis. His lack of determination dismayed Churchill.[16]

Daybreak on May 3 brought more British airplanes swarming over the plateau—forcing frightened Iraqi gunners under cover. Elsewhere in Iraq, British bombers struck various targets, and destroyed much of the Iraqi air force on the ground.[17]

In Berlin that day, Ribbentrop advised Hitler that "If available reports are correct regarding the relatively small forces the English have landed in Iraq so far, there would seem to be a great opportunity for establishing a base for warfare against England through Iraq." He proposed immediately dispatching a fighter and bomber squadron to support the Iraqis. Aircraft in Greece could be flown to Iraq through Italian-controlled Rhodes and Vichy-controlled Syria. Hitler—though skeptical about available fuel in Iraq—gave permission to proceed with Luftwaffe preparations.[18]

At Habbaniya during the next two days, British air strikes harassed the besieging Iraqis day and night, while levy patrols harried Iraqi outposts.[19]

Wavell radioed London on April 5 that he was assembling an incomplete mechanized brigade near the Iraqi border. Emphasizing that the relief force would not be ready before May 10, he expressed doubts as to whether it would be strong enough and also whether Habbaniya could sustain its resistance. "I am afraid I can only regard [the relief effort] as an outside chance," he advised.[20]

Incensed, Churchill remarked caustically that Wavell had "kept the cavalry division in Palestine all this time without having the rudiments of a mobile column organized!" "I am deeply disturbed by General Wavell's attitude," he admitted. "In spite of the enormous numbers of men at his disposal . . . he seems to be hard up for battalions and companies. He gives me the impression of being tired out." By comparison, the British leader was favorably impressed by Auchinleck's readiness to rush more reinforcements to Basra.[21]

On May 5, the HMAS *Yarra* escorted another convoy up the Shatt-al-Arab—carrying the 21st Indian Brigade to Basra. Passing Abadan, she again received a piped salute from the Iranian warships; but this time the Iranian guns were uncanvassed, and a company of Iranian soldiers with antiaircraft artillery warily eyed the passing ships. The Iranian message was clear to the men of the *Yarra:* The shah would countenance no infringement of Iranian sovereignty.[22]

Daybreak on May 6 found the plateau above Habbaniya deserted. The Iraqis were gone. Their spirit broken, they had fled during the night. The British garrison quickly attacked a residual force that was blocking the road east of the station, and took several hundred prisoners. That afternoon, British warplanes caught an Iraqi relief column nearing Habbaniya on an open road. Methodically bombing and strafing the trapped vehicles, the pilots destroyed the entire convoy; hundreds of Iraqis perished in the conflagration.[23]

Dispirited by the news from Habbaniya, Rashid Ali beseeched the Germans to find a means to supply urgently needed arms to his army. The

Nazis immediately hatched a scheme to pass arms intended for Iran over to Iraq instead. Because Turkey would never permit the direct passage of arms to Iraq, the Germans needed the cooperation of the shah of Iran. On May 6, Reich Foreign Ministry Under Secretary Ernst Woerman cabled the German minister in Tehran, Erwin Ettel, that "We have reason to believe that the Iranian Government is on Iraq's side even if it does not acknowledge it openly."[24] Woerman directed Ettel to approach the Iranian government confidentially and secure its cooperation in dealing with the Turks. "We regard an exhaustive investigation of all possibilities of getting arms aid to Iraq as so critical that we are willing to run the risk of a negative reply by the Iranian Government, even if this means that the English will sooner or later learn of it."[25]

Woerman had incorrectly assessed the shah's attitude toward Iraq. Far from siding with the rebels, the shah was in fact deeply disturbed by the neighboring turmoil. Convening his Supreme War Council, he suggested dispatching two Iranian divisions to crush the revolt. Such action, he explained, would win Iran the goodwill of the British. At first, the generals were hesitant to question their monarch's idea. Finally, they gained courage and disagreed, pointing out that such an expedition would be costly and difficult. The shah dropped the matter.[26]

Ettel responded to Berlin two days later that, indeed, the Iranian government would not openly acknowledge its support of Iraq. The only person who could make the decision sought by Berlin was the shah himself, he cautioned. Not even the prime minister was certain how the monarch would react, but the shah was clearly angry at Germany's failure to satisfy Iran's arms requirements. "The Iranian Government," Ettel concluded, "would not permit any arms that have arrived on Iranian territory to be taken out again."[27]

On May 7, Churchill jubilantly congratulated the Habbaniya garrison for a "vigorous and splendid action [which] has largely restored the situation. We are all watching the grand fight you are making. All possible aid will be sent. Keep it up." A hastily organized relief force—dubbed HABFORCE, and consisting of lorry-borne infantry and artillery with no armor—assembled in Palestine. On May 9, Churchill ordered Wavell to aggressively "exploit the situation" due to the "desperate straits" of the Iraqis.[28]

The worsening predicament of the Iraqi rebels disturbed Hitler, who decided that a great opportunity would present itself if the situation could be turned around. Three Heinkel-111 bombers—the advance element of a larger force—landed at Aleppo in northern Syria on the afternoon of May 9, to the surprise of local Vichy French officials. Aboard was a small military liaison staff and two important Foreign Ministry officials: Fritz Grobba and Rudolph Rahn. The next morning, Grobba departed with two Heinkels for Mosul in northern Iraq, while Rahn was flown aboard a French aircraft to Damascus where he persuaded the Vichy governor-general, Gen. Henri

Dentz, to supply arms to Iraq. Grobba reached Baghdad early on May 11. On conferring with the Iraqi leaders, he developed a fear that their resolve was weakening. Immediately, he cabled Berlin, and urged the "immediate appearance of German fliers, if only for purposes of demonstration."[29]

In answer, Maj. Axel von Blomberg, leader of the Luftwaffe expedition to Iraq, flew his Heinkel bomber toward the Rashid aerodrome outside Baghdad the next morning. On the tarmac waited Grobba and a delegation of Iraqi dignitaries. But as the aircraft descended onto the runway, it was mistakenly fired on by Iraqi gunners. The bomber touched down and rolled to a stop. When the Iraqi welcoming committee looked inside the cockpit, they found the young Luftwaffe officer dead with a bullet through his neck.[30]

In Iran, meanwhile, the presence of five German and three Italian merchant ships stranded at the Iranian port of Bander-i Shapur raised British fears that the vessels might attempt to scuttle themselves in the entrance to the Shatt-al-Arab—thus blocking British naval traffic to Basra and Abadan. On May 11, the Foreign Office asked the Admiralty to direct the Senior Naval Officer Persian Gulf (SNOPG), Com. Cosmo Moray Graham, to take the steps necessary to intercept the German ships.[31]

The Admiralty agreed, admitting that it was "absolutely vital that every necessary step be taken to prevent the Rooka Channel being blocked." "If this happened," they warned, "no oil could leave Basra and no troops or material could be sent there." The Admiralty urged strongly that "no political considerations should now prevent aircraft reconnoitering at any time over Iranian territorial waters" from keeping watch on the ships. The Foreign Office now faced the problem of Iranian neutrality. Sir Horace Seymour, assistant foreign secretary, believed that "a decision to reconnoiter over Iranian waters would be a serious one and might lead to the Persian air force at Ahvaz interfering." "On the other hand," he noted, "the closing by German ships of the Rooka Channel would be most serious, and they are very likely to try it." Seymour decided on a limited number of reconnaissance flights over the Iranian port. The Admiralty immediately directed Commodore Graham to take offensive action—if necessary—inside Iranian territorial waters, to prevent the Axis from sailing.[32]

On May 13, Churchill admonished Wavell to "beat down Rashid Ali's forces with utmost vigor." "What matters is action, namely the swift advance of the mobile column," he ordered, "for the Germans may not be long." The Middle East commander flaggingly responded that "we will do our best to liquidate this tiresome Iraqi business. Shortage of transport is causing difficulty."[33]

At Mosul in northern Iraq on May 14, German agent Rudolph Rahn surveyed the dismal situation that faced the incoming Luftwaffe units. There were no gasoline, bombs, or spare parts to service the German aircraft arriving daily. But what most alarmed him was the lack of firm Iraqi leadership. Nevertheless, he started preparing for the eventual arrival of German motorized infantry.[34]

Col. Werner Junck arrived at Mosul, meanwhile, to take command of the Luftwaffe forces in Iraq—altogether, some two dozen fighters and bombers. He found everything lacking—especially aviation fuel. The gasoline available was of the wrong octane for German aircraft. Already, losses and crack-ups had whittled his force to only a handful of aircraft. Worst of all, because of Blomberg's untimely death there was almost no liaison with the Iraqi High Command—leaving Junck to operate with incomplete information. The Luftwaffe commander nevertheless launched strike after strike against the Habbaniya air station and other British targets.[35]

On May 16, the German Navy ordered their merchant vessels trapped at Bander-i Shahpur to scuttle themselves in the Rooka Channel, but their closely watched captains were unable to comply.[36]

Advance patrols of HABFORCE from Palestine linked up with the Habbaniya garrison on May 17. Patrols from the garrison had already attacked and secured the vital iron bridge over the Euphrates at Falluja—opening the way to Baghdad.[37]

In increasing desperation, the Germans tried to pressure the shah of Iran into supporting the Axis effort in Iraq. On May 17, German Minister Ettel was directed to ask the Iranians to resubmit their list of required arms and munitions—which, Ribbentrop promised, would receive "immediate study . . . in an accomodating spirit [if] the Government in Tehran meets our wishes regarding Iraq."[38]

But the shah was determined to maintain strict neutrality with respect to all belligerents. When a British aircraft accidently overflew Iranian territory on May 18, the Iranian government lodged a protest with the British legation. The next day, Iranian antiaircraft fired on an unidentified airplane that was preceding a British convoy up the Shatt-al-Arab. Though the aircraft turned out to Iranian, the message was clear.[39]

The next day—May 20, 1941—the greatest airborne invasion in history commenced. Elite German paratroops and mountain troops of Gen. Karl Student's Eleventh Air Army—22,000 strong—assaulted the Greek island of Crete, which was defended by some 40,000 poorly equipped and demoralized British, Australian, New Zealand, and Greek troops. With massive numbers of transport aircraft at his disposal, General Student planned for the swift seizure of Crete to be followed by rapid, successive leaps to Cyprus, Vichy-controlled Syria, and ultimately Iraq and the Persian Gulf.[40]

But the initial wave of 3,000 German paratroops met dogged resistance, and suffered staggering losses. By nightfall of May 20, the Germans had seized none of the airfields needed to land follow-on reinforcements. Fierce fighting continued through May 21, as the Germans gained a tenuous but contested hold on Maleme airfield. Student immediately began airlifting reinforcements to Crete. Junker transports landed amid exploding shells, which extracted a stiff toll of men and aircraft. Still, the Germans slowly gathered strength.

Meanwhile, the German and Iraqi governments—in a desperate effort to choke off British reinforcements to Basra in southern Iraq—urged the Iranian government on May 21 to close the Shatt-al-Arab waterway to British warships. The shah's government flatly refused. The "Iranian Government do not question [Britain's] treaty rights," Acting Foreign Minister Djevad Amery assured the British minister, Sir Reader Bullard. But Amery also confided that the Iranians were deeply frightened of Nazi retaliation—particularly because German Minister Ettel had terminated further discussions, creating an "ominous" silence. Bullard hurriedly warned London that the "Iranian Government are confident that the German Government will seize upon the slightest pretext to accuse [Iran] of partiality towards us." He relayed the shah's "hope that we will do everything in our power to assist them." The shah was willing to stand up to the Germans if the British would back him militarily. Bullard assured Amery that his government would "assist the Iranian Government within the limits of military necessity."[41]

The following day—May 22—proved fatally decisive for both the Iraqis and the Germans in their efforts to drive the British from Iraq. In Iraq, the Iraqi Army launched a desperate counterattack in an attempt to reach and destroy the vital Falluja bridge over the Euphrates—which would delay the British advance on Baghdad. The Iraqis advanced to within sight of their objective, only to be driven back by intense British resistance. The Luftwaffe—whose support for the operation might have proven decisive—never appeared, due to poor coordination. The Iraqis' one chance to forestall the British was lost.[42]

On Crete the same day, more German forces landed at Maleme airfield—expanding their embattled airhead. The New Zealand defenders launched a determined counterattack to regain the airfield, but faltered at the edge of the airstrip. The initiative passed to the Germans. Days of grinding combat remained before Allied resistance was overcome. For the Germans, Crete was a tactical victory, but a strategic defeat. The enormous losses in men and transport aircraft so appalled the fuehrer that he suspended further airborne operations in the Mediterranean.[43]

The sole remaining hope for the Iraqi cause lay with the Luftwaffe's ability to strike at the British from Mosul. More German air units were due to arrive in Iraq within days. But these would be useless, because the fuel situation at Mosul had become so critical that many of Colonel Junck's aircraft were grounded. British air attacks had destroyed the limited Iraqi oil supplies. German fuel experts were even dispatched to Iraq to locally refine the proper grade of octane. Desperate for fuel, the German Foreign Ministry ordered Erwin Ettel on May 22 to seek oil from Iranian reserves. The German minister in Tehran was told that 2,000 tons was needed immediately. He was to assure Iran's prime minister that—in exchange—"the Reich Government would show its appreciation."[44]

Iranian Prime Minister Ali Mansur flatly refused the request. The Iranian government had no stocks of its own, he told Ettel; it obtained what it needed from the AIOC. Dissatisfied with this response, the German envoy pressed for the fuel. Cornered, the nervous official explained that—were Iran to provide the fuel—England would regard the action as hostile, and would invade. A British attack would in turn spark a Soviet invasion—which would mean the "end of Iran." The shah believed that Rashid Ali's actions were rash and premature, Mansur added, and the monarch doubted the success of the uprising. Mansur also admitted that, unless the Turks openly sided with Germany, Iran would maintain strict neutrality. He urged the Germans to understand his government's difficult situation.[45]

By the evening of May 22, 1941, the Iraqi rebel cause was irrevocably lost, and Hitler's golden opportunity to strike directly toward the Persian Gulf had passed. If the Iraqis had recaptured the vital bridge at Falluja and thus delayed the British advance until German aid (which was imminent) could arrive, if General Student's airborne forces had captured Crete swiftly and with little loss, if the shah had provided the fuel desperately needed by the Germans, and/or if the Germans had closed the Shatt-al-Arab by scuttling their ships in the narrow Rooka Channel, the outcome of the Iraqi revolt—and perhaps of the war itself—might have been different.

Only now—when it was too late—did Hitler realize that the looming calamity in Iraq was destroying a precious opportunity to outmaneuver the British position in the Middle East. On May 23, he issued a directive declaring that "The Arab Liberation Movement is our natural ally against England." The Arabs were to be encouraged to cast off the "British yoke" and achieve "self-determination." The order stipulated, however, that "whether and how the British position between the Mediterranean and the Persian Gulf . . . shall later be . . . defeated is to be decided only after BARBAROSSA."[46]

In Baghdad the next day, the Grand Mufti complained bitterly to the Italian minister that too few aircraft had arrived. He warned that the next two weeks would be decisive. Unless the Axis sent enough assistance before then, the entire anti-English Arab movement in the Middle East would collapse.[47]

At sunrise on May 28, the British force at Falluja commenced its final advance on Baghdad. Fritz Grobba left the Iraqi capital early the next morning to organize resistance at Mosul. By May 30, the British were closing on Baghdad from the west and north. Inside the city, the Iraqi colonels were losing control of their own men. Two battalions mutinied. Amid imminent collapse, Rashid Ali along with the mufti and three dozen other followers fled by auto to the Iranian border, where they were granted asylum. The mayor of Baghdad assumed control and requested a truce with the British.[48]

Berlin cabled Grobba at Mosul on May 31 that fresh Luftwaffe units would be arriving on the following day. The German Army had also alerted an infantry battalion for immediate dispatch to Iraq. But these actions came too late. The few remaining German aircraft were grounded for lack of fuel. Even the local Iraqi commander had lost heart. Grobba radioed back that the Luftwaffe should not land at Mosul, and advised instead that further German air operations would have to be based in Vichy-controlled Syria.[49]

The capture of Mosul was foremost in the minds of the British Chiefs of Staff, but for reasons other than just to capture Grobba and the few German pilots there. The British urgently needed an airfield from which they could threaten the Baku oil fields. As the British Chiefs of Staff warned General Wavell on May 31st,

> We have firm indication that Germans are now concentrating large army and air forces against Russia. Russian resistance may be strongly influenced if they think that should they submit to Germans we shall attack Baku oil. If we are to use this threat to exert pressure on Russians, we must control Mosul before Russians and/or Germans forestall us. Most energetic action . . . be taken to get control of Mosul.[50]

The British dispatched a mechanized column from Habbaniya, and it occupied Mosul on June 4. But Grobba and most of the German airmen had already slipped into Syria.[51]

The British government had been closely monitoring the German buildup in Poland. Hitler's intentions remained uncertain to both London and Moscow. Some believed that Hitler intended to invade the Soviet Union, but many thought that the fuehrer's real purpose was to extract stiff demands from Stalin—including Soviet action against the British in the Middle East.

"The Chiefs of Staff have come to conclusion that Germany is prepared to attack Russia," Sir Alexander Cadogan, permanent under secretary of the Foreign Office, wrote in his diary on May 31. "I agree, but I believe that Russia will give way and sign on the dotted line. I wish she wouldn't, as I should love to see Germany expending her strength there. But they're not such fools as our General Staff. But we must consider how we can use threat or fact of bombing to Baku."[52]

But this perception was incorrect. Not only was Hitler prepared to attack the Soviet Union, but he fully intended to. Stalin—also—mistook Nazi intentions, and decided to view the German concentrations as a show of force, possibly intended to pressure a Soviet move against the British in the

Middle East. Only days before the German invasion, a Soviet radio broadcast declared that "the dispatch of German troops into the east and northeast areas of Germany must be assumed to be due to motives which have no connection with Russia."[53]

Stalin obstinately ignored all warnings of Nazi intentions from the British, the Americans, and even his own intelligence service. As Churchill subsequently explained, "Nothing that any of us could do pierced the purblind prejudice and fixed ideas which Stalin had raised between himself and the terrible truth."[54] The Soviet dictator knew that his country must eventually fight Germany, but he was determined to gain as much time as possible to build up Soviet military might while the Germans expended theirs fighting the West. It appears that, to avoid war with Hitler, Stalin was prepared to tacitly meet the terms presented by Ribbentrop in November 1940 and move Soviet forces southward toward the Persian Gulf.

To this apparent end, Soviet relations with Iran grew tense during April. Germany's minister in Iran, Erwin Ettel, cabled Berlin on April 13 that "Official Soviet sources, both at Moscow and Tehran, have recently gone to almost ridiculous lengths to blow up entirely meaningless incidents . . . so as to make major political affairs out of them." Prime Minister Mansur told Ettel that the Iranian government was suspiciously following these Soviet activities, which "were apparently intended to furnish a pretext under which Soviet Russian designs on Iran could be carried out."[55] The British military attaché in Tehran warned London on April 28 of the "General uneasiness here caused by . . . fears as to . . . Soviet moves." He had learned from a "reliable German source" that the Germans expected "events to happen in Iran within seven weeks."[56]

In late May 1941, the Red Army began its final preparations for the invasion of Iran. Maj. Gen. M. N. Shahrokhin, the general staff sector chief for the Near Eastern theater (Iran and Iraq), arrived in Tbilisi, Georgia, with a team of General Staff officers to monitor a major staff exercise in the Transcaucasus Military District. A key member of the team was Lt. Col. Sergei Shtemenko, the architect of the General Staff invasion study of Iran.[57]

The commander of the Transcaucasus Military District, Lt. Gen. Dimitri Timofeevich Kozlov, met Shahrokhin and his staff. Kozlov seemed a logical choice to direct an operation in the Middle East theater. He had fought the Moslem Basmachi rebels in Central Asia during the 1920s, taught tactics at the Frunze Military Academy, and—most recently—commanded an infantry corps during the Finnish campaign.[58] For the purposes of the exercise, Kozlov's district was designated a front—a grouping of armies—whose primary striking force was the 28th Mechanized Corps, which included two tank divisions.[59]

The day after the General Staff team arrived, Kozlov was summoned urgently to Moscow. The reason is not known; but his counterpart in the

Central Asian Military District—Gen. Mikhail Kazakov—was also recalled to Moscow, in order to finalize his district's operational plan against Iran and to brief the commissar for defense. Presumably, Kozlov's purpose was the same.[60]

The Transcaucasus Military District contained not only the powerful forces added the previous year, but was being further beefed up with units from Siberia. On May 26, the Soviet General Staff ordered the 16th Army transferred from the Transbaikal Military District to the Transcaucasus. The deployment was conducted in the greatest secrecy. On June 3, trains carrying the 16th Army departed for the Transcaucasus—with their doors sealed and nobody permitted to detrain en route.[61]

Kozlov's Front was unlikely to encounter serious resistance from the meager British force in Iraq. If the Soviets could seize the Abadan refinery and its surrounding oil fields, Britain would be effectively knocked out of the war. But most importantly, Stalin could demonstrate good faith to Hitler by keeping the supposed bargain made in November. An expeditious Soviet move toward the Persian Gulf might also preempt a similar Nazi stroke. If Hitler were to move swiftly through Syria and Iraq—which seemed possible at the time—Stalin's position would be outflanked from the south.

The Transcaucasus war games ended in early June. General Shahrokin's staff debriefed Kozlov's staff, and then crossed the Caspian Sea to Mary in Central Asia—where they were met by Lt. Gen. Sergei Georgivich Trofimenko, commander of the Central Asian Military District, and his chief of staff, Maj. Gen. Mikhail Illyich Kazakov. This set of exercises occurred along the frontier with northeastern Iran.[62]

The Central Asian Military District formed its tank, infantry, and cavalry divisions into an single operational army, which was moved toward the Iranian border. General Kazakov, the district chief of staff, directed the army. Colonel Shtemenko from Moscow took this opportunity to familiarize himself with the region on which his study had focused. "During the exercises, for the purposes of studying the theater of operations," he wrote later, "I traveled extensively along the [Soviet–Iranian] frontier from Serakhs to Ashkahbad, and then across the Kizyl-Atrek as far as Gasan-Kuli."[63] General Kazakov later noted of the exercise that "it appeared that the General Staff representatives were no more concerned than we about the situation on our western borders."[64]

In London, meanwhile, British leaders feared that Hitler might compel Stalin to move against Iran and Iraq. On June 2, British Foreign Secretary Anthony Eden urgently summoned Soviet Ambassador Ivan Maisky, who arrived looking distinctly uneasy. Eden warned Maisky that the Germans were constantly intriguing in the Middle East in hopes of bringing the Soviet Union and Britain into conflict. The foreign secretary stated bluntly that England would defend its position in the Middle East—including Iran and Afghanistan—against attack. Pointing to the suppression of the Iraqi revolt as evidence, he warned Maisky that Britain was using all means available to reinforce its forces in the Middle East.[65]

Eden then relayed reports of increasing German concentrations along the western Soviet frontier, but Maisky found it difficult to believe that Germany planned any military action against the Soviet Union. The Red Army was clearly too well equipped, Maisky stated. He regarded the German buildup as part of a "war of nerves." Eden agreed, suggesting that possibly Hitler hoped to force concessions from the Soviets "which it was not in their national interest to give."[66] This was a carefully disguised warning. Both men knew that Britain's only trump against the Soviet Union in the Middle East was the threat to the Caucasus oil fields.

Eden asked Maisky to elicit an assurance from his government that it did not intend to join with Germany against Britain in Iran or Iraq. But Maisky displayed more interest in the Nazi airborne threat to Syria and Iraq. He asked if the situation in Iraq was under control and if Britain could deal with Vichy-controlled Syria. Eden responded that Iraq was secure and that the British were now well placed to handle Syria. Three days later, the two officials met again. Maisky still had no answer regarding his government's policy toward Iran and Iraq. After a long talk, Eden recorded his fear that "there is tremendous German pressure on Soviets. I continue to believe that latter will give way [against Britain] unless their skin is asked of them."[67]

Eden learned from British intelligence on June 9 that the Germans were heightening invasion preparations against the Soviet Union. He mulled various ways of encouraging Soviet resistance to German pressure, but realized that Britain could do very little diplomatically until Stalin's attitude toward the Middle East became clear. The next day—June 10—Ambassador Maiksy informed Eden that the Soviet government was not negotiating with Germany. He assured the foreign secretary that the Soviets did not intend to ally themselves militarily to the Germans. Even so, Maisky still had no response to the question of Soviet policy toward Iran and Iraq.[68]

In Soviet Central Asia, meanwhile, military exercises were proceeding along the Iranian border. On June 11, in the midst of the maneuvers, General Kazakov was urgently recalled from his army forward command post to Moscow. A Soviet SB bomber flew him to district headquarters at Tashkent where he boarded a passenger aircraft for the Soviet capital. While flying over the vast desert of Central Asia, Kazakov observed a number of military trains heading west. "I knew very well that no troops had been dispatched from our military district," he recorded later, "and that there were no plans to do so." The trains—he soon learned—carried units from the Transbaikal Military District.[69] Originally destined for the Transcaucasus, the 16th (Transbaikal) Army was redirected en route to the Kiev Special Military District.[70]

The Soviet General Staff—despite Stalin's optimism—was finally worried about German intentions. Soviet armies from the Urals, Volga, and Transbaikal Military Districts were being redeployed to assembly areas behind the western frontier. On June 10, the 19th Army arrived in the Ukraine from the North Caucasus Military District. This district normally supplied support forces to the Transcaucasus Military District. The Soviet high command—seeming to want to cover both the German and Iranian contingencies—retained control of this army directly under the commissar for defense.[71]

When General Kazakov reached Moscow from Tashkent, he was directed by General Vatutin, the deputy chief of the General Staff, to update the Central Asian Military District's operational plan in order to brief the commissar for defense, Mar. Semen K. Timoshenko. As he hurriedly incorporated changes in personnel and units into the plan, Kazakov noticed a flurry of activity. Another general confided to him that the Finns were mobilizing, while the Germans were ready to invade. Kazakov asked when war might begin. "We'll be lucky if it doesn't begin in the next fifteen to twenty days," his friend replied confidentially.[72]

But Stalin remained determined to do nothing that might provoke the Germans. When Marshal Timoshenko requested permission on June 13 to raise the combat readiness of the frontier forces, Stalin refused it. "You propose carrying out mobilization, alerting the troops and moving them to the Western borders?" he asked accusingly. "That means war! Do you understand that or not?" When his generals pointed to reports of German preparations, Stalin answered that "you can't believe everything in intelligence reports!"[73]

On June 14, TASS denounced the "rumors of an impending war" in the "English and foreign press" as "a clumsy propaganda maneuver of the forces arrayed against the Soviet Union and Germany."[74] The announcement made it clear that Stalin still viewed Britain as his more immediate potential foe. Unfortunately for the Soviets, the TASS article created a false sense of security.

At the General Staff, these attitudes puzzled General Kazakov, who wondered why the high command was concentrating on exercises directed toward its southern border rather than western border.[75]

Similarly bewildered was the chief of British Army Intelligence in Baghdad, Capt. Somerset de Chair. De Chair had learned that British intelligence was warning of a possible German attack on the Soviet Union—which he did not find too surprising. But what confused him was that one of his most reliable and well-informed agents was also relaying repeated information pointing to an imminent Soviet move into Iran. To ferret out the incongruity, De Chair asked his key agent—an Englishman with wide contacts—to verify the separate reports. The agent reported back several days later that his sources confirmed Germany's intention to attack the Soviet Union within the week. He had also found some basis for expecting a Soviet attack on Iran. However, when De Chair reported these findings to his superiors, they dismissed them out of hand.[76]

In the northeastern Iranian city of Tabriz—a mere 50 miles below the Soviet border—the British consul, Mr. Cook, was recording in his June diary that the Soviets were believed to be reinforcing their posts along the border. During the previous month, he had received reports of increased Soviet troop concentrations in the Caucasus and of attempts by the Soviets to infiltrate the Iranian Army. The Iranian police, he noted, were closely watching the local garrison.[77]

In Egypt, meanwhile, disaster beset the British army. Launching Operation BATTLEAXE on June 15, General Wavell hoped to drive the German Afrika Korps well into Libya and relieve the beleaguered British garrison at Tobruk. The British made some initial headway before meeting strong Axis resistance. Then Rommel's panzers swept out of the desert—smashing Wavell's exposed left flank. The British withdrew, leaving 100 tanks smoldering on the battlefield.[78]

Wavell's offensive capability was devastated. Troop morale plummeted. Staff officers in Cairo hastily prepared plans to evacuate Egypt; they were unaware that Rommel was being restrained at the border by Hitler. When reports of the setback reached London, Gen. Sir John Dill, chief of the general staff, confided to a friend, "I suppose you know that we shall lose the Middle East."[79]

In Berlin, Adolph Hitler felt so certain of quick victory in the coming campaign against the Soviet Union that, on June 19, he issued Directive Number 32: Preparations for the Time after BARBAROSSA. "After the Soviet Russian armed forces have been crushed," the Fuehrer declared, the German military would continue "the struggle against the British position in the Mediterranean and the Near East." "The possibility of exerting strong pressure on Turkey and Iran improves the prospect of utilizing these countries for the fight against England," the order explained. Once the Red Army collapsed, the Wehrmacht was to form in the Caucasus a "motorized expeditionary corps . . . to open the way . . . through Iran to Basra."[80]

In Moscow on June 19, Generals Kazakov and Vatutin prepared to brief Marshal Timoshenko on the Central Asian Military District operational plan. Kazakov was anxious to get back to Tashkent; he feared that war with Germany might break out at any moment, Finally that evening, the two generals were ushered into Timoshenko's office, where they watched a German propaganda film. Afterward, the commissar for defense hurried off to dinner and then went to bed. The next morning, Kazakov tried again to obtain an audience, and finally settled for presenting his questions to Gen. Georgi K. Zhukov, chief of the General Staff. Zhukov reviewed the plans thoroughly. Satisfied, he dismissed Kazakov, who flew back to Tashkent the following morning, June 21.[81]

At the same time, a train arrived in Moscow from Tashkent; it was carrying General Shahrokhin and the other members of his General Staff team, freshly returned from the staff exercises in the Transcaucasus and Central Asia. The staff officers turned in their exercise documents, and then received two days leave. But their rest would prove to be short lived.[82]

Along the Polish–Soviet frontier that evening, German infantry and tanks moved into forward assembly areas under cover of darkness while, at nearby airfields, bombers and fighters were being rigged and loaded. On the Soviet side, all was normal. Troops lolled in their barracks, and aircraft were lined up on runways in peacetime fashion. But in Moscow, the indications of imminent attack could no longer be ignored. German merchant ships were abruptly departing Soviet ports. A Nazi sergeant had crossed the border; he warned that the invasion was set for 3 A.M.[83]

Shortly before midnight, Marshal Timoshenko belatedly ordered all Soviet forces to combat readiness. Telegrams were dispatched to military districts and fleet commands. But the directions were contradictory. Soviet forces could defend themselves if attacked, but were not to respond to German provocations.

The alert came too late. At the first glimmer of dawn, Stuka dive-bombers descended on their targets while German shock troops stormed the frontier bridges—clearing the way for the onrushing panzers. From the Baltic to the Black seas, more than 1 million Axis troops launched the greatest invasion of history. The extensive but largely unmanned Soviet frontier fortifications were quickly pierced. Hundreds of Soviet aircraft were destroyed on the ground and in the air. Mass confusion reigned among the Soviet forces along the border.

Meanwhile—at almost the same moment that German troops began storming the Soviet borders—in Cairo, General Wavell's chief of staff, Lt. Gen. Arthur Smith, was awakened and given an urgent telegram from the prime minister. Smith dressed and rushed to Wavell's quarters, where he found Wavell shaving in the bathroom. Smith read the cable aloud. "I have come to [the] conclusion that [the] public interest will best be served by [the] appointment of General Auchinleck to relieve you," Churchill wired, ordering Wavell to assume Auchinleck's post as commander in chief, India.[84]

Following the failure of Operation BATTLEAXE and Wavell's lack of resolve during the Iraqi revolt, Churchill had lost confidence in his Middle East commander. But Wavell's reassignment would shortly have major repercussions for Iran, because the German invasion was suddenly reversing the polarity between Britain and Russia that, for nearly two centuries, had kept them at arm's length over Iran.

Winston Churchill—for one—wasted no time in embracing the Soviet Union as an ally. At 9 P.M. on June 22, 1941, he broadcast to the British people that

> No one has been a more consistent opponent of Communism than
> I have. . . . I will unsay no word that I have spoken about it. But all

this fades away before the spectacle which is now unfolding. The past, with its crimes, its follies, and its tragedies, flashes away. . . . We have but one aim and one single, irrevocable purpose . . . to destroy Hitler and every vestige of the Nazi regime. . . . The Russian danger is, therefore, our danger, and the danger of the United States.[85]

A new mutual struggle now brought the two erstwhile foes together. The danger posed by Nazi infiltration of the Middle East now affected both of their causes—and nowhere more so than in Iran.

4

The Germans Must Be Expelled from Iran

Herr Wulf, the German schoolmaster in Tabriz, excitedly awakened the German vice-consul, Bertold Schulze, at 6 A.M. on the morning of June 22, 1941. "Have you heard the news?" he asked. "It came over the five o'clock news. War with Russia! German troops marched in last night." Schulze was stunned but not entirely surprised, because he had been warned of the invasion three months earlier by Adm. Wilhelm Canaris, chief of the Abwehr (German Military Intelligence). Schulze was—in reality—a major in the Abwehr and the chief German military intelligence agent in northwestern Iran.[1]

The mission that Canaris had given to Schulze was to gather intelligence on Soviet oil facilities and military activities in the Transcaucasus. To this end, Schulze had arrived in Tabriz under diplomatic cover, and had quickly established a network of agents among various pro-German Iranian and anti-Soviet Russian émigré underground organizations. He routinely dispatched agents over the Soviet border on surveillance forays. In fact, a team of young Iranian agents had just returned from scouting the air base at Kirovabad.

Following Herr Wulf's announcement, Schulze hurriedly dressed, summoned the consulate limousine, and cruised about Tabriz with small Nazi flags fluttering boldly from the hood. The city was quiet. Clusters of men milled about the streets talking in whispers. Returning to the consulate, Schulze was given a note from an agent demanding an immediate meeting. The agent—a disreputable onetime tsarist officer named Nasarow—had been foisted on Schulze by Herr Maffey, his counterpart in the Sicherheitdienst (SD).

The SD was the foreign intelligence apparatus of the GESTAPO. Directed by the ruthless SS general, Reinhardt Heydrich, it operated in competition with the Abwehr. Its agents were dedicated Nazis, in contrast to the Abwehr—some of whose members, such as Admiral Canaris, secretly opposed Hitler.[2]

Schulze viewed SD agents as dangerous amateurs. Herr Maffey—for example—had indiscreetly revealed Schulze's true identity to Nasarow— which forced Schulze to handle the Russian. To minimize the damage, Schulze identified himself to Nasarow as "Captain Schmidt"—indicating that his real name was a pseudonym. He then dispatched the Russian on a number of small assignments, for little cost.[3]

Schulze agreed to meet with Nasarow; and the Russian appeared that afternoon in the consulate garden, with the smug report that he possessed information on new airfields in the Caucasus. Schulze offered him only a paltry sum. Nasarow demanded more money, and muttered that "Times have changed. We're at war and a trip over the frontier is a matter of life or death." Schulze flatly refused, and turned to leave. "I warn you," Nasarow threatened. "Don't drive me too far! What do think the Soviets would pay me if I gave them the news of your nice little spies' nest here in Tabriz, Captain Schmidt?" Schulze lunged at Nasarow with a stone. The terrified Russian fell to his knees, pleading for his life. Schulze disgustedly tossed the stone aside and allowed the man to flee.[4]

Too late, the Tabriz police arrested Nasarow—for the next morning, Schulze's Iranian secretary asked him excitedly, "Did you listen to the Baku radio last night? In Tabriz there exists a German spy center under a certain Consul Schmidt. The Russians warned they will soon be crossing the frontier to wipe out the whole nest."[5]

The German invasion of the Soviet Union suddenly focused international attention on the large German community in Iran. To the Allies, the situation seemed ripe for the usual Nazi fifth-column activities. Nearly 1,000 Germans resided in Iran that summer. Most had arrived before the war. Iranian police records indicate that 616 were employed by the Iranian government as technicians in various industries such as railways, mines, and agriculture or as advisors in government ministries. A few were professors in Iranian colleges, and several were merchants or doctors. About 60 were German seamen stranded aboard five merchant ships in the port of Bander-i Shahpur. There were a number in the Tehran legation and the Tabriz consulate. The rest were wives and children of the above.[6]

The German colony was tightly controlled by the slight, sinewy German minister, Erwin C. Ettel. Ettel—a protégé of Hitler—was the former Nazi party leader in Italy; he held the rank of oberfuehrer (brigadier general) in the notorious SS. German cultural activities centered around the "Brown House"—a recreation center and club in downtown Tehran.[7]

Both the SD and the Abwehr were active in Iran. The chief of the SD in Tehran was a handsome blond man named Roman Gamotha. His principle assistant was a 26-year-old, humorless Bavarian named Franz Mayr, whose black hair and mustache gave him a sinister appearance. Mayr was a fanatical Nazi who held the rank of untersturmfuehrer in the Waffen SS. The two men had arrived in Tehran in 1940—posing as representatives of the Shenkers Transport Firm. They established an import–export enterprise called the Nouvelle Iran Express as a cover for their underground activities. Mayr traveled extensively within Iran and abroad, establishing contacts and identifying safe houses.[8]

The Abwehr had several agents in Iran. Major Schulze and a man named Jacques Graewer both worked for Branch I (Espionage). A Herr Kuhl conducted operations for Branch II (Sabotage).[9] Iran provided the Abwehr with an ideal base to spy on the Soviet Union and the British oil facilities in the Persian Gulf.

The inadequate state of German military intelligence in the Near East greatly concerned the German Military High Command (Der Oberkommando der Wehrmacht, or OKW) as they began preparing for operations following the conquest of the Soviet Union. To address this problem, the OKW chaired a conference in Berlin on May 6, 1941—attended by representatives of the Foreign Ministry and other military agencies. The conferees proposed creating a covert "Kampforganisation" in Istanbul to direct intelligence operations in the Near East, including Iran. They also desired to establish a military "base of operations" in Iran, but concluded that the shah of Iran would never permit an official German military mission.[10]

They gauged the shah correctly, for he was keenly sensitive to foreign subversion—particularly by the Germans, who regularly invited top Iranian military leaders to countless diplomatic parties. The shah curbed this approach in March 1941 by forbidding foreign embassy's from inviting Iranian officers to their parties.[11]

Despite such measures, the Soviet and British governments almost immediately zeroed in on the perceived German menace in Iran, following the German attack on the Soviet Union. On June 26, the Soviet ambassador in Tehran, Alexei Andreivich Smirnov, delivered a note to the Iranian Foreign Ministry; it warned that his government had "serious evidence" of a planned German coup d' état, using elements within the Imperial Iranian Army. Smirnov then protested the harboring of German agents in Iran.[12]

On June 28, the U.S. minister in Tehran, Louis G. Dreyfus, Jr., replied to a query from Washington that neither he nor the British possessed reliable information on the internal organization of a Nazi fifth column in Iran. He described the German colony as large and well organized with agents and branches throughout the country. It was rumored, Dreyfus added, "that 500 tough and well-armed men could be placed on the streets of Tehran within a few hours." Doubting that a "skeleton General Staff exists in the German legation," he explained that the Iranian police were closely watching and restricting the movements of German agents. But he remarked that their efforts were "too desultory and weak to prevent the building up of an efficient organization which is ready to strike at the proper moment." That moment, he believed, would be "when German forces penetrate into the Caucasus."[13]

The shah's government quickly announced its neutrality in the Russo-German war on June 26, 1941.[14] But the invasion of the Soviet Union had already altered basic Iranian attitudes toward Germany—as if cleansing the Germans of past sins. Britain's minister in Tehran, Sir Reader S. Bullard, informed his government on June 25 that "Iranians generally are delighted at [the] German attack on . . . their ancient enemy Russia."[15] As Nazi successes in the Soviet Union mounted, crowds of Iranians gathered in Tehran's Sepah Square to cheer loudly each time a loudspeaker announced the fall of a Soviet town or city.[16]

The Iranians viewed the Germans as saviors from the hated Bolsheviks. The notion that Iran might itself fall victim to Nazi conquest seemed inconceivable. Unknown to the Iranians, however, the German Military High Command in Berlin had ordered on June 30, 1941, that—after the defeat of the Soviet Union—the British position in the Middle East would be subjected to a "concentric attack" that would include a possible motorized advance through Iran.[17]

In London on June 30—that same day—Iranian Minister Mohammed Moggadam gleefully expressed his hope to Foreign Secretary Anthony Eden that the Germans and the Soviets would kill each other off, and British power would increase. Eden tried to persuade the Iranian envoy that, if the Germans reached the Caucasus, it might have serious consequences for Iran. He asked Moggadam to urge his government to "rid herself" of the many Germans working in Iran.[18]

Moggadam replied that these men were all technical experts, whose expulsion could have a deleterious effect on Iran's economy. He added that his government had been unable to obtain such men from Britain. Eden informed Moggadam—as incentive—that, within a few months, Britain would deliver parts for the manufacture of 12 Hurricane fighters by the British-operated aircraft factory in Tehran. He expressed hope that this act would gratify the shah.

Because the Soviet Union had—in the course of one day—turned into an ally of Britain, the British now focused their security concerns in the Persian Gulf almost solely on the Germans, whom they expected to penetrate the Caucasus and enter Iran within weeks. Responsibility for the defense of Iran and Iraq had shifted to India on June 18; Gen. Archibald Wavell assumed command of British and Indian forces there on July 5. On June 24, the Indian General Staff had directed Brig. F. E. C. Hughes, commander designate of the British Persian Gulf Force, to reconnoiter the Persian Gulf jointly with the Royal Navy and the RAF to determine the requirements for its defense.[19]

Back in Cairo, meanwhile, Gen. Claude Auchinleck's Middle East Command prepared contingency plans to check a German breakthrough of the

Caucasus or Turkey by defending northern Iraq and advancing forces into northern Iran.[20]

Unknown to Auchinleck and Wavell, details of plans against Iran were being leaked to both the Germans and the shah by Egypt's corpulent, venal monarch—King Farouk. With Rommel's army posed on the Egyptian frontier, Farouk was terrified of losing his throne, and was eager to undermine his British "ally." For some time, he had maintained secret contacts with Berlin through his father-in-law—Zoulfikar Pasha, the Egyptian minister in Tehran. On June 29, Farouk secretly informed Pasha that he possessed definite information about a British General Staff decision to occupy the Iranian oil field region in order to protect it against German attack from the Soviet border. The British General Staff was reportedly allowing two months to prepare the invasion, and had asked for 500,000 men to conduct it. According to the information, they planned to occupy not only the AIOC concession area and the Persian Gulf ports, but also Kermanshah. The British further planned a second advance from Revandus in Iraq through northern Iran to Julfa on the Soviet border. Farouk instructed his father-in-law to inform the shah of the British plans and also to relay the information to the German minister, Erwin Ettel, "as proof of an attitude of candor and good faith toward Germany."[21]

Zoulfikar Pasha informed Farouk's brother-in-law, Crown Prince Mohammed Reza. He, in turn, alerted his father—the shah. Reza Shah initially refused to believe the report, but his son insisted on his source's reliability. The monarch then cabled his minister in London to ascertain Britain's true intentions.[22] On July 2, the Egyptian minister also dutifully apprised German Minister Erwin Ettel, who alerted Berlin of the alleged British plans.[23]

On July 3, Britain's secretary of state for India, Leopold S. Amery, privately advised General Wavell that action against Iran was necessary because of Germany's need for oil. He contended that the invasion of the Soviet Union had been "forced upon Germany largely because she must get oil." The Germans, he asserted, had failed to achieve this goal by operations in the eastern Mediterranean, "now their second string is Baku and Transcaucasia. . . . Once there they will be pretty close to your troops in Iraq and ready for every kind of mischief in Iran. [What] all that means [is] pretty close cooperation between ourselves and the Russians." He noted how "no one is better qualified than you to handle that."[24]

Amery was trying to plant the notion with Wavell for a coordinated British and Soviet campaign in Iran. Five days earlier, he had suggested to Eden—with little success—that the British government consider a joint Anglo–Soviet "action" in Iran. But Amery realized that Wavell was less concerned with diplomatic niceties than Eden and would support whatever military action necessary to secure his theater of operations.[25]

General Auchinleck, meanwhile, warned the War Office on July 7 that the Germans might reach the Caucasus by mid-August. The British would then have to defend Iran, Iraq, and Syria. Feeling that Turkey might not cooperate, he proposed maintaining a foothold against heavy German odds by defending only the vital belt covering Palestine, Basra, and the Iranian oil fields.[26]

Both Generals Auchinleck and Wavell believed—as did the British General Staff and the U.S. War Department—that Soviet resistance to the Germans would crumble within six weeks. Even the optimists gave the Soviets only three months. But President Franklin D. Roosevelt disagreed, deducing instead that—if the Soviets could hold until October—the fierceness of the Russian winter would delay German victory at least until spring. During that time, U.S. military aid could be rushed to the U.S.S.R.[27]

But such aid required a secure transit route. On July 7, British Minister for Economic Warfare Hugh Dalton suggested to Leopold Amery that Iran be occupied jointly with the Soviet Union, since Iran would be the only route remaining for Anglo–American supplies to the Soviet Union if the Japanese blocked Vladivostock. Dalton considered it vital for Britain to control the rail and road networks in southern Iran, while the Soviets could control the same in the north. Amery agreed, mentioning that he had made a similar suggestion to Eden on June 27.[28]

The viceroy of India, Lord Linlithgow, proposed similar action against Iran; he advised London on the following day that "in our view [a] positive policy to secure elimination of enemy centers in Iran is a matter of most vital importance." He further urged halting the delivery of warplanes to the shah.[29]

In Moscow that afternoon, Ambassador Sir Stafford Cripps personally delivered a note from Churchill to Stalin; it promised to the Soviets everything that "time, geography, and our growing resources allow." Though appreciative, Stalin expressed his worry over Iran, and claimed that there were "six to seven thousand Germans in Iran." He feared that Axis elements might attempt acts against both Baku and British interests in Iran, and recommended that the British and Soviet governments take some form of action. Cripps acknowledged that his government was aware of the Axis danger. He suggested that a jointly worded demarche be presented to the Iranian government in complaint about the German presence. Stalin agreed, and Cripps immediately advised Eden to "encourage the Soviet Government to backup . . . [the] demarche by troop concentrations on the northern Iranian border"; he asked that Britain consider staging a similar military threat along the southern Iranian frontier.[30]

In Tehran on July 9, Erwin Ettel learned that the shah was reacting to reports of British invasion plans by reinforcing Azerbaijan and Kermanshah. Reinforcements were also reportedly being dispatched to Khuzistan. Prime Minister Mansur confided to the German envoy that his government would seek German aid if attacked by Britain. He carefully added that, were Germany the aggressor, Iran would seek British aid. Ettel dismissed the notion of German aggression against Iran as purely "theoretical," and claimed that Germany wanted to avoid any extension of the war. But he warned Mansur that a "feeble" or "tacit" consent to a British invasion would make the "worst possible impression" on Germany's leaders. Afterward, Ettel expressed his belief to Berlin that "Iran will counter a British attack with resolute military resistance" and would "appeal to Germany for help." He added, however, that the "danger of a British attack on Iran has become less acute" because of the shah's firm military and diplomatic measures.[31]

The next day, General Wavell complained to London about its "complaisant attitude" over Iran, stating his view that

> It is essential to the defense of India that [the] Germans should be cleared out of Iran now. Failure to do so will lead to a repetition of events which in Iraq were only just countered in time. It is essential [that] we should join hands with Russia through Iran, and if the present Government is not willing to facilitate this, it must be made to give way to one which will. To this end the strongest possible pressure should be applied forthwith while [the] German–Russian struggle is in doubt.[32]

Wavell's proposal contrasted markedly with his previous views. Earlier, he had opposed intervention in Iraq. Now, with even scantier forces on hand, he was advocating a large-scale operation in Iran. But his perspective from India, where Iraq and Iran were his primary focus, differed markedly from Cairo, where his fronts and forces had been far flung. Ironically, Wavell had been among the most vocal opponents of a Soviet advance into Iran. But now he believed that the Red Army would be defeated within a matter of weeks; and therefore, he saw little long-term danger in a temporary Soviet presence in Iran.

The immediate concern of the British Chiefs of Staff was a German penetration of the Middle East. They apprised General Auchinleck on July 10 that the Wehrmacht might reach Caucasia by the middle of August, at which point the Germans might attempt to deny Britain its use of the northern Iraqi airfields. They also assumed that Iranian authorities would cooperate with Germany and allow it to use their airfields. The Chiefs of Staff feared that the Germans would simultaneously launch a land offensive against Iraq from either Iran or southern Turkey. If the attack came from Iran, they estimated that the Germans would push four divisions from Tehran and one from Tabriz. Because of Iran's limited communications and difficult winter weather, such an attack was unlikely to develop before April 1942.[33]

The Chiefs of Staff agreed with Auchinleck's proposal to abandon the defense of northern Iraq and to concentrate on a line east and north of

Baghdad and running through the mountains to Kermanshah in Iran. Meanwhile, mobile British forces would continue to operate in the far north, to maintain use of the airfields. To defend the region—including Syria—they estimated that at least ten divisions and thirty air squadrons would eventually be required. Their immediate plans, however, focused on a maximum scale attack through Iran to the Caucasus once the Germans arrived.

Soviet Ambassador Maisky advised Foreign Secretary Eden on July 10 that his government desired immediate measures to "check the serious threat to both countries" posed by "German infiltration" in Iran. Eden suspected that Stalin might merely be using the German presence in Iran as an excuse to attain long-sought Soviet objectives. But when he asked what action the Soviet government proposed, Maisky suggested a joint demand that Iran expel the Germans because of their "danger to neighboring countries." Eden pressed to find out what further action Moscow considered taking if the Iranians claimed that they could not dispense with the Germans. Maisky admitted that the Soviet Union and Britain would have to "clear their minds" on this issue before taking the first step, and suggested possible economic measures.[34]

The next day, the British War Cabinet asked the Chiefs of Staff to consider the problems involved in a joint Anglo–Soviet military action, should the Iranian government refuse to expel the Germans.[35]

From Tehran that day, Sir Reader Bullard cabled his concerns over British intentions, and noted his previous assurances to Iran's prime minister that reports of British plans to "send troops into Iran" were "contradicted by His Majesty's Government policy of respect for neutral states." He therefore asked rhetorically, "Would a demand for the departure of all Germans be compatible with that policy? I think not. We can produce surprisingly little proof of fifth column activities here although we are sure they must be going on." He advised instead threatening economic sanctions as part of proposed representations to Iran, and added that he would try to speak to the shah personally in regard to the Germans in Iran.[36]

The shah's minister in London, Mohammed Moggadam, appeared that day at the Foreign Office to complain about the insulting treatment that his ruler was receiving in the British press. "Really," he exclaimed, "your newspapers seem to refer to the Shah in worse terms than they refer to Hitler." Though his charges were obviously exaggerated, his real purpose was to ferret out British intentions toward Iran. When asked which article he referred to, Moggadam produced a clipping of a July 5 *News Chronicle* item calling the shah "cyncial, ruthless and money loving." Moggadam was told that the British press should never have published such a statement about "the ruler of a friendly country," and was assured that the Foreign Office would do what they could about it.[37]

Three days later, on July 14, Sir Stafford Cripps urged an immediate military show of force against Iran. Minimizing the question of Iranian neutrality, he argued that the

> present map of Europe provides an enlightening commentary on the policies of both Germany and ourselves towards small neutral states; and in the one case, Norway, where we were prepared to abandon our traditional policy [of respecting neutrality], we were not quick enough off the mark. Time factor is at least as important now, since in a few weeks the USSR may no longer be in a position to threaten Iran at all. [The] method of gradually increased infiltration is obviously inadequate in such circumstances. There seems no reason why any demands . . . should not be simultaneously reinforced by military demonstrations. If these fail of their effect and we then feel unable to take positive military action, it will not be the first time . . . that a military threat has not been pushed to its logical conclusion.[38]

But Eden remained unconvinced, noting that "Cripps' suggestions go beyond [British] policy and probably beyond what is at present practical."[39] That afternoon, Eden again met Maisky. The two agreed to first attempt a joint diplomatic approach to Iran, to be followed if necessary by economic pressure.[40]

The discontented viceroy of India considered diplomatic measures inadequate. "We wish to protest in [the] strongest terms," he cabled on July 16, "against the apparent failure . . . to take into account our considered representations regarding policy in a country where we are most directly interested, and from which [a] most dangerous threat to India's security may develop."[41]

Meanwhile, the Germans stepped up their covert activities in Iran. The Abwehr directed Schulze in Tabriz to "Watch troop movements in the frontier zone. . . . Report any new appearances of fighter squadrons. . . . Watch and report on any Allied transfer of troops from the Persian Gulf to the Caucasus." In Mid-July, a new German consul named Wussow arrived in Tabriz. Schulze knew of Wussow's reputation as a specialist in fifth-column "shock" tactics—Wussow having been a key player in delivering the Norwegian port of Narvik to the Nazis and in engineering the surprise attack on Yugoslavia.[42]

On July 17, the chief of the Abwehr's sabotage department, Col. Erwin von Lahousen, alerted his agent in Iran—Herr Kuhl—that a Major Strojil would soon be arriving in Tehran. Kuhl was instructed to contact Ali Azertekin, a member of an underground anti-Soviet Azerbaijani organization. Kuhl was to ask Azertekin how effective his organization in Iran was and what reliable contacts it had over the Soviet border. The Abwehr's intention was to prepare the organization "for action." The Azerbaijanis would report on the situation in their homeland and "carry out the directions of Abwehrabteilung II [Sabotage] in Berlin."[43]

Ambassador Cripps still wanted quick action against Iran. On July 17, he urged that

> maximum pressure, economic and military if necessary, can be applied before the opportunity passes as it may do with a German advance into the Caucasus. I suggest that it is the occasion to use . . . maximum pressure immediately and not to allow the matter to be dragged out . . . as no doubt [the Iranians] will attempt to do.[44]

The following day, the British Chiefs of Staff recommended adopting a firm attitude toward Iran. If military action was required, they advised that it be confined to southern Iran. At least one division—supported by a small air component—would be required to secure the oil fields. The chiefs estimated that the Soviets had five divisions available in the Caucasus, and three more east of the Caspian. Against this combined Ango–Soviet force, the Iranians were estimated to have nine divisions, of which only the two in Tehran were "moderately efficient." The main concern was that "this [Anglo–Soviet] force would have to come from Iraq, where at present we have insufficient troops for internal security." They noted, however, that "if the Russians cooperate with us . . . Iran is in no position militarily to resist a joint . . . demand for expulsion of the Germans."[45]

The next day—July 19, 1941—General Wavell advised that,

> to block advance of Germans toward India . . . we are in [a] position to enforce strong economic and political pressure on Iran in conjunction with Russians, and should not hesitate to do so. Failure to do this will allow German penetration supported by air forces and finally mobile troops right up to the frontiers of India with [the] connivance and active support of Iranian and Afghan governments.[46]

But Eden was "not clear"—he wrote to Horace Seymour on July 19—"whether the Chiefs of Staff are prepared to make forces available to go into south Iran should the need arise." "I hope that it may be explained to General Wavell," he added, "that there is no question of our pursuing a policy of appeasement toward Iran. It is equally of no use to indulge in threats involving military action until we know that forces are available to give effect to that threat." Regarding complaints that Iran was being supplied with modern aircraft, he explained that "the only purpose of supplying aircraft to Iran was to enable the British factory to keep going"—not to supply "finished" aircraft to Iran.[47]

In Tehran that day, British Minister Sir Reader Bullard and Soviet Ambassador Andrei Andreevich Smirnov presented jointly worded Anglo–Soviet demarches to Acting Foreign Minister Djevad Amery. The notes emphasized the desire of both governments to maintain Iran's independence, but noted that they could do so only if the Iranian government took precautions to preserve its freedom from foreign control. Britain and the Soviet Union requested the expulsion of specified Germans; and Bullard hinted that the British might withhold goods and services if Iran did not comply. Amery argued in response that his government had no grounds for acting against the Germans. To do so would violate Iran's neutrality and embroil Iran with Germany.[48]

Unimpressed by Iran's reply, Bullard immediately urged London to increase the economic pressure on Iran. Smirnov made similar suggestions to Moscow; he recommended that his government refuse to ship the German goods consigned to Iran that were lying at Baku.[49]

In London, Eden confided to Ambassador Maisky that he saw little hope of the Germans being expelled unless the shah believed that the British and the Soviets would back their requests with vigorous military action. The possibility of such action, he realized, depended on the military situation. He admitted that his military chiefs were studying the problem—and added that, if Moscow agreed, both governments could jointly examine the possibility of military action. The foreign secretary also asked Maisky what could be done to reassure the Turks, who were certain to be nervous about a Soviet move into Iran.[50]

On July 21, Bullard described his and Smirnov's impressions that "the Iranian Government, though conscious of German danger and already trying to reduce numbers gradually, will not effect [a] large reduction either at once or within a short time."[51]

Now it was up to Prime Minister Winston Churchill to decide what to do. He apprised Wavell on July 21 that "I am in general agreement with your view, and would like to give the Persians an ultimatum from Britain and Russia to clear out the Germans without delay or take the consequences. Question is what forces we have available in case of refusal?"[52]

Eden shared these concerns. "The more I examine the possibilities of [pressuring Iran]," he wrote Churchill on July 22 "the clearer it becomes that all depends upon our ability to concentrate a sufficient force in Iraq to protect the Iranian oil fields. It would be highly dangerous even to begin economic pressure until we were militarily in a position to do this, for the Shah is fully conscious of the value of the oil fields to us, and if he sees trouble brewing he is likely to take the first step." Noting reports that Iran was reinforcing its frontiers, Eden urged immediately strengthening British forces in Iraq. "If we can do this before the Russians suffer a severe reverse in the south, there is a reasonable chance of imposing our will on Iran without resort to force." He advised not to "move diplomatically ahead of our military strength or we shall court disaster."[53]

The War Cabinet agreed on July 22 to prepare for joint Anglo–Soviet military action while still exploring economic pressure. Wavell was informed the same day and, in turn, instructed the general officer commanding (GOC) in Iraq, Gen. Edward P. Quinan, to be prepared to seize and secure—without damage if possible—the Abadan refinery and the Khuzistan and Naft-i Shah oil fields.[54]

Quinan was a seasoned professional with extensive experience along India's wild northwestern frontier. Gaunt and gray-haired, he once served as the personal aide-de-camp to the king of England. Despite his royal connection, he was known throughout the army as a soldier's general. Casual about rank and prerogatives, he eschewed protocol and enjoyed the company of his Indian sepoys.[55]

Anticipating Wavell's directive, Quinan had already prepared a contingency plan—code-named COUNTENANCE—for seizing Abadan, Khorramshahr, and Bander-i Shahpur. But his only available forces—less than two divisions—were far flung, and he needed time to gather more troops from India and Syria. Nevertheless, he immediately alerted his key commanders—Brig. John A. Aizelwood, commanding the Second Indian Armoured Brigade at Kirkuk, and Maj. Gen. Noel de la Poer Beresford, commander of troops at Basra. That evening, Beresford informed Com. Cosmo M. Graham, commander of the Persian Gulf Squadron at Basra, that the strongest available forces were to be ready by July 29 to seize Abadan and Khorramshahr.[56]

Whether or not the British proceeded with their invasion plans now depended on the feasibility of economic measures against Iran. On July 24, representatives of the Foreign Office, the Ministry of Economic Warfare, and the India Office met and ruled out this option. They determined that economic sanctions were unlikely to succeed and would take too long to be effective. Recognizing that time was on Iran's side, they concurred that everything now depended on the possibility of coordinated military measures.[57]

Britain's Chiefs of Staff accordingly advised Wavell on July 25 that "there is general agreement that the Germans must be expelled from Iran as soon as possible," preferably by Anglo–Soviet diplomatic pressure backed by a military show of force. Otherwise, "it would be necessary to use force." They directed Wavell to deploy up to four bomber squadrons to Iraq for use against military objectives at Tehran, while keeping a fighter squadron available for defense of the southern oil fields. A ground striking force consisting of an infantry division, a mechanized cavalry brigade, and two Indian armored regiments was to be concentrated in southern Iraq to occupy the Abadan refinery and the Khuzistan oil fields. A small naval force of three or four sloops was to be assembled to transport two companies of infantry to seize the port of Bander-i Shahpur. Meanwhile, further demands would be levied on Iran. If Iran failed to comply, Wavell was to be prepared to conduct simultaneous military actions.[58]

At Basra, on the morning of July 25, Commodore Graham ordered his naval squadron to prepare a waterborne assault to seize Abadan. The plan— code-named DOVER—envisioned ferrying two Indian battalions to Abadan aboard two paddle steamers, an auxiliary minesweeper, and several dhows and motor launches. There they would land at jetties under covering fire from two sloops. He coordinated this plan with the 18th Indian Brigade commander, Brig. Rupert G. Lochner, and the Abadan Refinery's general manager, Mr. J. M. Pattinson.[59]

But as Britain moved closer to invading a friendly neutral nation, the questionable nature of the venture caused second thoughts in London. On July 26, Assistant Under Secretary for Foreign Affairs Sir Horace Seymour warned Foreign Secretary Eden that a "difference of objective" existed "between the Russians and ourselves." The Soviet goal, he explained, was to eliminate the Germans "whose numbers they exaggerate, but who are almost all in northern Iran." Seymour considered Nazi activities in Iran a "very minor matter" for the British "compared with the security of the oil supplies from southern Persia." He further argued that

> So long as the Russians are in complete control of the Caucasus and their forces there are intact, there is no greater threat to the oil fields than there has been since the war began. If the Russians lose control of the Caucasus, the threat to the [Iranian] oil becomes immediate, and this is the case whether the Germans . . . in Iran have been expelled or not. It follows that our own object, as distinct from that of the Russians, will not be accomplished simply by the removal of the Germans from Iran. It also seems to follow that, if we are to act in the long range assumption that the Russians will lose control of the Caucasus, it will at some stage be necessary for us to take over the protection of the oil fields, whether the Germans are expelled or not. [Therefore,] it may not be wise to base any threat to the Persians on the presence of the Germans in Iran.[60]

Eden agreed with Seymour that "our and the Russian objectives are not the same," but contended that

> the immediate thing to do is to assemble the force. If when it is assembled, we are still arguing with the Persians about the expulsion of the Germans, it will reinforce our argument. If at a later date, a Russian collapse in the Caucasus produces a direct threat to the oil supplies, we could then take direct action to occupy the oil fields.[61]

The Iranian government, however, was unmoved by diplomatic pressure. Prime Minister Mansur explained to Sir Reader Bullard on July 27 that to send away four-fifths of the Germans—as requested by the Allies—would contradict Iran's neutrality and her commercial treaty with Germany. He assured Bullard that Iran recognized the need for vigilance and was doing its utmost to reduce the number of Germans. He outlined plans to reduce the German presence in Iran—noting how Iran intended to replace Germans in government ministries and factories, take over the German-run Tehran radio station, and expel six Germans whose resident permits had expired. Ten more were to leave within ten days. Mansur was summoning the Tabriz director of police, and would issue him strict orders to list all Germans there. Lastly, a second gunboat was being posted to watch the German merchant ships in Bander-i Shahpur. Bullard responded bluntly that his government would not consider these measures satisfactory, and he warned that the matter was urgent—a question of weeks, not years.[62]

The shah himself was in a quandary as to what the British and Soviets were really after. He hoped that the minimal actions being taken against the Germans would placate—if not satisfy—the Allies. He found the notion that Britain and the Soviet Union might be preparing a joint invasion difficult to accept, considering historic British opposition to Soviet intervention in northern Iran. Therefore, he initially forbade any new troop deployments, but eventually agreed to concentrating forces along the approaches to Kermanshah. The 12th Division at Kermanshah was deployed to defend the mountainous frontier with Iraq. Maj. Gen. Hassan Moggadam, commanding the Fifth Kurdistan Division, was appointed commander to the western forces; he was dispatched to Kermanshah along with elements of his division.[63]

When Eden again met Maisky on July 28, both men knew that the Iranian response to their notes would be unsatisfactory. The foreign secretary proposed a strategy of presenting to the shah a jointly worded ultimatum demanding immediate expulsion of the Germans. If this was refused—as was expected—the military forces of Britain and the Soviet Union would enter Iran to enforce their demand. Maisky's government concurred with this course, but he suggested that the Allied demands should include the right of passage for Soviet troops and war matériel across the trans-Iranian railway. Eden balked, pointing out that such a demand was inconsistent with the argument that Iran was jeopardizing its neutrality by allowing the presence of so many Germans. But Maisky argued that the Allies could cite as a precedent the right of transit that Sweden was permitting the Germans. The War Cabinet considered his suggestion, but decided to limit demands to expulsion of the Germans.[64]

The controversial direction of British policy toward Iran continued to concern British Foreign Office officials. Second Secretary Posonby Moore

Crosthwaite believed that his government's policy toward Iran lacked honesty of purpose. On July 28, Crosthwaite provided the foreign secretary with a frank, thorough, incisive, and highly critical written analysis of the situation. This important and prophetic memo—tinged with sarcasm—reads as follows:

> Phase 1: We and the Russians assemble forces and then tell the Shah to get rid of the German colony. He will not like this but will temporize, in which case we should then proceed to: Phase 2: The occupation of the oil fields and the bombing of Tehran. The Russians will come in from the north and there would, or might be chaos all over the country. It will, I think, be agreed that we have no interest in promoting a state of confusion in Persia. . . . Therefore . . . we should now consider afresh what our real aims in Persia are and how far the use of force will advance them. . . . The most important of our aims is the security of the oil fields, and after that . . . our desire to open the Trans-Iranian route to Russia. . . .
>
> Would it not be best . . . to come out into the open and say frankly that we must ourselves look after the oil fields for the duration of the war, and take special steps to ensure that the railway functions in accordance with our requirements. Even if we do this, we could not . . . keep up pressure about the Germans in Persia, but I cannot help thinking that it would be a mistake to make this the main issue. . . . I submit that even if the Shah turned every one of them out of the country, it would not really get us much further.
>
> A straight forward demand for the right to station troops in Persia obviously has disadvantages from the point of view of world opinion. However, it is at least more honest, and might in the end be easier to explain to our sympathisers in the world . . . than if we were to get involved in an attack on Persia over the question of the German colony. Everyone would assume . . . we were going [in] to protect the oil fields, and I suggest that we might just as well say so and make the best of it.[65]

The Foreign Office discussed his memo with the Chiefs of Staff the following night, but Crosthwaite's suggestions went unheeded.

Meanwhile, British preparations against Iran proceeded. On July 28, 1941, General Wavell communicated his general agreement with the Chiefs of Staff proposal for military action. But because of his scanty forces, he recommended that "as additional infantry brigades arrive [in] Basra on August 10th and August 18th, respectively, it might be best to postpone operation till August 26th."[66]

On July 29, Maj. Gen. Charles O. Harvey, commanding the Eighth Indian Division headquartered in Kirkuk, received orders to transfer his headquarters to Basra in readiness for invading Iran. The frail, wizened general had only the incomplete 18th Brigade, the 11th Field (Artillery) Regiment, and a company of sappers to conduct the operation. A battalion of the Second Gurkha Rifles reached Basra that day—but these tough little warriors were unaccustomed to the torrid Iraqi summer, and 63 suffered heat prostration during the march to camp. To flesh out his forces, Harvey proceeded to collect troops from throughout Iraq.[67]

Quinan's chief of staff informed the U.S. minister in Baghdad, Paul Knabenshue, of plans to occupy Abadan and the oil fields—and possibly bomb Tehran—during the first week of August. Knabenshue hurriedly relayed this information to the State Department, which was also gleening British plans from the minister-counselor of the British embassy in Washington, Neville Butler.[68]

Butler met with Wallace Murray, chief of the department's Near Eastern affairs division, on the morning of July 29 to discuss British policy toward Iran. Butler described the Iranian reply to representations urging the expulsion of the Germans as "noncommittal." Then, referring to a request by Ambassador Halifax on July 8 that the U.S. government stop shipping warplanes to Iran, Butler explained that his government wished to prevent—to the extent possible—any aircraft being transferred to Iran, for fear the planes might be used against the Allies should the Axis occupy Iran.[69]

He described how the British were operating an aircraft factory in Tehran only to prevent the shah from turning to the Axis for aircraft. Further, to keep the shah "sweet," the British had agreed to ship parts for 12 Hurricane fighters to Tehran for assembly during the coming year. But Butler's logic eluded Murray, who asked why the British should object to shipment of antiquated aircraft to Iran when the British themselves were providing first-line fighters. Butler argued the need to keep the shah in good humor and to keep British mechanics occupied. But in the end, he admitted that it was illogical and unfair to expect the U.S. government to restrict its exports. Murray reminded Butler that—at Britain's request—the United States had refused export licenses for many items requested by Iran. He then emphasized that the U.S. government also desired the shah's goodwill. Cornered, Butler stated that the goodwill of the shah was more important to Britain than to the United States. Murray—uneasy about the direction of events—agreed to study the British request.[70]

The State Department's suspicions regarding British intentions were further heightened by a cable that night from the U.S. minister in Tehran, Louis Dreyfus, who reported that rumors of an impending British attack were rife—an action that Dreyfus did not consider "out of the realm of possibility." He noted that many well-informed observers believed that Allied propaganda was greatly exaggerating the size and strength of the German fifth-column movement in Iran. "Many of [the Germans] are honestly employed by the Government or business concerns while others have ostensible employment in various German companies." Few, if any, were "tourists" and the Iranian police "are keeping [the] Germans under strict surveillance, restricting their movement within the country."[71]

The invasion rumors had considerable foundation. On July 30, the British Chiefs of Staff alerted General Wavell that the shah would likely be presented an ultimatum on August 12, 1941. Military action would follow immediately if the Iranians did not capitulate at once. Wavell was to keep his forces on immediate notice should the Iranians attempt to sabotage the Abadan refinery or oil fields during negotiations.[72]

Despite public British concerns over the German presence in Iran, a British War Office weekly intelligence summary on July 30 dismissed rumors of German coup-plotting in Iran—deeming this unlikely unless supported by the Iranian Army, which was steadfastly loyal to the shah. British intelligence believed the Germans capable only of sabotage. The summary also concluded that the Soviets were planting rumors of German sabotage as an excuse to justify occupying Iran.[73]

In fact, Moscow was keenly sensitive to the German agents known to be operating from northern Iran. Pro-Nazi Iranians had crossed the border during the previous weeks—making the Soviets uneasy about their vulnerable oil fields and pipelines. In response, at the end of July, the Soviet General Staff ordered the Transcaucasus Military District to bring its forces along the Iranian and Turkish borders to full alert.[74]

The Transcaucasus Military District's force structure had been completely reorganized in late July. Gen. Dmitri Kozlov's three infantry and one mechanized corps were reformed into armies as part of the wartime mobilization. The 44th and 47th Armies were deployed along the Iranian border, while the 45th and 46th Armies took up positions opposite Turkey.[75]

While Allied forces were deploying along the Iranian frontier, Prime Minister Winston Churchill began developing doubts about the rushed action against Iran. On July 31—as he prepared to depart for an important conference with President Roosevelt—he created a special cabinet committee under Sir John Anderson, the lord president of the Council of Ministers, to handle the matter of "Persia" (as he insisted on calling Iran). His instructions to the committee outlined his concerns:

> I cannot feel that this operation, involving war with Persia in the event of non-compliance, has not been studied with the attention which its far-reaching character requires. While agreeing to its necessity, I consider that the whole business requires exploring, concerting, and clamping together. . . . We must not take such grave steps without having clear-cut plans for the various eventualities [such as,] what happens if . . . Persian troops . . . seize [AIOC] employees and hold them as hostages? . . . What happens to the British residents in Tehran[?] . . . Is there danger of the oilwells

being destroyed[?] . . . Are our available forces strong enough to occupy the Ahwaz oilfields in the face of . . . Persian opposition? How far north do we propose to go? . . . How is the railway to be worked if the Persians refuse to help[?][76]

He therefore directed the Anderson committee to review all possible alternatives and consequences, and report to the War Cabinet during the first week of August.

Churchill's and Eden's concerns over the risks involved with invading Iran soon began to materialize. The Royal Navy lacked sufficient shipping to support simultaneous landings at Abadan, Khorramshahr, and Bander-i Shahpur. On August 1, Com. Cosmo Graham urged his superior, Vice Adm. Ralph Leatham, commander in chief, East Indies, to supply additional naval forces as soon as possible. Graham was further worried that the element of surprise might be compromised by delaying the operation. He radioed General Quinan on August 1 that operational success depended entirely on surprise—emphasizing that any delays would dramatically increase the risks.[77]

The whole situation concerned Foreign Secretary Eden greatly. He frankly informed his fellow War Cabinet members on August 1 that he agreed with British intelligence estimates downplaying the German danger in Iran. While acknowledging that the Germans were well organized, he believed that they "did not appear to have much political influence," and specifically cited how "they had been unable to make the Shah take steps to support Rashid Ali."[78]

But, in fact, the Germans were starting to exert strong pressure on the shah. On the evening of August 1, a worried Prime Minister Mansur confided privately to U.S. Minister Dreyfus that the German minister was threatening to sever diplomatic relations if Iran accepted Britain's demands. Dreyfus afterward alerted Washington of "growing indications in the last few days that Iran is being forced [by Allied pressure] into closer cooperation with the British." He referred specifically to the expected deportation of two dozen Germans, with more—according to rumors—preparing to leave. He also cited how the official Pars News Agency was becoming more conciliatory toward the Allies.[79]

In London on August 4, 1941, Sir John Anderson convened his special ministerial committee to discuss Iran. The ministers decided against submitting an ultimatum, but rather a "firm but friendly" note—which, if not acceded to, would enable military action. They feared that an ultimatum would alert the Iranians. As incentive to the shah, they proposed doubling the oil royalties paid to Iran. The military chiefs briefed that they were preparing a division and two armored regiments in Iraq, along with a mechanized regiment from elsewhere, to back up the final joint demarche. Six RAF squadrons would support the ground forces. The committee possessed no details of Soviet military plans and intentions. "It would be important," one member urged, "to discourage the Soviet Union from gratifying ambitions they might have of occupying north Persia." The committee agreed to explain to their Soviet allies that "our intentions were limited to ensuring the Persian Government exercised their neutral rights without detriment to our interests." The War Office indicated that it intended to exchange liaison missions equipped with wireless sets with the Red Army.[80]

That afternoon, Eden asked Ambassador Maisky for any information regarding Soviet plans to concentrate its forces as a backup for the joint notes to Iran. Maisky said he had just learned that the Soviet force would be ready and in position by mid-August and that it would be twice the size of the British force in Iraq. The Soviet envoy agreed that military missions should be exchanged to facilitate coordination between the two armies. His government, Maisky noted, wanted the Germans expelled before discussing right of transit with Iran. Eden—expressing concern that the Germans might, in turn, demand transit through Turkey—encouraged the Soviets to reassure the Turks. The foreign secretary then explained that the joint demands on Iran must not appear like an ultimatum, but rather a "firm but friendly request." "We must use every precaution," he warned, "to insure our attitute to Persia does not rouse memories of the Ango–Russian policy of 1907." Maisky agreed, assuring Eden that his government had no territorial aspirations in Iran.[81]

British forces in Iraq, meanwhile, deployed into forward positions in readiness for the invasion. General Harvey and his staff reached Basra on August 4, with elements of his Eighth Indian Division arriving over the following days. His troops had to assemble rapidly and be ready for action by August 11—the date still set for delivery of the final note to Iran. Commodore Graham received welcome reinforcement on August 4 with the arrival of the 12,000-ton armored merchant cruiser HMAS *Kanimbla*. Despite its large size, the ship was needed for the Bander-i Shahpur operation because it possessed the berthing space needed for the landing party.[82]

At dusk on August 4, another large vessel—the giant battleship, *Prince of Wales*—steamed slowly out of the Scapa Flow naval base north of Scotland. Aboard the dreadnought, Winston Churchill sought out President Roosevelt's personal envoy, Harry Hopkins, who had just returned from a special mission to Moscow. Hopkins had been dispatched several days earlier to learn the true situation on the Russian front—which Soviet officials had been withholding from their allies.[83]

Hopkins described to Churchill his conferences with Stalin. By assuring Stalin that Roosevelt wished to aid the U.S.S.R. against Hitler, Hopkins had broken through the Soviet veil of silence. Stalin provided Hopkins with a surprisingly frank and detailed evaluation of his military situation, and assured the U.S. envoy that—when winter arrived—the line would stabilize within 100 kilometers of its present position. But the outcome of the following spring campaign, he cautioned, would depend on how well the Red Army could be equipped. When Hopkins asked which supply routes would be best for transferring U.S. matériel, Stalin replied that each of the three possible routes—Archangel, Vladivostok, and Iran—presented its own risks, but all had to be used. Hopkins's report pleased Churchill, who then—two days later—received the Anderson committee recommendations on action against Iran.[84]

The British and Soviet governments were now determined to proceed with their diplomatic and military strategy against Iran. Unexpectedly, however, other countries had recognized the Anglo–Soviet intentions, and they were reacting in a manner that threatened the entire operation.

5

Seeking a Magic Formula

Britain's envoy to Turkey grew uneasy when the Foreign Office seemed to ignore or discount his repeated warnings of Turkish anxiety over the Anglo–Soviet pressure on Iran. The Turks were pro-British, but distrusted Soviet intentions toward Iran. Finally, on August 5, 1941, British Ambassador Sir Hughe Knatchbull-Hugessen desperately urged his government to officially inform the Turks of the proposed Anglo–Soviet measures against Iran.[1]

Still, he received no response. Then, on August 7, Turkish Foreign Minister Sukri Saracoglu heatedly grilled the hapless British diplomat—asking pointedly just how many Germans were there in Iran. "I understand," Sir Hughe replied uncertainly, "that there are between three to five thousand." Saracoglu seemed skeptical. He noted that the Soviet ambassador had given the exact same number—saying this as if the Soviet allegation was automatically to be discounted. His own information, he remarked, pointed to no more than 580 Germans in Iran. "We could hardly consider this small a number so dangerous as to justify such stringent methods." Before Sir Hughe could respond, Saracoglu dropped his polite manner, and stated bluntly that he "disliked the whole business." The real Anglo–Soviet objective, he suggested, was to join forces in northern Iran in anticipation of a German move toward Iran. Sir Hughe cautiously admitted that it was "obviously important, if the Germans penetrated that far, that there should be a force ready to meet them." Saracoglu agreed, but insisted that the Soviets secretly harbored territorial designs in Iran. To bolster his thesis, he pointed out several recent Soviet takeovers. Knatchbull-Huggesson tried weakly to cite the Soviet argument that this was "merely recovery of territory which had formerly been Russian," but Saracoglu was not swayed.[2]

Following the audience, Sir Hughe emphatically advised London not to easily dismiss Turkey's role in the Iran matter. German victories in the

73

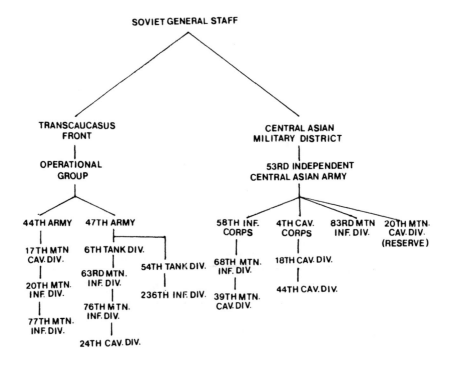

Figure 5.1
British and Soviet Command Structure for the Invasion of Iran

Soviet Union were kindling considerable sympathy toward the Third Reich; and, if Nazi pressure became too great and Turkish public opinion swung too heavily, the Turkish government could be compelled to permit the transit of German troops, and perhaps even to enter the war on the Axis side. To avoid this possibility, Turkish concerns had to be allayed before proceeding against Iran.[3]

This warning galvanized the Foreign Office. That same evening, Foreign Secretary Eden presented to Ambassador Maisky the draft of a joint note reassuring Turkey of Allied intentions. The note foreswore Soviet ambitions in the Dardanelles by reaffirming the 1936 Montreux Convention and avowing respect for Iran's neutrality and territorial integrity. Maisky agreed that Turkey must be placated.[4]

Eden insisted that both governments deliver jointly worded notes of assurance to Turkey by August 11 at the latest, in order to precede the final demarches to Iran by at least a small gap in time. Eden and Maisky therefore fixed August 15 as the provisional date for presenting the final notes to Iran. Maisky proposed requesting that Iran expel four-fifths of the Germans by August 31. He also recommended giving Iran three days to respond, and suggested that the British minister in Tehran "make it plain" that the current situation was unacceptable—and that, if a prompt reply was not received, His Majesty's government would be "compelled to proceed to other measures." Thus the "friendly" note would in fact be an ultimatum.[5]

The next afternoon—August 8—the British Defense Committee approved their proposal, and agreed that it would be a mistake to proceed too hastily in issuing demands that, if rejected by Iran, would entail "forcible action." Britain would delay representations to provide more time for the improvement of Soviet–Turkish relations.[6]

The Chiefs of Staff immediately informed General Wavell that "there may be some delay in presenting our note owing to Turkish suspicions of Russia and to the obvious need for squaring them before making them [Turkey] unhappy." Wavell was also instructed to prepare a liaison mission for departure to the Soviet Union. The chiefs noted that "it is considered impolitic to approach the Russians to perfect arrangements." This would be accomplished once "His Majesty's Government decided on military action in Persia."[7]

That afternoon, Eden presented the proposed text of the final note to U.S. Ambassador John Winant, and explained that Britain's minister in Tehran would deliver the memo on August 16. Realizing that the proposed actions lay on shaky moral and legal grounds, Eden sought U.S. backing, if not involvement. The draft note endorsed Iran's neutrality while declaring that Britain harbored no designs against Iran's political independence. The Iranians would be told that the "excessively" large numbers of Germans in the country presented a "serious" danger to both Iran and Britain. Therefore, the Iranian government should remove all but a small number of irreplaceable German technicians "without further delay"; they should leave the country by August 31.[8]

Eden noted that no time limit for an Iranian response was being inserted because Britain did not want to give the note the "character of an ultimatum." He then urged the U.S. government to instruct its minister in Tehran to make similar representations. Eden explained that he hoped "direct action" would not be necessary, but that he had to anticipate the possibility of the German Army reaching the Iranian border—in which case Britain could not allow the "dangerous nucleus of German technicians and political agents" to remain in Iran.[9]

From Tehran the same day, Sir Reader Bullard apprised London that he was being assured by Acting Foreign Minister Djevad Amery that the "necessary measures" to remove the Germans were being taken—although no specific numbers were given. The Germans, Amery confided, were accusing Iran of acting under British pressure. "The Shah seems to suppose," Bullard explained sarcastically to the Foreign Office, "that he can eliminate enough Germans to satisfy His Majesty's Government without the German Government noticing it."[10] The next day—August 9—Bullard reported that Iranian authorities were so intimidated by British and Soviet pressure that, "even if the Germans wanted to bring off a coup in Iran," Iranian surveillance was so close that "it seems unlikely they would give much trouble."[11] British intelligence supported this view by reporting that, according to decrypted Italian diplomatic messages, German attempts in Iran to organize a sabotage operation against the Soviets were encountering difficulties.[12]

But Bullard's views only infuriated the viceroy of India, Lord Linlithgow, who immediately complained to London of his "impression that [the] Persians believe themselves to have Bullard in their pocket." He emphasized his hope that the "local complacency will not be permitted to divert His Majesty's Government from pressing home their demands on Persia."[13]

The confusing and conflicting situation facing the British over Iran seemed to grow more complicated by the hour. The delivery of the notes and accompanying military action had been delayed several days due to Turkish concerns. Now the Iranians were becoming more cooperative— but not entirely—thus further undermining Britain's position vis-à-vis neutrals like the United States. The British assumption that the Americans would support their position without question was proving unfounded. The State Department was developing serious concerns over Anglo–Soviet policy toward Iran; these needed to be resolved before Britain or the Soviet Union could proceed.

Churchill realized that U.S. cooperation on this touchy matter should best be addressed at the highest level. Fortunately, the prime minister's meeting with President Roosevelt in the waters off Newfoundland fortuitously facilitated this. On August 11, 1941, President Franklin Roosevelt boarded the battleship HMS *Prince of Wales* to confer with Churchill. The two leaders had already formulated a draft declaration of principles by which their wartime policies were to be guided. The Atlantic Charter—as it came to be called—foreswore British and U.S. territorial ambitions while seeking peace among all nations and calling for the right of all peoples to choose their own form of government.[14]

The conference also spanned a wide range of strategic issues. Roosevelt's personal envoy, Harry Hopkins, gave a full report on his mission to Moscow, and convinced Roosevelt that the Red Army could hold out against the Nazis until winter. The president became determined to expedite military assistance to the Soviets by any means available. Churchill used this opportunity to broach a number of delicate issues with Roosevelt. These included a sensitive scheme to violate Spanish neutrality and seize the Canary Islands should Germany intervene in Iberia. Seeing its potential necessity, the president offered no objections to the plan.

Thus, the moment had come to raise the problem of Iran. Exactly what Churchill told Roosevelt is not on record—although he apparently pointed out the dangers posed by the large German presence in Iran, described the political and military measures proposed by Britain and the Soviet Union, and noted the importance of Allied control of the vital trans-Iranian railway as a means of supplying U.S. arms to the Soviet Union. The president's reaction clearly encouraged the prime minister, for he radioed Foreign Secretary Eden four days later that "I told the President about our plans in Persia and he seemed quite content with them."[15]

But U.S. reservations about Iran could not be so easily brushed aside. On August 11, the Iranian minister in Washington, Mohammed Shayesteh, called on the State Department's assistant secretary for Near East affairs, Wallace Murray, to discuss the "critical situation" facing his country. Shayesteh compared current developments with the 1907 Anglo–Russian partition of Persia, and insisted that the number of Germans in Iran was being greatly exaggerated merely to provide a pretext for invasion. If Iran fell victim to Anglo–Soviet aggression, he asserted, his country would naturally expect moral support and—if possible—material assistance from the United States.[16]

Murray listened sympathetically, and then patiently explained to Shayesteh that he could do little without more information on the precise number of Germans in Iran. Shayesteh contended there were only 600 or 700 but Murray demanded exact information. Murray then asked if Shayesteh believed that the shah would consent to a British or Soviet request for passage of troops through Iran. The Iranian responded stoutly that the shah's pride and character would refuse such a demand, even if it resulted in a disastrous defeat. Murray further inquired whether the shah might permit arms and munitions to pass on the Iranian railway. The question seemed to surprise

Shayesteh, who had no immediate answer. Before departing, the Iranian warned that he would request a personal audience with Secretary of State Cordell Hull if the crisis were not resolved soon.

The Turks were also unconsoled. On August 12, Foreign Minister Saracoglu bluntly told Ambassador Knatchbull-Hugessen that he did not believe the true Anglo–Soviet objective in Iran was to eliminate the "German Fifth Column." The British envoy replied emphatically that it was—and pointed to examples of Nazi subversion in Europe. The Turk remained suspicious. The next day, London saw that Turkish newspapers were belittling the "alleged danger from a few foreigners" in Iran, while praising the shah's policy of neutrality.[17]

The moral complexities of the situation increasingly perplexed Foreign Secretary Eden; he now feared Iran might argue that it could not expel the hundreds of Germans while still permitting the presence of an equally large British colony. He instructed Bullard on August 12 to "point out" [to the Iranians] that it is logical to differentiate between Germans and other foreigners" by explaining the Nazi pattern of attacking neutral countries by introducing agents disguised as technicians or tourists. "There is no analogy," he claimed, "between such persons and the British subjects who have in many cases worked for years in Iran."[18] In fact, there most certainly was an analogy, because key AIOC officials were quietly cooperating with the British Army in developing plans to seize the Abadan refinery.[19]

On August 13, London learned from its military attaché in Tehran, Maj. Gen. W. A. K. Fraser, that no "serious step" had yet been taken by Iran "to get rid of [Nazi] agents now in Iran." He warned that certain Iranian circles foresaw a compromise with the Allies that would enable the Germans "to continue their dangerous work." "Only a few German families have left Iran," he added, noting that the "Germans were carrying on normally."[20]

The situation demanded immediate action. Therefore, Eden and Maisky finalized the text of the final notes to Iran that day. Eden believed that the notes would be presented on the following morning, August 14. The implied deadline of August 31 cast no doubt that the notes were a disguised ultimatum. However, Eden directed Bullard to assure the Iranians that they were not an ultimatum—thus providing the shah with a face-saving means of capitulating. If Iran's reply turned out to be unsatisfactory, the invasion would commence between August 18 and 20. Maisky assured Eden that Soviet forces would be ready to move once the notes were presented, but not without the British.[21]

Then another delay was forced on the British, as a result of poor Soviet coordination. Sir Reader Bullard—learning that his Soviet counterpart had been directed to deliver his note on August 16—obtained Eden's concurrence for a postponement to that date.[22]

In Iraq, meanwhile, the British were hurriedly attempting to complete their invasion preparations. By August 10, Maj. Gen. Charles Harvey had assembled virtually all of his Eighth Indian Division at Basra. Two more infantry battalions arrived that morning from India—giving Harvey nine infantry battalions, an armored car regiment, and a field artillery regiment.[23]

Harvey's plan envisioned simultaneous attacks on Abadan, Khorramshahr, Bander-i Shahpur, and Ahvaz. He counted on a swift advance to occupy most of Khuzistan Province on the first day, and expected little resistance from the weak and scattered Iranian forces. Elements of the 24th Indian Brigade, under Brig. Roger E. LeFleming, would seize Abadan and Bander-i Shahpur by waterborne assault. Brig. Rupert G. Lochner's 18th Indian Brigade was tasked with securing Khorramshahr by overland march. The primary objective of the 25th Indian Brigade, commanded by Brig. Ronald G. Mountain, was Ahvaz.[24]

But the assembly of the Eighth Division had been so hasty that little time was available to rehearse a complex amphibious assault. Thus, the freshly arrived Second Battalion, Sixth Rajputana Rifles—designated as the primary assault force for Abadan—had to immediately commence boating and embarkation practice.[25]

Commodore Graham's naval squadron—working under the initial target date of August 11—feverishly readied itself for the invasion. In the port of Basra, the crew of the Australian sloop HMAS *Yarra* busily erected sandbag screens around their deck guns and other exposed positions. The Shatt-al-Arab waterway teemed with activity as small, U.S.-built Eureka launches scurried back and forth while larger paddle wheelers transported troops upriver to Ashar—where a dirt road led to the main British Army encampment at Tanuma, near the Iranian border.[26]

Commodore Graham completed his plans on August 10 for Operation BISHOP—the waterborne assault on Bander-i Shahpur. The purpose of BISHOP was to seize intact the eight German and Italian merchant ships stranded at the Iranian port. The captain of the merchant cruiser HMAS *Kanimbla*, Capt. Walter L. G. Adams, would direct the operation. Adam's small squadron, which was deployed near the head of the Persian Gulf, included the corvette HMS *Snapdragon,* the gunboat HMS *Cockshafer,* the tugboats *Saint Athans* and *Arthur Cavanaugh,* the dhow *Naif,* and an RAF launch. Boarding parties were drawn from the crews of the various vessels. On August 11, the sloop HMIS *Lawrence*—carrying two companies of about 300 men of the Third Battalion, Tenth Baluch Regiment, from Basra—joined Adams aboard the *Kanimbla*. The Baluchis would seize and occupy the port of Bander-i Shahpur.[27]

BISHOP was risky. To achieve surprise, Adams's vessels would have to negotiate their way up the treacherous Khor Musa Channel in the dark. The channel zigged and zagged through mudflats that offered no points of reference. The navigational lights had been extinguished by the Iranians to prevent a surprise attack. If the British vessels did safely reach the anchorage area off Bander-i Shahpur, they would then have to seize two Iranian gunboats—the *Karkas* and *Chahbaaz*—before boarding the Axis vessels. The largest of the German ships was the 15,000-ton *Wiessenfels,* followed by the smaller *Hohenfels, Marienfels, Sturmfels,* and *Wildenfels*—all of the German Hanza line. In addition, three Italian tankers—the *Bronte, Cabota,* and *Barbara*—were trapped in the port when Italy entered the war.[28]

The long internment had given the crews plenty of time to prepare their ships for scuttling. The Germans placed high explosives below the waterline next to the hull, running a long Bickford's fuse from the charges to the quartermaster's watch station on the upper deck where matches and shortlights were kept ready. Once the fuses were lit, charges would ignite within 15 minutes. Tar and kerosene were kept ready for dousing the dunnage in the hold, to be ignited by black powder bombs or shortlights tossed into the hold. As a final measure, the Germans intended to open the main inlet valve and flood the compartments below deck.[29]

The Italians set up temporary switchboards on their ships, through which switches were wired to TNT and gelignite charges placed next to the hull. In addition, Bickford fuses ran to powder bombs interspersed among ten-gallon kerosene drums in the holds. Scuttling procedures on both the German and the Italian ships were carefully and regularly rehearsed. A deck watch was maintained around the clock, with a loud alarm nearby.

Captain Adams's small naval force—floating a mere three-score miles from Bander-i Shahpur—desperately needed the element of surprise. Therefore, they made every effort to disguise or conceal their vessels. The dhow *Naif* was rigged to appear as a harmless fishing vessel. Its suntanned Australian crew garbed themselves in a motley assortment of costumes from the *Kanimbla's* theatrical club—giving the appearance of Arab pirates.[30]

Nevertheless, British fears regarding the exposure of the operation were already being realized. An Iranian businessman named Majid Movaghar—who had been sent by Prime Minister Mansur to Basra to arrange the movement of some railroad cars by lighter to Khorramshahr—observed the arrival in Basra of large numbers of British and Indian troops along with munitions and pontoons. Convinced that the British were preparing a waterborne operation against Iran, he hurried to Khorramshahr to warn the Iranian naval commander, Rear Adm. Golam Ali Bayendor, who politely brushed aside the report. Undeterred, Movaghar continued to Tehran, and obtained a personal audience with the shah. But the monarch, too, assured Movaghar that there was nothing to worry about.[31]

Although outwardly calm, the shah knew that British forces were concentrating along the frontier. General Moggadam at Kermanshah was reporting the assembly of British forces at the border town of Khanaquin. The British unit in question was the Second Indian Armoured Brigade, which had been hastily dispatched from Kirkuk to Khanaquin in readiness to seize the Naft-i Shah oil fields. General Moggadam's information was solidly based on reports from the garrison commander at Qasr-i Shirin and the Iranian consul at Khanaquin, along with border guards and tribesmen. Nevertheless, the still-skeptical Iranian General Staff asked Moggadam, "How do we know this information is true?"[32]

The shah and his generals hoped that the ostentatious British military movements were no more than an open show of force to back up ongoing political pressure. But at the same time, the threat posed by the British could not be allowed to pass without some deterrent response. The Iranian General Staff therefore hastily dispatched infantry, tank, and artillery units from the Tehran Central Garrison to Kermanshah and Ahvaz. Iranian entrenchments were constructed to block key passes and approaches. The British vice-consul at Khorramshahr reported that six classes of reservists were being called up, and that Iranian troops were digging a trench on the road to Basra.[33]

Recognizing the strategic importance of Khorramshahr and Abadan, the shah appointed Rear Adm. Golam Bayendor to direct the area's defense. The portly, baby-faced Bayendor was among the monarch's most trusted officers, the two having served together in the Persian Cossacks. Bayendor held Iran's highest award for bravery—the Medal of Zolfegar—and was considered exceptionally able. He had personally organized and trained the shah's infant navy. Many of his fellow generals, however, resented his meteoric rise and his closeness to the shah. They also derided his marriage to an Englishwoman and his openly pro-British sympathies.[34]

At Bayendor's disposal was his small Italian-built fleet of two 750-ton sloops armed with four-inch guns, and four 500-ton gunboats with three-inchers. To defend Khorramshahr and Abadan, he had 1,000 sailors at the Khorramshahr naval yard, plus a brigade from the Sixth Division commanded by Colonel Nakhjevan. The brigade included the 43d Infantry Regiment at Abadan and two battalions of the 30th Regiment at Khorramshahr.[35]

Working with the local army commanders, Bayendor supervised the construction of extensive entrenchments and positions. An antitank ditch was dug around Khorramshahr. From the Iraqi border on the Shatt-al-Arab to Khorramshahr, 50 men were stationed at several machine-gun posts. Five more such posts—with as many men—were located between Khorramshahr and Abadan. These posts could alert authorities of British movements, and could fire on British craft approaching either port. South of Abadan, two field guns were emplaced at Kasba point, where part of an Iranian battalion was garrisoned.[36]

Around the Abadan refinery itself, security measures were tightened. Although no Iranian troops were posted inside the refinery and tank farm area—which was surrounded by a high metal fence—police continually patrolled the outside. Aside from six police posts around the refinery, troops of the 43d Regiment established machine-gun and antiaircraft gun posts all along the waterfront from Braim Creek to Jetty 11, where the Iranian warship *Palang* was moored. Unless a waterborne attack achieved complete surprise, the attackers would be exposed to murderous fire.

The British military attaché in Tehran, Major General Fraser, alerted the War Office on August 13 that "Early British occupation of Khuzistan is anticipated everywhere," and added that "Iranian military intelligence appears well aware of our movements in Iraq." Fraser noted that the elite First Pahlavi Infantry Regiment along with 12 medium tanks and as many light tanks had been dispatched by train to Ahvaz. Seven classes of reservists were reportedly being called up. He described troop morale as "low."[37]

Although Iranian intelligence was detecting the relatively undisguised British military buildup with little trouble, it was completely unaware of similar Soviet moves. Both the British and the Soviets had agreed to a military show of force to back their demands. But the Soviets were instead secretly concentrating their forces a good distance from the frontier.[38]

Not only did Iranian military intelligence fail to detect the Soviet buildup north of Iran, but the Abwehr fared no better. Maj. Bertold Schulze in Tabriz—acting on orders from Berlin to closely watch the border area for signs of Soviet military activity—had accordingly redirected his surveillance efforts to the frontier region. Thus far, however, he had received no clear evidence of heightened military preparations. He would later learn that this was because the highly mobile Soviet forces had assembled well behind the frontier.[39]

For several reasons, however, Schulze sensed an invasion in the offing. For one, the British had suddenly withdrawn their citizens from Tabriz. Also, strange, unmarked aircraft were appearing regularly over the city. His most substantive indication was a report from across the border that eight Soviet ships were disembarking troops at Lenkoran—just north of the border—and were practising landing exercises for an attack on the port of Bander-i Pahlavi.[40]

This report was fairly accurate for—in mid-August—the commander of the Caspian Sea Flotilla, Rear Adm. F. S. Sedelnikov, received orders to be prepared to conduct amphibious landings at Bander-i Pahlavi and other points along the Iranian coast. To perform this operation, he had available three 750-ton gunboats (*Sovietsky Dhagestan, Markin,* and *Bakinsky Rabochy*), two 700-ton gunboats (*Lenin* and *Krasny Azderbaizhan*), a 1,000-ton gunboat (*Sergo Ordzhonikidze*), three floating antiaircraft batteries (*Polyus, Merdian,* and *Ekvator*), four auxiliary escort patrol boats, three hospital ships, one transport, and a few small patrol craft, submarine chasers, and torpedo boats. Most of Sedelnikov's vessels dated from the tsar's era.[41]

The Caspian Sea Flotilla's mission was to transport and land on the coast of Iran the 105th Mountain Infantry Regiment and an artillery battalion of the 77th Azerbaijan Mountain Infantry Division.[42] Lacking sufficient transport ships of his own, Sedelnikov arranged through the Caspian Merchant Marine Commissariat to divert several freighters and tankers to assist the Red Navy.[43]

The remainder of the 77th Division, which included the 276th, 324th, and 239th Mountain Rifle Divisions, were concentrated along with the 17th Mountain Cavalry Division at Lenkoran. From this site a few miles above Iran, these units of Maj. Gen. A. A. Khadeev's 44th Army would cross the Iranian border and push down Iran's Caspian coastline.[44]

For this operation, Khadeev's 44th Army was subordinated to a task-organized Operational Group that also included the 47th Army. The Transcaucasus Military District commander, Lt. Gen. Dmitri T. Kozlov, organized the Operational Group—assigning it nearly half the forces under his command. Kozlov appointed his chief of staff—the barrel-chested Maj. Gen. Fedor Ivanovich Tolbukhin—to direct the Operational Group.[45]

General Tolbukhin established his forward headquarters in the city of Nakhijevan, near the Iranian border. The Soviet forces were told that, in order to "liberate" Iran, the U.S.S.R. was preparing to invoke article five of the 1921 Irano–Soviet Treaty by introducing forces into northern Iran to deal with "Hitlerite" agents active along the southern Soviet border. Iranian bands were reportedly being created to instigate sabotage and terrorist activity inside the Soviet Union, while the Iranian Army was maintaining arms depots near the Soviet border.[46]

Quietly and admid the highest secrecy, General Tolbukhin assembled his heavily mechanized force well north of the border. To conduct the primary thrust through Tabriz toward Tehran, he assigned the powerful 47th Army under Maj. Gen. Vasily Vasilyevich Novikov. Novikov's juggernaut force included the Sixth and 54th Tank Divisions, the 63d Georgian and 76th Armenian Mountain Infantry Divisions, and the recently formed 236th Infantry Division. He was further reinforced by the 24th Cavalry Division and a squadron of the Seventh Independent Armored Train Battalion— bringing his army to about 40,000 men and 1,000 tanks. They opposed an Iranian force totaling only 20,000 infantry and cavalry.[47]

General Novikov—a lean, bald man with shaggy eyebrows—was among the Red Army's most experienced tank commanders. Previously, he had commanded the Fourth Mechanized Regiment and the 28th Mechanized Corps. Gregarious and full of humor, he so admired good music that he drafted the entire Tbilisi Opera Company into his headquarters company. Among his close friends was Soviet Army chief of staff, Gen. Georgi K. Zhukov, who felt that Novikov had the keenest memory of anyone he had ever met.[48]

Novikov planned a three-prong advance. His two tank divisions—the 76th Armenian Division and the 24th Cavalry Division—would carry the main assault through Tabriz to Kazvin. The 63d Georgian Division would conduct a supporting advance to occupy Rezeiyeh and penetrate into Kurdistan. To isolate the Turkish frontier, a small regimental-size force would thrust westward to seize Maku.[49]

Plenty of air support was available for Tolbukhin's Operational Group. The Transcaucasus Military District had 409 combat aircraft available, including heavy bombers. The 44th Army's air organization alone consisted of four fighter regiments, numbering 72 aircraft.[50]

Across the Caspian Sea, the Central Asia Military District was concentrating forces all along the Iranian frontier to conduct a simultaneous advance into northeastern Iran. The district commander, Lt. Gen. Sergei G. Trofimenko, formed the 53d Independent Central Asia Army in early August, under his own command. Forward headquarters was established at Ashkhabad. The 53d Army consisted of the 58th Infantry Corps, the Fourth Cavalry Corps, and the 83d Mountain Infantry Division, with the 20th Mountain Cavalry Division in reserve. Trofimenko's invasion plan also envisioned a three-prong assault. Maj. Gen. M. F. Grigorivich's 58th Infantry Corps was to cross the Atrek River near the Caspian Sea and advance through Gorgan and Semnan toward Tehran. Col. A. A. Luchinsky's 83d Mountain Infantry Division would advance from Ashkhabad to Quchan, and then on to the holy city of Meshed where it would link up with the Fourth Cavalry Corps—under Lt. Gen. T. T. Shapkin—which was advancing from the border town of Sarakhs.[51]

The whole Soviet invasion force—numbering some 120,000 men and more than 1,000 tanks—was deployed into its staging areas by mid-August. When assembled, the combined Soviet invasion force would number six times that of the British. The invasion was unlikely to take place, however, until the concerns of powerful neutrals such as the United States were resolved. The State Department increasingly viewed the intended Anglo-Soviet action against Iran as not fully justified, given the facts at hand.

On August 13, the chief of the department's division of Near Eastern affairs, Wallace Murray, expressed his belief to Secretary of State Cordell Hull that the British intended to invade Iran and were using their demands as a pretext. He further accused the British of being vague on the details of the alleged German menace. If the United States were to join the Allied representations in Tehran—as the British had requested—Murray contended that this would constitute endorsing British and Soviet military action against Iran. The moral reputation of the United States was at stake, he pointed out—particularly considering the imminent public release of the statement of principles that had been endorsed by the president. Impressed by these arguments, Hull agreed that more details on the German threat in Iran were needed before the United States could support Britain's action.[52]

Two days later, Murray apprised Ambassador Halifax that the department was having difficulty in dealing with the planned representations in Iran because of the insufficient information and background against which the representations had to be considered. The State Department knew that the British were disturbed over the number of Germans in Iran, suspicious of the Iranian government, and anxious lest the Iranian military be strengthened with U.S. aid—he noted—but the department needed more specific facts regarding the basis of British assumptions in these areas. Halifax immediately advised London to provide the United States with as many details as possible.[53]

The State Department's concerns were heightened early the following morning—August 16—when they received a cable from Dreyfus describing the notes to be delivered to the Iranian government. Dreyfus learned from Bullard that Iran must expel at least four-fifths of the Germans "by the end of August but certainly no later than the middle of September." The Iranians were to be told verbally that an answer was expected within three days. "The verbal demands and the implied threat of military action make the notes a virtual ultimatum," Dreyfus contended, "although the British Minister stresses that they are not intended as such." Bullard "left no doubt in my mind," Dreyfus added, "that unless the demands are complied with the Russians will occupy the north of Iran and the British the remainder." "Although predictions are dangerous, it would seem likely," he prophesied, "that the demands will be refused, that the country will be invaded and that the Iranians will put up a weak gesture of resistance. . . . I consider it not unlikely that if invasion comes the Shah will lose his throne."[54]

On receiving this dispatch, Cordell Hull convened an urgent meeting to discuss Iran. The United States had to take a stand. Hull's Near Eastern affairs staff warned that endorsing the Anglo–Soviet action would only embarrass the United States. Hull agreed, and informed London that the U.S. minister in Tehran would not participate in the joint representation—although he was to keep them in mind during conversations with the Iranian government.[55]

Just prior to levying the final demands on Iran, the British and Soviet governments assuaged Turkish fears by assuring Ankara that neither nation harbored designs on Iranian territory or independence. Moscow further reaffirmed its respect for the Montreux Convention and its peaceful intentions toward Turkey.[56]

In Tehran on the morning of August 16, Ambassador Andrei Smirnov delivered the Soviet Union's demarche to Prime Minister Ali Mansur. Mansur nervously read the contents, and then refused to accept the note; he recognized it as a disguised ultimatum. He also declined a personal copy for the shah. Only when Smirnov threatened to seek a personal audience with the shah did Mansur relent. When Minister Bullard arrived that evening to deliver the British demarche, both Mansur and Acting Foreign Minister Amery tried to persuade him not to leave his memorandum. However, Bullard's task was eased by the earlier success of his Soviet colleague. Mansur depicted the Allied notes as an ultimatum, and accused the British of objectives other than eliminating the Germans. The Iranian complained that London was blind to the difficulties facing Iran, and he assured Bullard that "serious steps" were being taken to eliminate the Germans. More than 30 had left in the previous three weeks, he noted, and more were departing "imperceptibly."[57]

Unimpressed, Bullard responded that "at this rate it will take two years to effect a serious reduction." Mansur then offered confidentially that two key German agents—Mayr and Gamotta—would be leaving soon. He characterized the program for removing the Germans as "highly successful," and as being so discreet that the Germans were unaware to it. Bullard responded acidly that, "it is a waste of time to look for a magic number so large as to satisfy His Majesty's Government and so small as to be imperceptible to Germany."[58]

The shah—on receiving the notes—summoned his generals to address the crisis. He found the Soviet demarche particularly worrying because his intelligence had given no indication of unusual Soviet military preparations. He naturally attributed this to Soviet preoccupation with the German invasion. In fact—to avoid provoking the Soviets—he had specifically restricted his northern garrisons to their barracks, except for minor patrols.[59]

Although Prime Minister Ali Mansur tried to downplay the seriousness of the demands, the implied ultimatum contained in the notes was clear.[60] Even so, the shah still had no clear picture of what was really happening, or why. As Sir Reader Bullard later explained, "wrapped in suspicion, [the shah] cut himself off from foreigners and saw only his ministers and chief officials, who had good reason to know that he did not welcome unpleasing news."[61] For this reason, the shah clung to the sensible—if outdated—belief that Britain would never allow the Soviet Union to dominate northern Iran. As he explained to his generals that day, he could not understand "how England would allow communism to conquer Iran and thus contaminate the whole Middle East and India."[62] What he failed to grasp was the extent to which Britain was seconding its traditional rivalry with Russia over Iran to the immediate task of defeating Germany.

Still—unable to ignore the threatening tone of the notes—he weighed his alternatives carefully. To defiantly reject the Anglo–Soviet demands could be disastrous. On the other hand, capitulation was unthinkable. This would only lead to more demands—eventually reducing Iran to Allied tutelage. Plus, to meekly submit would only infuriate the Nazis, who were inflicting staggering defeats on both the Soviets and the British. Within weeks, German armies could reach the Iranian border. To anger the expected victor would be suicidal.[63]

Therefore, only one course remained. Temporizing. At least until the present crisis passed. Somehow, the shah had to find a formula by which the Iranians could placate the Allies without angering the Germans. Meanwhile, Iran would have to press its case with other neutrals—particularly

Turkey and the United States. The sympathetic Turkish government and press had been able to do little. But the shah was only beginning to approach the Americans, whose outspoken sense of international justice would naturally have to favor Iran.

The shah's goal was to buy time until the war's outcome could be decided on the battlefield. If the Soviet Union were defeated quickly, then Britain could be dealt with more easily. On the other hand, if the Allies somehow prevailed, then the modest German presence in Iran would become irrelevant. In fact, it was largely Hitler on whom the shah now depended to save him.

In fact, the shah's fate weighed heavily on the fuehrer at this time. On August 18, at Hitler's headquarters in East Prussia, the Nazi leader strolled through the woods and enjoyed the warm air outside his damp concrete bunker. During the past few nights, he had suffered a recurring nightmare: a huge blaze consuming the Rumanian oil fields—his primary source of fuel. Certain that his dreams were an evil omen, he determined to obtain fresh sources of oil as quickly as possible. Therefore, when—during a staff meeting that day—his military leaders proposed an immediate advance on Moscow because they would need two months to secure the city before winter, the fuehrer rejected the plan outright. Instead, he ordered a continued drive into southern Russia. Depriving the Soviets of their oil and arms industry was far more urgent, he told his generals—and added that a thrust toward the Caucasus would also strengthen Iran's resolve to resist the British and the Soviets.[64]

The shah's government had not yet replied to the notes of August 16 when, on the morning of August 18, Soviet Ambassador Maisky discussed the next step with British Foreign Secretary Eden. Eden believed that both governments must assume the expected answer to be negative, and asked Maisky what should be done next. Maisky suggested that Iran be presented a 48-hour ultimatum to "modify its attitude" or the Allies would resort to "other measures." Or, he added, Britain and the Soviet Union could begin military action without warning, while simultaneously presenting notes explaining why. Maisky stated that he personally favored the 48-hour approach, although he had no specific guidance from Moscow. But Eden did not believe that the shah would capitulate, and argued that "further delay" would only give the Iranians more time to appeal to Turkey and the "rest of the world" for help. The day before, Eden had received a warning from Vice Admiral Leatham that any further delays would placed the operation at risk. Therefore, diplomatic objectives had to be achieved by August 31. Eden and Maisky agreed to act without warning. The Soviet envoy suggested the morning of August 22 as a suitable date to attack, for it gave both armies time to complete final preparations.[65]

Eden composed a draft text of the note to be presented at the time of attack, and transmitted it to Tehran.

It is regretted that the Iranian Government have not seen fit to return a satisfactory reply to the memorandum of 16 August. It is evident that the Iranian Government attaches greater importance to retaining these German nationals in Iran than they attach to meeting the wishes of His Majesty's Government in a matter which is becoming one of increasing urgency as a result of the developments in the war situation. The Iranian Government must bear full responsibility for the consequences of their decision. In these circumstances, His Majesty's Government now feel themselves obliged to take appropriate measures to safeguard their own vital interests and to deal with the menace arising from the potential activities of the Germans in Iran. The Iranian Government may be assured that these measures will in no way be directed against the Iranian people. Any military measures which British forces may be obliged to take are of a temporary nature and are directed solely against the Axis powers.[66]

But, in fact, the planned Allied military measures were very much directed against Iran.

At the U.S. embassy in London that same day—August 18—United Press bureau chief Fred Kuh met with Ambassador John Winant, and conveyed his hope that the English would be "hardboiled" in taking any "necessary action" against Iran.[67]

In Tehran that day, Acting Foreign Minister Amery outlined an oral counterproposal to Sir Reader Bullard. Iran would deport the principal Nazi leaders—Mayr, Gamotha, and Dr. Eilers of the German-Iranian Institute—and would continue its program of removing about 30 Germans a month, as they could be spared. Bullard replied that London would reject such a proposal, which would require a year to realize any appreciable reduction.[68]

U.S. Minister Louis Dreyfus also spoke with Amery, and "gained the distinct impression"—he informed Washington—"that the Iranians are temporizing and parrying without realizing the seriousness of their situation." They seemed to be "seeking a magic formula which will satisfy [all] parties," he noted, adding that "Unless they . . . face immediately the realities of the situation, they will perhaps within a few days find it is too late."[69]

On August 19, Iranian Minister Mohammed Shayesteh conveyed a note to the State Department in which he refuted the British charges about a German menace in Iran. The Iranian government contended that "the number of Germans is not so great as pretended, and it scarcely touches the figure of 700 in all Iran." The note detailed various measures taken to control the German community and to hasten their departure. The note accused the British of instigating "harmful propaganda" and trying to "terrify the Iranians by their pressure." Iran called on the American "spirit of international justice and equity" to prevent a repetition of the "great misfortunes of the last war . . . famine and epidemics caused by foreign intervention." Shayesteh requested a personal appointment with the secretary of state to present Iran's case. He stated that his government opposed "under any circumstances" the passage of British troops through Iran to the Soviet Union. Regarding the transhipment of war material, he evaded a specific response, but indicated that the Iranian railway could not carry heavy arms and tanks. He contended that "aggressive action" by Britain against Iran was "unthinkable," and further observed that the Soviet Union "seemed to have her hands full at the present time." If the Soviets did attack, Shayesteh believed that Iran would put up a "desperate" and "successful resistance."[70]

On August 19, Churchill was aboard the HMS *Prince of Wales* still en route to Britain when he learned of the joint Allied decision to proceed with the invasion. He immediately radioed Eden that "I think the Russian view is reasonable, and we ought to move with them while there is time."[71]

That afternoon, Eden assured Turkish Ambassador Tevfik Rustu Aras that neither the British nor the Soviets harbored ulterior motives in their representations to Iran. The Turks strongly suspected otherwise, and Aras offered his hope that the British would "mingle reasonableness with a display of strength" in their dealings with Iran. The Turkish diplomat suggested that the shah might be persuaded to dispense with the Germans and to request U.S. technicians in their place. Eden cautioned Aras to understand that "there was no question of waiting while an elaborate negotiation took place" over such a possibility. The Germans must leave first, he insisted. Afterward, other matters could always be discussed. Aras admitted that he understood the British position.[72]

In Tehran on August 19, German Minister Ettel met with Prime Minister Mansur, and inquired the nature of the Allied demands. "They always demand one thing," Mansur replied, "namely the removal of the Germans." The Iranian stated his belief that the demands served merely as a pretext for aggressive action. He admitted frankly that, although his government was threatening to offer resistance if attacked, Iran was "isolated." Attempts to elicit a public stand from Turkey had failed, and German forces were too far away to offer effective aid, he admitted. If Iran were facing only one of her enemies, it might be easier. "Unfortunately," he stated, "the Soviet Union still lives." Because the approaching winter would place further obstacles between the Germans and Iran, he believed that Iran had to gain time.[73]

Ettel assured Mansur that the shah could rely on the loyalty of the Germans in Iran, and he pointed to the seizure that day of Nikolayev near the Black Sea as proof of imminent German victory. Neither the Soviet Union nor England would survive for long, Ettel insisted. The Iranian government must therefore remain steadfast in the face of Allied pressure. He warned subtly that, if the British intervened, Germany might be forced to strike into Iran.

Ettel offered to help alleviate the Allied pressure by removing a number of specialists who were urgently needed in Germany. The disruption of German supplies to Iran, he admitted frankly, made the presence of many Germans unnecessary. But Mansur urged that none of them be removed; it was vital, he insisted, that his government not convey the impression that the Anglo–Soviet pressure was successful. Instructions from the German legation—even if only for the departure of women and children—could have a devastating effect on the morale of the Iranian people, he warned. The prime minister urged a gradual departure, which could be attributed to economic difficulties—thus gaining valuable time.

Ettel asked if England had not already detected that Iran's policy was aimed at gaining time. "Probably," replied Mansur, but both he and the shah "knew how to talk to the British." "Every week gained, during which the German forces victoriously advance has improved Iran's position," he asserted. Describing Iran's friendship with Germany as "sincere and firm," Mansur avowed that "Iran would never join the camp of Germany's enemies." Ettel wired Berlin that his planned departure of women and children would be delayed. Only technicians and families who were no longer needed in Iran would leave.[74]

That afternoon, the shah arrived at the Iranian Military Academy summer camp outside Iran to deliver the commissioning speech to the graduating cadets. Standing before the crowd, he looked tired and depressed. After handing out the diplomas, he congratulated the cadets for completing the course, and expressed his hope that their "performance of duty will earn you many future promotions." His tone turned grave. To the surprise of everyone present, he announced that the cadets' normal 30-day leave was canceled and that they were to report immediately to their units. He added ominously but obliquely that "later we think you will understand the reasons for this" and the "reasons will strengthen your feelings of sacrifice."[75] The cadets cheered loudly; but the shah departed solemnly, speaking to no one. The audience was alarmed and confused. Few Iranians knew of the grave crisis facing their nation. U.S. Minister Louis Dreyfus explained to Washington that the shah's speech was significant "because it is his first public statement in the present emergency and since it indicates his appreciation of the gravity of the situation."[76]

Meanwhile, the British and Soviet armies were completing final preparations for the invasion when an unexpected hitch developed. Their respective high commands decided at the last minute to accompany the intervention with a massive leaflet-dropping campaign. But this imposed a serious logistic burden on both armies. When the Soviets informed the British that they were not ready to drop leaflets, the War Office directed Wavell on August 19 to prepare a drop over the Soviet zone. Wavell replied that he was printing 1 million leaflets, but warned that the first 300,000 could not be dispatched to Baghdad by air until August 25—which thus threatened still another invasion delay.[77]

Sir Reader Bullard learned meanwhile from an "unimpeachable source"—as he cabled to London on August 20—that Prime Minister Mansur had assured Ettel that "the Persian Government would not accept the British demands." This confirmed his suspicion "that the [Iranians] counter program . . . was being drawn up in consultation with the Germans."[78] The Foreign Office now felt more confident in its suspicions of the shah. They informed their ambassador in Washington the same day that the "exact number of Germans in Persia is not accurately known" but was estimated at about 3,000—including some 1,000 men. "What we are up against," they explained, "is [a] familiar process of placing Germans in key points where their services would be of great value whenever [the] general war situation requires their use."[79]

The British Chiefs of Staff cabled a warning order to General Wavell at 8 P.M. on August 20. Deeming the Iranian reply unsatisfactory, they explained that "His Majesty's Government have decided to authorize Operation COUNTENANCE and are agreeing date of move with Soviet Government . . . is likely to be 22 August."[80]

British air reconnaissance commenced over Bander-i Shahpur and Ahvaz the next morning. Soldiers of the Iranian 45th Infantry Regiment were exercising outside their barracks at Ahvaz when a black, unmarked aircraft appeared from the south and passed over the Karun River. Their division commander, Maj. Gen. Mohammed Shahbakhti, alerted Col. Hedayat Gilanshah, commander of the Fourth Air Regiment. But the aircraft disappeared before any planes could be scrambled. The plane's appearance demoralized Shahbakhti's men, who were mostly poorly trained and unmotivated conscripts. Nevertheless, Shahbakhti was determined to do everything possible to defend Khuzistan.[81]

Shahbakhti—a gray-haired, stern-faced man in his fifties—was a harsh and fearless martinet. Commanding the Iranian Sixth Division, he was tasked with defending Khuzistan Province. Because of distances and communication difficulties, Admiral Bayendor was responsible for Abadan and Khorramshahr. To defend Ahvaz, the oil fields, and Bander-i Shahpur, Shahbakhti had the 45th and elements of the 30th Infantry Regiments plus units of the First and Second Infantry Regiments from Tehran, along with eight medium and eight light tanks and ten armored cars. The Fourth Air Regiment at Ahvaz had 18 obsolete biplanes. Ten U.S.-built P-40 fighters had arrived at Ahvaz, but most were still in their crates. Shahbakhti's greatest shortage was officers, with many companies commanded only by sergeants.[82]

On August 21, Wavell alerted General Quinan in Baghdad that operations against Iran might commence on the morning of August 22. Quinan immediately directed all subordinate commands to move into assembly areas. The orders were greeted with relief. After many days of preparation, training, and waiting, the troops were eager for action. Ships shifted into position, while trucks were loaded with munitions and supplies. Troops prepared to march to the docks for embarkation.[83]

At the same time, the British War Office radioed its plan of action to the military mission in Moscow. One infantry division supported by four bomber squadrons would advance from Basra to Ahvaz. The Soviets were advised that a British liaison mission was ready to join the Soviet headquarters in the Caucasus. The Soviets were asked where and when the liaison staff should arrive. Was the Soviet military liaison ready to arrive at Mosul?

However, what the War Office really sought were details on the Soviet invasion, for the British military mission was instructed to find out what forces the Soviets would employ and when they would be ready. What would be their objectives and lines of advance? What air force units would be employed, and from what bases? At this late date, the British still had precious little information on Soviet plans.[84]

That evening, Maisky alerted Eden that Moscow wished to postpone the operation until August 25, but the Soviet ambassador could provide no additional details. Not questioning the request, the British immediately ordered their forces to stand down, just as they were preparing to move off.[85]

The delay provided a badly needed breather for Iran, for the State Department was starting to tilt toward Iran. "I am of the opinion," Minister Louis Dreyfus cabled Washington at 4 P.M., "that invasion by both the Russians and the British will come within a few days." Although Iran had not yet formally replied to the demands, he noted that "the British Minister informs me that . . . the reply will be unacceptable."[86]

Dreyfus estimated that there were 2,500 Germans in Iran—"almost none are tourists," and "most . . . have legitimate employment." While emphasizing the dangers posed by the Nazi fifth column—and noting his own efforts to warn the Iranians—he nevertheless admitted concern that "the British propaganda campaign against Iran, abetted by private individuals and newspaper men, has reached an intense pitch." "This has resulted," he complained, "in the dissemination of distorted or false news as, for example, a report from Delhi that a trainload of Germans had arrived in Iran, that from Cairo as to rebellion in the Iranian Army." "Newspapermen have assisted the campaign by accepting such British inspired news as true," he explained, noting that "The Iranian side of the story has never been told." Dreyfus emphasized that

> I do not minimize the fifth column danger. I am convinced, however, that the British are using it as a pretext for the eventual occupation of Iran and are deliberately exaggerating its potency as an isolated arm. I have come to the conclusion that the British and Russians will occupy Iran because of overwhelming military necessity no matter what reply the Iranians make to their demands. I

must add emphatically to avoid misunderstanding that I am in full agreement with the British action and believe it to be vitally necessary for the furtherance of our common cause.[87]

On August 21, the Iranian government delivered its formal response to the notes of August 16. Written only in Farsi, the reply took note of British assurances to respect Iran's neutrality and maintain friendly relations. The note assured Britain that "the number of foreigners in Iran had lately been specially reduced and their number would soon show a remarkable diminution." But, it added, Iran would not abandon its "neutral course" or "accept any proposal . . . contrary to [Iran's] policy of neutrality."[88]

The next morning, Ambassador Maisky confirmed to Eden his government's request to postpone the invasion until August 25—citing reasons "of a technical nature." The delay was probably related to a Soviet decision to drop their own leaflets. Consulting with Churchill and Chief of Staff Gen. Sir John Dill, Eden informed the Soviet envoy that his government agreed to the postponement and would issue orders accordingly.[89]

The British unsuspectingly granted Iran a three-day reprieve. No serious impediments to their plans seemed to remain. The Americans—the British believed—would raise no public objections. The Foreign Office was aware of Roosevelt's nod to Churchill off Newfoundland.[90] But the British had underrated U.S. sentiment for Iran; and this brief delay was about to jeopardize their impending invasion.

6

Say One Word to the British, They Would Not Invade Iran

British and Soviet intentions toward Iran were hardly a secret by the morning of August 22, 1941. The New York *Times* front-page headline exclaimed, "BRITISH AND RUSSIANS POISED TO MOVE INTO IRAN." The paper's lead article predicted that,

> Should Iran refuse [the Anglo–Soviet demands], as is expected, Great Britain and Russia have already warned that they will take steps to protect themselves. Of course, it is not said what these steps will be, but it would appear they mean sending in troops, and such action can be expected. It is clear that Iran is not something about which the British and Russians are bluffing. In fact, it might be that deep in the hearts of the statesmen of the two nations one might almost find a hope that Iran will not accept the protest and will keep the Germans. It may be that the British and Russians would feel safer if they actually had the country under their military control.[1]

The U.S. press found itself suddenly concerned with Iran's fate. Reporters gathered for a press conference at the Roosevelt mansion in Hyde Park, New York—some eager to question the president on his role in the Iranian affair. A cheerful Franklin Roosevelt entered the room; he fielded questions on several subjects until one journalist finally raised Iran. "Mr. President, on another subject, this Iran situation seems to be fairly hot," the reporter remarked, referring to the morning headlines, "and one press association out of London yesterday said that you had been kept fully in accord—were in accord—on the policy that the British were adopting. Can you say anything about that?" The president paused, then quipped smilingly that "except that is an illustration of freedom of the press in London. It's not true. I don't know anything about it."[2]

But his facetious response masked serious concern. Although in a technical sense he was not being "kept fully in accord" with British plans, the president was certainly aware of their intentions from his conversation with Churchill. Undoubtedly, he never suspected that his nod to the prime minister would cause a clamor. But somehow, United Press in London had learned of the discussion.

The president faced a perplexing dilemma. He did not want to undercut the British and the Soviets, whose larger purpose in Iran seemed clear. On the other hand, if Roosevelt openly supported Anglo–Soviet military actions against a country with which the United States maintained friendly relations, it could make a mockery of his outspoken opposition to Axis aggression. Therefore, he contacted Secretary of State Cordell Hull after the press conference, and officially denied the accuracy of the UP report.

At 11 A.M., Hull—having no reason to doubt the president's veracity—accordingly informed Iranian Minister Mohammed Shayesteh of the president's denial.[3] This encouraged the desperate Iranian envoy, who knew that a British invasion appeared imminent. Having exhausted all diplomatic avenues in trying to placate the Allies, his government now pinned its final hope on Shayesteh's persuading the United States to intervene on Iran's behalf.

Shayesteh cited how Secretary Hull and other U.S. officials had often proclaimed the principles of peaceful international relations. What therefore, he asked pointedly, did the U.S. government intend to do to prevent the threatened British invasion of Iran? Hull—cornered—replied that "British military authorities, of course, plan all of their strategy without any consultation with officials of the American Government." He did allow as how the possibility of a German invasion of "that general area of the world" could necessitate "defensive" actions by the British, but he insisted that Britain had nothing against Iran. As to the U.S. government, Hull declared that it could not develop any new or contingent policy based purely on the "theoretical military situation" presented by Shayesteh. Describing U.S.–Iranian relations as "thoroughly friendly", Hull assured the Iranian that Americans "feel most kindly toward the people of Iran." The secretary then warned that the Germans had no respect for neutrality and would throw any neutral state into "serfdom or semi-slavery." It was the British—aided by the United States—who were "struggling desperately" against Hitler.[4]

Shayesteh realized with mounting hopelessness that he could not persuade the U.S. government to invoke its respected moral authority. He therefore assured Hull that Iran would defend its sovereignty by force if it were invaded. Rising solemnly to leave, the envoy beseeched Hull once more in meek desperation: "If your Government would say but one word to the British, I believe they would not invade Iran."[5]

Hull remained silent. He plainly disliked the uncomfortable moral position in which his government was being placed by the high-handed British. The Foreign Office was attempting to entangle the United States in the Iran affair, perhaps to better justify their own questionable intentions. The State Department's suspicions of British motives were further heightened by Dreyfus's reports and by the blatant British propaganda campaign that was clearly exaggerating the number of Germans in Iran. Hull therefore decided that the time had come to make the British fully justify their position regarding Iran.

In London that morning, another key American was disturbed by Britain's policy toward Iran. UP bureau chief Fred Kuh arrived at Ambassador Winant's office, ostensibly to discuss the Allied Economic Conference; but instead, he raised the subject of Iran. Winant could add little to what was known, except that he understood the Iranian reply to Britain's demands to be considered unsatisfactory. Kuh—reversing his position of three days earlier—stated that it would be a "great mistake" if British troops invaded Iran. He believed that the United States might deter this action by offering to replace the German technicians in Iran. Winant let the suggestion pass, but wondered how Kuh's views could have changed so dramatically in only three days. That evening, he casually asked Anthony Eden if Eden had received any suggestions about sending U.S. technicians to Iran. The foreign secretary answered that he had received just such a suggestion that same day from the Turkish ambassador, but had given it no weight.[6]

While much of the world—including some Iranian officials—realized that Iran faced imminent invasion, one key person stubbornly refused to fully accept the looming danger: the shah. Sequestered in his palace, Reza Pahlavi remained oblivious to the warnings in the Western press. Despite assurances from his advisors that all was well, he nevertheless sensed that the situation was becoming serious. But he was not certain exactly why. Summoning Prime Minister Ali Mansur on August 22, he ordered the expeditious departure of all nonessential Germans. Believing that the Anglo–Soviet demands actually concealed a more important demand, he also directed Mansur to learn from the British minister the nature of this more serious demand.[7]

Ali Mansur himself was already certain that the Allies' true intention was to secure a channel of communication through Iran. He had privately admitted this to Dreyfus, but he feared his tempestuous monarch too greatly to express his views.[8]

That evening, Acting Foreign Minister Djevad Amery assured British Minister Sir Reader Bullard, that the Iranian government was hastening the removal of the Germans; Amery cited an expulsion order issued for 16 (in Sir Reader's view, unimportant) Germans—mostly barbers. The positive effect of this action on Britain was negated, however, by a fiery editorial that night in the newspaper *Ettalaat*—which called for action and sacrifice to save Iran's honor.[9]

Meanwhile, the British military chiefs postponed the invasion a second time, on August 22. The repeated stand-downs were affecting not only morale and security. The shortage of water aboard the vessels lying in the steamy Persian Gulf worried the squadron commander, Com. Cosmo Graham. The HMAS *Kanimbla* reported that its crew and the men of its Baluchi detachment were suffering from a critical water shortage exacerbated by relentless heat.[10]

The conditions aboard the gunboat *Cockschafer* and the dhow *Naif* were just as intolerable. The *Cockschafer* had filled her tanks with water from the Shatt-al-Arab, normally fresh at ebb tide. For some reason though, the water was very salty and was driving the crew crazy with thirst. No one could shave or wash. Torrid heat made the decks unbearable. Even bathing was impossible, for the waters were filled with sea snakes and stingrays. The *Naif* was overloaded with 28 men and three officers. The below-decks were crammed with rifles, pistols, ammunition, supplies, and boarding gear. The men could not withstand such conditions much longer. Gratefully, the squadron was shielded by a massive dust cloud, which limited visibility to less than three miles.[11]

While the Royal Navy waited impatiently for the final go-ahead, Soviet naval forces were assembling for their own amphibious operation against Iran. The merchant steamships *Kasflot* and *Kasptanker* were under way in the Caspian Sea on August 22 when they received orders to proceed directly to Baku. Arriving shortly thereafter, they joined other merchant vessels including the passenger line *Dagestan*, the freighters *Kuybyshev*, *Osetin*, *Baksovet*, and *Spartak*, and the tanker *Komintern*—all of which were being outfitted with antiaircraft guns and machine guns in preparation for transporting troops.[12]

Along the central portion of the Iranian–Iraqi border, Brig. John G. Tiark's newly arrived Ninth Armoured Brigade joined Brig. John Aizelwood's Second Indian Armoured Brigade at Khanaquin. Tiark's "armoured" force consisted of the famous First Household Cavalry Regiment and the Wiltshire and Warwickshire Yeomanry Regiments—all transported in 30-hundredweight Morris trucks.[13]

Aizelwood nevertheless welcomed the new arrivals, who added considerable reinforcement to his meager command of two Gurkha battalions, a light-tank regiment, and a field artillery regiment. A former cavalry officer, Aizelwood had developed a plan of attack that envisioned seizing the nearby Naft-i Shah refinery and the Iranian town of Qasr-i Shirin, followed by a limited reconnaissance toward the vital Paitak Pass. With Tiark's brigade, his force was now strong enough to advance on the city of Shahabad. But his task was complicated by recent Iranian reinforcements along his planned route of march. The day before, he had learned that elements of the 12th and possibly the Fifth Iranian Divisions had moved into the Paitak Pass.[14]

The Iranians belatedly—if hastily—attempted to strengthen their positions bordering Iraq. In Ahvaz, General Shahbakhti directed the immediate dispatch of reinforcements to Abadan. A young lieutenant named Moggadam received sealed instructions during lunch on August 22 that ordered him to gather all available conscript soldiers in the 30th Infantry Regiment and to proceed downriver to Abadan. Hurrying from company to company, Moggadam tried to round up the soldiers, but their commading officers offered little assistance. By 11 P.M. that night, he had assembled only 180 men, whom he herded aboard a waiting naval vessel and ferried downriver to Abadan.[15]

The next day—August 23, 1941—the British military attaché in Tehran, Maj. Gen. W. A. K. Fraser, reported to London that artillery from the Tehran Central Garrison had reinforced the 12th Division along the Qasr-i Shirin–Kermanshah road.[16]

The British also received a cable that day from the chief of their military mission in Moscow, Maj. Gen. Noel MacFarlane, who advised that the Soviets were interested in British intentions once they reached Ahvaz, Dizful, and Kermanshah. The Soviets feared, he explained, that the British were underestimating their task. The Soviets apparently hoped to persuade the British to confine their advance to Iran's southern border region. Strangely enough, the two countries had not yet demarcated their zones within Iran. Also the Soviets doubted that the scanty British forces in Iraq were sufficient.[17]

This view highlighted a glaring contrast in philosophies between the two armies. The Soviets intended to employ massive, brute force to crush or intimidate any opposition. The Red Army had staged some 120,000 men and 1,000 tanks, which were opposed by only 37,000 Iranian infantry. By comparison, the British planned to outmaneuver their opponents, and had only 19,000 men and 50 light tanks positioned to handle a well-entrenched force of 30,000 Iranians reinforced by 16 tanks.[18]

General Wavell in India and General Quinan in Baghdad received a warning order from London at 5 P.M. on August 23 that outlined Britain's true political and military objectives in Iran:

ONE. His Majesty's first object in Persia is by military action to bring pressure to bear on the Persian Government to expel German nationals and later with Russian help to control communications. Question of communications is not, repeat not, to be publicly mentioned at present.

TWO. For the first object your forces will occupy and hold the oil producing areas in Khuzistan and Naft-i Shah.

THREE. Further military operations must depend on the attitude of the Persian Government when the oil bearing areas have been occupied and whether they agree to use of their railway.

FOUR. The plan and objective of the Russian forces are as yet undisclosed. Urgent enquiry has been made and reply will be cabled to you in near future.

FIVE. It will then be necessary to agree with [the] Russians limits of areas in which their forces and yours will operate.[19]

The Soviet General Staff, meanwhile, formally activated the Transcaucasus Front on August 23. Maj. Gen. Fedor Tolbukhin's Operational Group was assembled near the Iranian frontier. The months of planning and rehearsal were to finally pay off. The Soviet divisions in the Caucasus—kept up to strength, though in reserve until now—were about to enter the war.[20]

The growing controversy in Washington over Iran was being affected by apparently inflated British reports on the number of Germans in Iran. Unbeknown to the U.S. State Department, to the British Foreign Office, and even to Britain's minister in Iran (Bullard), an error in a cable from Bullard on August 8 had caused the British government to claim that there were 3,000 Germans in Iran, when Bullard had meant to report only 2,000.[21]

Consequently, Sir Reader himself was confused by the numbers officially cited by the Foreign Office. He advised the Foreign Office at 9:30 A.M. on August 23 that, in dealing with Washington, it would be "better to avoid totals, as my estimate of 2,000 Germans including women and children is lower than yours." He urged London to "concentrate on positions occupied" by the Germans. Noting that nearly all the males were of military age, he asked rhetorically, "How could they be spared from Germany?" He cited the employment of Germans in railways, construction, mines, agriculture, factories, ports, and the Tehran radio station. Some were "combatant soldiers" or "ex-officers," he alleged, claiming "positive evidence of some engaging in intrigues in neighboring countries."[22]

Bullard's U.S. colleague, Dreyfus, continued to fuel the controversy. A cable from Dreyfus at 10:30 that morning described a meeting the day before between himself and top Iranian officials. He believed that "the Iranians are doing everything they can to control the fifth column activity but their action is too weak and desultory to offer [an] effective check to the efficient Germans." Both the Iranian prime and foreign ministers had expressed their willingness "to expel [the] Germans gradually from Iran," but deeply resented "being pushed around by the British." Foreign Minister Amery complained to Dreyfus that the British were behaving in a "high-handed rather than a friendly way" and had never even suggested "closer cooperation or the forming of an alliance." "In short," Dreyfus concluded, "the Iranians are willing to cooperate in what they consider a reasonable program for the expulsion of the Germans but refuse to be cowed into accepting the arbitrary British–Russian demands. It is considered almost certain in well-informed circles here that the British and Russians will invade Iran. The only speculation is as to whether an ultimatum will first be delivered."[23]

This cable helped to convince Secretary of State Hull that the time had arrived for the U.S. government to clearly disassociate itself from Anglo–Soviet actions. At 5 P.M., Hull alerted U.S. representatives in Britain, Turkey, and Iran that "the President has denied the accuracy of the [UP] despatch" implicating Roosevelt in the British scheme. He directed Ambassador Winant in London to "ascertain if possible the source" of the report and to "voice the regret of this Government that such a report should have been circulated." Winant was also to state that the U.S. position outlined on August 16 had not changed—namely, that the United States was not participating in the Allied program toward Iran. The envoys also were told that the U.S. government was not a participant to the Allied actions, although it agreed with removing the Germans from Iran. That evening, Winant relayed to Hull a memo from Eden, and stated "how seriously they view the German threat in Iran. The British are certain that their negotiations with the Iran Government are being directed by the Germans. . . . I felt Mr. Eden was simply asking for a sympathetic understanding of their problem."[24]

British suspicions of Iranian–German intrigue were not without foundation. Ettel's August 19 cable to Berlin—which had alluded to fealty on the part of the Iranians—sparked the fuehrer's personal interest. Drafting a secret memo to the shah, Hitler offered his personal "sentiments of sincere friendship," and urged the monarch to "continue [his] present policy of neutrality and to defent Iran's sovereignty . . . until this brief period of danger . . . passed away." Boasting of the Wehrmacht's "victorious advance" into the Ukraine, the fuehrer assured the shah that "the Reich Government is firmly resolved to occupy the entire southern territories of the Soviet Union in the course of this summer." Studying the draft message, Hitler decided that his promise to reach Iran by late summer was clearly unobtainable. His army was hundreds of miles away; and his immediate objective was the Kiev salient, which was defended by 1 million Soviet soldiers. The advance toward the Caucasus would have to wait. He therefore revised his memo to read "occupy further territories of the Soviet Union in the course of the autumn."[25]

In Tehran, Sir Reader Bullard received instructions during the afternoon of August 23 to deliver the note announcing Britain's intervention to the Iranian government on the morning of August 25. Eden instructed that "the actual time should be concerted with your Soviet colleague, but should be as early in the morning as you both consider reasonably possible."[26]

The following morning was Sunday, August 24. In the large Caspian port of Baku, Soviet cavalry units, howitzers, and various items of military equipment were loaded aboard transport ships. The assault troops of the 77th Division's 105th Mountain Infantry Regiment would board later that night.[27]

In the Persian Gulf shortly before noon, the boatswain aboard the HMAS *Kanimbla* loudly announced, "Zero hour at Bander Shahpur—dawn the twenty-fifth." The news spread immediately from craft to craft—each crew cheering raucously in turn. Within minutes, the dhow *Naif* raised sail and slid away toward the entrance to the Khor Musa Channel. Her mission was crucial: to place hurricane lamps on the channel buoys to light the treacherous channel. The buoys were normally lit from Bander-i Shahpur, but the Iranians had severed the lines. As they drifted past the *Kanimbla*, the dhow's crew salaamed and grimacingly drew their fingers across their throats. The *Kanimbla*'s crew cheered wildly at this display. The skipper, Capt. Walter Adams, quipped, "No enemy spy could take that dhow and its band of cutthroats for anything but lousy Arabs." Adams's crew were painting "SURRENDER" in both German and Italian on *Kanimbla*'s sides.[28]

In Basra at 4:30 P.M., Lt. Comdr. Winifred Harrington mustered his crew on the mess deck of the HMAS *Yarra*. Outlining the plan on a blackboard, he explained that the HMS *Falmouth* and the *Yarra* would proceed downriver that night to seize the Iranian naval headquarters and warships moored at Khorramshahr. A company of Baluchis would constitute the boarding party. One platoon would embark aboard *Yarra*, and the other two on *Falmouth*.[29]

The *Yarra*'s crew finished dinner, and then went to their stations at 6:30 P.M. Forty minutes later, the Baluchis marched aboard. On deck, seamen dismantled awnings, hoisted small boats, positioned brows to be run out, and laid out grapnels and heaving lines. Along the Basra piers, meanwhile, vessels quietly assembled one at a time at embarkation jetties, so as to not arouse attention.[30]

Sepoys of the Second Battalion, Sixth Rajputana Rifles boarded lorries at 9 P.M., and were driven to the Basra waterfront. Their mission was the most dangerous and risky: a direct waterborne assault on the Abadan oil refinery. To muffle tramping feet crossing the sharf, the troops wore gym shoes, and carried their boots slung over their backs. The men—clad only in khaki shirts and shorts—were chilled by the night air. There was no moon; but the sky was clear, and the stars bright. Their commander, Lt. Col. Rupert E. Ridley, boarded the auxiliary minesweeper HMIS *Lilavati* with his staff and with A and B Companies—264 men altogether. C Company's 143 men and D Company, with 108, embarked aboard six Eureka launches and four dhows.[31]

The other battalion to land at Abadan—the First Kumaon Rifles—embarked 600 officers and sepoys aboard the paddle-wheel steamships *Ihsan* and *Zenobia*. The Kumaons were to land north of the refinery at Braim Creek. Commodore Graham's flagship—the armed yacht *Seabelle*—would escort the flotilla downriver, and would carry Brig. Roger LeFleming and his 24th Indian Brigade staff.

Shortly after midnight, the Eurekas and dhows quietly departed Basra one by one, followed soon after by the larger vessels. The sepoys crouched silently in the launches, and scanned the dark, tree-studded shoreline of the Shatt-al-Arab. Neither frightened nor anxious, they merely looked forward to finally participate in some real fighting. Aboard Dhow Two, the commander of D Company, 2/6th Rajputanas—Capt. Patrick M. Kent—paced the deck impatiently, watching the Eureka launches ahead of his dhow. After a time, he grew tired and went below decks for a short nap; he nipped on a hip flask of gin to help him relax.

Not far behind the Abadan-bound vessels chugged the second group of ships destined for Khorramshahr. The *Falmouth* led, followed by the *Yarra* and the tug HMIS *Investigator*. Some of the *Yarra*'s crew treated their mission as a lark, but others were more sober. By 12:45 A.M. on August 25, 1941, all of Commodore Graham's vessels at Basra were under way.

At the Abadan oil refinery, George Wheeler—the AIOC chief engineer—remained at his post throughout the night, and awaited the attack. His role in the assault was vital. He was to alert selected British AIOC employees, who would then proceed immediately to key positions within the refinery and prevent sabotage. On receiving warning that the landing was about to occur, he was to sound the fire alarm—the signal for the personnel to report to their stations. He would then meet the British commander at Jetty Three and guide him and his men into the refinery. Wheeler worried that the handful of employees involved in the plan were not enough. He had asked the general manager, Mr. Pattison, if 20 employees could be brought into the scheme. His request had been denied for reasons of security. Wheeler was also on edge because of the repeated postponements. Only the day before had he learned that the operation would definitely occur on August 25.[32]

Meanwhile—400 miles north of Abadan—more reinforcements were reaching the border town of Khanaquin late in the afternoon of August 24. Accompanying Brig. Charles Weld's 21st Indian Brigade was the commander of the Tenth Indian Division—Maj. Gen. William J. Slim—who had been recalled en route to Palestine two days earlier by General Quinan and directed to take immediate command of the forces advancing into central Iran. Slim assumed command of the forces under Brig. James Aizelwood, and amalgamated the two brigades present into his division.[33]

Aizelwood—though disappointed at losing command on the eve of battle—briefed Slim on his plan of attack in a professional manner. His plan envisioned a night march to Naft-i Shah that evening by the 2/7th Gurkhas, and an artillery troop to seize the oil refinery at first light. Simultaneously, A Column—which included the 1/5th Gurkhas, the 10/14th Hussar light tanks, and 15th Field (Artillery) Regiment—would cross the border and seize the Iranian city of Qasr-i Shirin. This force would then advance and reconnoiter the vital Paitak Pass. To its south, meanwhile, B Column—consisting of the Warwickshire Yeomanry, a tank squadron, and a 25-

pounder troop—would pivot right at the border, and motor through the village of Gilan toward Shahabad. This latter movement would outflank the Iranian defenses at the Paitak Pass. With no time to alter the plan, Slim readily approved it.[34]

Back at the main British camp at Tanuma outside Basra, Brig. Rupert Lochner's 18th Indian Brigade prepared for a cross-country attack on Khorramshahr. His lead battalion—the 5/5th Mahrattas—formed up at 6 P.M. Dubbed "Rapier Force" because they were to sweep out of the desert from the north and surprise the Iranian defenders of Khorramshahr, the Mahrattas were joined by a Guides Cavalry armored car squadron and an artillery troop.[35]

Rapier Force was part of an overall plan for a three-prong attack on Khorramshar from the north and northwest. Rapier Force would navigate across the open desert to a preselected point, and then pivot south—while, farther south, the First Battalion, Second Gurkhas would parallel Rapier Force on a more direct route. Last, the 2/3d Gurkhas would move directly down the Basra–Khorramshahr road. All three columns would converge on the Iranian defenses north of the city. Rapier Force's 157 vehicles rolled out of camp at 8:15 P.M.—heading westward—while the other two battalions finished dinner and prepared to move out.

The Mahrattas of Rapier Force crossed the Iranian border at 11 P.M. on August 24, and then turned right—heading due east. They sighted Iranian picket posts to their north and south, but passed undetected. Each vehicle had a towel tied to the rear, so as to enable the truck behind to follow in the darkness. In the leading armored car, 2d Lt. John W. Humphries navigated the column by periodically checking his compass bearing. A lean, red-haired subaltern, he commanded a troop of Guides Cavalry who were tasked with screening the column, which bumped uncomfortably across the desert at four miles an hour. At 1:45 A.M., Rapier Force reached its final pivot point, and wheeled south. Humphries prayed that his navigation be accurate.[36]

The second column of the 18th Brigade—the lorry-borne 1/2d Gurkha Rifles—crossed the frontier north of Duaiji village at exactly midnight. Back at Tanuma, meanwhile, the 2/3d Gurkhas began departing along the main road to Khorramshahr.

British plans were formally revealed to U.S. Minister Louis Dreyfus that evening in Tehran. Sir Reader Bullard stated that he would deliver a note to the Iranian government at 8 A.M.; it would announce Britain's intervention, encourage Iran not to resist, and reiterate His Majesty's government's pledge of having no designs on Iran's sovereignty. Maj. Gen. W. A. K. Fraser, the military attaché, added that military operations would commence at dawn. Dreyfus hurriedly cabled Washington.[37]

The scheduled delivery of the British note changed later that night, when Ambassador Smirnov informed Bullard that the Soviet note was to be delivered at 4:15 A.M. The British envoy agreed to advance his time in order to present the two notes together. Smirnov and Bullard then passed the remainder of the night discussing their instructions and the possible consequences of the Allied action.[38]

The Iranians themselves were unaware of the forces descending on them that night. Along the border with Iraq, Iranian forces were at a medium state of alert; many were deployed in trenches and prepared positions. At Abadan, key posts along the waterfront were continuously manned throughout the night; but most of the garrison was in its barracks east of town, where their weapons were locked in the armory. There the commander of the 43d Infantry Regiment, Colonel Massoumi, entertained his officers until late into the night with tales of campaigns against the mountain tribes. Among the officers was Lieutenant Moggadam, who had arrived the day before with his conscripts from Ahvaz. At 1 P.M., the officers finally turned in.[39]

Iran's northern garrisons remained in their barracks that night, and displayed no unusual vigilance. At the port of Bander-i Pahlavi along the forested Caspian Sea coast, a heavy rain fell outside as soldiers of the Iranian 36th Infantry Regiment cleaned the barracks for inspection by their commander, Lieutenant Colonel Iranpur. Their barracks were situated on a small, heavily wooded island in Murdab Bay, a large lagoon behind the port.[40]

Some 200 miles directly north of Bander-i Pahlavi at Baku, soldiers of the Soviet 105th Mountain Infantry Regiment boarded the transports of Rear Admiral Sedelnikov's Caspian Sea Flotilla at 2 A.M. Artillery and cavalry were already aboard. Space was tight, and troops were either billeted in cabins or assigned space on deck. Without a moon for navigation, the flottila would have to await first light before getting underway at top speed for their objectives on the Iranian coast.[41]

All along the Irano–Soviet border that night—from Lenkoran on the Caspian coast to Nakhijevan near the Irano–Turkish border—Soviet tanks, trucks, and troops of General Tolbukhin's Operational Group were advancing through the darkness toward final assembly points. Maj. Gen. A. P. Rodionov's 77th Mountain Infantry Division and elements of the 77th Mountain Cavalry Division—both of the 44th Army—wound their way through from Lenkoran through a pass in the Talyshkive Gory Mountains enroute to the Iranian border town of Namin, north of Ardabil. Farther west, Maj. Gen. V. V. Novikov's 47th Army concentrated in two groups: one near the Soviet border town of Dzulfa, and the other near Nakhijevan.[42]

In Moscow at 3:30 A.M. on August 25, the Soviet commissar for foreign affairs telephoned and awakened Iranian Ambassador Mohammed Saed, and demanded his immediate presence at the Kremlin.[43]

At the same moment, north of Khorramshahr, Rapier Force came to a halt. The guide—Lieutenant Humphries—checked his position a final time; but, in the darkness without landmarks, he could not be certain of the column's location. The force could only wait for sunrise to burn off the thick haze. Back at Tanuma camp in Iraq, the men of the 25th Indian Brigade rose for breakfast at 3 A.M. The brigade's mission was to cross the border, seize the fort at Qasr Shiekh, and make it impossible for any Iranian reinforcements sent from Ahvaz to reach Khorramshahr. The lead battalion—the 2/11th Sikh—along with two armored car squadrons, was to capture Qasr Sheikh, which was located astride the Ahvaz–Khorramshahr road.[44]

Some miles south of Tanuma, at the RAF's Shaiba Air Station outside Basra, six Blenheim bombers of Number 84 Squadron and several Hurricane and Gladiator fighters of 261 Squadron warmed their engines in readiness to strike at the aerodrome at Ahvaz, in hopes of knocking out the Iranian air force on the ground. Nearby on the Shaiba tarmac were 85 sepoys of B Company, 3/10th Baluch Regiment—with their commander, Capt. J. Michael Forster—waiting to board six Valentia transports for a 120-mile airborne insertion behind Iranian lines. Forster's company was to be airlanded at the deserted airfield at Haft Khel, to prevent the Iranians from taking hostage the British AIOC employees and families at Haft Khel and at Masjid-i-Suleiman.[45]

Meanwhile, British and Indian naval vessels were converging on their targets. The sloop HMS *Shoreham* departed the Iraqi port of Fau (at the mouth of the Shatt-al-Arab) shortly before 1 A.M. on August 25, and steamed upriver toward Abadan. Her captain, Comdr. Robert E. T. Tunbridge, Royal Navy Reserve, had orders to attack the Iranian sloop *Palang* at Abadan, so as to prevent her from interfering with the British landings.[46]

Not far from Fau, the British dhow *Naif* sailed silently up the treacherous Khor Musa Channel toward the port of Bander-i-Shahpur. The stillness was broken only by water lapping against her bow and the muffled chugging of her engine. Close behind her came an RAF picket boat, with its machine guns ready to provide cover. The *Naif* picked its way slowly and carefully up the channel. Its mission was to install lighted buoys to guide the squadron behind. But luck was with the British, because the *Naif* sighted channel buoys blinking ahead. A British agent ashore had reconnected the disabled circuit. Farther back down the channel, the giant shadow of the HMAS *Kanimbla* glided, starkly silhouetted against the night sky. Behind her—in close column—steamed the other vessels.

Shortly before 4 A.M., the dhow *Naif* slowed to a dead halt near Buoy 13. Bander-i Shahpur lay just around the next bend in the channel. The dhow's engine was emitting a faint glow, which—if she proceeded further—might compromise the squadron. The lights of the port were visible across a small bay. The remainder of Adams's force soon arrived, moving into a line abreast and awaiting the signal to race toward their targets.[47]

To the north 100 miles, the flotilla carrying Brigadier LeFleming's 24th Brigade drifted quietly down the Shatt-al-Arab. Some 20 miles downriver from Basra, the Eurekas and dhows neared Satan's Gap, the boundary between Iraq and Iran. To avoid detection by shore posts, the small craft swung to the right of Um Al Labani Island, and hugged the dark Iraqi shoreline for the next five miles. Emerging just south of Khorramshahr, the small boats rendezvoused and formed into groups of three in order to reduce the apparent number of craft going downriver.[48]

Meanwhile, the larger vessels—forced to use the main channel—crept carefully past the Iranian outposts north of Khorramshahr. On deck, the densely packed men nervously watched the darkened shoreline. The night was so still that every sound seemed like a thunderclap. The *Seabelle* and *Lilavati* breathlessly passed Khorramshahr without challenge. A few minutes later—at 2:45 A.M.—they rendezvoused with the *Zenobia* and *Ihsan* in the lee of Um Al Labani Island, and then continued downriver. A short distance ahead, the smaller craft were encountering difficulties. Attempting to negotiate the narrow channel to the right of Qatah Island, the lead group of Eurekas and dhows ran aground, and were followed blindly by the second group. The crews worked feverishly to free the craft, so as to arrive at zero hour.

Upriver, the ships bound for Khorramshahr were also having trouble. As the tide began to fall, the HMS *Falmouth* struck an uncharted sandbar near Margil, not far from Basra. Aboard the *Yarra*, Lieutenant Commander Harrington considered trying to tow her loose, but decided that it would take too long and might jeopardize arriving by zero hour. As the *Falmouth* struggled to get free, the *Yarra* proceeded boldly on to Khorramshahr—determined to single-handly sink the Iranian Navy and capture the naval base.

The *Yarra* reached the mouth of the Karun River at 4:08, only two minutes before zero hour. A British freighter—the *Varela*—was docked on the north side of the river, and luckily shielded the *Yarra* from the view of her main target: the Iranian sloop *Babr*. The *Babr* was moored to a T-shaped jetty at the naval base. Harrington slowed the *Yarra* to a dead stop in the lee of the *Varela,* and awaited the flashes or booms from Abadan that would signal the *Shoreham*'s attack on the *Palang*. His gun crews stood ready by their mounts—their guns loaded with high explosive shells; and the three-incher, with armor piercing. Zero hour arrived—but still no flashes to the south. To Harrington and his anxious crew, each passing minute seemed like an hour.

At Abadan, the *Ihsan* and *Zenobia* carrying the 600 Kumaons were off Braim Creek at zero hour. Right behind them came the HMIS *Lilavati* with part of the Rajputana battalion, and the HMS *Seabelle*. Most of the launches and dhows followed, carrying the remaining two Rajputana companies.

Several hundred yards downriver, the HMS *Shoreham* approached the *Palang,* which was tied to Jetty 11 just south of the refinery. All was dark and quiet, and the British saw no Iranians ashore. Complete surprise had been achieved. In the dim predawn light, the *Shoreham*'s forward battery ranged their four-incher on target. At 4:13 A.M., a flash and a loud thunderclap pierced the vanishing darkness as the *Shoreham* slammed a shell directly into the *Palang*. The Iranian warship erupted in a massive ball of flame. Commander Tunbridge—fearing that the explosion might spread to the refinery—ordered the *Shoreham*'s guns to cease fire.[49]

Aboard the *Palang,* the gunnery officer, Lieutenant Kahnemooei, was sleeping when the shell hit. Awakened by the explosion, he rushed onto the blazing deck, and ordered the terrified crewmen spilling from the hatchways to return fire. He rushed to a gunmount, but was mortally wounded when a secondary explosion severed one of his hands. Shouting "Fire! Fire!," Kahnemooei collapsed and died. The captain, Lieutenant Commander Milanian, lay bleeding nearby from shrapnel lacerations. Those of his crew not killed or wounded in the explosions fled ashore. War had come to Iran.[50]

In Tehran at that moment, the streets were still dark and quiet. Two cars drove slowly along Shahreza Street; each fluttered a small flag from its hood—one a Union Jack, and the other a hammer and sickle on a red field. Reaching the intersection with Shimran Road, the cars pulled to the left curb, and parked. British Minister Sir Reader Bullard and Soviet Ambassador Andrei Smirnov emerged and walked up to a large iron gate in front of the elegant home of Prime Minister Ali Mansur. They rang the bell at 4:15 A.M.[51]

A few moments later, a servant appeared at the gate. The two men presented their personal cards, and asked to see the prime minister. Ushered immediately into the guest room, they waited impatiently while Mansur was informed of their presence. Dressing hastily, he hurried to meet his unexpected guests. The two envoys were brief and blunt. The Iranian government, they stated, had ignored the Allied notes of July 19 and August 16 requesting the expulsion of the Germans. Regretfully, their governments had no choice but to act by force. British and Soviet troops were at that very moment entering Iran, they announced. Mansur was speechless. He tried to assure them that everything could be settled if only their troops were pulled back, but Bullard and Smirnov were in no position to negotiate. Handing their notes to Mansur, they promptly departed. Mansur's impulse was to notify the shah immediately. But then he noticed the time and realized that Iran's monarch was still asleep.

His mortal fear of the shah exceeded his concern for the immediate danger facing his nation. Mansur had deliberately misled the shah as to the seriousness of the Allied demands, in hopes that some miraculous solution could be found before it was too late. Now he would have to face the ruler with the tragic news. But not until after the shah had finished breakfast. Holding the two notes nervously in his hand, Ali Mansur sat down to wait out what was surely the longest 90 minutes of his life.

7

They're Blowing Her Up!

At 4:10 A.M.—zero hour—on August 25, 1941, the HMAS *Kanimbla* signaled "full speed ahead" to the waiting craft of Capt. Walter Adams's squadron. From his bridge, Adams shouted, "Good luck, lads. Do your stuff!" Cheers erupted across the water as the vessels chugged into the opening bay of Bander-i Shahpur.[1]

The tugs and dhows entered first. For a few moments, the Axis merchantmen did not react. Then the sloop HMIS *Lawrence* rounded the bend; her silhouette with four-inch guns was unmistakable. The deck watch aboard the *Hohenfels* was the first to sight the *Lawrence*, as it overtook the smaller craft. Blast after blast was sounded on the *Hohenfels*'s horn—which was answered within moments by frantic gongs from the other Axis vessels.

The British vessels fanned out, speeding pell-mell toward their assigned ships. The tug *St. Athans* reached the *Hohenfels* while her Klaxon was still blaring. The British believed the senior Axis officer to be aboard. Grappling hooks and Jacob's ladders shot onto her deck as a boarding party of several seamen and eight Punjabis from the Baluch detachment—knives tucked in their belts, and tommyguns swinging from their shoulders—clambered up her side onto deck.

German seamen roused from their bunks scampered on deck to meet the boarders. Tossing grenades while swinging jackknives and blackjacks, the Germans exchanged curses and shouts with their attackers. Blades slashed, and a revolver discharged—but, within ten minutes, it was all over; and, at 4:15 A.M., the Royal Navy's White Ensign replaced the Swastika on the ship's mast. Two Germans lay dead, and one wounded, but none of the boarders were injured.

Alongside the *Hohenfels*, the *Sturmfels* spit machine-gun fire at the racing British craft. A billow of smoke suddenly erupted from her afterhold. At

109

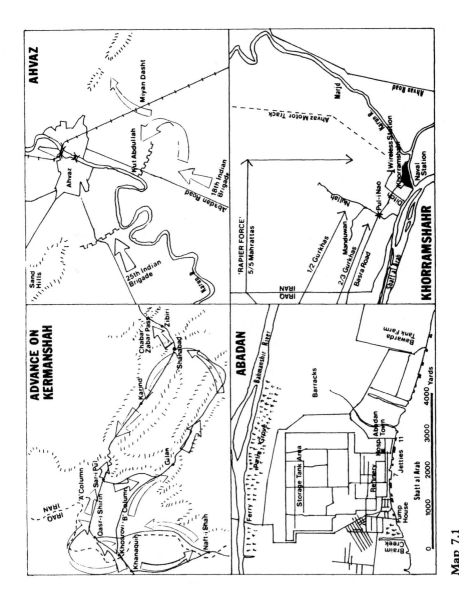

Map 7.1
British Operations in Central and Southern Iran, 1941

ADVANCE ON KERMANSHAH

IRAN
IRAQ
'A' Column
Qasr-i-Shirin
Sar-i-Pul
Karind
Chabar
Zabar Pass
Zibiri
Shahabad
Khosrov 'B' Column
Khanaquin
Gian
Naft-i-Shah

AHVAZ

Sand Hills
Ahvaz
Kut Abdullah
Miyan Dasht
Abadan Road
18th Indian Brigade
25th Indian Brigade
Karun R.

ABADAN

Bahmanshir River
Ferry
Refinery Gravel
Barracks
Storage Tank Area
Hosp.
Abadan Town
Refinery
7 Jetties 11
Pump House
Braim Creek
Bawarda Tank Farm
Shatt al Arab
0   1000   2000   3000   4000 Yards

KHORRAMSHAHR

Marjd
Ahvaz Road
Ahvaz Motor Track
Karun R.
Wireless Station
Khorramshahr
Naval Station
Ditch
Pul-i-Nao
Mullah
Manduwan
1/2 Gurkhas
2/3 Gurkhas
Basra Road
'RAPIER FORCE'
5/5 Mahrattas
IRAQ
IRAN
Shatt al Arab

the same moment, the lights of Bander-i Shahpur went out. The crew of the HMS *Snapdragon* scaled ladders onto the deck of the *Sturmfels*. Flames leaped from the hold, and smoke permeated the deck as the boarders struggled with the German crew.

The Axis ships were primed for scuttling, and explosion followed explosion. Flames began leaping from the three Italian tankers. The gunboat HMS *Cockshafer* bore down on the *Weissenfels* as loud German shouts followed by a rocking blast shook the vessel. Sheets of fire erupted from her deck—followed by agonizing squeals from the cargo of 40 pigs. "They're blowing her up! Blast them!" an officer aboard the *Kanimbla* shouted.[2] Thus deterred from her blazing target, the *Cockshafer* instead sped over to a large floating dry dock, and disarmed an Iranian naval detachment without resistance.

Amid the Axis ships, Lt. Comdr. Henry E. Passmore-Edwards maneuvered the *Lawrence* alongside two Iranian gunboats—the *Karkas* and the *Chahbaaz*—which were moored to buoys. Seaman Mashkur Ali leaped aboard the *Chahbaaz;* he was followed by Lt. Walter Coltham and three other crewmen. Before the rest of the boarding party could follow, a strong current dragged the *Lawrence* away—leaving Coltham and his men to round up the surprised Iranian crew. Seaman Ali rushed below deck and aft to the officers' quarters where—revolver in hand—he awakened the startled ship's captain, Lt. Comdr. Faradjonnash Resai, and his two officers. Sub-Lt. Mariott Harper meanwhile secured *Chahbaaz*'s engine room while Lieutenant Coltham locked up the crew on the mess decks. Coltham's men then leaped onto the gunboat *Karkas,* which was tied alongside.

Aboard the *Karkas,* Capt. Jafar Fosuni was awakened by the loud gonging and whistles. Fosuni commanded not only the *Karkas,* but all naval forces at Bander-i Shahpur. Grabbing his pistol, he rushed on deck and fired a warning shot into the air. Through the fog, he could not tell whether the boarders on the *Chahbaaz* were English or Germans. His only option was to scuttle the *Karkas* before it could be seized. He and his officers raced to prearranged stations. While Fosuni carried a can of gasoline to the ship's armory, another officer went to disable the generator. Coltham's men were too quick, however. They swarmed over the *Karkas* within moments, and apprehended the crew at gunpoint before they could implement scuttling procedures.

The *Kanimbla* cruised slowly past the first German ships, and watched the struggles on the smoke-filled decks. British boarders sometimes had to rush below and cut burning fuses just as they were about to reach the explosives. The Australians of the dhow *Naif* cheered wildly as they climbed the sides of the Italian tanker *Barbara.* The angry Italian crewmen met them head-on— scratching, biting, and screaming—but resistance was quickly overcome.

Boarders from the tug *Delavar* meanwhile scrambled up ladders onto the *Marienfels,* and engaged in still another violent spree. Silhouetted against the flames, a tall German engineer tossed burning flare after flare into the blazing hold, until a British tommy-gun ripped through his chest—killing him instantly. When the White Ensign was raised aft, the crew of the *Kanimbla* shouted, "*Marienfels* is ours!"[3] But a larger problem now confronted the *Kanimbla*. Flames spurted from the tanker *Bronte*, where stacks of kerosene tanks had been ignited amidships. Captain Adams quickly shifted the *Kanimbla* alongside as the Italians abandoned ship—some of their life rafts capsizing in the *Kanimbla*'s wake. Fire control parties battled to gain a foothold on the blazing *Bronte*, but were beaten back repeatedly by rushing flames. Adams maneuvered his vessel back and forth, with hoses gushing water onto the *Bronte* to douse the flames before they could reach the ship's bridge.

The gathering sunlight revealed a bay spotted with blazing hulls and small Axis life rafts paddling madly toward shore. To save the burning *Caboto*, the *Lawrence* left prize crews aboard the gunboats and steamed directly to that vessel. Commander Passmore-Edwards secured the *Lawrence* to the *Caboto* while a fire-fighting party prepared to board. But the blaze was so far beyond control that he had to back off and proceed to the *Barbara*, where the crew worked furiously with hoses and buckets to douse a fire under the bridge.

While the *Lawrence* battled flames on the *Barbara* and the *Caboto*, the *Kanimbla* continued to spray water on the blazing *Bronte*. The dhow *Naif* pulled up alongside the *Kanimbla*, meanwhile, with a load of Italian prisoners from the *Barbara*, and was joined shortly by a captured Iranian tug. Captain Adams decided to use these craft to help in seizing the port itself. He originally planned to dock the *Kanimbla* at the long wooden pier, but it was occupied by two U.S. merchant ships—the SS *Puerto Rican* and the SS *Anniston City*. Maj. William Maxwell, the landing force commander, crammed A Company and two bren gun teams aboard the dhow and tug. No room remained for D Company, which he instructed to wait for the next lift.

Meanwhile, several aircraft appeared through the haze and smoke surrounding the burning ships. The *Kanimbla*'s crew—mistaking what were British fighters for Iranian planes—opened fire with three-inch guns. The planes kept at safe distance, and suffered no damage.

Maxwell's force reached the pier—his sepoys walking single file over a rickety ladder and onto the jetty. On the dock, Maxwell encountered the garrison commander, Col. Abdullah Zeile, who surrendered his sword and the port. But the fighting was not over, because two platoons of the Iranian 18th Infantry Regiment doggedly took defensive positions around the railway station.

As Maxwell's men moved out toward the station, a locomotive chugged out of the station yard. Aboard the *Kanimbla*, Captain Adams spotted the train, and—suspecting that Axis seamen were trying to escape—began lobbing six-inch shells at the moving train. The rounds impacted closely—straddling the train for nearly a mile. But the boggy salt marsh dulled their effect. The locomotive opened its throttle and raced across the marshland out of range.

At 7:30 A.M., Capt. Hamid Khan led A Company, 3/10th Baluch, along the right bank of the rail line toward the train station. His Platoon Nine came under fire from the locomotive shed some 150 yards away; one sepoy was wounded. As Platoon Nine gave covering fire, Platoon Seven out-flanked the Iranians—killing two, and driving the rest some 300 yards back behind some railway buildings. Platoon Seven pressed the attack; and the Iranians panicked, ducking behind the railway embankment and fleeing into the marshlands beyond. Meanwhile, D Company landed at the pier, and the port was secured by 8:30 A.M.

While the British secured Bander-i Shahpur with minor loss, a more serious struggle ensued around the Abadan oil refinery.[4] The explosion of the *Palang* alerted the Iranian garrison. All along the waterfront, Iranian soldiers manned their posts, and trained their guns on the approaching British vessels, which were illuminated by the blazing warship. In the AIOC office building just outside the refinery fence, chief engineer George Wheeler sounded the fire alarm, which signaled key employees to man their stations. Wheeler had expected—but never received—advance warning of the landing.

At the Iranian barracks east of Abadan, the men were just awakening from 4 A.M. reveille when two green rockets were spotted over the river, followed by the explosion of the *Palang*. The soldiers panicked and fled the barracks without guns or ammunition. Lieutenant Moggadam ran to the armory to get weapons, but found the door locked and the lights off. No one could open the vault until daylight. The buzz of aircraft overhead terrified the unarmed Iranians, who sought cover in a palm grove near the Bahmanshihr River.

The paddle wheelers *Ihsan* and *Zenobia* carrying the First Kumaon Battalion arrived off Braim Creek at precisely zero hour—4:10. But the Eurekas and dhows carrying the Rajputanas were nowhere in sight. Two dhows remained aground upriver. *Ihsan* and *Zenobia* ran directly into the small inlet, and leveled fire from their three-pounders on the Iranian machine-gun posts at the corners of the creek.

The *Ihsan* struck shore on the right bank, and was followed by *Zenobia* slightly forward on the left bank. A platoon from C Company jumped ashore on the right bank, and captured a light machine-gun post in the south corner of the creek—its crew having fled under fire. On the opposite bank, D Company quickly disembarked and advanced on the nearby aerodrome; they captured it and two aircraft at 6:15 A.M.

The two dhows and four Eurekas carrying most of C and D Companies of the 2/6th Rajputanas appeared just as the *Ihsan* and *Zenobia* touched shore. Soldiers lined the decks of the dhows; they were poised for quick exit. The waterfront was dimly lit by flames from the *Palang*. To Capt. Patrick M. Kent, the D Company commander, the burning Iranian vessel seemed afire from stem to stern. Eurekas R74 and R76 came ashore unopposed to the right of Braim Creek at 4:15, and disembarked the first group of Maj. W. G. Mortimore's C Company. As the two craft withdrew, Iranian machine-gun fire splashed all around, without effect. Five minutes later, Dhow One reached Braim Creek, but found its landing point blocked by the *Ihsan*. As bullets whizzed past, the dhow moored alongside the *Ihsan*, and disembarked C Company across her deck.

Eurekas R73 and R75 carrying sepoys of D Company, 2/6th Rajputanas, landed at the same moment at Jetty One amid heavy rifle and machine-gun fire from the roof of the pumping station. The boats returned fire bren guns, and managed to unload their parties without casualty. Right behind came Dhow Two, carrying Captain Kent and 40 sepoys plus the mooring party for the *Lilavati*. Bullets sprayed the dhow as it touched the pier. One ripped the throat of Kent's signaler—killing him instantly. Several of the crew were grazed. The boat squadron commander was shot in the face and arm. But by 4:23, Kent's men were across the jetty without further casualty.

Captain Kent's reserve platoon—already ashore from the two Eurekas—scurried to shelter in a large bungalow opposite the jetty. Joining them inside, Kent encountered Mr. Cope—the works assistant manager—and his wife, who were both in nightgowns. Just east of the Copes' home, a strong Iranian machine-gun position atop the pumping station kept D Company pinned down. Kent's men could do little to dislodge their opponents, who were concealed behind high parapets. Inside the pumping station, British and Iranian employees remained steadfastly at their posts despite the crossfire outside. Their functions were essential. If the station were to cease pumping its thousands of gallons of water into the refinery cooling system, the entire complex would explode.

Several hundred yards downriver, the HMIS *Lilavati* attempted to berth at Jetty Seven only to discover two ships—the Norwegian SS *Nidaros* and the American SS *Pronto*—already moored at the pier. The remaining berth was partially occupied by barges. Fortuitously, the two ships shielded the packed decks of the *Lilavati* from murderous fire as she tried to maneuver into the pier. Lt. Harold Gahan finally steered the *Lilavati* alongside Jetty Seven at 4:30. Several of his Indian crew braved the heavy Iranian fire to lash the vessel to the pier.

The commander of A Company, 2d Lt. Charles G. Morrison, led a platoon onto the jetty; they were followed by the battalion commander, Lt. Col. Rupert Ridley, and his staff. The British had barely stepped onto the pier when an Iranian machine-gun post on the jetty loosened a murderous volley—killing Morrison outright. Ridley was hit in the thigh as he stepped off the ship, while 2d Lt. R. MacPherson was killed next to him. Subadar Udai Singh led the rest of A Company ashore, but was immediately pinned by intense fire. Their narrow frontage of 15 yards offered no cover except for a few small railway wagons and oil drums. Within minutes, three sepoys were wounded. Rifleman Mangal Singh finally charged the Iranian post, single-handedly storming the position—with a rifle, a bayonet, grenades, and finally a bren gun—and killing eight Iranians.

Heavy fire continued from a machine-gun post at the west end of the jetty as Capt. Charles W. Auchmuty brought B Company ashore and tried to advance with two platoons through the refinery to work their way behind the Iranian position. When they could not get close enough to be effective, the HMS *Shoreham* silenced the last Iranian post on Jetty Seven with machine-gun fire.

Back at Braim Creek, B Company, First Kumaons, disembarked from the *Ihsan* onto the south bank at 4:30 A.M., and moved south 100 yards into a palm grove. They encountered stiff opposition from a company of 60–70 Iranians in the trees and around several small barracks. The Kumaons fought at close range for an hour and a half; they lost two men killed, before clearing the woods. The Iranians withdrew, leaving 25 dead and ten prisoners. To their left, A Company advanced through the European area west of the refinery, toward the main police station. They encountered machine-gun fire from inside the police post at 5:15 A.M. They cleared the area around the station, but—even with mortars—could not budge the well-sheltered defenders inside.

At Braim Creek, most of C Company, 2/6th Rajputanas, came ashore with the Kumaons, and then moved along the shoreline into the European bungalow area. Several Iranian posts atop bungalows slowed their advance. The Iranians fought fiercely, losing 30 men killed. Inside the cottages, English AIOC families huddled in fear as the battle raged around them. The Rajputanas met strong resistance at Bungalow 55 where an Iranian anti-aircraft gun and a machine gun leveled intense, close-range fire that wounded two sepoys.

At the nearby nurses' quarters, British nurses lay breathlessly on the floor for more than an hour while bullets tore holes in their bedroom windows and cupboards.[5]

Farther east, around the Copes' bungalow, Kent's D Company continued to exchange fire with the Iranians atop the pump house. Two platoons worked their way around, and proceeded down the waterfront toward Jetty Seven. Not far from the pumping station, the sepoys approached the refinery manager's office, where another Iranian post was reportedly located. From the bund, the Punjabis spotted three men in blue uniforms outside the front door.

Inside the building, chief engineer George Wheeler was briefing eight British employees on their duties when he heard shots. Three British office messengers outside—dressed in the AIOC's blue uniforms—had been mistaken for Iranian soldiers and gunned down. The wounded men were brought into the office building—Wheeler not knowing what had happened—telephoned the fire station to send an ambulance. Meanwhile, two of the messengers died.

Minutes later, the ambulance pulled up in front of the building. Marked with a red crescent—per Iranian law—rather than a red cross, the ambulance was mistaken by the Punjabis for Iranian. As Wheeler watched in horror, three Iranian corpsmen were shot down as they stepped out of the vehicle. Wheeler rushed back inside, with charging sepoys close behind.

Bullets sprayed through windows as the British civilians—trying to find safety—cowered in a narrow hallway. A moment later, Indian troops with fixed bayonets burst through the door into the dimly lit room. One soldier spotted figures huddled in the hallway and opened fire with a tommy gun—wounding six men. Wheeler desperately shouted the prearranged password—"Bombay"—but the rampage continued. Wheeler crawled to his office to telephone the works manager, Mr. Pattison; but a sepoy with a tommy gun appeared at the door, and fired five shots into his groin.

The impending massacre was only narrowly avoided when an AIOC official, Mr. E. B. F. Auld, appeared through the main entrance and shouted at the sepoys in Hindustani. With the help of two Indian soldiers, Auld pulled Wheeler and another wounded British employee through a window and into his car. He then drove the wounded men through the refinery to the AIOC hospital.

At the Iranian barracks south of the refinery, the Iranian brigade commander, Colonel Nakhjevan, arrived shortly after sunrise to assess the situation. Most of his troops had fled without weapons into the palm groves along the Bahmanshihr River. Nakhjevan ordered the armory doors broken open, but had no way to distribute the weapons and ammunition to his scattered and disorganized garrison. Movement was restricted by the British aircraft that were attacking the barracks and the palm groves.

Nakhjevan was out of contact with both Admiral Bayendor at Khorramshahr and General Shahbakhti at Ahvaz. Deciding that an organized defense was no longer possible, he ordered all available trucks loaded with ammunition and staged for a withdrawal north to Ahvaz. Trucks were assembled to transport as many troops as possible. Proceeding to the Bahmanshihr ferry, Nakhjevan ordered the truck-mounted antiaircraft guns withdrawn immediately.

In the midst of this, Major Tayfuri—who was commanding the infantry battalion and artillery battery at Kasbah, 18 miles south of Abadan—arrived seeking orders from Nakhjevan. Nakhjevan angrily chastised Tayfuri for leaving his post without orders and directed him to return immediately to Kasbah, gather his men and guns, and then retreat toward Ahvaz. Tayfuri drove back to Kasbah only to find that his troops had panicked during his absence, and dispersed. He spent the rest of the day reforming his scattered unit.

Back at Abadan, A and B Companies of the 2/6th Rajputanas cleared Jetty Seven only to receive machine-gun fire from Iranian posts east of the jetty. Lacking any reserves, they formed two platoons from the headquarters company, and proceeded to clear the waterfront toward Abadan town of all resistance except a few snipers.

The HMS *Shoreham* continued its 50-caliber machine-gun fire and an occasional, carefully directed four-inch round against the remaining Iranian rooftop posts. The *Lilavati* joined in at 8:00 A.M.—engaging rooftop snipers with machine guns and cannon. Several Iranian posts fought to the last man. A serious fire broke out meanwhile on Jetty Seven. A *Shoreham* fire control party—assisted by hoses from the Norwegian ship *Nidaros*—extinguished the blaze.

At 5 A.M., Brig. Roger LeFleming and his staff disembarked onto Jetty Seven from the HMS *Seabelle*. He quickly assessed the situation, and decided that the heavily engaged forces around him needed urgent reinforcement. Heedless of the fighting, he rather casually strolled down the waterfront to the pump house, where Captain Kent's D Company was still pinned down by Iranian fire.

At the Copes' bungalow, a dead sepoy lay outside front door. Finally, one of Kent's Punjabi riflemen rushed the pump house, climbed a steel ladder on the side of the building, and threw two grenades over the parapet. The explosion ceased all resistance. Two more Iranian posts east of the pump house near the main telegraph exchange remained to be mopped up.

Captain Kent—leaving the Copes' house to reorganize his scattered company—ran into Brigadier LeFleming. LeFleming directed Kent to quickly move his men down the bund to assist in clearing the area east of Jetty Seven. He then contacted the First Kumaons, and ordered them to assist the Rajputanas in clearing the waterfront. Two Kumaon companies advanced through palm groves toward the waterfront. When fired on near the nurses' quarters, they outflanked the defenders and forced the Iranians to surrender.

At 9 A.M., Brigadier LeFleming learned that the Iranian garrison was concentrating northwest of the main storage tank farm, near the Bahman-shihr ferry. He immediately ordered the Kumaon battalion to form up northwest of Braim Creek for an attack on the ferry. A platoon from A Company remained behind, to cover the stubborn police station. AIOC officials provided vehicles to transport the Kumaons to their attack position.

While the Kumaons gathered their forces, the Rajputanas finished clearing the waterfront between Jetty One and Jetty Seven by 9:45 A.M. A and B companies then moved westward around the refinery's wire fence to secure the artisan barracks and the AIOC hospital by 10:30 A.M. Firing continued to come from Abadan town. The Rajputanas reconnoitered through the streets as far as the motor transport park, where one platoon was already in position. The troops continued mopping-up operations along the streets leading north and west into the town.

In the palm groves near the ferry, hundreds of Iranian soldiers huddled beneath the trees. British aircraft had strafed the area—killing several men. Those with guns returned fire. Lieutenant Moggadam from Ahvaz was sheltering among the trees when a soldier appeared and told him that the Sixth Division chief of staff was calling the Ministry of Justice building in Abadan and wanted to speak with an officer. Moggadam hurried through the embattled streets to the Justice building, but found the telephone line cut. The building was under British fire, and the defenders were trying to withdraw. He and another officer helped to remove a machine gun from the roof. The Iranian troops began evacuating the town, but had no means of removing the many dead soldiers lying in the streets.

Back at the palm grove, Colonel Nahkjevan ordered his men to retreat to Ahvaz before they could be surrounded and taken prisoner. While Nahkjevan and his staff crossed the river by auto, a Major Bakhtiar formed up the remaining troops, and moved them to the ferry. Few trucks were available. Several had been destroyed by British air attack near the ferry. Bakhtiar left a small rearguard in the palm grove to screen the withdrawal.

While fighting raged at Abadan, another battle ensued eight miles up the Shatt-al-Arab at the port of Khorramshahr.[6] When the first, distant explosions were heard at 4:13 A.M. from downriver, the sloop HMAS *Yarra* lay in midstream of the Shatt-al-Arab, in the lee of the *Varala*. While waiting for zero hour, Lieutenant Commander Harrington decided to shell—rather than board—the Iranian sloop *Babr*, in order to discourage the Iranians ashore and to prevent the remaining two gunboats from escaping.

Around the bend of the Karun River—about 300 yards up from the *Babr*—the captain of the Iranian gunboat *Shahrokh*, Lt. Shamsedden Safavi, was rudely awakened by distant explosions. Peering through a porthole in his cabin, he observed flashes to the south, and overheard another officer exclaim, "Some ship is firing in Abadan!"[7]

The *Yarra* meanwhile cleared the *Varala*, and illuminated the *Babr* with its searchlight. At the order to fire, the two forward guns—depressed below the safety cutoff—misfired. Gun Two quickly reloaded its battery, and loosened a four-inch round directly into the moored Iranian warship. Nine more salvos followed, as the three-incher joined in.

Aboard the burning *Babr*, gun crews rushed to their mounts at the first sound of firing. The *Yarra*'s crew watched anxiously as the Iranians hurriedly loaded and trained their forward gun. A moment later, a shell from the *Yarra* blew them apart. Two Iranian sailors appeared on deck and rushed onto the concrete jetty, with shrapnel exploding on all sides. The men turned and ran back aboard the *Babr*—vanishing a moment later amid the explosion of a four-inch shell. Hit below the waterline, the *Babr*—her deck torn and shattered—heeled to port, and came to rest partly submerged in the river mud. Mooring lines prevented her from capsizing.

Ashore, whistles in the barracks alerted the naval station. Rifle and machine-gun fire rang out from the barracks and the naval staff building. The *Yarra* lobbed a well-placed three-inch shell into the barracks, and silenced the whistles.

Aboard the *Shahrokh*, Lieutenant Safavi pulled on his tunic and trousers, and then rushed onto the quarterdeck. Looking downstream, he watched as the seemingly enormous dark profile of the *Yarra* turned up into the Karun River. His own small ship was undergoing refit, and had no ammunition for its forward three-inch gun. The officers of her sister gunboat, the *Simorgh*—moored inboard of the *Shahrokh* to a concrete "T" jetty—were on shore leave.

Downstream from the gunboats, the Iranian training ship *Ivy* opened rifle fire on the *Yarra*. Moments later, withering machine-gun fire from the *Yarra*'s twin 50-calibers tore the *Ivy*'s wooden superstructure to pieces.

Across the river in Khorramshahr proper, Rear Adm. Ali Bayendor was awakened by the explosions. Donning his white dress uniform, he left his frightened English wife and young son, and rushed to a nearby waiting motorboat. The launch sped across the river toward a small pier above the two gunboats—passing obliquely in front of the *Yarra*. The first shell from the *Yarra* passed overhead, but the second lifted the launch from the water. It landed on a mudflat. Bayendor scampered ashore and down the waterfront to the gunboats—shouting at Lieutenant Safavi from the jetty, "What happened?" Safavi answered, "They are attacking *Babr*. I heard explosions and saw flashes at Abadan." Bayendor queried Safavi's status. "We are undergoing repair," came the reply. Saying nothing more, the admiral disappeared; he crossed back to the north shore to investigate the situation there.[8]

Five miles directly north of Khorramshahr, meanwhile, Rapier Force sighted gun flashes far to the south shortly after 4 A.M. Several minutes later, there were closer flashes. It was still dark, and the haze-covered landscape left them unsure of their position. From the direction of the flashes, the Mahrattas appeared to be on the correct bearing. Receiving the order to advance, they rolled forward in their trucks—opening out gradually into daylight formations as the light increased. The 12 armored cars of Maj. W. A. Gimson's Guides Cavalry squadron swept ahead. Lt. John Humphries scanned the featureless landscape from the hatch of his armored car for some landmark to guide by. As the horizon brightened and the mist began to lift, he discerned in the distance a tall mast—the Khorramshahr wireless tower. Rapier Force was precisely on target.[9]

Back at the Khorramshahr naval yard, the *Yarra* approached the two Iranian gunboats berthed ahead of the training ship *Ivy* and an armed tug.

Small-arms fire kept the Iranians away from the loaded Maxim machine guns mounted aft on both vessels. A gun crew aboard the inboard-moored *Simorgh* rushed to the forward battery, and hurriedly trained it on the *Yarra*. But all were mowed down by *Yarra*'s machine guns before they could fire a round.[10]

Pulling alongside the *Shahrokh*, the *Yarra*'s Gun Crew One drew the two vessels together with grappling hooks. Two Australian naval officers led a boarding party onto the upper deck. The *Shahrokh* began vibrating violently from its engine's convulsions. Lieutenant Safavi started up the ship's ladder to the bridge. Near the top, he came face-to-face with several Australians wearing dark plastic capes. One had a pistol in each hand, and fired directly at Safavi—knocking his cap off. Hurrying down to the trembling lower deck. Safavi stuck his head through a hatchway and ordered the engine stopped. A moment later, he felt a pistol at his back, and heard the order, "Hands up!"[11]

Complying, he turned to face his captor, who asked if he was the ship's captain. Answering in the affirmative, Safavi and his two officers were taken aboard the *Yarra* for questioning. As they crossed onto the quarterdeck, Australian sailors ceremoniously "piped" them aboard. They were taken to the wardroom and offered coffee. There Safavi met another prisoner—an Italian engineer, who was so hysterical that he could not stand without assistance.

While the *Yarra*'s crew were securing the two gunboats, the tug HMIS *Investigator* engaged an Iranian tug that was lying between the gunboats and the *Ivy*. Iranians concealed between decks and behind portholes on the tug opened rifle fire on the exposed deck of the *Investigator,* and struck its captain near his elbow.

While *Investigator*'s crew replied with bren guns, Sub-Lt. Nilakanta Krishnan and four ratings armed with rifles and bayonets stood ready as the tug was steered alongside a barge secured to the Iranian tug. Krishnan leaped onto the barge, only to have his tug and boarding party swept away by the current. Alone, he suddenly faced three armed Iranians in the barge, while others on the Iranian tug sniped away. One aimed his rifle directly at Krishnan, who whipped out his revolver and killed the man. Wounding a second Iranian, he frightened the third into dropping his rifle. As bullets pinged around him, Krishnan boarded the Iranian vessel in search of better cover. The *Investigator* pulled alongside again, and unloaded the rest of the boarding party. The Iranians divided into several parties below decks. The Indians slammed down the afterhatch on one group, and left a guard there while the rest exchanged fire at close range with the other Iranians.

Dashing across the deck, Lieutenant Krishnan closed the door through which the Iranians were firing. Meanwhile, his men bolted closed the watertight doors over the forward hold and lower decks—trapping the enemy below. Carrying a torch, Krishnan inspected an open hold that appeared to be empty. But as he turned to leave, something moved. Flashing his torch, he spotted three Iranians who were so unnerved that they dropped their rifles and surrendered.

More Indians boarded the tug, and Krishnan's reinforced party charged into a defended compartment on the upper deck. After a brief scuffle, they captured eight more Iranians. Krishnan came upon the forward hold, which was pitch dark; the only means down was by rope ladder. Knowing that several Iranians were concealed below, he shouted, "Here's a bomb. Come up or I will kill you."[12] The Iranian sailors dropped their rifles and surrendered.

Now only the ship's bridge—where an Iranian naval officer had been observed earlier—remained unsecured. Krishnan and a seaman cautiously entered the compartment. Lieutenant Harischi, the tug's captain, was secluded in a small cabin—waiting with pistol in hand to ambush anyone who approached. As Krishnan stepped warily through the bridge compartment, he passed Harischi in the darkness. The Iranian aimed his pistol to fire just as the seaman behind Krishnan shouted a warning. Krishnan wheeled, and the two men fired their weapons at the same moment. Harischi missed, but Krishnan's round mortally wounded Harischi in the neck.

It was now 4:59 A.M., and all was momentarily quiet. Aboard the *Yarra*, Harrington decided to delay landing his Baluchi party until the *Falmouth* arrived. The HMS *Falmouth* entered the Karun River at 5:30 A.M. Coming alongside the *Ivy*, she poured 50-caliber fire onto the deck—smashing what resistance remained. While *Falmouth* landed her Baluchi contingent across the *Ivy*, the Baluchi landing party from the *Yarra* went ashore across the gunboats.

The Baluchis of C Company's Platoon 15 established a beachhead—while Number 14 Platoon moved up on its right and Platoon 13 on its left. Led by their company commander, 2d Lt. James M. Vokes, they attacked and silenced an Iranian post covering the waterfront. As the company began advancing toward the barracks, Platoon 14 came under fire from several buildings, and a sepoy was wounded. His attack having been met with heavy fire, Lieutenant Vokes dashed across open ground through heavy rifle fire to get within grenade-throwing range. A bullet struck and mortally wounded him. Dying, he urged his men on, as they stormed the Iranian position.

On seizing the buildings, the Baluchis sent out a patrol to clear the area within 800 yards. Platoon 15 searched the central buildings to their front; they captured 30 Iranian naval personnel, who were placed on the *Yarra*. Meanwhile, Platoon 13 cleared the remaining buildings—inflicting several casualties on the remaining holdouts. The base garage was seized along with 30 vehicles, 400 rifles, and four machine guns.

While fighting ensued at the naval yard, Admiral Bayendor returned to his quarters, where his car and driver waited. Taking along his black morocco jewelry case filled with gems—should he need to escape—he drove to the Iranian army post at the Pul-i Nao bridge, on the road to Basra. He ordered a Captain Abdi to divide his forces in two. One battalion would defend the outer approaches to Khorramshahr while the other withdrew to defend Hafar, the main munitions depot and ferry crossing. Then Bayendor and Capt. Mokri Nejad—the Sixth Division artillery commander—drove to the wireless station, where they would radio the situation to Tehran.[13]

Just to the north, the armored cars and trucks carrying Rapier Force neared the wireless station. Shortly before 6 A.M., Iranian troops opened fire with machine guns and rifles from palm groves to the right of the invading forces. An antitank ditch—two meters wide and deep—lay between the Indians and the Iranians. The ditch stretched from the Shatt-al-Arab to within 300 yards of the wireless station.[14]

Debussing under fire, the Mahrattas were pinned down by fire from positions seemingly behind the antitank ditch. The Guides' armored cars rolled forward, spewing machine-gun fire at the defenders while artillery and mortars were brought into action. To get better cover, the Mahrattas rushed forward to the antitank ditch, where they stumbled onto a number of Iranian soldiers in the trench. Fighting with bayonet and submachine gun at close quarters, the Mahrattas cleared the ditch—killing several Iranians, and capturing eight. Iranian soldiers in foxholes behind the ditch either fled or were overrun.

The Mahrattas then advanced on the wireless station 1,000 yards away, from which no fire had been received. Assuming the station to be undefended, they cautiously approached the compound, which had a high mud wall and an arch for a gate. An NCO carrying a white flag was sent to parley with those inside. On entering the compound, he was immediately gunned down and killed. Under the Guides' covering fire, the enraged Mahrattas stormed the station at bayonet point, and slew everyone inside without mercy.

Lieutenant Humphries was observing this attack when a radio signal from another armored car announced that a staff car flying a pennant was leaving the compound at high speed. Humphries ordered a warning volley fired in front of the car. The auto ignored the burst, and a chase ensued. A second machine-gun volley brought the car to a stop. The driver fled into the bush, while Admiral Bayendor and Captain Nejad exited out the right side. An armored car gunned the two officers down. Nejad was killed instantly. Bayendor was helped into his car where he died. Lieutenant Humphries arrived the next moment and was surprised to discover the identity of his victim.[15]

A short distance west of the tower, Lt. Col. Osmonde Lovett's 1/2d Gurkhas occupied a recently deserted Iranian police post at 6:45 A.M. near the Manduwan Nullah. Then, spreading out across the open desert, Lovett's trucks charged the main Iranian defenses at Manduwan at 30 miles an hour. With the sun to their backs—which blinded the defenders—the British convinced the Iranians that tanks were attacking. The defenders panicked and deserted after firing a few shots; many discarded their weapons and uniforms, and fled directly into the hands of the Mahrattas of Rapier Force. Hundreds of prisoners were rounded up.[16]

Lovett's charge was brought to a sudden halt when his trucks entered date plantations crisscrossed by small canals. His men dismounted and moved on foot to make contact with the other units. Capt. A. D. R. Geddes—commanding A Company—initially leaped over the countless ditches; but he wearied quickly, and was soon climbing in and out of the canals.

At the same time, Lt. Col. Charles Gray's 2/3d Gurkha Rifles were advancing along the main road to Khorramshahr. Crossing flat desert covered with scrub, Gray's battalion was approaching the bridge at Pul-i Nao shortly before 6 A.M. when they were shelled by an Iranian artillery battery. One of the first bursts killed a Gurkha in Capt. Neal Ford's A Company. Another shell struck the oil pipeline to Basra to their left, and ignited a powerful blaze that illuminated the morning landscape. The shelling continued for 15 minutes. The Gurkhas hugged the ground—feeling intense heat from the nearby conflagration.

The shelling ceased; and several minutes later, an Iranian auto bearing a white flag approached Gray's unit. An Iranian captain came forward to surrender his company of about 150 men. The 2/3d Gurkhas linked up with the 1/2d Gurkhas at Pul-i Nao at 8:15 A.M. Mahrattas and Guides Cavalry entered the city at about 7:30.

Meanwhile, 50 miles to the north, RAF aircraft were pounding the Ahvaz aerodrome. Arriving over Ahvaz at 5:42 A.M. at an altitude of 6,000 feet, Hurricanes of Squadron 261 dropped a ton and a half of bombs on the aerodrome and hangers, but without effect. Caught by surprise, Colonel Gilanshah immediately ordered his aircraft up in the sky to oppose the British. Iranian pilots scrambled into three waiting biplanes; but, as they warmed their motors for takeoff, British fighters roared in at low level—strafing all three planes.[17]

A few minutes later, six Blenheim bombers from 84 Squadron flew over at 2,000 feet, and dropped 3,000 more pounds of bombs squarely on the aerodrome. When the attack ended, two hangers were destroyed, while five Iranian planes lay in shambles and two others were damaged. Near the railway tracks, American-supplied P-40 Tomahawks lay useless in their crates, except for one that had been constructed by U.S. mechanics. No sooner had the British departed than a U.S. technician who had been assembling the P-40 jumped into the fighter and flew off to safety in Iraq.[18]

In the skies west of Ahvaz, six Valentia transports neared the abandoned Iranian landing field at Haft Khel at about 8 A.M. The aircraft carried 87 men from C Company, 3/10th Baluch Regiment. The men were mostly Pathans—fiercest of the northwestern frontier tribes. Their commander,

Capt. J. Michael Forster, had spent 19 years commanding a company near the Khyber Pass.[19]

At 7 A.M., the escorting long-range Hurricane circled the landing ground—signaling the transports that the "safe to land" strip markers placed by the local AIOC manager were visible. The RAF had precious little information on the condition of the field. The Valentias approached the airfield in two flights of three aircraft. The first flight landed perfectly—despite an unexpected slope—and wheeled right, to make room for those behind. Platoons 10 and 12 disembarked and quickly secured the perimeter of the strip. The second flight then touched down; but the center and left aircraft taxied too far down the strip, and crashed into a nullah. Forster and his orderly ran over to extricate the survivors. Although the wreckage was severe, the aircraft did not explode, and—miraculously—no one aboard was seriously hurt. The sepoys of Platoon 11 scrambled out with only a few cuts and abrasions among them. The four undamaged aircraft taxied around and took off ten minutes later.

Forster surveyed the area for some sign of the AIOC manager and his trucks, which were supposed to be ready to take his men to Haft Khel and Masjid-i-Suleiman. Walking over to where Number 10 Platoon had taken up position, he noticed five Iranian policemen approaching. When the Iranians were 15 feet away, Forster ordered the man in charge to surrender his pistol. The Iranian officer suddenly drew his revolver and fired five times at Forster's chest—shouting the while for his comrades to get away. With his submachine gun, Forster's orderly instantly gunned down the Iranian officer and another hapless policeman.

Forster—though stunned—was unhurt. Examining the Iranian's revolver, he discovered five misfires. The assailant lay dying on the ground—begging vainly for Forster to shoot him through the head. Forster's sepoys quickly surrounded the police station, and disarmed those inside. The AIOC manager then arrived to report that he had no trucks with which to move Forster's men to Masjid-i-Suleiman. But he advised the British captain not to worry. The manager at Masjid-i-Suleiman had telephoned that everything was normal and there appeared no need for an evacuation. Having no other choice, Forster told the manager to gather all British and Indian citizens into the Haft Khel compound, where his company established a defense perimeter.

Back at the Abadan refinery, the First Kumaon Rifles were assembled by noon for the advance on the Bahmashihr ferry. A 45-millimeter howitzer battery, which had been brought ashore to support the attack, laid fire in the vicinity of the ferry. Within minutes, a large plume of smoke rose in the distance—raising fears that a pipeline had been hit. The guns had actually hit an Iranian munitions truck.[20]

At 12:40 P.M., the Kumaons crossed the open desert with C and D Companies in the van. An Iranian rear guard fired a few shots, but were quickly mopped up. The rest of the garrison had already crossed to the north side, and escaped. A Company of the Kumaon Rifles with a section of howitzers returned to clear the police station. The defenders resisted fiercely, killing one Kumaon and wounding another. The British guns shelled the station from 100 yards, and slowly reduced its resistance. The position was not fully cleared until almost 6 P.M.

A dozen miles north of Abadan at the village of Marid on the west bank of the Karun River, B Company of the 2/3d Gurkhas along with the Ninth Field Company Sappers and Miners arrived late on the morning of August 25 to reconnoiter a ferry-crossing site. At about noon, they sighted the retreating survivors of the Abadan garrison, who were on the opposite shore—moving north in trucks and vehicles. The British had no means of intercepting the enemy force. Meanwhile, 25 miles directly north of Marid, another battle was being fought around the Iranian police fort at Qasr Shiekh.

Lieutenant Dehtaziyani of the Iranian Navy had left Ahvaz early that morning—with his wife, two children, and two servants—for duty at the Khorramshahr naval station. He had driven to within 30 miles of his destination when, at 4:15 A.M., he discerned the flash and rumble of cannon fire in the distance. Realizing that the British were attacking Khorramshahr, he pulled over and sought shelter at the police fort of Qasr Shiekh.[21]

The fort was a square mud structure with high walls—much resembling a Foreign Legion post from *Beau Geste*. Concealed entrenchments defended by a battalion of the elite First Pahlavi Infantry Regiment from Tehran surrounded the ramparts. The Pahlavi Infantry wore pith helmets and mustard-toned desert uniforms, and carried the latest Czech weapons. Their officers graciously provided Lieutenant Dehtaziyani and his party shelter in the fort.

Meanwhile, some 25 miles to the southwest, the 25th Indian Brigade crossed the Iranian frontier on a beeline toward Qasr Shiekh. A "mobile group" consisting of the 13th Lancers, an antitank battery, and a Sikh platoon forayed ahead of the main body. The Lancers had departed Tanuma at 3:30 A.M., and entered Iran at 5:20 A.M. en route to the village of Saudiyeh near Qasr Shiekh. An hour later, they approached four armed Iranian trucks, which retired swiftly on sighting the British.[22]

Thirty minutes behind the Lancers came the brigade's main body led by the Second Battalion, 11th Sikhs. In the vanguard was Maj. Colin H. McVean's C Company. Four armored cars screened the column's advance about 100 yards ahead of McVean. To his rear some 400 yards came the battalion main body in four long, parallel columns. A battery of aging 18-pounder antitank guns brought up the rear of the column.

Fifteen minutes into Iran, the Sikhs rolled into a customs post and captured a few Iranians, who reported that Qasr Shiekh was defended by an Iranian battalion. An RAF biplane scouted the objective. Returning, the pilot dropped a message to Brig. Robert G. Mountain—warning that a line of possibly defended trenches stretched south from the fort. Mountain altered his direction of march so as to approach Qasr Sheikh from the west, and outflank the defenders. The column rolled out again, with the First Mahrattas and Third Jat battalions behind the Sikhs. The going was rough, over small sand dunes and through coarse marsh grass.

At 8:30, Major McVean's advance guard reached a large nullah some 4,000 yards from the fort. As he halted his company to permit the armored cars and navigating party to locate a crossing, a shot rang out from the direction of Qasr Shiekh. The armored cars and the truck carrying the navigating officer turned about and scurried out of the nullah. More Iranian long-range rifle and machine-gun fire followed. McVean signaled his men to dismount and take cover in the nullah. The turbanned Sikhs leaped out of their lorries—whose drivers immediately reversed gears and sped back to the battalion main body, about a half mile to the rear.

McVean's battalion commander, Lt. Col. Arthur E. Farwell, came forward to find out why the column had halted. When Iranian fire recommenced, he hastily approved deploying one of McVean's platoons to a small hill across the nullah.

Meanwhile, Brigadier Mountain arrived, standing calmly in the open with Farwell—heedless of the bullets whizzing past. McVean grabbed two signalers, and walked briskly across the open desert as bullets zinged past and kicked up dust all around. Colonel Farwell sent his adjutant to bring up the main body.

The 13th Lancers were to the northwest; they could hear the firing from the fort as they reached Saudiyeh village. The armored cars immediately sortied toward Qasr Shiekh. Major McVean watched as the B and C Lancer squadrons commenced their attack. The armored cars mistakenly directed some of their machine-gun fire toward McVean's position. McVean frantically waived a signal flag, but only attracted another burst.

C Squadron moved right, and soon bogged down in heavy sand—the commander's car being stuck very near an Iranian trench. Heavy fire poured onto the stalled armored cars; a troop leader and his driver were wounded. To the left, B Squadron was halted by stiff opposition. A Squadron was then sent on a wide detour to the right. Iranian 75-millimeter howitzers that were emplaced north of the fort shelled the Lancer's reserve. The regiment's attached antitank troop fired back. B Squadron withdrew north a short distance, and then cut sharply west and south in a wide circle around the fort.

By this time, all of the Sikh battalion had reached the nullah, and debussed. Colonel Farwell strolled across the nullah to join Major McVean on a small hill overlooking the fort. Farwell ordered an immediate attack, and directed McVean to guide his company on the fort. Two columns were formed. McVean's C Company advanced on the right—followed by Capt.

Robert B. Penfold's A Company—while, to the left, 2d Lt. James Franklin's D Company led 2d Lt. Dennis Rimmer's B Company. Mortar detachments mounted in trucks covered the forward companies, with a machine-gun section on the flank.

At 9:30, Colonel Farwell waved for Major McVean to begin his advance. A line of men rose and walked stolidly forward across the grassy plain. Iranian machine guns opened fire immediately. Major McVean felt large and vulnerable, but his fear abated when a herd of gazelle brazenly pranced across his front.

Iranian howitzers began shelling the battalion's transport, but their bursts were either too high or too short. Farwell grumbled to his attached artillery officer that his own 25-pounders were too slow getting into action. Moments later, the ground shuddered from the intensity of the British artillery salvos. McVean jumped at the roar, as he watched the shells explode on the fort.

Only five rounds were expended before the British ceased fire—having sighted friendly armored cars near the fort. The Lancers' B Squadron had passed behind the Sikhs, and circled south and then east of the fort to attract Iranian fire away from the advancing infantry. Not taking the bait, the well-sited Iranian light machine guns poured voluminous but inaccurate fire on the attackers—kicking up dust all around C and D Companies.

D Company was slowed, but C Company continued to advance. The fire was coming mainly from McVean's front and left flank, where the Iranian positions were hidden by high grass. Falling prone behind a small scrub, he tried to locate the hidden enemy positions with his binoculars. A terrific punch struck his left shoulder just below the armpit. After squirming for a moment, he realized that his wound was not serious, and he continued forward.

An orderly bandaged McVean's wound. He then decided that the time had arrived to wheel his company left and attack the Iranian positions enfilading his men. McVean had barely issued his attack order when, to his left, he saw Lt. James Franklin's D Company surge toward the enemy machine guns that were firing at his own company. As the Iranian fire switched toward Franklin's force, McVean and his men pressed forward. A Company—under Captain Penfold—meanwhile passed to McVean's right at 9:50 A.M. Catching the same fire as C Company, Penfold was wounded in the thigh.

A runner from C Company informed Farwell—as he moved his headquarters forward—that Major McVean had been wounded and that the Iranians were holding up the advance from hidden positions in a grassy depression between C and D Companies. Farwell ordered B Company to clear this gap—not realizing that D Company had already begun an assault. The two left platoons were held up by fire to their front, while Platoon 16 pressed forward on the right. Lieutenant Franklin had reached the lip of the

Iranian trench when he and a Sikh rifleman were killed. His enraged sepoys pummeled furiously into the ditch with bayonets, tommy guns, and grenades—extracting a terrible revenge from the defenders. One sepoy bayoneted seven Iranians single-handedly. The trench was quickly cleared. Three more sepoys were wounded; 38 Iranians were killed, with ten others taken prisoner. B Company and some armored cars assisted D Company in overrunning another position and capturing 90 more prisoners.

McVean's advancing C Company now had a clear view of the concealed Iranian positions. As McVean watched, a trench filled with Iranian soldiers surrendered to a Lancer car—several of which were moving about the trenches. Iranian fire was still coming from a position in front of C Company. McVean requested mortar support, but the fire slackened before the mortars arrived.

Reaching an Iranian trench, McVean spotted a havidar leaning on his rifle and slowing pushing his bayonet into a hapless Iranian who was beyond resistance. A sepoy stood at the edge of the trench—shooting at the Iranians lying on the bottom. McVean chastised his soldiers for not properly treating a surrendered enemy.

By 11:15 A.M., the firing had all but stopped. McVean watched armored cars circle the fort—like the Hollywood Indians in a Western movie—and then fire into it with machine guns. His lead platoon joined the platoon attached to the Lancers in storming the undefended post. As McVean rushed up, his men were firing wildly about the fort. The major was warned that there were still people inside the structure. A sepoy tossed a grenade into an outbuilding.

Several persons streamed out of the burning hut, only to be gunned down immediately by the Sikhs. Among them was Lieutenant Dehtaziyani—who, as he lay wounded, was bayoneted through his back by an Indian soldier. By some miracle, no vital organs were damaged, and he survived. His terrified wife was dragged from the burning house by an hysterical Indian officer, who shouted that he would not spare her at any price. Appalled, McVean slapped the officer, and forced him to release her. The woman threw herself thankfully into the arms of the extremely embarrassed major, as his sepoys cheered their lustful approval.

McVean restored order, and directed his men to provide the wounded Iranians with shade and water until the arrival of a doctor. McVean helped Dehtaziyani and his wife into his car, where he offered them a flask of tea. Outside the fort, an Iranian captain wearing polished boots and a German-style officer's hat came forward to surrender the post to Capt. Robert J. Henderson, the battalion adjutant. Six Iranian officers and 300 men were captured, while 60 Iranian bodies were discovered. Several Iranian officers reportedly fled toward Ahvaz when the fighting began. British losses were two dead and 20 wounded in the battle that secured the road to Ahvaz.

Meanwhile, 300 miles northwest of Qasr Shiekh, Maj. Gen. William Slim's Tenth Indian Division advanced into central Iran that morning. During the preceding night, A and B columns moved into position outside Khanaquin for a parallel advance through the Paitak Pass and the Gilan valley.[23]

South of Khanaquin, the Second Battalion, Seventh Gurkha Rifles, assembled shortly before dawn at the Iraqi border town of Naft-i Khaneh. The force struck quickly across the border just before 4 A.M.—reaching the oil fields at Naft-i Shah at 4:30. The Gurkhas debussed and attacked before the small Iranian detachment could organize a defense. Shots were exchanged, and several Iranians wounded; but the Gurkhas secured the site without casualty.

Meanwhile, 25 miles to the north, Capt. George Nightingale led B Company, 1/5th Gurkha Rifles, across the frontier near the Khosrovi customs station. First cutting the telephone lines to Qasr-i Shirin, Nightingale's force then rolled up to the post, where the 20 customs officials and border guards were caught asleep. One startled customs official awoke to find a kurki blade poised over his head. All were taken without resistance. Nightingale kept one officer prisoner, released the others, and then pushed on toward Qasr-i Shirin.

Close behind, the rest of the 1/5th Gurkhas crossed the border at 5:15, and raced north to catch up with Nightingale. During the night, light tanks of the 14/20 Hussar Regiment negotiated their way through very difficult terrain west of Qasr-i Shirin. Zero hour—4:15 A.M.—found them in position astride the main roads leading out to the northwest, north, and east from town. Alerted to their presence, Iranian troops fired small arms at the tanks, and damaged several support trucks.

At about that moment in Kermanshah, a servant awakened Maj. Gen. Hassan Moggadam, the Iranian corps commander. Colonel Tabatabai—commanding the 39th Infantry Regiment at Qasr-i Shirin—was calling to report that English forces were invading Iran. Moggadam dressed quickly and assembled his staff. He realized that the British would advance toward the Paitak Pass, which was defended by General Puria's 12th Division. But he also knew that the enemy would attempt to bypass Paitak through the village of Gilan to the south. Expecting this, Moggadam emplaced a full infantry regiment supported by antitank guns and artillery on the ridges east of Gilan. Before 5 A.M., he and his staff were driving west from Kermanshah to join the forces deployed at Gilan.[24]

South of Qasr-i Shirin at 5:05 A.M., Captain Nightingale's lorries encountered heavy Iranian fire as they approached the town. A Gurkha was slightly wounded. B Company debussed and pushed forward to seize the ridges covering the road. The rest of the battalion arrived and deployed on either side of the road. At 7:30, two companies attacked and seized the prominent hills astride the road—driving the defenders into the encircled town.

Shortly before 10 A.M., A and C Companies advanced into Qasr-i Shirin as the Hussar tanks attacked from the opposite side. The cornered garrison panicked and fled westward into the hills. Entering the town, the Gurkhas encountered a surprisingly warm reception from its inhabitants. Two hours later—at 11:50 A.M.—they received orders to push on toward the Paitak Pass.

At Naft-i Shah, meanwhile, the 2/7th Gurkhas left a small detachment to protect the oil fields, and—at 10:30 A.M.—resumed their advance north to rejoin A column. Fifteen miles north of Naft-i Shah, the battalion motored through the village of Chicha Surkh, whose small garrison had fled east into the hills at the approach of the British. After a brief stop, the Gurkhas continued their advance northward at 1:15 P.M.

B Column had meanwhile crossed the frontier shortly after A Column, and had wheeled right at Khosrovi toward Gilan. B column included the Warwickshire Yeomanry, a squadron of 12 Hussar tanks and bren carriers, a battery of the 15th Field Regiment, and a company of miners and sappers. Entering Iran, they found the same flat desolate desert as in Iraq. But after traveling eastward several miles, they began a steady climb into a valley of the Zagros Mountains, where the terrain changed dramatically. The mountain ridges were green and wooded, while the fresh-flowing streams crisscrossed the valley. Their route curved to the southwest as they neared the village of Gilan. On either side of the road, Iranians could be seen working in the fields. Some farmers—looking ragged and undernourished—approached the road to stare at the passing convoy.

At about 12:15 P.M., the column rumbled through the deserted village of Gilan. Ahead, the valley narrowed as mountains rose sharply on either side. B Column passed quietly through Gilan, and moved toward the Koh-i-Wazhlan ridge—a hogsback jutting perpendicular to the southern slope of the valley. Just beyond Gilan, the tanks and bren carriers were ambushed by machine guns, antitank guns, and artillery in concealed positions along the ridge and on the valley slopes. The bren carriers pulled to either side of the road in search of cover. As one carrier reversed off the road, it knocked over its sergeant—running over his leg with its tracks. Trucks carrying the Yeomanry halted abruptly as shells rained down from the ridge. One shell caused several casualties. A frightened radio operator signaled, "This is getting a bit too hot! I'm going under my truck, over." "I am under my truck! Out!" came the response.[25] The Hussars pulled back while the 18-pounder battery was unlimbered and wheeled into action. The tanks charged forward, spotting and knocking out an antitank gun. But the other guns were too well concealed and difficult to approach. Intense fire drove the attackers back. Iranian soldiers on the steep hillsides braved exploding British shells to push boulders down onto the road, in a vain attempt to create a roadblock. After two more attempts and with darkness approaching, the British pulled back to await reinforcement.

While British forces advanced into southern and central Iran, their Soviet allies were being equally aggressive in northwestern Iran. Thousands of Soviet troops, tanks, and trucks were streaming across the Iranian border.

8

The Russian Armor Has Broken Through!

Early on August 25, 1941, Iranian border guard Hossein Dashi was on duty in his border post at the village of Pol Dasht, a few miles up the Araxes River from Nakhijevan. Shortly after 4 A.M., he heard noises, and—walking to a small cliff—spotted approaching Soviet soldiers in green woolen uniforms with steel helmets, rifles, and submachine guns. Dashi aimed his rifle and began picking them off, until the last of his few rounds were expended. The Soviets then closed in and killed him with machine-gun fire.[1]

Securing the border crossing at Pol Dasht, a Soviet force of probably regimental size led by light T-26 tanks advanced quickly westward toward the northwestern Iranian city of Maku. Wedged on a narrow strip of land between the Soviet and Turkish borders, Maku was a historic gateway into Asia—possessing a strategic importance far greater than its population of 10,000.[2]

The city quartered the Iranian 17th Infantry Regiment, whose soldiers were just rising for 4 A.M. reveille when they heard the approaching drone of aircraft. A flight of Soviet bombers swept through the narrow Zangemar River gorge, and unloaded a string of bombs on the city. As explosions awakened the garrison, a bewildered Iranian soldier shouted, "What's happening? We're not at war with any country!" Frightened troops darted about the barracks in confusion until a company commander—Lt. Kenami Zadeh—screamed at them, "What are you waiting for? Let's fight!" Zadeh led the soldiers to the armory, where he handed out guns and ammunition. He was soon joined by another company commander, Lt. Ettehadieh Shargi, who rose from his sickbed.[3]

The garrison gathered trucks to transport men and supplies to positions outside the city, where the Zangemar River valley widened and emptied onto a broad plain that extended to the Soviet frontier. The valley entrance

132

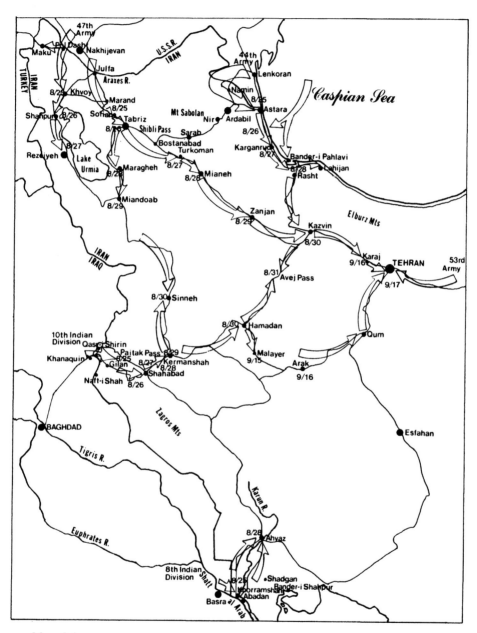

Map 8.1
British–Soviet Movements in Western Iran, August–September 1941

was blocked on the north by cliffs and on the south by steep hills. The Iranians hurriedly dug firing pits to prepare for the approaching Soviet force, which was still some hours away.

The Soviet unit advancing westward on Maku was part of a larger force consisting of the 63d Georgian Mountain Infantry Division, which itself composed the left wing of Maj. Gen. V. V. Novikov's 47th Army. The main body of the 63d Division crossed the Araxes River near Nakhijevan, and advanced south toward Khvoy and Rezeiyeh.[4]

Ahead of the 63d Georgian Division, Soviet warplanes attacked the cities of Khvoy and Rezeiyeh. At Khvoy, the 1,800 Iranian cavalrymen of the 17th Division, which garrisoned the city, mounted their horses and fled toward the Turkish border as the Soviets approached. Farther south at Rezeiyeh, Soviet bombers swept across Lake Urmia to unleash their bombs on the garrison that was headquarters for the Iranian Fourth Division. The first bombs fell on the Ministry of Education building and other adjacent structures. Antiaircraft machine-gun fire from the nearby barracks revealed the garrison's location to the attackers. The bombers immediately veered toward the location of the gunfire, and targeted a string of bombs directly onto the main barracks, which collapsed the large building and buried 30 Iranian soldiers inside.[5]

Following the attack, the Fourth Division commander, Maj. Gen. Ali Moini, called for army reservists to report for duty. Most of his division was scattered into outlying garrisons, with only a portion actually posted at Rezeiyeh. Moini was short of troops, weapons, and ammunition. A convoy of 14 trucks that was carrying desperately needed munitions from Tehran had failed to arrive. It was intercepted en route by the advancing Soviets.[6]

The right wing and main portion of General Novikov's 47th Army thrusted into Iran at Julfa. In the predawn twilight, Soviet troops dashed across the 100-foot wooden bridge over the Araxes River, and seized the small wooden shack that served as border post; it was manned only by a sleeping guard armed with an old rifle. Within minutes, a long column of tanks, armored cars, and trucks that were crammed with troops rolled across the bridge and into the sleeping town—down streets lined with small, shuttered shops and flat-roofed, whitewashed buildings. Exiting the city to the south, Novikov's main force—which consisted of the 76th Armenian Mountain Infantry Division, the 24th Mountain Cavalry Division, and elements of the Sixth and 54th Tank Divisions—drove south toward Tabriz.[7]

At the Iranian barracks on the southeast edge of Tabriz, meanwhile, Cpl. Tomic Romson of the Engineer Battalion was standing in ranks with the other 8,500 men of the Third Division—all of them saluting the Iranian flag during 6 A.M. formation—when a flight of three four-engined Soviet bombers swept overhead. Bombs were released, missing the barracks and exploding in a dry creek bed beyond. The soldiers broke ranks and scattered in all directions. Iranian antiaircraft guns fired on the succeeding waves of attack, and struck one aircraft. The others veered off and dumped their bombs outside the city.[8]

The sound of antiaircraft guns and exploding bombs awoke German Vice-Consul (and local Abwehr chief) Maj. Bertold Schulze. Hurriedly dressing, he dashed to the consulate, where he met Consul Wussow. Having assembled the consulate staff, Wussow calmly issued instructions for the evacuation of all Germans in Tabriz. Calls were placed to the Germans who had telephones—who, in turn, alerted other of their countrymen. All were ordered to report to the consulate, where transportation was being arranged.[9]

Meanwhile, at the American Presbyterian Mission Hospital in Tabriz, Dr. Charles Lamme was dressing that morning, when he heard the drone of aircraft and distant explosions. He thought at first that the Iranian Army was conducting war games. But as he came down for breakfast, his Iranian servant excitedly announced that large foreign aircraft were bombing the city. Lamme rushed to his roof where he watched wave after wave of bombers—usually two or three to a flight—drop explosives around Tabriz. Fortunately, none fell near the hospital.[10]

Back at the Iranian barracks, the dispersed soldiers were recalled by their officers, and were formed into their proper units. Corporal Romson and the rest of the Engineer Battalion lined up with other units at the munition's depot, where they were issued only five rounds of ammunition and no food. The men readied kits for march.

Their division commander, Maj. Gen. Ephraim Matbooi, telephoned the aerodrome north of the city, and ordered Colonel Shaybani, the commander of the Second Air Regiment, to fly north to determine the direction and strength of the Soviet advance. Shaybani's unit consisted of only 14 obsolescent Hind and Audax biplanes. Because of the danger of Soviet fighters, Shaybani decided to fly the mission himself. He called for volunteers among his pilots to accompany him. A Lieutenant Irvani stepped forward, and the two men were soon navigating their way northward. Shaybani soon found the fast-moving Soviet column.[11]

Fourteen miles south of Julfa, Novikov's army entered the narrow, four-mile-long Daradis Gorge. Though vulnerable, the column was protected by antiaircraft pom-pom guns carried on trailers that were pulled by tractors. The only plane in the vicinity, however, was being flown by Colonel Shaybani on his reconnaissance mission. He sighted hundreds of tanks and other vehicles. Many of the trucks were commandeered farm vehicles. There were not enough vehicles for the whole army; therefore, some infantry units marched on foot.[12]

The Soviet force soon exited the gorge, and rolled onto a wide plateau leading to the town of Marand. Five miles beyond lay the 6,000-foot Yam Pass, where the road ascended steeply through the Mishou-Dagh Mountains. The pass was known to be fortified but unmanned. Novikov's army needed to reach it before the Iranians got there.[13]

Colonel Shaybani completed his scouting foray, and flew back to Tabriz to report his findings to General Matbooi. Matbooi was greatly disturbed by the strength and speed of the Soviet advance. He had no tanks, few trucks, and insufficient artillery or ammunition. His foot infantry could not reach the Yam Pass before the Soviets. The Third Division's main defense line lay 20 miles south of Tabriz at the Shibli Pass—where the road was mined, the pass was fortified, and the artillery observation posts were connected by telephone. However, Matbooi decided against withdrawing in this direction when he received a report that another Soviet force had crossed near Ardabil and could cut his line of retreat toward Tehran. Therefore, only one course remained: to withdraw the division southwest through Miandoab toward the Turkish border. Orders were issued accordingly, and the troops prepared for the march.[14]

Far to the east of Tabriz, about 15 miles inland from the Caspian Sea, motorized infantry and cavalry of Major General Khadeev's 44th Army emerged from the Talyshskive Gory Mountains, and crossed into Iran north of Ardabil shortly after 5 A.M. The Soviets chose this winding mountain route in order to bypass the easily blocked Hadshi-Amir Pass above the port of Astara, and because the old and decaying wooden frontier bridge across the Astara River could not support tanks and heavy vehicles. The 44th Army's motorized advance guard crossed the frontier near Namin, a small city of 2,000 clay houses surrounded by gardens.[15]

Shortly before 6 A.M., the Soviets reached the paved Ardabil–Astara highway—three miles south of Namin—and encountered a small Iranian cavalry patrol. A bloody skirmish ensued, during which most of the Iranians were killed. The Iranian survivors galloped south toward the foothills of Mount Sabolan, a towering feature that dominated the Ardabil plain.

Although Ardabil lay 15 miles farther south, the 44th Army's immediate objective was the Caspian port of Astara, which was over the mountains to the east. While motorized infantry of the 77th Mountain Infantry Division and mounted columns of the 17th Cavalry Division ascended the Hadshi-Amir Pass en route to Astara, small screening patrols scouted toward Ardabil.[16]

In Ardabil, Soviet bombers swept over the city at 5:50 A.M.; they caused little damage but roused the garrison, which included the 15th Division headquarters and two infantry regiments—totaling about 3,000 men. To escape further air attack, the commander of the Iranian 11th Infantry Regiment—Colonel Sadiq—hurriedly assembled his troops and marched them south to the village of Nir, an easily defensible bottleneck on the road through the foothills of Mount Sabolan. The other infantry regiment followed shortly behind.[17]

The 15th Division had only 20 light and 15 heavy trucks to transport its artillery, ammunition, food, and water. Supplies were being loaded for the retreat when the division commander, Brig. General Gaderi, appeared and ordered some of the ammunition dropped into the Bowlagi Chay River in order to make room for his personal furniture and household goods.[18]

The Soviet advance on Astara, meanwhile, was being supported by vessels of the Caspian Sea Flotilla, carrying the 105th Regiment of the 77th Mountain Infantry Division. Admiral Sedelnikov's amphibious squadron steamed southward from Baku at first light on August 25. Gunboats, torpedo boats, and subchasers escorted the merchant ships transporting the troops. Speed was urgent, for the Iranian coast lay more than 100 miles away. The vessels cruised at maximum speed. The slower merchant ships pushed their engines to 18 knots—exceeding the normal top speed of 14 knots.[19]

Well into the morning, the amphibious squadron rendezvoused off Kuriskiy-Kamen Island, near the mouth of the Kura River—still north of Iran. The ships' captains opened sealed packets containing their respective destinations. The flotilla then separated into two groups. One force headed toward the coastal village of Khevi—18 miles south of Astara—where a Soviet force would land to support the advance along the coast. The main amphibious force, meanwhile, sailed directly toward Bander-i Pahlavi—intending to land and occupy that key port.

Nearing the Iranian coast, the Soviet ships sighted an unidentified aircraft. The plane approached from the coast, circled the fleet, and then disappeared back over the mountains. The Soviet crews remained alert against air attack. In midmorning, the western group of ships approached the coast south of Astara. The barren shore near the mouth of the Khiva River was unequipped for landing operations. The transports therefore had to run their bows up into the sand in order to lower their sterns enough to off-load troops and equipment into small launches and fishing boats, which ferried them ashore.[20]

While the landing was in progress, 12 large bombers approached the Soviet squadron from over the mountains. Mistaking the aircraft for German Junkers, the gunboats opened fire. But the planes were neither German, whose nearest air bases were too distant, nor Iranian, who did not possess such bombers. The Red Navy opened fire on their own bombers en route to bombard the Iranian port of Bander-i Pahlavi. The Soviet bombers reacted to the antiaircraft fire by unloading a string of bombs from high altitude—all of which fell harmlessly into the Caspian Sea.

Meanwhile, down the coast at Bander-i Pahlavi, the director of Shilat—Iran's caviar industry—drove across a concrete causeway onto Mijan-Pushte Island in Murdab Bay, and pulled up in front of the barracks of the Iranian 36th Infantry Regiment. The official located the chief of staff—Captain Golcheem—and warned him that he had just received a telephone report from Shafarud (a village 20 miles to the north) that eight Soviet ships had been sighted off the coast. The Soviets were reportedly ferrying soldiers ashore in small boats, and were pitching tents.[21]

Captain Golcheem immediately telephoned the 11th Division Headquarters at Rasht. The only reply was to "watch." Moments later, a whistle blew in the barracks, and soldiers rushed to gather their rifles and ammunition. Golcheem hurried toward the gate to inform his regimental commander, Lieutenant Colonel Iranpur. On reaching the gate, he spotted the local Soviet consul parking his car across the street in front of a small palace owned by the shah. The consul noticed the flurry in the barracks, and hurried off in his auto.

An hour later, Colonel Iranpur arrived at the barracks, where troops and supplies were already prepared for march. However, lacking enough trucks to move his whole force, Iranpur dispatched a patrol to scour the city for trucks, cars, and gasoline. The patrol proceeded directly to the Customs House where they again encountered the Soviet consul, who departed on their approach.

Iranpur meanwhile telephoned the situation to the commander of the naval station, Capt. Morteza Daftary. The naval yard lay on the east, or Qazian, side of the channel leading to Murdab Bay. Daftary's small squadron included the sleek, Dutch-built Royal Yacht *Chahsavar,* and three small patrol craft armed with heavy machine guns. One patrolboat was commanded by Lt. Yadulah Bayendor, younger brother of Admiral Bayendor. Daftary immediately hurried to his headquarters to alert his naval force of 100 officers and men.[22]

Presently, a Soviet bomber appeared high over the port. Captain Golcheem spotted the plane, and ran to the barracks to warn Colonel Iranpur. Bombs were already falling before he reached the building. The first exploded on the Caspian shore, and killed several soldiers at an observation post. Meanwhile, a report reached the barracks that the Soviet consulate had raised four red flags as a signal to the attacking aircraft. Learning this, Colonel Iranpur immediately ordered his regiment to deploy half a kilometer from the barracks.

In Tehran at 6:30 that morning, a black car whose license bore a large "1"—symbol of the prime minister—hurried along Pahlavi Street. Daylight brightened quickly as the auto entered the large gate of the Saadabad Palace. The driver parked near a cluster of large trees. Prime Minister Ali Mansur emerged—visibly pale and shaking—and walked nervously toward a building. After a few steps, he spotted the shah standing idly near a tree.[23]

Mansur's terrified expression alarmed the shah, who demanded, "What is the matter? Why are you so pale? Is something wrong?" Mansur paused to gather his thoughts, then replied in a trembling voice, "Yes, Your Majesty. Something terrible has happened. At 4 o'clock this morning, I was informed by the Soviet and English ambassadors that their military forces have invaded Iran." Reza Pahlavi was stunned, for he had not believed the situation to be this extreme. Suddenly tired, he walked with Mansur toward one of the buildings, where he rested in a chair and lit a cigarette.[24]

"That is incredible," he exclaimed. "Our friends, England and Russia, are giving us exactly the same treatment Hitler gave to Belgium and Mussolini gave to Greece. I cannot understand how, while we were prepared to give England whatever she asked for peacefully, Great Britain and Russia should so foolishly resort to the invasion of a peaceful and small country." He directed Mansur to have certain selected officials report to the palace immediately.[25]

The shah's special council convened at 8:30 A.M. to discuss the crisis. Those present included Prime Minister Mansur, Acting Foreign Minister Amery, Army Chief of Staff General Zargami, and Tehran Chief of Police Colonel Mokhtary. Situation reports filtered in as the conferees debated the political, military, and security measures to be taken. Initial reports indicated that the British were attacking Abadan, Khorrmahshar, and Bander-i Shahpur while the Soviets had crossed the border at several places and were advancing on Tabriz with 1,000 tanks. Soviet planes were striking cities across the northwest—including Tabriz, Maku, Khvoy, Ahar, Miandoab, Mahabad, Rasht, Baneh, and Mianeh. The casualties were mostly civilian.[26]

After being briefed by his council, the shah summoned Ambassador Smirnov and Minister Bullard to a special audience at 10 A.M. When the envoys entered the room, the shah angrily held out the diplomatic notes given earlier to Mansur, and exclaimed, "What is this? I have given my assurance that most of the Germans will be expelled from Iran. I find this morning that you have attacked both the north and south of my country and seized eight Axis ships in the Gulf."[27]

Without awaiting a reply, the shah sarcastically suggested that, if the reason for the attack was that Germany had seized most of Europe and therefore Britain and the Soviet Union wished to seize Iran, then his country was too weak to resist. If, however, the real object was to eliminate the Germans in Iran, then the necessary measures were already being effected. The shah claimed to have directed his ministers to expel the Germans. "I am ready to send away all Germans within one week, with the few exceptions such as are mentioned in your memoranda [of August 16]," the shah assured the two Allied representatives. "Only, what will His Majesty's and the Soviet Government do if I send the Germans away?" He demanded that, "to avoid bloodshed, hostilities must cease pending the receipt of your [government's] reply." The shah promised that he was "doing everything" possible to eliminate the Germans. "I gave orders yesterday," he claimed, "that all Germans in Tabriz be sent away. But what is the good of that if today your forces attack me?"[28]

Bullard gained the impression that the shah, who seemed tired and feeble, was completely surprised by the invasion. The monarch seemed to have sincerely believed that everything was proceeding normally. Both Bullard and Smirnov were certain that the shah's ministers had not kept their ruler fully informed. The two envoys therefore described to the shah details of the Nazi menace in Iran. Much of the information seemed new to him. The shah then asked if Britain and the Soviet Union were at war with Iran. Bullard assured him that, per his own government's communiqué, "these measures will in no way be directed against the Iranian people." The monarch advised the two envoys that Iran must continue to resist the invasion. He insisted that nothing more could be done until he received a reply from their two governments.[29]

At the Kremlin early that morning, Ambassador Mohammed Saed was ushered into the office of Commissar Molotov. The Soviet official coldly handed him a copy of the same note delivered in Tehran.[30]

The note cited the provisions of the 1921 treaty permitting Soviet intervention in Iran, and described the alleged activities of some 50 German agents in Iran. Noting that Iran had ignored three requests made to remove this danger, the memorandum stated flatly that the Soviet government

> has been forced to . . . march troops temporarily into Iranian territory for purposes of self-defense. The Soviet Government has no intentions whatever against the territorial integrity and independence of Iran. The military measures taken are solely against the danger created by the hostile activities of Germans in Iran. As soon as this danger which threatens the interests of Iran and the Soviet Union are averted, the Soviet Government will immediately withdraw its troops.[31]

Saed had spent many years in the Soviet Union and he realized that military resistance to the Soviets was useless. Carrying the note back to his embassy, he immediately composed a dispatch urging the shah to withdraw all forces from the frontier and submit to Allied demands.

In London, meanwhile, Foreign Secretary Anthony Eden was called on by Iranian Minister Mohammed Moggadam, who had not yet learned of the developments affecting his country. Moggadam offered a proposal to Eden that he hoped could resolve the differences between their countries. He suggested that Iran expel citizens of the belligerent powers from those areas designated by the British, such as Azerbaijan or the Caspian Sea. This approach, he cleverly explained, would affect mainly the Germans while seeming to affect all belligerent nationalities. Eden found himself in an uncomfortable and embarrassing position. Drawing a piece of paper from his desk, he read aloud the text of the note delivered that morning to the Iranian government. Moggadam was stunned. Eden assured him that His Majesty's government had no designs on Iranian territory. The Iranian envoy tried to argue that the Germans were no danger and that it was necessary for Iran to remain strictly neutral. The foreign secretary could only advise that Iran accept the British proposals for expelling the Germans at once.[32]

Although the invasion was now a fait accompli, the Foreign Office was still being plagued by discreet State Department objections to British high-handedness. During a Foreign Office meeting that day to discuss ways of handling the Americans, someone mentioned that Roosevelt had approved Churchill's action, at Argentia. If so, the president could quiet his own troublesome officials. A memo was submitted to Eden noting that,

> during the Atlantic Conference, the Prime Minister mentioned the question of Persia to the President, but we have no information here as to exactly what was said. The State Department are being rather sticky on the whole question and it might be useful, if the Prime Minister thought it sufficiently important, if he were to send a short personal message on the subject to the President.[33]

Eden disapproved the suggestion. The invasion was an accomplished fact, and there was nothing the Americans could now do to stop it.

In Washington, D.C., that morning, Under Secretary of State Sumner Welles received Iranian Minister Mohammed Shayesteh. A cable that morning from Dreyfus had informed the department of the invasion. Shayestah, however, was clearly not aware of this development, nor did Welles dare apprise the Iranian of his own foreknowledge. Instead, the State Department official listened passively while Shayesteh again urged U.S. political action to avert British and Soviet intervention in Iran. It was obvious—the Iranian complained—that the two powers were merely using the presence of the Germans as a pretext to occupy the country.[34]

Assuring Shayesteh that the president was fully aware of the developments affecting Iran, Welles admonished him to remember that the United States was committed to assisting—within the limits of its announced policy—the defeat of Nazi Germany. Whatever happened in Iran—Welles told Shayesteh—he was certain that its outcome would be the "maintenance intact of the independence and integrity of Iran." Welles added that—no matter what "temporary measures" the British might undertake—he was sure they would eventually restore the liberties of the Iranian people. He noted that, by comparison, the Germans would never relinquish their domination, once achieved.[35]

At 11 A.M., more Soviet bombers attacked Tabriz. One explosion killed 15 people. Several badly wounded men, women, and children were brought to the American hospital, where Doctors Charles Lamme and Joseph Cochrane treated wounds caused by bomb fragments. A few patients died before reaching the operating table.[36]

Toward noon, the Tabriz garrison began evacuating its barracks. The soldiers of the Third Division marched out in tight formations—one regiment following the next. Mountain artillery loaded on pack mules trailed behind. Their discipline had been shaken by the bombings, but it remained in evidence. General Matbooi himself wasted little time in loading his family into his car and roaring out of the city—evidently hoping to reach the Turkish border before it was closed.[37]

About 25 miles north of Tabriz, meanwhile, the main force of the Soviet 47th Army rolled into Marand, where General Novikov established a temporary headquarters and radioed a progress report to General Tolbuhkin in Nakhijevan. Just ahead lay the Yam Pass, which was possibly defended by the Iranians.[38]

Back in Tabriz, Major Schulze and Consul Wussow climbed onto the roof of the German consulate from where they could see pillars of smoke rising within the city and in the outlying countryside, from the heavy bombardment. They also heard the distinct rumble of artillery to the north, where the Red Army was apparently shelling the Yam Pass before continuing its advance. In the consulate courtyard, smoke swirled upward from the ashes where secret documents were smoldering. Schulze went into the building, dispatched a final coded message to the German legation—saying, "We're pushing off to Tehran"—and then destroyed his encoder. Outside, German citizens pale with fear stood waiting with packed suitcases. Only hushed whispers were heard as they waited anxiously for mechanics to hotwire their bus. The keys had disappeared with Herr Maffey, the SD representative—who had departed the previous evening for the Turkish border after receiving warnings of the impending invasion.[39]

Consul Wussow told Schulze that two Germans were still missing: a Herr Heinemann and Sister Elizabeth Garms, who administered a hospital for blind Armenian children. Wussow and Schulze drove to fetch them—passing through deserted streets with shuttered shops, outside which stood small clusters of men. "Vultures waiting for their prey," Wussow remarked. They found Heinemann seriously ill and wanting to be allowed to die in peace. Wussow readily acquiesced, stating, "We must think of the healthy."[40]

Continuing on, Wussow and Schulze arrived at the hospital for Armenian children, outside the city. Sister Elizabeth Garms—a young, blue-eyed nun—admitted them somewhat coldly. Wussow commanded her to pack her bag at once and accompany them. Taken aback, she asked, "By what right do you . . . ?" "I am the German Consul," he interjected, "and responsible for the evacuation of the German colony. Be good enough to hurry. Time presses." The nun responded, "And if I say no? You see, I'm responsible for forty blind children." Wussow told her not to "talk rubbish." "When the Russians arrive," he warned, "you won't be left twenty-four hours with your children. And then they will have to get along alone." At that moment, two small blind children walked uncertainly up to the sister, and clung to her dress. "I'm staying where God has placed me," she answered firmly. Wussow warned that her habit would not protect her.

"You don't know war. You'll be . . . sent off to Siberia . . . or even worse." She still refused.[41]

In frustration, Wussow and Schulze returned to the consulate, where the bus was loaded and ready to depart. At that moment, a policeman arrived and warned the Germans that prisoners had broken out of the city jail. Wussow's convoy of 30 cars and a bus sped out of the compound, and drove circuitously through the city. The Iranian army was gone, and the police were deserting. The Germans watched lawless groups begin plundering stores and breaking windows. One old man ran berserk down the street—blood streaming from his face.

Leaving the chaotic city behind, the Germans sped southward in a cloud of dust. Outside Tabriz, they encountered an open car carrying three Iranian army officers, who excitedly warned them that "The Russian armor has broken through. Ardabil has already fallen. You must try and reach the Bostanabad road before the Russian advance tanks get there." The Germans roared off, ascending the Shibli Pass and on to the apparent safety of Tehran.[42]

In Tehran at the Saadabad Palace, the shah's advisors concluded their meeting at 1 P.M. Military reports left no doubt that the invaders could not be stopped or repelled. Therefore, the Iranian people had to be officially informed of the invasion. The conferees agreed to have Tehran Radio make a brief announcement stating that the country had been attacked in both the north and the south. The speaker of the Majlis, Mohtasham al Saltanah Esfandiary, was also telephoned and requested to convene an emergency session of Parliament at 2:30 P.M., at which the press was requested to attend.[43]

The shah then retired briefly for lunch. Although his children sat around the table, their father was so tense and serious that none dared speak. "What I knew was inevitable has happened," he exclaimed bitterly. "The Allies have invaded Iran. I think this will be the end for me. . . . The English will see to it." His own prime minister, the shah grumbled, had not warned him that the invasion was imminent. The Iranian envoys in Europe had cabled the intentions of the Allies, but Mansur had not relayed these to the shah. Mulling Mansur's motives, Pahlavi mistakenly attributed them to a possible secret agreement between his enemies and the Allies.[44]

At Bander-i Pahlavi at 1 P.M., Iranian soldiers were resting not far from their barracks when the Soviet consul approached one of the sentries. Diplomatic immunity precluded his arrest, even though his purpose was clearly to spy on the army's activities. Because their position was now compromised, the infantrymen marched across a bridge to the Qazian side, where they took up positions in the forest near the beach. Lieutenant Sadeghian emplaced his four-gun artillery battery to cover the approaches to the harbor. Although fortifications for shore batteries had been constructed, the coastal guns had never arrived from Rasht.[45]

At the naval station, Captain Daftary was taking defensive measures of his own. The antiaircraft machine guns on his patrol craft were armed and ready for action. To prevent the Soviet Navy from entering the harbor and landing troops, Daftary had scuttled a German-supplied dredger between the two long, concrete moles protecting the harbor entrance. No ships could enter the port, and the beaches were poorly suited for landing operations.[46]

In Tehran, meanwhile, people were still unaware of the invasion, and were going about their business when—at ten minutes past two o'clock—seven Blenheim bombers appeared overhead. The planes circled for several minutes—disgorging thousands of leaflets, which the crowds below rushed to grab and read. The leaflets proclaimed: "Iranians! Thousands of Germans are living in your country. By a calculated plan, they are holding important positions in industry. When Hitler gives the word, they can sabotage the main sources of your revenues. They are organized by the German Legation and every man has his orders." Iranian authorities were accused of ignoring repeated warnings about the German threat. Therefore, Britain and the Soviet Union were determined to throw the Germans out. Iranians were assured that there was "no quarrel with you nor have we any designs on your country."[47]

The leaflets frightened and confused the people, most of whom knew nothing about the crisis facing their country. Moments after the aircraft departed, a U.S. Presbyterian minister, the Rev. William M. Miller, was walking across the missionary compound in Tehran when a fellow missionary, Mr. Fisher, called for him to come over quickly. Miller raced into Fisher's room in time to hear a radio broadcast from London announcing that British and Soviet troops had crossed the Iranian border at 4 A.M. that morning. Tehran Radio soon repeated the announcement, but assured the people that "our forces are defending the national territory."[48]

At the Majlis, Prime Minister Ali Mansur walked nervously to the speaker's platform at 2:30 P.M. Standing before the assembled deputies, he paused briefly—his hands trembling—and then stated gravely that "What I am going to say concerns the current situation. I request that the members of the Majlis leave anything they have to say until the next session." He described how, since the start of the war in Europe, the Iranian government had been trying to maintain its policy of neutrality. He referred to the notes of July 19 and August 16 urging the deportation of the Germans. "The Government of Iran," he explained, "assured them that we were watching all foreign agents and no danger existed. We also asked the Government of Germany to reduce their citizens in Iran. Unfortunately, all our efforts failed and the Governments of Britain and the Soviet Union informed me at 4 A.M. this morning that their forces were invading Iran."[49]

Mansur briefly described the British and Soviet actions that had occurred that morning. Discussions were under way with the two foreign governments, he indicated, and the Majlis would be kept informed. He then urged that the people of Iran face the situation firmly and calmly. The session was over in ten minutes.

Word of the invasion spread rapidly through the city. Banks closed, and food merchants shuttered their shops to avoid panic. The streets turned eerily quiet as many people hurriedly hid their automobiles to prevent requisitioning by the army. At the Baghe Shah barracks of the First Guards Division, soldiers were playing sports and listening to music on the exercise ground when rumors of the invasion started being whispered from man to man.[50]

At the palace that afternoon, Crown Prince Mohammed Reza—believing that the Iranian Army could not defend Tehran—handed his twin sister Ashraf a pistol, and told her to "keep this gun with you, and if troops enter Tehran and try take us, fire a few shots and then take your own life. I'll do the same."[51]

The editors of Tehran's two leading papers were summoned to the palace by the shah, who was conferring with top officials and reading translated foreign news reports when they arrived. Holding a transcript from Radio Berlin urging the shah to stand fast until German aid arrived, the monarch shouted angrily, "Did you read this? Why do the Germans say our victory is very near? I have no military treaty with Germany, only economic agreements." Turning to the editors, he commanded, "Go and deny these reports." As the journalists started to leave, the shah called out to them, "But don't write in such a way as to displease the Germans."[52]

German Minister Erwin Ettel was then summoned to the palace. Ettel handed to the shah the fuehrer's cable of August 18—which urged the shah to resist English attempts at embroiling Iran in the war. The shah thanked Ettel for the communiqué, and then described the day's events. He detailed how Iranian cities and towns from the Caspian Sea to the Persian Gulf had been bombed; ships, sunk; and ports on the Persian Gulf, occupied. More than 1,000 tanks and several hundred aircraft were reportedly involved in the operation. Because his army could not conduct a successful campaign on two fronts, the shah did not intend to request assistance that Germany could not yet render. He instead urged that the Turkish government be encouraged to influence the British and Soviets to cease hostilities and grant safe conduct for the Germans in Iran. The Allied accusations against the German colony were, he contended, merely a pretext for the invasion. Ettel left with the clear impression that the shah was no longer determined to offer serious resistance to the invasion.[53]

At 4 P.M., the army chief of staff, Major General Zarghami, arrived at the palace to report the latest military developments. Tired and irritated, the shah ordered Zarghami to deploy the Tehran Garrison to defend the outside of the city. He directed that his War Council be formed, but had no guidance for the remote garrisons under attack.[54]

On leaving the palace, Zarghami ordered Brig. Gen. Karim Aga Buzarjemehri, commander of the First Division, and Major General Naghdi, commander of the Second Division, to issue a confidential circular directing all officers to report to their posts and remain there pending further instructions. As word of the invasion circulated, officers and soldiers hurried back to their barracks. Buses and taxis carried them without fare. A number of young men who were seeking to enlist reported to the garrison also.[55]

At the U.S. legation in Tehran, U.S. Minister Louis Dreyfus, nervously paced the floor—chain-smoking one cigarette after the next, and fretting because he had taken no provisions to evacuate the U.S. citizens in Tabriz. The missionaries there lay in the path of the advancing Red Army. Dreyfus worried that he would be held responsible if any harm came to them.[56]

Dreyfus soon received a telephone call from the Iranian Foreign Ministry. The director, Sayah, urged Dreyfus to communicate to the State Department an official request that "the President of the United States use his good offices with the British and Russian Governments to bring about the immediate cessation of hostilities." The Iranian government was willing to offer assurances that most of the Germans would be expelled. Shortly thereafter, the Iranian Foreign Ministry forwarded a personal appeal from the shah to President Roosevelt; it accused the British and the Soviets of crossing the Iranian border "brusquely and without previous notice . . . occupying certain localities and bombarding a considerable number of cities which were open and without defense." The shah assured Roosevelt that Allied concerns over the Germans were unwarranted, given the Iranian assurances that the Germans would soon leave Iran. Therefore, he could "no longer . . . see for what reason they have proceeded to those acts of aggression." He appealed to Roosevelt's sense of moral justice—noting "declarations which Your Excellency has made . . . regarding the necessity of defending principles of international justice and the right of peoples to liberty."—and beseeched the president to help spare from war a "neutral and pacific country which has had no other care than the safeguarding of tranquillity. . . . I beg Your Excellency to take . . . urgent . . . steps to put an end to these acts of aggression."[57]

In northern Iran, at the village of Nir—25 miles south of Ardabil—the two infantry regiments of the Iranian 15th Division arrived late that afternoon after a long and grueling march. The troops were constructing defenses when the division commander, General Gaderi, arrived and directed their commanders to withdraw to a more defensible position at Sa'in Gaduki—eight miles farther up the winding mountain road. Gaderi promised to send back food and supplies, and then drove away with no intention of returning.[58]

Fortunately for the 15th Division, the Soviet 44th Army was not pressing its advance in their direction. General Khadeev's column had followed the well-paved highway that paralleled the Soviet frontier—crossing the Hadshi-Amir Pass and following the course of the Astara River. Descending from the heavily forested Busgush Mountains, the long column of trucks, tanks, and horsemen passed extensive, swampy rice fields. By late afternoon, they had reached the humid coastal plateau—marching unopposed into the port of Astara.[59]

To the west 175 miles, General Novikov's large mechanized column crossed the undefended Yam Pass, and approached the town of Sofian—their night's encampment. In the morning, the juggernaut would roll across the Talkeh River valley and into Tabriz.[60]

Southwest of Tabriz, meanwhile, the retreating soldiers of the Iranian Third Division were entering the broad, arid basin where the Talkeh River drains into Lake Urmia. Fatigued and famished, their once disciplined marching ranks became stretched out and ragged. The artillerymen had already cast aside their cumbersome pack guns. Junior officers maintained enough control to prevent the troops from deserting or turning into a mob. But their commanding general and other senior officers had disappeared. Despite the heat, the hunger, and the sore feet, the men tramped inexorably forward, driven by one obsession: to escape capture by the Russians.[61]

At the Tabriz aerodrome, meanwhile, Colonel Shaybani waited for further orders from General Matbooi—unaware that his commander had fled. In desperation, he finally cabled the army chief of staff in Tehran directly, and requested instructions. Army headquarters replied that Shaybani was—if possible—to evacuate the entire Second Air Regiment to Zanjan. Shaybani feared to fly out in daylight, because the Red Air Force had mastery of the air. On the other hand, the Tabriz aerodrome lacked the field lights necessary for taking off at night.[62]

Assembling his officers and men, Shaybani stated that their only choice was to fly out during the night. Because of the extreme danger, he offered to allow anyone and all to flee by auto, if they preferred. As for himself, he would fly out alone if necessary. All of his pilots volunteered to try saving their aircraft from capture. The takeoff time would have to be just before dawn the next day in order to reach Zanjan shortly after sunrise. Shaybani's pilots then settled down for a long night, with the Red Army only 20 miles away.

In the extreme northwest of Iran that afternoon, a column of Soviet infantry preceded by a screen of light tanks neared the city of Maku. Entrenched and waiting on both sides of the narrow valley entrance were soldiers of the Iranian 17th Infantry Regiment. The Iranians opened fire, slicing into the invader's ranks. The Soviets attacked, trying to outflank the Iranian position. Daylight was fading quickly as the battle ensued.[63]

Lieutenant Kenami-Zadeh's company came under attack on the southern ridge. As the Soviets advanced toward them, an Iranian machine gun jammed. The gunner called for Kenami-Zadeh to come and help unjam it. As the officer started to crawl from his position, a soldier named Khoda Karam held him. "If you are killed," he admonished his commander, "we'll be without a leader. I know how to repair it." Karam crawled across the open ground. As he neared the machine-gun pit, a shell exploded and killed him.[64]

Casualties on both sides mounted. At least several dozen Iranians were killed, and an unknown number of Soviets. Lt. Ettehadieh Shargi was shot through the leg, but remained at his post until evacuated to a hospital—where he died. The fighting subsided slightly by 7 P.M. Darkness fell on the battlefield; it would hide Soviet attempts at infiltration. Seven of Zadeh's men had already been killed, and his position was surrounded on three sides. In the twilight, he gathered his surviving troops—all of whom were tired, hungry, and thirsty. He explained that their only hope of escape was to cross the mountains and attempt to reach Rezeiyeh. Under cover of darkness, they slipped away, and eventually reached their destination. The Soviets then advanced and occupied Maku.

In the late afternoon of August 25, the British Army was continuing its advance into central Iran. The First Battalion of Fifth Gurkha Rifles motored into the dusty, squalid village of Sar-i Pul near the entrance to the Paitak Pass at 3:45 P.M. A screen of light Hussar tanks took up position facing the pass. The division commander, Maj. Gen. William Slim, and his Second Indian Armoured Brigade commander, Brig. John Aizelwood, arrived to survey the mountainous obstacle in front of them.[65]

Standing atop his station wagon, Slim scanned the escarpment. The road from Sar-i Pul climbed sharply up a 3,000-foot gorge, which twisted and turned until it reached a high plain beyond. The easily defensible pass was known to be defended by several thousand Iranians, though he discerned no sign of the enemy. Nevertheless, Slim decided against an immediate assault. The RAF would have to soften up the defenders the next day. In the meantime, he needed to push troops around the pass to Shahabad.

However, attempts to bypass Paitak Pass through Gilan had failed. The vanguard (B Column) of HAZELFORCE had attacked the Iranian defenses east of Gilan three times that afternoon, only to be repeatedly driven back by artillery and machine-gun fire. The assaults were suspended at 6:30 P.M,. with darkness approaching. A squadron of the Wiltshire Yeomanry was brought forward to reinforce B Column, but this was still not enough to eject the estimated 2,000 Iranians defending the Koh-i Wazhlan ridge.[66]

Back at Sar-i Pul, Slim and Aizelwood pored over a terrain map, and noted a small track leading south from Sar-i Pul to Gilan. Slim directed the Second Indian Armoured Brigade to move to Gilan by this route early the next morning. From there, they would push through the Iranian position to Shahabad, and outflank the defenders at Paitak. Meanwhile, Slim would assemble the 21st Indian Brigade at Sar-i Pul for a frontal advance up the pass. To support this scheme, the main body of A Column—consisting of the remainder of the Second Armoured Brigade—moved out of Qasr-i Shirin, and drove eastward through the dark along a twisting, dusty road to

Sar-i Pul. In the absence of any Iranian air threat, Slim had given the convoy permission to proceed with their lights on. They had not proceeded far, however, before an irate officer drove by from the opposite direction and ordered their lights out. Continuing the remaining 20 miles at a slow pace, the column did not reach Sar-i Pul until midnight.[67]

At Abadan that evening, the First Kumaon Rifles and the 2/6th Rajputanas bivouacked around the oil refinery. The Iranian barracks and part of the town were still unsecured, but the refinery itself had been cleared after several tedious and dangerous hours of hunting snipers from building to building. The last pocket of resistance at Bungalow 55 surrendered at 5:30 P.M. Two howitzers, four armored cars, and 350 prisoners were captured.[68]

The Soviet Caspian Sea Flotilla meanwhile neared the port of Bander-i Pahlavi. At 6 P.M., several Soviet aircraft flew over the port, without attacking. The Iranian 36th Regiment was hidden in positions among trees on the Qazian side. At 8 P.M., an Iranian observer in the port tower reported to Lieutenant Colonel Iranpur that eight ships were nearing the coast. Iranpur instructed the observer to report when the vessels were 500 meters from shore. His artillery commander, Lieutenant Sadeghian, received directions for his battery to fire on order. Moments later, the tower telephoned that the ships had doused their running lights and disappeared in the darkness. The Soviet commander was probably frustrated because the seas were choppy and his ships could not pass between the two harbor moles because of the scuttled dredger. He moved his gunboats and transports closer to shore.[69]

Thirty anxious minutes passed for the Iranians. The watchtower called and reported that the ships were within 400–500 meters, and closing. Four Iranian 75-millimeter guns fired two volleys in succession at the vessels. No hits were scored, but the Soviets returned three volleys. The Iranian battery was not hit, but remained silent lest it give away its position. The Soviet commander withdrew. The risk of a night landing in difficult surf against determined opposition was too great. The Soviets decided to wait until sunlight.

At Tabriz, Soviet bombers returned several times after dusk to drop incendiary bombs, which ignited fires throughout the city. At the American hospital, Dr. Lamme passed the night in the lower hall—ignoring the raids. The nurses stayed in the basement.[70]

In Tehran that evening, Rev. William Miller went to his regular Monday-night prayer class, and found his Iranian parishioners poring over late-afternoon newspaper editions. This was unusual, for few people read the heavily censored press. But that afternoon, the editions had sold out as fast as they reached the street. People fought to purchase papers, even though the information inside was sketchy. Miller led his small congregation in prayer that night—asking for God's guidance and protection during this difficult time. After the service, he ate supper and started toward Mr.

Fisher's room for the 9:30 P.M. news broadcast. Before he could reach the door, total darkness descended on the city. Tehran was experiencing its first blackout.[71]

Confusion, fear, and despair seemed to reign in the city. Procedures for a blackout had never been established or rehearsed. Even the police were without guidance. The people—hungry and afraid—were on the verge of panic.[72] For 20 years, their all powerful shah had controlled their lives. Now, sequestered in his summer palace, the exhausted and dejected monarch could no longer perform the superhuman feats of the past. In fact, he was now facing a situation completely beyond his control.

9

Handling a "Red-hot Iron"

Thirteen biplanes of the Iranian Second Air Regiment revved their engines for takeoff from the Tabriz aerodrome in the 3 A.M. darkness of August 26, 1941. The pilots gunned their motors, and the aircraft roared one after another along the runway and into the night sky. Colonel Shaybani flew the lead plane. Each pilot raced his engine to gain height and avoid the treacherous mountains around Tabriz.[1]

Shortly after sunrise, Colonel Shaybani's plane touched down safely at Zanjan airfield, 150 miles southeast of Tabriz. Minutes later, ten more aircraft landed on the runway. Shaybani scanned the sky for the remaining two planes, but they never appeared. The pilots had crashed their aircraft into a mountainside south of Tabriz. Miraculously, both survived and eventually reached Tehran.

Shaybani—certain that the Soviets would soon detect their departure and pursue them to Zanjan—hurriedly refueled his aircraft, and took off for Tehran. In fact, Soviet aircraft appeared soon after, and bombed the Zanjan airport. Closer to Tehran, the Red Air Force bombed the undefended city of Kazvin.[2]

East of Tabriz some 100 miles, soldiers of the Iranian 15th (Ardabil) Division reached the Sain Gaduki Pass—eight miles up the road from the village of Nir—at 4 A.M. on the morning of August 26. Their division commander, Brigadier General Gaderi, had driven off ten hours earlier and not returned—leaving his men hungry and without food. The commander of the 11th Regiment, Colonel Sadiq, sent an officer to the town of Sarab in search of food and ammunition. Finding Sarab deserted except for an old man at a coffeehouse, he returned to inform the division that no food would be forthcoming. Dispirited, many soldiers dropped their rifles and deserted in search of sustenance. Those who remained awaited the arrival of the Red Army—unaware that the Soviets had, thus far, bypassed Ardabil.[3]

In fact, Maj. Gen. A. A. Khadeev's 44th Army was advancing slowly but inexorably down the Caspian shore that day. Departing Astara that morning, motorized infantry of Maj. Gen. A. P. Rodinov's 77th Mountain Infantry Division and mounted troopers of the 17th Mountain Cavalry Division negotiated their way over poor roads, and forded numerous streams. A highway connecting Astara to Shafarud had been started in 1928, but never completed. Only a bare roadbed remained—poorly suited for vehicles.[4]

Anticipating this problem, Rodinov had brought along heavy road construction vehicles, which improved the roadstead for the motorized forces. The Soviets pushed through marshy terrain, rice fields, and rain forests—ever deeper into the province of Gilan (which, in Farsi, means "swamp"). During the day, the main force linked up with elements of the 105th Mountain Infantry Regiment, which had landed the day before at Khevi. By evening, the 44th Army had penetrated to the Lissar River—32 miles south of Astara.[5]

Offshore, Rear Admiral Sedelnikov's Caspian Sea Flotilla resumed shelling the port of Bander-i Pahlavi at 8 A.M. The Soviets made no attempt to land troops, however, apparently because the harbor entrance remained blocked and the Iranians still had artillery hidden in the trees. Three hours later, several Soviet aircraft attacked the woods east of the port. The Iranian battery commander, Lieutenant Sadeghian, believed that the planes were searching for his howitzers, and therefore ordered his gun crews to hold their fire. Unable to find targets, the aircraft turned and attacked the naval station—meeting heavy machine-gun fire from the three small patrolboats moored there. Antiaircraft fire kept the attackers at a distance; but bombs did fall among the gunboats and killed one of the captains, Lt. Yadoolah Bayendor—the younger brother of Admiral Bayendor.[6]

Soviet bombers returned to Tabriz that morning—dropping leaflets and sporadically bombing sections of the city. Dr. Charles Lamme of the American hospital walked down a main street and noticed that the people seemed dazed. Shops were shuttered, while small groups of men talked and watched the Soviet aircraft circling overhead.[7]

General Novikov's 47th Army resumed its march that morning, and was nearing the city. Word of the Soviet approach reached a village outside Tabriz where a young Iranian army lieutenant had taken refuge with his wife. Panicking, he borrowed a horse, told his wife that he was only going to see what was happening, and rode away.[8]

Shortly before noon, Soviet T-26 tanks rolled into Tabriz—accompanied by marching groups of helmeted Soviet soldiers. An Iranian rushed to the American hospital to warn Dr. Lamme. In the distance, occasional rifle and machine-gun shots were heard. Several snipers fired on the Soviets from side streets. The Soviets returned fire liberally in all directions. The Iraqi consul was standing in the window of his consulate—watching the Soviets march past—when the Soviets fired into the window and killed him.[9]

Dr. Joseph Cochrane, a colleague of Dr. Lamme, was treating an Iranian wounded during the bombings when he heard several shots in the distance. Climbing onto the roof of his house, he watched in surprise as dozens of Soviet tanks and vehicles began filling the vacant lots located beyond the hospital compound wall.

Many Armenians in the city—chafing from years of Iranian rule—greeted their cousins from the north as liberators. A small group of Armenians appeared at the American hospital, and demanded that Dr. Lamme surrender his auto. When he refused, they left and returned later with a Soviet-Armenian soldier. The Armenians then broke the padlock to the garage, but were persuaded not to take the car.

Dr. Lamme then walked downtown to seek help from the British consul, Mr. Cook. With Cook's assistance, he sought a paper from the Soviet commandant and the Soviet civilian counterpart that would authorize the doctor to retain his car. After repeated requests, Soviet authorities finally gave him the necessary paper, and even offered to provide armed sentries to protect the hospital compound. Returning to the hospital, Lamme passed near the city prison, where he saw a Soviet truck and many Soviet soldiers. The prison had been opened, and the prisoners released. The Soviets intended to release only certain political prisoners. But when they could not identify them, they simply released the whole lot—between 600 and 800 convicts.

One of the prisoners released was Schulze's nemesis—Nasarow—who led a Red Army detachment to the deserted German consulate. Meanwhile, Sister Elizabeth Garms—who ran the Armenian Blind Children's Hospital—was arrested by the Soviet secret police and taken to the city prison, where she perished during interrogation.[10]

Some 60 miles southwest of Tabriz, thousands of famished men from the Third Division swept like a swarm of locusts through the ripened grape vineyards along the shores of Lake Urmia.[11]

The city of Rezeiyeh was quiet following the brutal bombings of the day before. Dead bodies littered the streets, but few people dared leave their homes to bury them. The city hospital was crammed with wounded, dead, and dying. At 10 A.M., Soviet bombers again swept over the city, and bombarded the outskirts. The garrison was in disarray; its commander—General Moini—had fled south.[12]

North of Rezeiyeh, the 63d Georgian Mountain Infantry Division continued its southward advance from Khvoy, and occupied the city of Shahpur that afternoon. The scattered garrisons of the Iranian Fourth Division collapsed or deserted in the face of the Soviet advance.[13]

In southern and central Iran, meanwhile, the British forces resumed their advance that morning. Rolls Royce armored cars of the 13th Lancers rolled out of Rahmaniyeh—33 miles southwest of Ahvaz—at 6:20 A.M. Fanning out in a 12-mile semicircle, they reconnoitered toward Ahvaz—moving slowly over the poor roads and trails while cautiously watching for Iranian tanks.[14]

Over Ahvaz at the same time, patrolling British fighters spotted two Iranian planes. A Hurricane shot one down—watching it trail smoke until it crash-landed in a field southeast of Ahvaz. Its partner turned back to the Ahvaz aerodrome. Southwest of Ahvaz, meanwhile, a Vincent biplane was providing aerial reconnaissance support to the 13th Lancers when a Hurricane mistakenly pounced on it. The wounded pilot glided the aircraft to a bumpy landing. Lancers rushed to the rescue, and evacuated the two crewmen.

At Abadan early that morning, the 2/6th Rajputana Rifles occupied the deserted Iranian barracks, and recovered the rifles and ammunition that had been abandoned by the garrison. The Kumaon Rifles, meanwhile, boarded AIOC buses and cars, and drove off at 8 A.M. to clear the southern part of Abadan Island. Brigadier LeFleming, his staff, and a section of 45-millimeter howitzers joined the expedition, which arrived at Khosroabad an hour and a half later. Finding the Iranian barracks there empty, they had no idea that they had passed the Iranian garrison en route. Major Tayfuri had marched his battalion out of Khosroabad during the night, and had taken shelter in palm groves along the Bahmanshihr River—midway to Abadan. The Kumaons continued their patrol south to Kasba, which they also found deserted.[15]

A burial ceremony with full honors was conducted for Admiral Bayendor that morning in the Khorramshahr Naval Yard. Maj. Gen. Charles O. Harvey, commanding the Eighth Indian Division, attended. A Union Jack was ceremoniously draped over the casket, but just before the ceremony commenced, Lt. Shamseddin Safavi removed the flag and replaced it with the Iranian ensign that he had removed from his ship.[16] As General Quinan noted in a dispatch, Bayendor's death was a tragic irony: "This officer had an English wife and, while giving full allegiance to the Shah, was very friendly disposed towards us."[17]

At Bander-i Shahpur, the fires aboard seven of the eight Axis merchant ships were under control, with only the *Wiessenfels* a complete loss. Maj. William Maxwell—commanding the landing party ashore—learned that the Iranian police or military might attempt to arrest the small British AIOC community at Bander Mashur, an oil-loading area several miles upchannel. Using the two Iranian gunboats—operated by their own crews, under British supervision—he led a detachment to Bander Mashur to secure the facility. On arriving, the Iranian sailors learned of the fighting at Abadan, and—embarrassed by their own collaboration—refused further cooperation. Ninety-seven Iranian officers and ratings were placed under guard aboard the *Karkas*. The British persuaded an Iranian naval lieutenant to pilot the vessel to Basra, where the prisoners were incarcerated.[18]

At the AIOC compound at Haft Khel—east of Ahvaz—Capt. Michael

Forster led a platoon north that morning to rescue the British citizens at Masjid-i-Suleiman. Ten miles from their destination, the convoy was halted by a messenger who reported that the Iranian Army had occupied Masjid-i-Suleiman early that morning. Assured that the civilians were safe, Forster was advised not to interfere. Seeing no other choice, he withdrew, and continued improving Haft Khel's defenses.[19]

News of Forster's foray north soon reached General Shahbakhti's division headquarters at Ahvaz, where the strength of the small force became greatly exaggerated. Rumors that a full Indian battalion had parachuted into Haft Khel created anxiety among the Iranians. Shahbakhti entrenched his forces along the various approaches to Ahvaz. The hills to the southwest of the city were fortified and covered by artillery. These fixed defenses were backed by patrols of tanks, armored cars, and lorried infantry.[20]

But British air attacks were unnerving his troops, whose morale was further undermined by the shaken survivors from Abadan. Shahbakhti believed that only ruthless discipline could motivate his men to continue fighting. When one officer suggested preparing small boats for a possible withdrawal across the Karun River, he angrily slapped the man on the face. "I'll break the teeth of anyone who even talks about retreat," he barked sternly. "We don't need any boats. We'll die on this side of the river." Shahbakhti ordered the Karun River bridge prepared for demolition. When word of his plans reached the General Staff in Tehran, Shahbakhti received orders to halt any demolitions. This was the only guidance he received from higher command.[21]

Three hundred miles north, British tanks and bren carriers of the 14/20th Hussars probed and harassed the Iranian defenses on the Koh-i Wazhlan ridge east of Gilan early that morning. Heavy Iranian fire dissuaded any attack until the arrival of reinforcements. Gen. Hassan Moggadam personally directed the Iranian defense. His men, however, were hungry, demoralized, and rapidly exhausting their limited supply of ammunition. As the morning wore on, he realized that the position could not be defended much longer.[22]

Shortly before 9 A.M., the Iranians sighted the dust from a fresh British column to their northwest. Now having no choice, Moggadam ordered the position evacuated. Artillery was limbered to the available trucks. Those soldiers who could not be transported were dispersed into the hills. Moggadam rushed back to Kermanshah to organize a new line of defense. Before leaving, he directed that the road from Gilan to Shahabad be demolished at various points to delay the enemy advance. The British tanks and Warwickshire Yeomanry facing the ridge noticed at 9 A.M. that Iranian fire was slackening, and detected that the enemy was retreating.

Although Brig. John Aizelwood's Second Armoured Brigade departed Sar-i Pul at 5 A.M. that morning for Gilan, the vanguard of B Column at Gilan was not informed. Therefore, Maj. John Lakin—commanding B

Squadron of the Warwickshire Yeomanry—was unaware of the approach of Aizelwood's force. To cover the rear of B Column, he had deployed his men across the road coming south from Sar-i Pul, eight miles northwest of Gilan at the base of a pass; he had been told not to expect friendly troops from this direction.[23]

Several Mark VI Hussar tanks—the vanguard of Second Armoured Brigade—passed through the defile. Turning a corner, they came unexpectedly on the entrenched men of Lakin's B Squadron. The Yeomanry opened fire with machine guns—knocking off the lead tank commander's helmet. The mortar section, which was situated on high ground, immediately lobbed several well-aimed shells onto the road.

The tanks buttoned their hatches and sprayed machine-gun fire at the opponents. Bullets flew back and forth. Major Lakin peered closely at the "enemy," and finally decided that the tanks could only be British. Unfortunately, he had no means of contacting them, for his radio would communicate only with regimental headquarters. He concluded that only by "surrendering" could the shooting be stopped. Rising from his position, he walked cautiously toward the tanks—holding a large cigarette lighter over his head. The tanks ceased firing. A Hussar officer cautiously emerged from his hatch. The two men recognized each other from a fox-hunting trip that they had taken together, several years before.

East of Gilan, meanwhile, advancing Yeomanry troopers found the Koh-i Wazhlan ridge deserted. One Iranian soldier was taken prisoner, while another was found dead next to an abandoned antitank gun. The Household Cavalry arrived from Khanaqin at the road intersection northwest of Gilan, and then were held up there until 2 P.M. by trucks and tanks of the Second Armoured Brigade coming from Sar-i Pul. An advance party comprising the Warwickshire Yeomanry, 2/7 Gurkha Rifles, and an artillery battery pursued the retreating Iranians. The remainder of the force followed close behind.[24]

Back at Sar-i Pul, General Slim and Brigadier Aizelwood drove off in midmorning to reconnoiter the Paitak Pass. The empty road ran upward, disappearing around several turns. Curiosity drew them farther up the defile. They soon passed a placid, whitewashed coffeehouse at a sharp corner. Continuing up the road, both generals boldly (if somewhat recklessly) stood upright in the auto—poking their upper bodies through the open roof. At 11:30 A.M., Slim sighted an oil-pumping station that was marked on his map. At the same moment, he heard a large clap behind the car. An instant later, a second explosion showered them with dust and rocks. "By God, they're shooting at us!" Aizelwood exclaimed with great umbrage. Their driver jerked the car into reverse, and swung around—speeding around a corner just as more shells impacted exactly where they had been a moment earlier. Wasting no time, they sped back down the pass.[25]

The 2/4th Gurkha Rifles were meanwhile advancing cautiously up the same defile—moving astride the road in combat formation. Shells from Iranian heavy artillery exploded harmlessly well to their left. Lt. Col. William "Willy" Weallens, commander of the 2/4th Gurkhas, suspected that the Iranians were ranging their guns on likely avenues of approach. His adjutant, Capt. John Masters, carefully scanned the blackened mountainsides.[26]

The Royal Artillery soon answered the Iranian shells with slow fire. The firing of a bren gun put the Gurkhas on alert. The shot had been an accident, however—one that slightly wounded a Gurkha rifleman. Suddenly, a tan sedan came barreling down the road from above. The point rifleman dropped and took aim. Before firing, he spotted the red divisional flag atop the radiator cap. The car pulled up, and—to the astonishment of the officers—General Slim emerged.

"How the hell did he get past us?" Captain Masters muttered to himself. Colonel Weallens double-timed up to the general. "Morning, Willy," Slim greeted. "There's nothing until you get around the fourth hairpin. They've got an antitank gun there." Masters then noticed a gaping hole in the rear of the car. The officers saluted as Slim drove off, and then quickened their pace up the slope.[27]

Twelve Blenheim bombers from 45 Squadron blasted the summit of the pass that afternoon. Several Iranian machine guns opened fire on one of the aircraft. The train of bombs quickly scoured the Iranian position. As evening approached, Weallen's Gurkhas were nearing the summit, but had made only light contact. An Iranian machine gun near a pumping station had opened fire on a patrol.

In Tehran that morning, General Zarghami chaired a meeting of the shah's War Council in the Army Officers Club at the end of Hafez Street, to review the deteriorating military situation. The Soviets had occupied Marand, Sofian, Khvoy, and Maku, they learned. The British had seized Abadan, Khorramshahr, and Bander-i Shahpur; also, a battalion had reportedly parachuted near Masjid-i-Suleiman. The Iranian First and Second Divisions had deployed during the previous night to cover the western and eastern approaches, respectively, to Tehran. Army patrols were requisitioning civilian vehicles for military use. No operational instructions had been issued to the front-line units, nor were rear-guard actions being ordered. The only instructions given to the outlying commands—General Arfa learned to his amazement—forbade demolishing bridges, railways, and roads.[28]

Arfa therefore surmised that the shah had no intention of conducting a true defense, but only wanted to demonstrate token resistance so that Iran would not be treated as hostile if occupied by the Nazis. Arfa proposed that the important bridges be destroyed and that the powerful Tehran garrison withdraw to a mountain redoubt west of Arak, but the shah rejected this idea.

The streets of Tehran were devoid of vehicles that morning. Civilians were hiding their cars, trucks, and buses from the roving—and oftentimes abusive—military patrols. One truck driver leaving the city en route to Qum was stopped at an army roadblock and told that his truck was being confiscated. He bribed the sentries, and then turned his lorry around and headed back. A half mile later, he was halted at another post; this time he escaped with an even smaller bribe. Returning home, he locked his truck in the garage.[29]

People in Tehran were hungry that morning. Near riots broke out in the long bread lines. "We couldn't get bread," an Iranian told Rev. William M. Miller, "but I managed to find a little rice." Miller noted anger and bitterness among the street crowds; many openly cursed those in authority.[30] Frightened depositors started a run on the National Bank of Iran—forcing its temporary closure.[31]

Foreign Minister Djevad Amery appeared at the U.S. legation shortly before 8 A.M. to again urge the U.S. government to stop the hostilities. His government was so anxious to reach a settlement—he confided—that they were not only willing to deport the Germans, but were ready to meet any reasonable British requests, including changes to the shah's cabinet. Dreyfus listened, but could do nothing. Iran's predicament—he apprised Washington—was a result of their own failure to face realities. "They now awaken to find the perennial bogey of Russian invasion has become a reality."[32]

Toward noon, four large Soviet bombers circled Tehran for several hours—dropping leaflets. No Iranian planes rose to meet them, but they were fired on by antiaircraft guns. The thundering of the guns frightened the shah's second oldest daughter, Princess Ashraf. Cradling her son tightly in her arms, she began rushing toward the palace basement—only to be stopped by her husband, Ali Qavam, son of a prominent Iranian politician, who demanded that she give him the boy. "I'm going to take him to the British Embassy," he told her. "Never!" she cried. Ashraf despised her husband's family's close connections to the British. Her husband tried forcibly to take the child, but could not break her grip.[33]

General Zarghami drove his auto into the Saadabad Palace at 2:30 P.M.; he was carrying a situation report for the shah. The monarch perused the sheet closely several times. Its details were sketchy. Army Communiqué Number One read thus:

1. At 4 A.M. on the 3rd of Shahrivar [August 25], the Armies of the Soviet Union and Great Britain invaded Iran.
2. The following cities have been bombed: Tabriz, Ardabil, Rezeiyeh, Khvoy, Ahar, Maku, Mahabad, Rasht, Mianeh, Ahvaz, and Bander-i Pahlavi. There were many casualties. In Tabriz, one aircraft was shot down.

3. Soviet motorized units entered from the north and the British Army from the south.
4. The Soviet Navy attacked in the Caspian Sea and the British Navy in the Persian Gulf.
5. His Majesty's Army Divisions have stopped the invaders in the east.
6. The morale of the people is excellent, and in the north and east people are asking to be drafted and go to the front.[34]

Although the shah questioned the accuracy of the last sentence, he still authorized its release to the newspapers. Despite the false optimism of the report, Reza Pahlavi realized that his army was collapsing. There was no hope of a successful defense. The survival of his regime hinged on his appeal to President Roosevelt.

The shah did receive questionable moral support from Berlin and Rome that day. German and Italian papers strongly—if hypocritically—condemned the Allies' "unprovoked aggression against Iran." *Dienst aus Deutschland* focused its criticism on British "hypocrisy." The Italian daily *Stampa* placed partial blame for this "unjustified aggression" on the United States, and claimed that U.S. diplomats and businessmen were supporting the invasion.[35]

In Washington that morning, Secretary of State Cordell Hull called an emergency meeting with Sumner Welles and Wallace Murray to discuss the urgent telegram from Iran requesting U.S. intercession to stop the invasion. Hull likened the U.S. predicament to "handling a 'red-hot iron.'" Murray urged the State Department to "make every endeavor to induce the British to negotiate with Iranians" despite the "late hour." The British, he maintained, should seek Iranian collaboration in the common defense of their territory. "It would be far better for the British to be surrounded by a friendly, cooperative Iranian people than to have to face dogged opposition, sabotage and, perhaps guerrilla warfare."[36]

Welles disagreed completely, advocating instead that the United States should avoid—at all costs—using its good offices in this matter. He suggested that U.S. action be limited to forwarding the Iranian request to the British and inquiring in what way the department could be helpful to the British. The group finally agreed to urge Iran to seek "an amicable settlement with the British Government," while the U.S. government would "keep in close touch with the British with a view to being as helpful as possible to the Iranians."[37]

The Americans did not intend to try to halt the invasion. They would notify the British of the Iranian request—but "without comment"—and would take up separately with the British the "larger aspects" of the situation. In particular, they would request to know Anglo–Soviet intentions regarding the extent of the occupation of Iranian territory, what assurances the British intended to give that their Soviet allies would not conduct "widespread oppression, persecution and . . . confiscation of property" in their zone, and whether Britain would be able to take over full occupation of the country to allow the withdrawal of Soviet forces. The British were to be apprised that the invasion had "aroused nation-wide attention and discussion in this country" and that "the situation is a delicate one politically."[38] The shah's final hope was being dashed.

Wallace Murray returned to his office; he was displeased by the outcome. Before long, Iranian Minister Shayesteh arrived and requested an audience with Hull in order to propose that the president be urged to intercede with the British and Soviets for a cessation of the hostilities. Shayesteh pointed out that U.S. silence on the matter would appear to condone the Allied act of aggression—causing the United States to "suffer a great loss of moral authority in the world." Murray suggested that Iran open negotiations with the British to work out "some system of collaboration" on defending Iran against Nazi aggression. He pointed out that Iran could not defend herself against the Germans if they penetrated the Caucasus. Shayesteh was shocked by Murray's attitude, which he had expected to be more sympathetic. The U.S. government, he insisted, could not allow a "brutal act of aggression" to go without "some form of condemnation or effort to stop it." Murray was concerned. An "ideal solution" was not easy to find—he explained to the Iranian envoy—because "We regard the British cause as our cause." "In the common effort . . .," he explained, "we necessarily have to take account of the undoubted dangers of aggression spreading into areas of the Near East vital to the defense of the British Empire."[39]

Britain obtained further support that day from the New York *Times,* whose editors rationalized the invasion by stating,

> To beat Germany to a position which she was obviously plotting to seize at the first possible moment is reason enough for joint action by Britain and Russia. The Iranians are putting up at least a show resistance and this is a logical if futile reaction of a people who unquestionably desire to maintain their neutrality and independence.[40]

The editor admitted that "the British and Russians are invading armies"—but went on to say that the Iranians, who were "impaled on the horns of a cruel dilemma, can be consoled by their comparative good fortune. Their extraordinary luck is that the British got there first [before the Nazis]."[41] The paper tactfully did not contend that Iran was also lucky to have the Soviets as occupiers.

In southwest Iran that afternoon, British armored cars skirted south of Ahvaz, and met no opposition. B Squadron reached the east bank of the Karkheh River—northwest of Ahvaz—where they approached several Iranian vehicles, which promptly withdrew. They also discovered tank tracks along the riverbank. C Squadron reached the village of Tell-i Zibid, where they were fired on by Iranian artillery, machine guns, and small arms. They could discern the distant clanking of tanks. The various squadrons concentrated back at Umm-at-Tumair, and then—at 4:30 P.M.—returned to camp. The route selected, however, took them through thick sand dunes in the dark. Tired crews worked through the night digging out stalled vehicles. The Lancers did not reach camp until 2 A.M. the next morning.[42]

Outside Abadan late that afternoon, Major Tayfuri's battalion from Khosroabad reached the palm groves along the Bahmanshihr River where the British had directed them to remain until the following morning. Tayfuri himself stayed with the British in Kasba—leaving his men under the command of a Major Bakhtiar. At 6 P.M., Bakhtiar led the men across the ferry to the north bank; they had to abandon their four mountain guns and many weapons. On the north side, they waited through the night for the British troops to accept their surrender.[43]

To the north 300 miles, Brigadier Aizelwood's column—HAZEL-FORCE—worked its way through the darkness along dangerous cliffs and defiles leading to Shahabad. The troopers watched for ambush—expecting to encounter some of the Iranians who had earlier evacuated Gilan. No resistance was experienced, but their opponents had erected a series of obstructive—though undefended—roadblocks. The delays caused by felled trees and boulders dragged the advance on into the night. At one spot, a well-placed road demolition on the face of a 4,000-foot mountain blocked all vehicle movement. While sappers worked ferverishly through the night to clear the obstacle, the lightly clad and shivering British and Indian troops who were strung out along the mountain road waited several cold hours in their vehicles.[44]

Meanwhile, far to the northeast, a fresh Soviet army moved furtively through the early morning darkness toward the Iranian frontier. From the eastern shore of the Caspian Sea to the Iran–Afghanistan border, the Soviet 53d Independent Central Asian Army prepared to open a new front against Iran.

At 3 A.M. in the Iranian border town of Sarakhs—the extreme northeast corner of Iran—11-year-old Hassan Soburi was awakened by the distant crack of rifle fire. The shots came from the direction of the Soviet border about two miles away, where Iranian border guards had opened fire on Soviet troops crossing the parched Hari River. The Soviets returned fire with machine guns.[45]

Minutes later came a knock on the Soburis' door. Hassan's father answered. Outside stood three terrified men: the mayor, the chief of police, and the captain of the border guards. They sought sanctuary with Soburi, who spoke fluent Russian and had lived for many years in the twin Soviet town of Serakhs, across the river. The police officials surrendered their pistols to the elder Soburi, who directed Hassan to hide them. Hassan rolled them in a cloth and secreted them under an awning. The group then waited anxiously for the Soviets.

They did not wait long. The sputter of truck engines and clopping of horses was soon audible in the street outside. Hassan and his father cautiously emerged to meet the invaders. Mounted cavalry strode past their house. Two Soviet officers and a civilian approached the Soburis. Hassan's father recognized the civilian from Serakhs. The two men embraced warmly, recalling old times. Then the elder Soburi informed the Soviets that three officials were in his home. The Soviet officers followed Hassan's father into the house, and informed the three trembling men that they were under arrest and were to surrender their side arms. Hassan retrieved the pistols and gave them to the Soviets. Moments later, the door opened, and the two Soviet officers snapped to attention. Through it strode a towering Soviet general—attired in an immaculate, bemedaled white tunic—Lt. Gen. Timofei T. Shapkin.

Shapkin, commander of the Fourth Cavalry Corps, announced sternly that, under the provisions of the Irano-Soviet Treaty of 1921, the Red Army had entered Iran to remove the threat posed by German agents. The proclamation meant little to the Iranians—none of whom had ever seen a German.[46]

Outside, troopers of the 18th and 44th Cavalry Divisions marched through town en route to the provincial capital of Meshed, 100 miles to the west. A motorized detachment of two infantry companies was sent ahead to seize the vital Mazduran Pass, midway to Meshed.[47]

At the headquarters of the Iranian Ninth Infantry Division on the southeastern edge of Meshed, Major General Mohtashami received warnings of the Soviet crossing early that morning from border posts at Sarakhs and Bajgiran. The reports indicated that Soviet motorized columns were moving quickly. Although Iran had been under attack for two days in the west, Mohtashami had received no guidance from Tehran—only the army's bombastic war communiqué, which did little but buoy false hopes. On his own initiative, Mohtashami assembled his staff and issued orders; he realized that there was no time to waste if Iranian forces were to reach the key passes ahead of the invaders.[48]

The Ninth Division consisted of six regiments. Four of these—including two infantry and two cavalry—were garrisoned at Meshed. A cavalry regiment was stationed at Bojnurd, while the 28th Infantry Regiment was at Torbat-i-Jam. There was also a large detachment at Birjand, far to the south. Mohtashami divided his force into two mobile groups: a motorized column under Col. Mahmud Dollow, which consisted of an infantry and cavalry regiment along with two 75-millimeter and one 105-millimeter artillery batteries; and a second lorry-borne column under Lieutenant Colonel Afshar, which included a regiment each of infantry and cavalry along with one 75-millimeter and two 105-millimeter batteries.

Colonel Dollow's mission was to secure and defend the Mazduran Pass—the only defensible position between Sarakhs and Meshed—where sat a decaying, medieval fortress. Colonel Afshar's column was dispatched to Quchan to engage the Soviets wherever they met them.

Like the other Iranian divisions, the Ninth lacked sufficient vehicles to transport its troops and equipment. While his forces assembled outside the barracks, Mohtashami dispatched patrols to scour the city for trucks and buses. Word that the army was commandeering vehicles spread quickly through the streets. Owners hurriedly hid their trucks or flattened tires. Nevertheless, the army soon garnered enough transport to move the two detachments.

At 5:15 A.M., Soviet bombers attacked the Meshed airfield. Encountering strong antiaircraft fire, they caused little damage. They strafed the antiaircraft positions, but avoided hitting the large clusters of soldiers assembled at the nearby barracks. Shortly after dawn, the two Iranian motorized columns rolled through the city streets, and off in their respective directions. The paved highway to Quchan—90 miles distant—enabled Colonel Afshar's column to move quickly. The column under Colonel Dollow also made good time over a dusty secondary road.[49]

Back in Meshed, chaos reigned as thousands of panicky townspeople scurried into the countryside by car or foot. Some carried their belongings in horse-drawn droshkies or on mules and donkeys. The Red Air Force struck the city repeatedly as the morning wore on. At 9 A.M., 35 Soviet bombers raked the airfield and barracks—again meeting antiaircraft fire. One hanger received a direct hit, while six aircraft of the Iranian Third Air Regiment were demolished on the ground. Four Iranian soldiers were killed, and 18 wounded.[50]

Another Soviet offensive was also under way in Gorgan Province. Iranian border posts near Tangeli detected Soviet troop movements along the Atrek River at 4 A.M. They alerted the Iranian 23rd Cavalry Regiment at Gonbad-i-Kavus—40 miles to the southwest—that the Soviets were crossing the river. This warning was relayed to Colonel Motazedi, acting commander of the Tenth Division at Gorgan.[51]

One of Motazedi's infantry regiments was positioned along the Atrek River. Its scattered posts, however, offered no resistance. The Iranians dropped their guns and fled. Some were killed in the onslaught. Maj. Gen. M. F. Grigorovich's 58th Soviet Infantry Corps advanced on two axes. The 39th Cavalry Division with a regiment of the 68th Mountain Infantry Division pushed toward Gonbad-i-Kavus, while the rest of the 68th Division marched toward Gorgan.[52]

While the Soviets thrust into northwestern Iran, the British pressed forward their advance in central Iran. In the predawn darkness, the two Gurkha battalions of Brig. Charles Weld's 21st Indian Brigade scrambled up the sharp escarpment of the Paitak Pass. The assault was barely under way when General Slim received a report that HAZELFORCE was entering Shahabad behind the pass.[53]

There the Warwickshire Yeomanry rolled into the small but sprawling city on a high plateau shortly after dawn. On the road for 19 hours, they had crossed rocky and winding mountain passes. Behind them—strung out for miles—straggled the Wiltshire Yeomanry, Household Cavalry, Gurkhas, bren carriers, tanks, and field guns of HAZELFORCE. The Mark VI tanks leading the advance broke down so often that they were bringing up the rear. The main body did not even enter the city until 4:15 P.M. that afternoon.[54]

Back at Paitak, local people streaming down the pass told Brigadier Weld that the Iranian defenders had abandoned the pass at midnight. Weld drove on ahead by truck, and encountered only one or two minor, undefended roadblocks. Reaching the summit about noon, he discovered large amounts of ammunition abandoned by the Iranians. An advance brigade headquarters was established at the top of the pass. Slim arrived at Weld's field headquarters just as the brigadier was dispatching a pursuit party of two companies and one artillery troop toward the town of Karind (close to Shahabad). Nearby, a group of 50 ragged Iranian prisoners sat clustered by the road; they had been abandoned by their officers during the night withdrawal.[55]

In Shahabad, the advance guard paused only long enough to eat a hurried breakfast before C Squadron, Warwickshire Yeomanry, motored down the Kermanshah road to reconnoiter the Zibiri area and establish a roadblock. Believing that the Iranians had retreated in disarray, the column proceeded with little caution. The road climbed steadily from Shahabad. The Second Troop, commanded by 2nd Lt. John Arkwright, led the advance. Trooper Sam Croft—riding with Arkwright in the second truck—could feel the morning heat rise as he scanned the barren terrain on either side of the road.[56]

Eight miles from Shahabad, C Squadron entered a narrow defile where, suddenly, an Iranian light machine gun opened fire and sprayed the first two trucks. The Yeomanry had driven into an ambush laid by an Iranian cavalry patrol. Both trucks stopped dead—their tires shot out. The men dived to the right side of the road as rifle and machine-gun fire spat all around. Trooper Croft ran several paces and plunged to the ground facing the truck. Lieutenant Arkwright dropped next to him. Arkwright had been struck; he jerked around toward the truck and died. Croft felt blood on his own foot, but thought that it was caused by a stone kicked up by the bullets.

Trooper William Ward shouted to the section leader—Sgt. Jack Dunn— "They've got the troop officer, Sarge!" Dunn yelled back, "Who else has copped it?" Croft replied, "It must be me. My foot's gone numb!" Iranian cavalrymen emerged from behind the rocks and bushes on the crest of the ridge, and rushed the lead truck. Sgt. Joseph Dixon was taken prisoner along with Trooper Montgomery Banks, who was badly wounded. The six others in the truck ran back to Dunn's position.

Dunn ordered his driver to get into the abandoned third truck and turn it around. As he did, the group scrambled into the lorry and sped away. Sam Croft tried hopping after them on his good leg, but collapsed after several feet. As his comrades disappeared, he began crawling away, though painfully encumbered by his ammo pouches. Dropping all but his water flask— which he strapped to his hand—Croft turned over and pushed himself backward with his good foot.

Iranian gunfire continued, but was soon answered by the crump of British 25-pounders, deployed to cover C Squadron's withdrawal. Moments later, all firing ceased. Croft heard galloping. Up rode an arrogant-looking Iranian cavalry officer with a rifle in one hand. The officer eyed Croft closely until satisfied that he was incapacitated. Then the Iranian galloped toward another British truck, whose prostrate occupants were hugging the ground. There, he rounded up the small group of prisoners, raised his arm, and then galloped away. Iranian gunfire spattered around the handful of men, who immediately scattered. Miraculously, no one was hit, and the troopers escaped. Moments later, the 25-pounders began shelling again. An Iranian bugle sounded recall as the Iranian officer and his men hurriedly abandoned their ambush site. Croft was left on his own. Refilling his canteen from a discarded bottle, he inched his way along, for what seemed like hours.

From Shahabad, meanwhile, A Squadron, First Household Cavalry, was dispatched toward the Paitak Pass. They expected to encounter Iranian troops retreating from the pass. Instead, on approaching the outskirts of Karind, they came upon a Gurkha patrol from the 21st Brigade approaching from the pass. The 21st Brigade occupied Karind at 3 P.M., to a warm reception by the residents. "The local populace," noted a British officer, "seemed genuinely pleased at our appearance in place of the Shah's troops." The British arrested a German engineer who had been supervising construction of a hotel.[57]

On Abadan Island early that morning, two Rajputana companies cautiously approached the Bahmanshihr ferry to accept the surrender of Major Tayfuri's battalion from Khosroabad. At the crossing, they found only three envoys—an Iranian officer and two soldiers—who told Capt. Patrick Kent that the others had crossed to the north shore during the night. Kent dispatched messengers across the river to contact the recalcitrant Iranians.[58]

As Kent awaited their return, correspondent Alan Moorehead of the London *Daily Express* appeared. "About six hundred of the enemy got across in the ferry," Kent explained to Moorehead. "We have just sent messengers to them to say that unless they surrender in two hours' time, we will round them up." One of Kent's emissaries arrived minutes later—his brow covered with sweat—to report that the Iranians were having a conference. "They can't make up their minds what to do," he indicated.[59]

The British waited in vain, for the Iranians had decided to march northeast to the village of Shadgan—30 miles across an immense, barren, and sunbaked mudflat. As the sun rose high in the sky, the thirsty and disorganized soldiers from Khosroabad tramped wearily across the waterless desert. They soon became lost in the trackless waste. The heat soared, further parching the already dry throats of the weakened men. The few who were still carrying rifles discarded them.[60]

Many were near collapse. They had tramped some 30 miles since the previous morning, without food and with little water. The searing desert soon began to take its toll as—one by one—men succumbed to the heat and exhaustion. Their straggling comrades were by now too debilitated to help. Stranded miles from the nearest water, the survivors stumbled forward.

Forty miles to the north, Gen. Charles Harvey arrived at the 25th Brigade's camp at Rahmaniyeh on the Karun River. Dissatisfied with the Lancers' previous day's reconnaissance, he directed Brigadier Mountain to reconnoiter the Iranian defenses outside Ahvaz in greater detail. Mountain ordered a fresh patrol dispatched—consisting of officers from all three battalions. Their objective for the next day's attack, he explained, was Hill 110—or "banana ridge," as it was dubbed. Lt. Col. William Marshall, commanding the First Mahratta Light Infantry, was ordered to advance and seize the ridge at first light on August 28. "I don't know how many enemy there are," the brigadier admitted.[61]

Colonel Marshall turned immediately to his second in command, Maj. Allan J. F. Johnstone, and directed him to organize two companies to conduct the assault. Johnstone gathered his two company commanders; the attached battery commander then joined the mixed scouting foray as they motored off toward Ahvaz—escorted by a 13th Lancer armored car troop and a 5/5th Mahratta company.

In Tehran, Prime Minister Mansur entered Saadabad Palace at 8:30 A.M. to offer his resignation. The shah accepted, but instructed Mansur and his cabinet to remain at their posts until a new cabinet could be formed. The news of a fresh Soviet offensive against the Gorgan and Khorrasan Provinces further discouraged the monarch. His War Council was uncertain as to how they should react to the latest Soviet move. Initially, they ordered the Ninth and Tenth Divisions to defend the borders, and directed the 23rd Cavalry Regiment at Gonbad-i-Kavus to keep open the line of communication with Meshed through Shahrud, should a withdrawal become necessary.[62]

There was no vehicular traffic—not even buses—on the usually clogged Tehran streets. Widespread anxiety caused hoarding of food and kerosene. Fear of an air raid spread in the wake of the antiaircraft engagement the previous day. Radio Tehran urged people to be calm in such an event and to fall flat if bombs exploded nearby. First aid procedures were described, along with names of hospitals for the wounded.[63]

At Rasht near the Caspian coast, Soviet planes dropped leaflets that morning. Bazaars were closed, and people were terrified. The wealthy of the city were hurriedly removing their valuables to village estates before the Soviets arrived. Troops of the Iranian 11th Division remained in their barracks, and awaited orders.[64]

Forty miles up the coast, the Soviet 77th Mountain Infantry Division continued trudging along the difficult, marshy road toward Rasht. By evening, however, the Soviet force had only reached Karganrud—still short of its main objective.[65]

Farther northwest, other elements of the 44th Army—probably from the 20th Mountain Infantry Division—occupied Ardabil, but then stopped. The demoralized remnants of the Iranian 15th Division from Ardabil remained entrenched east of Sarab, although their ranks were thinning rapidly from desertions.[66]

Their line of retreat through Bostanabad was cut that day by General Novikov's fast-moving mechanized force. The lead element of the 47th Army—consisting mainly of the 24th Cavalry Division, reinforced by tanks and motorized infantry—rolled out of Tabriz that morning on its southward movement toward Tehran. The Soviets had improved their mobility by commandeering all available vehicles in Tabriz. Ascending the steep Shibli Pass, the Soviet tanks and trucks rumbled past extensive but unmanned Iranian fortifications and artillery emplacements. The advance continued to the village of Turkomanchai, 50 miles southeast of Tabriz.[67]

Farther west, the 63rd Georgian Division occupied Rezeiyeh. General Moini had fled, while his troops had either deserted or scattered. Near the lower end of Lake Urmia, the straggling clusters of retreating men that had once constituted the Third Tabriz Division continued their march southward.[68]

Back in Meshed that morning, British Consul Gen. Giles Squires was summoned by Governor Pakrevan of Khorrasan soon after the two Iranian army columns departed. Squires expected to be interned, or possibly confined to the consulate grounds and surrounded by a hostile mob. All of the British citizens in Meshed—including 30 Indian families—had sought refuge in the consulate.[69]

His reception by the governor, however, was surprisingly cordial. Pakrevan offered Squires tea and cookies, and politely apologized for any earlier hostile behavior—which he ascribed to orders from his "tyrannical" sovereign. Trying to ingratiate himself with Squires, Pakrevan hoped that the British might exercise a moderating influence over their Soviet allies. Squires lodged an official protest that the army had confiscated several Indian lorries. Pakrevan could do nothing; he explained that civil administration had broken down.

In the meantime, Squires' vice-consul, Mr. C. W. Hart, wandered the shuttered, nearly deserted streets of Meshed. Some Iranians greeted him warmly, in contrast to their previous coldness. The usual policemen who kept watch on the British were noticeably absent.

That afternoon, Soviet bombers again struck the Meshed aerodrome and cantonment, at 2 P.M. and later at 5:45. Soviet air reconnaissance also detected the Iranian column approaching the Mazduran Pass. Colonel Dollow's ill-fated expedition was nearing its objective when Soviet aircraft caught the convoy on the open road. Bombs rained on the packed trucks and buses—killing many. When the raiders departed, Dollow ordered the survivors back to Meshed, leaving the road from Sarakhs open to General Shapkin's cavalry. The other column—under Colonel Afshar—approached Quchan late that afternoon, only to discover it occupied by Col. Alexander A. Luchinsky's 83d Division. Soviet artillery opened fire. Some Iranian officers deserted on the spot, and fled back to Meshed. Afshar ordered a general retreat.[70]

In Meshed, General Mohtashami received a cable from Tehran at 4:30 P.M.; it announced the Soviet invasion, and directed that units be dispatched to defend the frontier—which he had already done, 12 hours earlier. Even then, his actions had come too late.[71]

In Washington that morning, Iranian Minister Mohammed Shayesteh personally called on Secretary of State Cordell Hull. Shayesteh again urged the U.S. government to invoke the eight principles of the Atlantic Charter in order to help preserve Iran's neutrality and peaceful sovereignty. Hull evaded the request by saying that he was "assembling the pertinent facts relating to the entire matter, including the opposing viewpoints." He blamed the Iranian government for not publicly recognizing the problem of German aggression "in sufficient time in advance of any possible military occupation" to get the "best possible advantage" for itself from the Allies. Shayesteh pressed for assistance from the United States "as a champion of the rights and sovereignty of small nations." Hull reiterated assurances of the long-standing U.S. friendship with Iran, but insisted that Shayesteh's government should recognize the "broad view and the significance of Hitler's movement to conquer all of Europe."[72]

At noon, Ray Atherton, acting chief of the division of European affairs, told British Minister-Counselor Herschel V. Johnson by telephone that the controversy over U.S. "moral support of the British position in Iran was constantly being raised here." The department lacked the "full information," including "factual data" and a "full statement of purposes," necessary to support that position. Johnson replied that "some statement in this sense had already been made." Atherton responded that, "unfortunately, this is not at hand"; and he urged Johnson to provide immediate information on British attempts to negotiate with Iran. The U.S. official stressed the importance of needing to be kept informed by London.[73]

In Tehran at 4 P.M., the shah asked Ali Foroughi—a respected scholar and former prime minister—to accept the post of prime minister and to form a new cabinet. Because Foroughi was known to be critical of the shah's regime, Reza Shah hoped that his action would both be popular with the people and please the Allies. Although he was in poor health, the 64-year-old Foroughi agreed, and quickly departed to select his slate of ministers.[74]

Southwest of Ahvaz that afternoon, the Mahratta company and three armored cars scouted ahead of the 25th Indian Brigade's reconnaissance group. Approaching to within 1,300 yards of the main Iranian position, they confirmed reports that the enemy line extended from the southeastern extremity of the Fuliabad hills—five miles west of Ahvaz—to a large bend in the Karun River near Karaishan. The five-mile front covered the narrowest approach to the city from the north bank of the Karun.[75]

The advance group heard the ominous clanking of tanks in the distance, and nearly panicked. The Lancers and Mahrattas wheeled about and rushed headlong to the rear. The officers' group was bumping along the main road to Ahvaz when the armored cars and lorries of the advance guard came racing back in a cloud of dust. "Tanks, Sahib!" a breathless armored-car section leader yelled to Capt. Robert Henderson of the Second Sikhs. Henderson's Sikh driver turned pale with fear. The officers' patrol withdrew.[76]

Across the Karun River, meanwhile, Brig. Rupert Lochner's 18th Indian Brigade completed its crossing of the hastily erected Marid ferry, and reached the Dorquain pumping station af 11:30 A.M.—five hours after an Iranian army detachment withdrew. The force then continued its march to Maqam Hasbeh, 25 miles south of Ahvaz.[77]

Late that day, hundreds of nearly delirious Iranian soldiers staggered into the village of Shadgan. Some were near death from heat prostration. In the searing mudflats behind, more than 100 of their comrades had collapsed and died.[78]

Also near the end of his tether that afternoon was British Trooper Sam Croft who, after being wounded in the ambush east of Shahabad, had crawled and inched his way along for almost five hours in the heat. Ahead of him, he saw a small ridge where he believed his squadron to be located. Seeing two heads pop up, he waved—but elicited no response. His comrades were only a few feet away, but darkness was rapidly approaching. Fortuitously, a British truck came racing down the road past Croft. A soldier in the back yelled back to him, "later!" The lorry returned soon afterward, picked up Croft, and carried him to a dressing station.[79]

C Squadron of the Warwickshires continued to advance; it had recovered the two lost trucks and occupied the Kuh-i-Bangar ridgeline overlooking the village of Zibiri by 6 P.M. Across a small valley, the Iranians had established a visibly strong defensive position on the steep but narrow Chahar Zabar Pass. The two sides exchanged artillery fire throughout the night. Toward morning, the Wiltshire Yeomanry came forward to relieve the C Squadron. Several of the Wiltshires braved Iranian shelling to rescue wounded Warwickshire troopers.[80]

Prime Minister Ali Foroughi introduced his cabinet of new ministers to the shah at 8 P.M. A brief meeting followed, during which the sovereign agreed to order all military forces to cease fire so that negotiations could commence. Foroughi would announce the cease-fire on the following morning. At 8:30 P.M., the tired-looking monarch left the room. His ministers then departed the palace, and drove home through darkened streets.[81]

In Meshed, Governor Pakrevan telephoned Consul Squires at sunset to state that he, his staff, and the police were departing for Tehran under orders. At 8 P.M. that evening, a telegram from the capital ordered the army in Meshed to retreat to Tehran via the town of Sabsevar. The shah's War Council had decided to withdraw all possible units for the defense of the capital.[82]

The orders meant little to General Mohtashami, whose forces were in disarray. Shortly after dusk, the same soldiers who had bravely sallied forth against the invaders that morning came fleeing back into the darkened city. Army officers tore off their uniforms and tossed them into ditches. Donning civilian clothing, they filled their vehicles with petrol, and then sped southward along the Zahedan road toward Birjand. Conscript soldiers—after being ordered to turn in their weapons and remove their uniforms—scattered toward their homes in the city and outlying villages.

General Mohtashami nevertheless gathered what troops he could, and decided to move out that night so as to avoid Soviet air attacks. Believing the road through Sabsevar closed, Mohtashami decided to move through the desert oasis of Tabas. Before they could depart, Mohtashami received fresh orders to return the troops to the barracks. Other Iranian reinforcements were en route to Meshed from Birjand. When they reached Torbat-i-Haidari, they were ordered by Mohtashami to withdraw southward toward Tabas.

At Gonbad-i-Kavus in Gorgan Province, Colonel Hanjani—commanding the Iranian 23d Cavalry Regiment—received orders from division headquarters at Gorgan to withdraw immediately to Shahrud. Hanjani assembled his officers, and issued instructions. Lt. Ali Farivari and two other lieutenants went immediately to their quarters, and gathered their belongings. Returning to camp, they assembled their troopers and horses, and prepared to mount. The order to withdraw was unpopular. Some soldiers actually cried at having to retreat without fighting. But at 2 A.M., the 700 cavalrymen rode out of the garrison and into the night—hoping to put distance between themselves and the Soviets, who were not far behind.[83]

Outside Kermanshah and Ahvaz as dawn approached on August 28, the British and Iranian armies prepared for major clashes. Although the shah desired a cease-fire, it remained likely that news of this decision would not reach the front before serious fighting erupted.

10

Why Should We Quit Fighting?
We're Winning!

At the village of Maqam Hasbeh—25 miles below Ahvaz on the south bank of the Karun River—Brig. Rupert G. Lochner's 18th Indian Brigade hurriedly prepared in the predawn darkness of August 28, 1941, for the final advance on Ahvaz. Truck motors sputtered as khaki-clad sepoys clambered aboard. Lochner personally led the column northward. The Second Battalion, Third Gurkha Rifles, advanced left of the Abadan–Ahvaz oil pipeline—near the river—while the 1/2d Gurkhas moved to the right.[1]

Directly across the river from Maqam Hasbeh, the 25th Indian Brigade under Brig. Ronald G. Mountain began its parallel advance toward Ahvaz at 5:15 A.M. A screen of armored cars and an antitank troop led the way, and was followed closely by the First Mahrattas and one antitank and two artillery batteries. Next in column came the Third Jat Battalion, trailed by the 2/11th Sikhs.

Thick haze made maps useless. The rugged track caused the column soon to become strung out. Within 15 minutes, the brigade halted to regroup. A scout reported sighting 12 Iranian tanks to the left. Mountain reinforced his flank and shortened the column by deploying the Third Jats left of the Mahrattas, and then resumed the advance. Following some distance behind were two battalions of the 24th Brigade. When a truck's horn stuck— creating a piercing clamor—the driver climbed onto the running board at 40 miles an hour to silence it.[2]

While British fighters circled unchallenged overhead, seven Blenheims bombed barracks and troop concentrations around Ahvaz. Iranian antiaircraft replied without effect. The 25th Brigade reached its attack starting point south of Ahvaz at 7:15 A.M. Maj. Allan Johnstone deployed two Mahratta companies and an armored car squadron for the assault on "banana ridge." An antitank battery scanned the left for Iranian tanks. The haze made visibility so poor that Johnstone could not discern his objective.

171

Back on the south bank of the Karun, armored cars of the Guides Cavalry—screening ahead of the 18th Brigade—encountered brief resistance at the Swaiyeh police post. But by 7:30 A.M., the 18th Brigade had reached its starting line, two miles south of Kut Abdullah. The 1/2d Gurkhas wheeled right toward the railway crossing at Miyan Dasht, and halted briefly to regroup before commencing a simultaneous assault with the 25th Brigade on the opposite bank. Ahead lay a gap in the hills east of Ahvaz. D Company, 1/2d Gurkhas, and a Guides squadron moved toward the fortified ridge, only to find that the defenders had elusively withdrawn.

On the left of the 1/2d Gurkhas, Lt. Col. Charles Gray's 2/3d Gurkhas deployed on a ridge facing Kut Abdullah. They knew that an Iranian company was entrenched on a slight rise about a mile ahead. While his supporting artillery troop of four 25-pounders deployed, Gray dispatched D Company to envelop the Iranian left flank through a gap between two hills. D Company crossed the gap at 9:40 A.M., and surrounded Kut Abdullah. Iranian artillery on the north bank of the Karun fired briefly at Gray's position, but the shells landed harmlessly in an open area.

While the Eighth Indian Division prepared to assault Ahvaz, Maj. Gen. William Slim's Tenth Indian Division was assembling west of Kermanshah to attack the Chahar Zabar Pass. At first light on August 28, four howitzers of the 15th Field Regiment pounded Iranian positions near the village of Zibiri at 15-minute intervals. Shortly after 6 A.M., a patrol from C Squadron of the Wiltshire Yeomanry forayed through Zibiri to draw Iranian fire and reconnoiter the Chahar Zabar Pass. Barely had the Wiltshires crossed the ridge at 6:45 A.M.—exposing themselves to enemy view—than Iranian shells began landing around them. The patrol quickly withdrew.[3]

From the crest of Zibiri Ridge facing Chahar Zabar, General Slim watched the patrol action through binoculars. The Iranian Army's 105-millimeter howitzers easily outranged his aging 18-pounders. Shortly, the Iranians started bombarding the road near Slim, and shells were exploding dangerously close to a cluster of Indian lorries. The drivers frantically dropped their breakfast, started their engines, and roared off. Moments later, a second barrage impacted squarely where the vehicles had been parked. Slim presumed the Iranian Army to be incapable of accurate artillery fire, and concluded that German advisors must be directing the operations. In reality, the excellent gunnery was performed by well-trained crews commanded by a Colonel Piruzan.[4]

Slim was anxious to silence Iranian resistance and seize Kermanshah. Earlier, he had received a report that British civilians were killed at Abadan; Slim wrongly assumed that they were murdered by Iranians. Consequently, he urgently sought to rescue the AIOC community at Kermanshah before they should suffer a similar fate.

Slim estimated the force facing him to be at corps strength. In fact, the Iranian forces around Kermanshah numbered 8,000, including units of the

Fifth and 12th Divisions and detachments from Tehran. Slim nevertheless issued orders at 8:30 A.M. for a general attack. A tank squadron of the 14/20th Hussars would lead the 1/5th and 2/7th Gurkha Rifles at 10 A.M. to seize the Chahar Zabar Pass.[5]

In the meantime, an Iranian cavalry brigade began assembling northwest of Zibiri Ridge, from where it could charge the exposed British left flank and rear. To the rear of Zibiri Ridge, the 1/5th Gurkhas were motoring through a valley that led up to the ridge, to join the impending attack. They heard explosions ahead, but were unaware of the mounted blow that the Iranians were preparing against their flank. No sooner did the gunfire ahead cease than a cloud of dust appeared from the same direction. A column of British Yeomanry emerged from the haze—barreling down the road. The Gurkhas pulled their lorries over. Orders were passed down the column to dismount and take defensive positions. The Yeomanry reached the Gurkhas, turned right, and drove straight for a ridge slightly to the north where they dismounted and ascended the crest—placing themselves between the Iranian cavalry and the Gurkhas.[6]

In Tehran early that morning, Brig. Gen. Hassan Arfa was busy working in his office at the military academy when he heard three successive explosions to the south of the city. He telephoned his English-born wife, who reported that a low-flying Soviet bomber had dropped three bombs near their estate. The raid was in apparent retaliation for Iranian antiaircraft fire against the Soviet leaflet-dropping operation on the previous day.[7]

In the city, the Majlis convened in special session at 9 A.M. Prime Minister Ali Foroughi—looking aged and tired—stepped up to the speaker's platform and introduced his new cabinet by name. Foroughi's integrity and honest reputation gave weight to his appointment. "His Majesty is deeply concerned about the invasion," he announced, and—because "we desire a policy of peaceful coexistence with our neighbors"—the military was being ordered to cease fire on all fronts in order "to demonstrate our good will to the whole world." The news came as a great relief to many. Although the deputies wanted more information—some even hoping that the shah would abdicate—they still unanimously endorsed Foroughi's cabinet.[8]

The shah's cease-fire order was quickly transmitted to all commands still in communication with Tehran.[9] But in Ahvaz, the directive incensed Gen. Mohammed Shahbakhti. "Why should we quit fighting? We are winning!" he cabled back to Tehran.[10] In his view, the situation was far from hopeless. His tanks had driven off a British reconnaissance party the day before. His defensive position seemed strong. An infantry regiment—backed by a reserve battalion—was entrenched along a ridge west of Ahvaz. A similar force was dug in on the east bank of the Karun. Tanks and cavalry were concentrated northwest of Ahvaz to strike the British flank.[11] However, his well-designed defense was already starting to fall apart.

Orders to attack the eastern portion of "banana ridge" reached Maj.

Allan Johnstone at 8:10 A.M. But the haze obscured both friend and foe. At 8:35 A.M., C Squadron of the 13th Lancers rolled forward—followed closely by B and C Companies, First Mahrattas in lorries, and a Jat reconnaissance group. As the forward troops neared the southeast extremity of the hill, several long-range but badly aimed rifle shots whizzed overhead. Below the ridge 500 yards, a Mahratta company debussed and assaulted through increasing rifle, machine-gun, and antitank fire. The morning mist impaired the defender's vision—and saved the lives of many sepoys.[12]

Iranian cavalry were sighted, meanwhile, about 2,500 yards to the left. An antitank gun troop opened fire and scattered the riders. The guns were poised to engage Iranian tanks, but none appeared. An artillery observer with Johnstone's attack force spotted a group of Iranians—possibly reinforcements—gathering on the summit of the hill. Several shells quickly dispersed them. To the right of the Mahrattas, A and B Squadrons, 13th Lancers, advanced and occupied an objective south of Tell-i-Zebid despite tire damage from Iranian antitank and machine-gun fire.

Johnstone's charging sepoys then stormed the forward Iranian trenches—laying heavy fire to keep the defenders' heads down. Overrunning the main trench, the Mahrattas killed or wounded almost 50 Iranians. One sepoy was slightly wounded. On clearing the position, the Mahrattas gathered some 250 prisoners. The remaining Iranians fled to the rear. Reaching the summit, Johnstone sighted more Iranians near the Ahvaz bridge—apparently reserve elements. Through the lifting haze, he also spotted a white flag fluttering from a pole in the town. He quickly relayed the news to Maj. Gen. Charles O. Harvey that the Iranians were surrendering.

The Jats had just received orders to clear another section of Iranian trenches when, at 10 A.M., a black sedan bearing a large white flag approached. Escorted to General Harvey's headquarters, the Iranian envoy delivered a message from General Shahbakhti citing the shah's order to cease resistance and noting Shahbakhti's desire to discuss terms personally with his British counterpart. Harvey dispatched his political officer, Lt. Col. Arnold C. Galloway, to parley with the Iranian commander.

On the south bank of the Karun, Lt. Col. Charles Gray—commanding the 2/3d Gurkhas—received a report from his forward artillery observation post that an Iranian vehicle was approaching from Kut Abdullah and was flying a white flag. Gray hurried to meet the Iranian envoy, and then radioed news of the Iranian surrender to Brigadier Lochner at 10:56 A.M.[13]

Another Iranian army emissary circled around the 25th Indian Brigade, and ran into a long-strung-out column of the 24th Indian Brigade moving north to reinforce the advance. Driving a blue civilian auto, the Iranian officer soon became intermingled in the long line of British vehicles. He proceeded from truck to truck—trying to surrender—but no one paid any heed.[14]

Across the river, the 1/2d Gurkha Rifles prepared to advance through the gap held by D Company, 2/3d Gurkhas. Brigadier Lochner suspended the attack, and sent two Gurkha platoons to Kut Abdullah to investigate the surrender. Lochner issued orders at 12:30 P.M. to cease all operations and remain in position.[15]

Colonel Galloway soon returned with his Iranian escort to the division command post, and led General Harvey to Shahbakhti's quarters in the city. An Iranian honor guard presented arms as he arrived. Shahbakhti agreed to Harvey's terms—which included confining the Iranian garrison to their barracks for 24 hours, releasing all AIOC personnel under guard, arresting and handing over any Germans or Italians in Khuzistan, and returning any AIOC property looted during the military operations. Shahbakhti offered to have his regimental band play during the British entry into Ahvaz.[16]

While Harvey established his headquarters at the AIOC offices and rest house, the rest of the division redeployed to Kut Abdullah. Lochner's 18th Brigade was encamped by 3 P.M. The Gurkhas disrobed and plunged into the Karun River. But their swim was interrupted by the presence of small freshwater sharks. Several men were badly lacerated, while one was reportedly dragged away completely.[17]

That afternoon at Haft Khel—50 miles east of Ahvaz—Capt. Michael Forster learned by radio of the Iranian surrender. His small, isolated company was much relieved. They had earlier received a report that an Iranian force was approaching their position. Forster had dispatched a platoon-size patrol to the north, and it had advanced as far as the Yamaha airfield—12 miles south of Masjid-i-Suleiman—without encountering opposition. Forster's constant motorized patrols had greatly exaggerated the size of his small force. They now had only to await relief. An RAF Vincent flew over Masjid-i-Suleiman, meanwhile, and sighted an "OK" sign on the roof of the AIOC manager's bungalow.[18]

At Zibiri—west of Kermanshah—nearly 2,000 Gurkha soldiers with 16 light tanks sat on the Kermanshah road awaiting General Slim's signal to attack. Shortly before 9 A.M., Slim returned to his observation post on Zibiri Ridge. He had just ordered the attack to commence when he spotted a black sedan cautiously approaching from the direction of Zibiri. As it drew nearer, he discerned white flags poking out from either side. Two tanks clanked forward and escorted the auto to British lines. The sedan halted, and out stepped Maj. Abdullah Massoud of the Iranian cavalry—attired in a dress uniform replete with medals.[19]

Massoud was escorted to Slim, who greeted him politely. As the Iranian major spoke little English, the two parleyed in French. Massoud announced that he was to deliver a message to the British commander in chief. Slim—feeling awkward in his scruffy khaki uniform—identified himself as such. Massoud was taken aback, until reassured by Slim's red collar tabs. He then explained that the shah—wishing to avoid further bloodshed—had ordered his field commanders to arrange a cease-fire. The Iranian terms were that both sides would cease fighting and remain in their present positions until their governments completed peace negotiations.[20]

Slim refused the terms—his chief concern being the safety of the British civilians at the Kermanshah refinery. Besides, he sensed that Massoud's overbearing confidence was a facade. He told Massoud he would not accept terms that limited his troops' freedom of movement. He demanded instead that both sides cease hostilities, that the Iranians withdraw when and where directed, and that his force be permitted unrestricted passage to Kermanshah. Most importantly, all British subjects in Iranian hands were to be delivered to him unharmed and well treated.

Major Massoud protested indignantly. His purpose was to arrange a cease-fire—not a surrender—he stated, and added that his men would rather fight than accept such terms. If the British rejected the cease-fire, he warned, then orders had already been issued for "overwhelming" forces to attack. The major gestured toward the Iranian cavalry regiment poised to charge. Slim replied coldly that he only hoped they would.

Massoud's bluff was called, and he began giving in to each condition in turn. Slim finally insisted that the Iranian major flatly accept or refuse all terms. Massoud temporized, behaving as if he lacked the authority to accept the terms. Slim gave him one hour to retrieve his commanding general, with whom Slim could deal directly. "It is not the custom in the Iranian Army," Massoud announced indignantly, "as it appears to be in the British Army, for the general to be in the front line!" At this, he succumbed to all points on behalf of General Moggadam. The major insisted, however, that there was insufficient time to withdraw his forces from their positions by the 2 P.M. deadline. Slim disagreed. Massoud stiffened, squared his shoulders, and announced that he—as a graduate of the military staff college—knew that such arrangements were impossible.[21]

"I too am an é lève de l'Ecole Supérieure de Guerre—" Slim responded, "not only an élève but I was professeur!" Deeply impressed, Massoud bowed and respectfully submitted to Slim's authority; he offered to evacuate Kermanshah within four days. Slim demanded two. Agreeing, Massoud assured him that the civilians at the refinery were in no danger, and noted that his general and the British refinery manager were the closest of friends. Slim remained adamant, however, and suspended his attack for two hours while Massoud telephoned the terms to his commander in Kermanshah.[22]

As Major Massoud departed amid many bows and handshakes, four Iranian horsemen galloped up to the British lines from the direction of Chahar Zabar. Brigadier General Puria, commanding the Iranian 12th Division, led the party; he sought permission to pass through British lines in order to halt the impending Iranian cavalry charge. With permission, they spurred their way forward, and intercepted their countrymen before the attack could commence.[23]

In Kermanshah, General Moggadam received Slim's conditions, and relayed them to the shah. The general realized that there was little else he could do but accommodate the British demands. Moggadam then drove to the refinery to visit the works manager, Mr. Robertson, whom he had met some days earlier at a wedding reception. When the fighting began, the two men kept in close contact, to protect the refinery against bandits. Robertson greeted the Iranian general warmly. Moggadam asked politely if Robertson and his senior staff members would accompany him to the British lines. "I want to convince the British general," he said, "that none of you has been ill-treated."[24] Robertson thought it absurd to pack the British into cars and cart them to the front. Moggadam agreed completely, but insisted that it was not his demand but that of the "mad English general."[25]

Robertson agreed to go himself, but could not take any of his staff. When Moggadam inquired why not, the Englishman replied matter-of-factly that they were on the golf course playing a foursome arranged at lunch. Moggadam sighed in disbelief.

At Zibiri, meanwhile, Lt. Gen. Edward P. Quinan arrived from Baghdad with two Soviet liaison officers. He approved the terms given by Slim to the Iranians—including the intended occupation of Kermanshah. British ground and air patrols meanwhile monitored the Iranian retreat. Before long, another car approached British lines. Slim expected to see Major Massoud returning with the Iranian response. Instead, a British civilian in a linen suit and sun helmet emerged, introducing himself as the refinery manager. Slim was amazed that Robertson had passed through hostile lines alone. Robertson brushed his concerns aside, and explained that he had decided to come by himself in order to describe the situation in Kermanshah and to spy out Iranian strength along the way.[26]

He described Kermanshah as orderly and peaceful. Everyone there—both military and civilian—were pleased that the fighting had ended, but rumors had reached the city of a Soviet advance from the north. The people were terrified of the Soviets, and were only too eager to be occupied by the British. Robertson then offered to take Slim into the city personally; the manager insisting that he could guarantee both the general's safety and a warm reception. Slim found the idea novel. He had planned to send a staff officer to negotiate, but now saw no reason why he should not go himself. Gathering a couple of staff officers and a small escort, he climbed into Robertson's sedan and sped off at 40 miles an hour.

On the British left flank, meanwhile, a minor panic occurred. The Household Cavalry were alerted that a cavalry attack was developing in the hills beyond their camp. Although the Iranians had ceased fire, it was possible that some units had not received the word. C Squadron was deployed in defensive positions, with the remainder of the regiment standing to. The cloud of dust raised by hoofs was eyed closely. To everyone's relief and amusement, the cavalry turned out to be a wandering herd of cattle.[27]

Robertson's car roared through the now deserted Chahar Zabar Pass and into the broad valley beyond. The English party swiftly overtook an enormous column of retreating Iranian soldiers. All wore new uniforms and carried the latest firearms. To Slim, they seemed a better lot than those captured at Paitak. In fact, they included soldiers of the Tehran Central Garrison. Robertson's Iranian driver slowed the vehicle to a crawl—honking his way through the astonished and insolent-looking horde. At one point, an Iranian officer stopped the car, but let them pass after exchanging a few words. The lines of men seemed endless to Slim, but eventually the car broke free of the column.[28]

The party skirted the city—passing numerous apathetic and poorly dressed local inhabitants—and soon reached the refinery. The sedan pulled up before a beautifully landscaped bungalow. Inside, the party was greeted by an Iranian butler who guided them into the drawing room; Mrs. Robertson was serving tea to the four Englishmen who had just returned from golf. Slim felt a bit foolish at his earlier concern for their safety. After tea, Robertson took Slim to General Moggadam's headquarters in Kermanshah. The Iranian general, his staff, and a guard of honor stood ceremoniously outside as the British party pulled up. Slim bluntly brushed aside any formalities—feeling he must impress the Iranians with arrogance, in the absence of his army.

Moggadam politely led Slim into his office, where they discussed the armistice terms over tea. Slim repeated his demand that all Iranian forces be withdrawn from Kermanshah within 48 hours, except for Moggadam's headquarters. The general agreed, but needed the shah's approval. Slim also demanded the arrest of a German doctor named Fuchs, who was wanted by British intelligence. Moggadam hesitated, fearing to offend the Germans. Finally, Slim offered to have his own men arrest Fuchs if the Iranians would only show them where he lived. Relieved, Moggadam supplied a guide, who accompanied two British staff officers to the German's residence.[29]

Slim was then confronted with an unexpected development. News had reached Kermanshah that two Soviet columns were advancing rapidly in their direction—one via Sinneh about 100 miles directly north, and the other from Kazvin through Hamadan. These reports had been brought by Iranian refugees, and Slim doubted their accuracy. But he also had little other information on the movements of their "ally," despite the presence of a Soviet liaison team.

Slim's doubts were justified. In fact, the Red Army had not yet reached either Sinneh or Kazvin, although they were moving steadily in both directions. That morning, a motorized column of Soviet-Armenian troops led by light tanks pushed out of Tabriz and southward along the shore of Lake Urmia in pursuit of the retreating Iranian Third Division. By evening, the column occupied the city of Maragheh. Farther east, General Novikov's 47th Army departed Turkomanchai that morning, and motored another 50 miles to halt in the city of Mianeh.[30]

North of Novikov's force, what remained of the isolated Iranian 15th Division was still holding the approaches to Sarab that morning when news of the cease-fire arrived. An orderly withdrawal was impossible with the Soviets controlling all the roads. The division therefore disbanded: The troops were released to their homes, while the officers attempted to reach Tehran as best they could.[31]

In Rasht near the Caspian coast that morning, a Soviet aircraft dropping leaflets was fired on by antiaircraft guns at the barracks of the Iranian 11th Division. The division knew of the armistice, but many soldiers were defiant. Later that morning, several bombers returned and attacked the crowded barracks. Collapsing walls killed almost 100 soldiers. Many of their furious comrades ignored orders to withdraw to Tehran, and instead took weapons from the armory and dispersed into the jungles. Some soldiers fled down the coast road to Ramsar.[32]

That afternoon, the Soviet 77th Mountain Infantry Division with units of cavalry entered Rasht and occupied the barracks. Russian Cossacks rode boldly through the streets—terrifying the residents. Soviet aircraft soared over the outlying forests in search of armed bands of Iranian soldiers.[33]

Meanwhile, a motorized battalion of Soviet Azerbaijanis left Rasht and took over the port city of Bander-i Pahlavi. Capt. Morteza Daftary was in his headquarters at the naval station when the Soviet column rolled into the compound. The Soviets lined up his sailors outside, under guard. Captain Daltary himself was interrogated at length as to the location of his submarines. He had difficulty convincing the Soviets that he had no submarines.[34]

At the opposite end of the Caspian Sea coast, in the city of Gorgan, an Iranian civilian named Daghestani arrived that morning at the Iranian Tenth Division headquarters with a telegram from Tehran ordering all Iranian forces to cease fire. Colonel Motazedi, the acting commander, was suspicious—and so, he wired Tehran directly. A reply was soon received, confirming the report. The colonel then issued orders for all forces to cease fire.[35]

One of Motazedi's units could not be reached. The 23rd Cavalry Regiment was on horseback all day, withdrawing through the Elburz Mountains toward Shahrud. Several miles behind rose dust trails from their Soviet pursuers. Occasionally, one of their light tanks could be spotted. The Soviets seemed in no particular hurry, and made no serious attempt to close with the Iranians.[36]

South of Meshed that morning, the Iranian Army column that had been called north the day before from Birjand was withdrawing back southward when attacked and bombed by Soviet aircraft. The soldiers dispersed off the road and took shelter in the hills. In Meshed itself, all was quiet that morning. No soldiers or police were evident in the streets. Soviet bombers appeared several times, but there were no longer any military targets of significance. At the Shah Reza hospital, the entire staff had deserted, leaving only the old German director and a Czech surgeon to tend the regular patients and wounded Iranian soldiers. Governor-General Pakrevan returned to the city after a short hiatus, and anxiously asked British Consul General Squires whether the Soviets would occupy Meshed. The Englishman knew no more than Pakrevan. At dusk, Meshed heard the shah's cease-fire order over Radio Tehran. The blackout ended, and the city's lights were turned on. Cinemas reopened, and uniformed men appeared again in the streets. Many believed that the Soviets had halted at Quchan and intended to advance no further.[37]

In Tehran, Sir Reader Bullard and Ambassador Andrei Smirnov were summoned separately about noon to meet the new foreign minister, Ali Soheili, who informed them officially of the cease-fire and indicated that his government was prepared to meet any Allied terms. Both diplomats rushed back to telegraph their respective governments for instructions. Smirnov boasted openly that, since his countrymen were making such rapid progress, their advance forces could reach Tehran within 24 hours. In reality, however, the nearest Soviet force was a two-day road march away.[38]

Rev. William Miller was returning to the Presbyterian Mission that afternoon when he learned of the cease-fire. All day, he had been hearing stories of the many people killed by bombings in Tabriz, Rasht, and other cities; and he was pleased that peace had come. "How happy the people were!" he wrote, describing the reaction to the announcement. "One could see that a great burden had been lifted and they were happier than they had been for a week."[39]

Their initial relief, however, would soon be proven premature. The Iranians are an emotional people, who are driven more by conditions of the moment than by a long view of events. For, as they began to examine the calamity that had befallen Iran, they discovered that a quick, ignominious surrender was worse than war itself.

11

There May Be a Revolution in Tehran

Tehran's feared and despised chief of police, Colonel Mohktary, was summoned to Saadabad Palace at 5 P.M. on August 28. The shah appeared tense and weary, as he confided his apprehensions to Mohktary, saying, "I am not sure what is going to happen, therefore I've decided to send my family to Esfahan. I will join them later if the situation worsens." He directed Mohktary to prepare the secret evacuation of the royal family.[1]

While the shah watched his Iran's situation deteriorate, leaders in the West started worrying about the menace posed by the sudden large Soviet military presence in Iran. From London late that afternoon, Ambassador John Winant relayed Britain's assurances to Washington that the occupation of Iran was only temporary and that there were no "private understandings" giving "Russia any sort of free hand in Iran or any tacit acquiescence in Russian troops remaining in Iran any longer than military necessity required."[2]

That same evening, the British and Soviet governments agreed to link up their forces near Kazvin, 90 miles northwest of Tehran. The following morning—August 29—General Novikov's long armored column drove forth from Mianeh on its southeastern push toward the city of Zanjan, which was its objective for that day. Overhead, a flight of Soviet bombers roamed ahead to bomb targets in the path of the column. At 10:30 A.M., the Soviet aircraft attacked the undefended city of Kazvin. Bombs struck an AIOC oil storage facility; they ignited 500,000 gallons of fuel oil—which, ironically, might otherwise have been used by the Red Army. The explosions and fire terrified the townspeople, and caused many of them to flee into the outlying villages.[3]

A lone Soviet bomber continued southward and bombed the city of Hamadan—killing some 15 people. Eight wounded Iranians were brought to the American Presbyterian Mission Hospital.[4]

Farther west, a Soviet mechanized column from Tabriz pressed south-ward into Kurdistan, and reached the Kurdish town of Miandoab just as thousands of weary Iranian troops of the Third (Tabriz) Division were trudging into the settlement. The soldiers, who had been on the march for four days, had not received word of the cease-fire. Their heavy weapons had long since been abandoned.[5]

As the Soviet tanks approached, Iranian officers ordered their men to take cover behind mounds of dirt and to open fire with rifles. Some crawled into position, but none fired—for their rifles were useless against tanks. The Iranians threw down their weapons and surrendered. Soviet-Armenian sol-diers rounded up the prisoners, stripped them of valuables (particularly watches), and began herding them back toward Tabriz.

In the northeastern city of Quchan on August 29, Col. Alexander A. Luchinsky, commander of the Soviet 83d Mountain Infantry Division, dis-patched patrols to Bujnord and also to seize the key road junction at Sab-sevar, which connected Tehran to Meshed. That morning, Luchinsky's superior, Maj. Gen. Mikhail Kazakov (the chief of staff of the 53d Indepen-dent Central Asian Army), was visiting Luchinsky's headquarters when the deputy commander of the Iranian Ninth Division—a colonel—arrived from Meshed to negotiate surrender. The Iranian officer assured the Soviets in the name of both General Mohtashami and Governor-General Pakrevan that his division was prepared to lay down their arms. He then presented his sword and requested conditions. Kazakov scribbled down several points regarding the transfer of weapons and forbidding the withdrawal of armed troops from assigned areas, and handed the demands to the Iranian colonel.[6]

In Meshed, people felt relief, for the Soviets seemed to have halted their advance. Shops reopened, while soldiers and police reappeared on the streets. But at noon, everything changed. Columns of Soviet infantry marched suddenly into the city from the direction of Sarakhs. Lt. Gen. T. T. Shapkin, commander of the Fourth Cavalry Corps, personally accompanied this advance guard of two Central Asian companies. Soviet soldiers quickly occupied key points throughout the city; they disarmed the police, and placed guards in front of government buildings. Tajik sergeants exhorted crowds in the streets to "throw off the yoke of your Shah and his Ministers," and depicted Iranian authorities as "pro-Hitler traitors from whose tyranny the benevolent Red Army has come to liberate you!"[7]

Several hundred miles to the west, the sole remaining unit of the Iranian Tenth Division—Colonel Hanjani's 23d Cavalry Regiment—trooped into Shahrud that Friday morning. They had crossed the Elburz Mountains during the previous night—closely pursued by Soviet motorized units. On reaching Shahrud, Hanjani learned of the shah's cease-fire order, and sent an officer to negotiate surrender with the Soviets—who had paused outside Shahrud at the village of Pol Dokhar. Despite Hanjani's surrender offer, the Soviet commander decided to wait until the following morning before entering Shahrud. This respite offered Hanjani's men an opportunity to flee the city. Many officers, troopers, and soldiers—including Lt. Ali Farivani—discarded their uniforms, donned civilian clothing, and hid from the Soviets. Shopkeepers closed their stands and fled into the gardens outside the city.[8]

In Tehran that morning of August 29, an auto caravan bearing the royal family departed the palace at 10 A.M., headed for Esfahan. Rumors quickly circulated through the capital that the shah and his entire family had fled. But the monarch remained behind with 21-year-old Crown Prince Mohammed Reza. Distressed by the continued Soviet bombings following the cease-fire, the shah dispatched his son-in-law's father—Ebrahim Qavam—to express the sovereign's concern to British Minister Sir Reader Bullard. Qavam also sounded out whether Sir Reader might offer the shah sanctuary in the British legation, should the Soviets enter Tehran. Bullard's response was not encouraging, however.[9]

The panic over food shortages in Tehran subsided when the government opened the warehouses and released grain to the people—which evaporated the long queues for bread. Frightened citizens continued to flee the city in large numbers, despite urging by the government to remain calm and ignore wild rumors.[10]

From London that day, Churchill cabled his pleasure to Stalin over the outcome of events in Iran—revealing the true, if publicly unstated, purpose of the invasion:

> The news that the Persians have decided to cease resistance is most welcome. Even more than safeguarding the oilfields, our object in entering Persia has been to get another through route to you which cannot be cut. For this purpose we must develop the railway from the Persian Gulf to the Caspian and make sure it runs smoothly. . . . We are instructing our advance guards to push on and join hands with your forces at a point to be fixed by the military commanders somewhere between Hamadan and Kazvin. . . . It would be better at this moment for neither of us to enter Tehran in force, as all we want is the through route. We are making a large-scale base at Basra, and we hope to make this a well-equipped warm-water reception port for American supplies which can thus surely reach the Caspian and Volga region.[11]

At Kermanshah on August 29, Iranian Generals Moggadam and Puria were concentrating their troops for withdrawal on foot. Major General Slim had ordered them to evacuate the city by 6 A.M. on August 30, and was permitting only a 200-man garrison to remain in the barracks—enabling Moggadam to save face with the shah. Moggadam himself intended to return to Sinneh with an infantry regiment of his Fifth Division. General

Puria's 12th Division and the troops from Tehran would have to tramp northeast to Hamadan.[12]

Slim had already sent an advance detachment to secure the AIOC refinery near Kermanshah. The rest of the force encamped outside the city, where they prepared for a triumphal victory march into Kermanshah on the following morning. Their general, however, had little time for parades—for he was suddenly preoccupied with the advance of his "ally." General Moggadam's chief of staff, Col. Ibrahim Arfa—the younger brother of Gen. Hassan Arfa—was keeping Slim apprised of Soviet movements. Arfa reported that the Soviets were nearing Kazvin and had bombed Hamadan that day. He assured Slim that the Soviets had every intention of occupying Hamadan, which lay on the British side of the demarcation line. Arfa also noted that another Soviet column was bearing down on Sinneh, 100 miles directly north of Kermanshah.[13]

Slim wanted to give his men two or three days rest before pushing on; but, if the Soviets reached these cities first, the British might have difficulty ejecting them. Plans were swiftly formulated to preempt them. Beginning on the following morning, Brig. John Aizelwood would rush his brigade to Hamadan, while Col. John G. Pocock would lead a smaller second column to Sinneh. They were to make every effort to arrive ahead of the Soviets. Slim instructed them to behave cordially toward their allies. If the Soviets did arrive first, the British were to politely suggest that they withdraw to their own assigned areas. Slim was to be kept continuously informed of developments.[14]

That night, Radio London began making personal attacks on the shah; it declared that there was no food in Iran because the monarch had sold it all to Germany. The BBC further criticized him for stealing land from the people. The British government was using the BBC to disassociate itself from the unpopular monarch because many Iranians believed that it was the British who had installed the shah and propped up his regime through oil subsidies.[15]

The verbal broadside surprised and delighted most Iranians, because open criticism of the shah was a serious crime. But the U.S. missionary Rev. William Miller knew that the British allegations regarding food shortages were untrue. The harvest was just in, and abundant food reserves existed in warehouses—although the authorities had been reluctant to release them.[16]

The radio attacks disturbed the shah, who feared that foreign invective might incite insurrection. He therefore ordered Prime Minister Foroughi to implement martial law in Tehran, and appointed Brig. Gen. Ahmad Ahmadi as military governor of the city.[17]

The Reverend Mr. Miller—returning from prayer meeting that evening—noticed military vehicles dashing about the city. An Iranian friend told him that the Soviets would likely arrive the next day, and predicted that "something interesting" was about to happen. Miller rose early the next morning—Saturday, August 30—and strolled through the still quiet streets. Trucks loaded with troops rumbled through the city. An infantry battalion assigned to the military governor was being deployed to protect strategic points. As Tehran came to life that day, rumors and fears abounded. Miller heard that the shah and his family had fled, leaving the city under military control. At 8 A.M., a terrified Jewish woman rushed into the missionary compound—crying that "they" were going to murder all the Jews.[18]

Iranian pilots at the Gala Morghi Military Airbase on the southeast edge of Tehran were seething, that morning, over an order grounding their airplanes. The air force had been denied virtually any role in the brief war. Like pilots everywhere, the aviators scorned death and were eager to rise in their antiquated machines to meet the foes. Their frustration and anger had passed its limit when the Soviets bombed undefended Kazvin the day before.[19]

Shortly before 9 A.M., the Iranian Air Force commander, Gen. Ahmad Khosrovani, arrived at the air base to calm the situation. The general assembled all pilots and officers, and began speaking. An insubordinate pilot—a Captain Vassighi—interrupted Khosrovani. The general's temper flared, and a fight ensued. Rebellious officers shot the general's adjutant, Major Afkhami, through the neck, and fatally wounded him. The rebels seized Khosrovani and placed him under guard. To keep news of the mutiny from spreading, they quickly arrested the army sentries who were guarding the airfield.

A Soviet bomber meanwhile neared Tehran. Captain Vassighi and a Sergeant Shoshtary took off immediately in two aircraft to intercept the approaching plane. The two pilots threatened to bomb the city unless the government resisted the Allies. Two bombs were dropped on the airfield, possibly by the rebels.

At the Baghe-Shah barracks, a dust-covered Iranian soldier rushed excitedly into the office of Capt. Kyhan Khadive, and announced that there was an uprising at the airfield. The soldier explained that he had barely escaped the mutineers. Captain Khadive telephoned his division commander, Brig. Gen. Karim Aga Buzarjemehri, who dispatched armored cars and tanks to suppress the rebellion. Orders were issued to shoot down the maverick aircraft flying over the city.

Downtown, a civilian named Daoud Amini was walking down Ferdowsi Street when he heard airplane engines overhead. A large Soviet bomber began spewing leaflets over the city. Then Iranian planes began zooming around the bomber just as Iranian antiaircraft guns commenced firing. As Amini watched, people panicked, believing that the city was under attack. Children cried and women screamed as the street crowd dashed about in terror. The Soviet plane escaped unharmed. An Iranian armored detachment entered the aerodrome and crushed the rebels, following a brief skirmish. Khosrovani was freed, and order restored—although the two rebel pilots escaped in their aircraft.[20]

The government publicly announced that martial law was being imposed in Tehran to prevent disorder and to maintain security. At the Army Officers Club, small groups of army officers gathered to whisper their concerns over the worsening situation. Predicting revolution and chaos, some discussed fleeing the capital.[21]

Meanwhile, in Kermanshah, the Iranian Army evacuated the city early on the morning of August 30. At 11 A.M., an eight-mile-long British column slowly entered the city, and then began increasing speed to 30 miles per hour. Thousands of sullen Iranians lined the streets as a diverse procession of turbanned Punjabi motorcycle riders, truckloads of Gurkhas, Madras sappers, Household Cavalry, and Yeomanry, along with Hussars in tanks and bren carriers motored briskly down the main thoroughfare. Some spectators seemed glum or hostile, but most displayed no emotion. Once through the city, the bulk of the division encamped a mile and a half beyond, near the refinery. The Household Cavalry took over the Iranian barracks from some 80 Iranian soldiers.[22]

Outside Kermanshah, two flying columns formed up for their race against the Soviets. Colonel Pocock assembled his officers and issued instructions; he explained the touchy diplomatic situation facing them in dealing with the Soviets. His column—composed of the 1/5th Gurkhas, an armored car section, and an artillery troop—then sped north on the Sinneh road. Pocock's station wagon took the lead; it was stuffed with champagne, and carried a large Union Jack.[23]

About ten miles north along the same road, Gen. Hassan Moggadam and his defeated men were trudging toward Sinneh when they encountered an unexpected sight. A car heading south pulled up, bearing Generals Matbooi and Moini—who had deserted their men at Tabriz and Rezaiyeh. They announced excitedly that the Soviets had entered Kurdistan and were moving rapidly toward Sinneh. Facing the Soviets to his front and the British to his rear, Moggadam decided to avoid a squeeze, and ordered his men to turn northwest toward the small city of Ravansur. They soon crossed the Qareh Su River and destroyed the only bridge behind them.[24]

In fact, a Soviet patrol of three armored cars and four troop-filled trucks entered Sinneh at 2 P.M. The city was quiet. Many people had fled to the hills in fear of their approach. After inspecting the barracks and the telephone exchange—and distributing photos of Joseph Stalin—they drove off to scout the countryside.[25]

Along the road leading east from Kermanshah toward Hamadan that morning, Brig. James Aizelwood's column began passing small parties of Iranian soldiers. Many had abandoned their weapons. Iranian 105-millimeter guns were being carried in large trucks. The Iranians moved off the road to allow the hurried British to proceed.[26]

General Slim and his aide, Capt. William Storey, followed closely behind. Eighty miles east of Kermanshah, their station wagon ascended the precipitous Shah Pass. The steep incline had taken its toll of British vehicles. Several disabled lorries and tanks were encountered. Aizelwood was obviously pushing his vehicles to the limit.[27]

Farther north, the Iranian city of Kazvin was nearly deserted when units of the Soviet 44th Army entered it after crossing the Elbruz Mountains from Rasht. From the northwest, meanwhile, advance elements of the 47th Army rolled into the city to link up with their Caspian counterparts. Maj. Gen. V. V. Novikov established his army headquarters in the city hotel.[28]

Of Novikov's original five-division army, only the 24th Cavalry Division—reinforced by a tank brigade—remained by the time he reached Kazvin. Though his combat losses had been nil, his line of communications stretched over 300 miles, and had consumed much of his force in garrison and security duties.[29]

Brigadier Aizelwood's tanks and lorries rolled into Hamadan shortly after dusk—at 7 P.M.—to a joyful reception by the greatly relieved populace, who swarmed around the large traffic circle in the center of the city. Seldom have invaders been treated more like liberators. The local Iranian garrison had fled as the British approached—but only after vandalizing their barracks and murdering some of their own officers. The British set up camp in a melon field beyond the city. General Slim soon arrived; he was pleased with the situation, but became anxious when he learned that the Soviets had reached Kazvin. He instructed Aizelwood to be ready to push north at first light, so as to establish contact with the Soviets.[30]

In Tehran, meanwhile, German Minister Erwin Ettel approached U.S. Minister Louis Dreyfus with a request for his help in ensuring the humane treatment of the 900 German citizens who had taken refuge in the German legation. Ettel feared for their lives if the Soviets should arrive, and much preferred that they be turned over to the British. Dreyfus assured him that the U.S. government would "look with great disfavor" if any Germans were mistreated. Afterward, Dreyfus secured the necessary assurances from his British and Soviet counterparts.[31]

The two allies more immediate concern, however, was not the fate of the Germans, but the question of occupation zones. The night before, Sir Stafford Cripps had met with Deputy Commissar Vyshinski to hammer out a final demarcation line between the two armies. The Soviets were demanding a more southern salient in the eastern Khorrasan region than Cripps thought would be in Britain's interest. Vyshinski argued that his government desired petroleum mining rights in the area. The mounting Soviet demands worried Cripps who, ironically, was previously the staunchest advocate of Soviet participation in Iran. Cabling the Foreign Office on August 30, he warned Eden that "any prolonged occupation of this northern part of Persia by Russia is likely to be dangerous, especially if they have in mind such things as Vyshinski mentioned. Once established there, a whole host of incidents may crop up, each of which will lead to their continued occupation."[32]

Now realizing that his trust in Soviet promises had been abused, Cripps cautioned that

> in view of our quite definite statement that all we went in for was to get the Germans out, I fear that we may be led into a continued occupation to counterbalance [the Soviet] occupation for a long time, and without any honest justification for it on the basis of our statement at the outset. . . . I observe that . . . we are preparing to insist on facilitating transit of war material . . . and that, while the Persian Government are to expel the Germans within a week, our withdrawal is not to take place till "the military situation permits."
> It thus seems clear that even His Majesty's Government themselves are tending to drift away from their attitude towards Persia as explained to the Turkish Government and announced to the world in general; and with such encouragement, the Russians may be relied upon to drift much further still to our own ultimate disadvantage.[33]

In spite of Cripps's warning, Churchill still hoped that sincere Anglo–Soviet cooperation was achievable. In this light, the formal Anglo–Soviet armistice terms were delivered to Prime Minister Foroughi and Foreign Minister Soheili at 5 P.M. on August 30. The British note demanded that the Iranian Army be withdrawn north of a line running from Khanaquin through Kermanshah to Khorramabad, from there to Masjid-i-Suleiman, then to Gach Saran, and on to Bandar Dilam on the Persian Gulf. In return, the British promised not to advance any further into Iranian territory and to remove their forces when the "situation permits."[34]

They further required that all Germans, except a few technicians, be expelled from Iran with one week; that no Germans be allowed to enter Iran; that the Iranian government provide facilities for the transit of war supplies and munitions, but not troops; and that Iran maintain a policy of strict neutrality and friendly relations with Britain and the Soviet Union. In return, the British offered to continue paying oil royalties and to assist the economic needs of Iran.

The Soviet terms were similar to the British in promising that the Soviet government had no designs on Iranian sovereignty. The Soviets required the Iranian Army to be withdrawn south from a line running easterly from Ushnu—on the Iraqi frontier—through Miandoab, Zanjan, and Kazvin, then northeast to Shahrud, and north to the Soviet border. They offered to help develop Iranian oil in the Khorian desert, and also the Caspian fishing industry.[35]

Ambassador Smirnov added one oral condition—the very one so disturbing to Sir Stafford Cripps—that the Soviets be allowed to maintain one brigade and 50 aircraft at Meshed, although he agreed that the Iranians could also keep troops in the city. Bullard noticed that this particular point made a "bad impression" on Foroughi and Soheili, who otherwise appeared relieved that Tehran was not to be occupied. The two Iranians expressed their hope that Allied troops would not advance beyond the limits mentioned. They were also anxious lest the Soviets continue bombing Tehran, particularly after the antiaircraft incident earlier that day.[36]

After the meeting, Foroughi and Soheili drove directly to the palace to deliver the terms to the shah. The monarch studied the notes closely, and then ordered his ministers to further analyze the demands in order to adjust them more favorably to Iran. Earlier, the shah had informed his ministers that he planned to join his family in Esfahan the next day, because he feared an imminent Soviet entry into Tehran. The new terms, which precluded an occupation of the capital, now gave him reason to reconsider.[37]

The shah expressed great disappointment to his ministers that President Roosevelt had not replied to his appeal of August 25. His concern was relayed to Washington, where—in response—Roosevelt directed Secretary Hull to prepare a suitable reply to the shah.[38]

Elsewhere in Tehran on August 30, a confidential circular was dispatched to all army units at 6 P.M.; it ordered the release from active duty of all conscripts, and directed that there be no resistance if the Soviets or British entered Tehran. The origin of this directive remains clouded in controversy. From the evidence, it seems that the new government was uncertain of the army's reliability and feared new disturbances, after the air force revolt. Therefore, the new minister of war, Maj. Gen. Ahmad Nakjevan, ordered that the conscripts be dismissed, and only a small professional force retained.[39]

The directive reached the Baghe-shah barracks at 7 P.M. The Second Division commander, Brigadier General Buzarjemehri, promptly ordered his conscripts to turn in their guns and ammunition, and then to proceed home before the martial law curfew was imposed at 9 P.M. The streets soon filled with poorly clad young soldiers who were only too happy to hurry home in long, irregular lines toward their villages.[40]

When Tehran's chief of police, Colonel Mohktary, learned that the army was releasing its men, he hurriedly summoned his senior police officials to warn them that the situation had become dangerous and that "there may be a revolution in Tehran." Fearing that the soldiers released from duty "might come and kill us," the police commandant announced that he was leaving the capital; he invited the others to join him. Those who agreed to go with Mohktary prepared to leave early the next morning for the city of Yadz.[41]

Along the dusty road from Kermanshah to Hamadan that evening, General Puria and the tired and demoralized men of his 12th Division marched into the village of Sahneh—35 miles east of Kermanshah—where they paused to rest. On arriving, Puria heard rumors to the effect that Tehran was in turmoil, the shah had fled, and the army had ordered its soldiers to return home. General Puria therefore released his men, after gathering up and abandoning their weapons.[42]

The first contact between the British and Soviet forces occurred at 11:45 P.M. that night, August 30. Colonel Pocock's column arrived in Sinneh well after dark, and met the Soviets on their reentry into the city from the north. The British broke out champagne to celebrate the occasion. The free-flowing nectar smoothed cooperation, and quickly put the Soviet soldiers in good spirits.[43] Admitting that they were out of their established bounds, the Soviets blamed poor maps and bad map reading. But Capt. George Nightingale found their excuses suspect, and commented to himself, "Some maps! Some map reading!"[44]

Gen. William Slim awakened early on Sunday morning, August 31, to the news of Colonel Pocock's meeting with the Soviets. Although encouraged by their willingness to withdraw from Sinneh, he also heard reports that the Soviet forces at Kazvin knew of the his arrival at Hamadan and were preparing to advance in strength. Convinced by the insistence of his Iranian sources, Slim ordered Aizelwood to form up the 2/7th Gurkhas and move out smartly.[45]

Slim impressed on the colonel commanding the Gurkhas that speed was essential in meeting the Soviets—regardless of how many trucks turned over or how many soldiers were injured. Relations were to be friendly, and the Soviets could even send a few officers to Hamadan under escort; but any large force was to be discouraged. The battalion commander then hurriedly briefed his own officers and sent them double-timing back to their men. Drivers revved their engines as the Gurkhas climbed aboard. The column sped off across a tilled plain toward the 8,000-foot Avej Pass, over which they must pass quickly to establish a defensible position before the Soviets arrived. While the column was racing across the valley at 50 miles per hour, Soviet aircraft appeared over Hamadan—dropping leaflets.

Slim finished his own business and raced to join the column. His car started to overtake the convoy near the foot of the Avej Pass. The lorries were careening perilously around tight bends. Following close behind a truck filled with Gurkhas, Slim noticed that the speeding vehicle was nearing a sharp turn above a cultivated field. Failing to slow down, the lorry jerked off the road, flew over an embankment, and flopped onto the field. The Gurkhas bounced into the air in unison, and landed with their ranks rigidly intact. The driver gunned his truck back onto the road, without losing any speed. Near the summit, several trucks overheated and broke down. One lorry plummeted over a ledge, rolled, and seriously injured three Gurkhas.

A short distance beyond the summit, the Gurkhas halted in a narrow gorge—an ideal defensive position. When Slim arrived, the soldiers were busily siting machine guns and digging foxholes to cover the approaches. A listening post was dispatched forward, with a radio to warn of any movement. The morning being early, the British settled in to await the arrival of their allies.

At Sinneh, meanwhile, the Soviet patrol that had entered the city a day earlier departed at 10:30 A.M. to their headquarters at Miandoab, 125 miles to the north. To demonstrate Britain's presence, Colonel Pocock led a flag march through the streets, and unlimbered two field guns in the city square. Townspeople flocked in from the hills—reopening shops, and exuding relief.[46]

In Tehran that morning, Rev. William Miller was presiding over his Sunday worship service when he noticed among his parishioners a government employee who should have been at his office. "Have you given up your work?" Miller asked. The Iranian replied emphatically, "Oh, no! But nobody is working these days. We don't go to the office, and there is no one to force us to work!"[47]

Elsewhere, the shah had changed his mind and decided not to leave the capital. Learning that much of his army had been dismissed without authorization, he drove immediately to the Baghe-shah barracks to investigate. General Bujerjemehri nervously greeted the fuming monarch, but behaved as if he knew nothing of what had happened. The shah strode angrily through the empty barracks—the anxious general scurrying three steps behind. The enraged monarch ordered all soldiers rounded up and returned.[48]

Prime Minister Foroughi convened the Majlis that morning to state that negotiations with the Allies were nearly concluded. He urged the deputies and the people to remain calm, and cited the harm done by the recent panics. At 9 A.M., 15 large Soviet bombers flew over the city to extract revenge for the previous day's antiaircraft fire. Seven bombs fell near the Doshan Tappeh military airport northeast of the city. More bombs fell on a cement factory to the southeast—killing two men, and wounding 14 people. U.S. Military Attaché Col. Francis Tompkings inspected two bomb craters about a mile from the airport, and noticed leaflets littered the area. Written in French, they assured the Iranians that the Soviets were their friends.[49]

The main body of General Shapkin's Fourth Cavalry Corps entered Meshed that day. For three hours, a division of cavalry on horseback paraded through the streets, which were lined with spectators. The Soviet soldiers sang marching songs until they approached the sacred shrine of the Imam Reza, where they turned reverently silent. A patrol continued 25 miles south of Meshed to occupy the junction of the Tehran and Zahedan roads. Meanwhile, a Soviet patrol from Quchan secured Sabsevar—thus severing Meshed from Tehran.[50]

At the same time, the Soviet 68th Mountain Infantry Division in Gorgan was extending its tentacles along the Mazanduran coast—occupying Sari, Shahi, and Babol.[51] The Iranian Army and Gendarmerie had fled these cities four days earlier. A Soviet patrol of one officer and a dozen young soldiers entered Babol and searched the deserted police station. As they continued through the streets, they were chided by children, who threw stones at them. The Soviet officer stormed angrily into the house of the mayor—the only official who had not fled—and warned that, "We have been mocked in the streets and so far, have done nothing in retaliation. However, if this happens again, you are responsible for what we do." The insults immediately ceased.[52]

In Tehran at noon, the shah drove through the streets to assure the people that rumors of his departure were false. Thousands of conscripts had already reached home. The General Staff informed the shah that finding and returning them to the barracks presented an almost impossible task. Furious, he summoned all senior general officers to the palace at 2 P.M.[53]

At the designated time, four men waited anxiously in a palace hallway: Minister of War Gen. Ahmad Nakhjevan, Army Chief of Staff General Zarghami, Military Academy Commandant Gen. Morteza Yazdanpaneh, and Air Force Commander Gen. Ahmad Khosrevani. Ten minutes later, the shah entered the corridor, glanced about venomously, and demanded the whereabouts of his other generals. Before anyone could answer, he began hurling obscenities and abuse at those present. Raising his cane, he whipped Nakhjevan and Zarghami about the face—accusing them of treason, and commanding them to drop their guns. Summoning his servants, he ordered them to remove the two men's shoulder straps and place them under arrest. Gen. Mohammed Nakjevan (no relation to Ahmad) was reappointed by the shah to his previous post as minister of war.[54]

Four more Soviet planes flew over Hamadan that afternoon. At the Avej Pass, Brigadier Aizelwood took a small escort of Gurkhas in several trucks and drove north to intercept the Soviets. At 3:30 P.M., while barreling across the desert plain, the British party spotted a large armored vehicle looming in the distance, and approaching fast. The six-wheeled Soviet BA-6 armored car—its 45-millimeter gun pointed straight ahead—halted when it sighted the British. The vehicle swiveled its cannon ominously toward the British—causing a great deal of concern. But the Soviets evidently spotted the large Union Jack flying from the lead truck. A sergeant and his crew emerged from the armored car, and exchanged greetings with their allies—although neither group could speak the other's language. The Soviet NCO then fired three green flares to alert his comrades who were following.[55]

The armored car led the British several miles down the road to a platoon of Soviet infantry. The Soviet officer in charge shook hands with his allied counterpart, while soldiers on both sides smiled shyly. Brigadier Aizelwood and four of his staff officers were escorted into Kazvin. Along the highway to the city, they passed frightened peasants and townspeople fleeing on foot or donkeys. In the city, Soviet mechanized columns rolled through the streets, while sentries guarded certain buildings.

The British observed tanks, armored cars, and tracked vehicles in abundance—and were somewhat surprised by the first-rate quality of the Soviet troops and equipment. They had assumed that Stalin would divert his best troops to oppose the Germans, and expected to encounter only second-rate reserve units. Certainly, the pathetic Iranian Army deserved no better. What they did not realize was that the Soviet mechanized army had been kept ready in the Transcaucasus for more than a year. Its original purpose had been not merely to crush the Iranians, but the British as well. Reaching Soviet headquarters, the five English officers were led upstairs to discuss demarcation with General Novikov and his staff.[56]

Meanwhile, a Soviet mechanized column was attempting to reach Hamadan. A squadron of armored cars leading a column of lorried infantry pulled up before the British roadblock at the Avej Pass. Several bewildered Soviet officers walked forward to be greeted by their English counterparts. Relations became politely strained when the Soviet commander announced his intention to advance his entire force to Hamadan. The British commander politely offered an escort for the Soviet officers, but assured them that—as there were sufficient British forces to handle any situation in Hamadan—Soviet reinforcements were not required. The Soviet leader persisted, but the Englishman remained adamant. The Soviet surveyed the strength of the Gurkha position, conferred briefly with his officers, and then decided not to press the issue. Turning their vehicles around, the Soviet squadron drove back toward Kazvin.[57]

In Tehran at 3 P.M. that afternoon, Prime Minister Foroughi informed the British and Soviet legations that his government accepted—in principle—the Allied terms. The next day—September 1—the British further demanded that all Germans except for the legation staff and certain technicians be turned over to the Allies for internment—pointing out that the Germans could no longer be "expelled," because Iran's borders were closed.[58] That evening, the Iranian government delivered a written acceptance of the original terms—while boldly requesting indemnities for damage incurred by the invasion, and ignoring the new demands.[59]

At the request of Sir Reader Bullard, U.S. Minister Louis Dreyfus agreed to act as intermediary between the British and Germans over the disposition of the Germans in Iran. To prevent the Germans from falling into Soviet hands, Bullard suggested that the German legation arrange to send its citizens to Ahvaz for internment in India. The British would allow certain Germans—including the legation staff—to remain in Iran. Ettel balked at this proposal; he was being presented at the same time with an alluring Turkish offer of safe transit back to Germany for all Germans.[60]

The Soviets, meanwhile, were already starting to violate their promises. In Meshed on September 1, the Soviet garrison ignored its agreement with the Iranian government, by which it was not to interfere with the local garrison. A summons had been posted, ordering all Iranian officers to report to Soviet authorities. When 110 officers presented themselves, they were loaded into Soviet army trucks and driven through Meshed en route to prisoner-of-war camps. Street crowds cheered loudly—expressing pent-up hatred for the arrogance and brutality of Iran's officer corps.[61]

In Tabriz that same day, thousands of Iranians captured at Miandoab were driven through the streets by their captors. Among them was Cpl. Tomic Romson who—being Armenian—had befriended a Soviet-Armenian sergeant during the long march back. As the straggling column winded down a narrow street, the Soviet NCO offered Romson a chance to escape. The Iranian corporal dashed into an alley, and then crept back to his home.[62]

Elsewhere in Tabriz that day, the Soviets assembled a crowd of local Armenians in an open-air theater, where they were treated to doses of propaganda encouraging Azerbaijani separatism. Many pro-Soviet Armenians had been armed by the Red Army in order to assist with security in Tabriz.[63]

Tehran remained quiet on Sunday, September 1. Poorly clad soldiers released from duty still filled the streets, although army and gendarmerie patrols were busily rounding them up and returning them to their barracks. Many shops had reopened, and more food was available—though bread remained scarce. Prime Minister Foroughi's promise that Tehran was not in imminent danger of Soviet occupation relieved many people.[64]

At 11:30 A.M., Erwin Ettel met with Foreign Minister Soheili to discuss the fate of the German colony. Soheili admitted that he had no definite instructions from the British or Soviets on the subject. Ettel hoped that the British would allow the evacuation of the entire colony through Turkey. Soheili admitted that the British minister was prepared to accept the Germans in Ahvaz, but would offer no guarentees for safe passage to Turkey.[65]

"The situation is entirely clear to me now," Ettel remarked cynically. "The English Government intends to intern the German colony in any event. If the Iranian Government were to expel the Reich Germans, it would amount to delivering them into the hands of the enemy." Ettel sternly warned Soheili that, if the Germans were expelled without safe conduct, the consequences for the Iranian government would be "very grave." Intimidated by Ettel's threats, Soheili excused himself and summoned Prime Minister Foroughi, who could only promise to urge the Turkish government to pressure the English into allowing safe conduct through Allied-occupied areas. Foroughi assured Ettel that he would seek the Soviet position on the matter. But the German minister was completely dissatisfied, and cabled Berlin that day: "I am no longer in any doubt that the Iranian Government is prepared to throw the German colony to the wolves." He indicated that he would prepare a contingency plan to move the Germans into the Turkish embassy. The Turks, however, refused to cooperate with Ettel; they claimed that the British and Soviets were not going to occupy Tehran.[66]

Elsewhere in Tehran that day, Rev. William Miller spent the afternoon calling on various Iranian converts. From then, he learned that the people felt betrayed and were turning against their ruler. What angered them most was that the shah had capitulated so quickly to the invaders. The people had endured years of great expense to build a large Iranian Army with aircraft, tanks, and ships to ward off invaders. They had provided their young men and payed exorbitant taxes on tea and sugar to support the army. Up to the last minute, the shah had exhorted the military to be prepared for the ultimate sacrifice. Then, when the invasion began, he forbade the army to fight. Many Iranians now felt that their country had been disgraced.[67]

Some families that had previously paid large sums to keep their sons from military service were now urging them to enlist and fight. Elements within the army were reportedly plotting to make a final stand. Miller heard some people suggest that the time had come for a "jihad" against the Soviet "infidels."[68]

That evening, Miller recorded his amazement at the bitter resentment expressed against the shah:

> For 15 years, people have been afraid to speak a word of criticism of anything the Shah said or did. The papers praised his every act as though it were that of a god. . . . But now that he is no longer supreme, people are beginning to open their minds, and one is startled by what is being said. All these years, he has been robbing the poor, enriching himself by taking away the lands and rights of the people. And now the day of reckoning is rapidly approaching. And when it comes, I fear it will be terrible. The man who completely controlled the life of this nation has utterly failed them, and they are going to turn on him. . . . The situation is getting ripe for a revolution of some sort and, with the Russians here to help, it will probably be a bloody one.[69]

That night, the British and Soviet radio stations heightened their propaganda offensive against the shah with fresh subject matter—the imprisonment of Gen. Ahmed Nakhjevan. Hearing of the broadcast, the shah summoned his new war minister, Gen. Mohammed Nakhjevan, and ordered the immediate court-martial of five leading generals. To preempt further propaganda against himself, he directed that the trials begin on the following day.[70]

The British broadcast that night included one other item apparently intended to diminish blame for Britain's role in the invasion. The radio announced that President Roosevelt had given Prime Minister Churchill approval of the plans for the invasion of Iran during the Atlantic Conference. Dreyfus immediaiely denied this, but the harm was done. The friendship felt by many Iranians toward the United States turned immediately to bitterness and a feeling of betrayal.[71]

In Washington that day, Roosevelt received a message from Churchill, who noted that the "good results which have been so smoothly obtained in Persia puts us in touch with the Russians." The British leader proposed to "double, or at least greatly improve, the railway from the Persian Gulf to the Caspian, thus opening a sure route by which long-term supplies can reach the Russian reserve positions in the Volga basin." He asked Roosevelt to lend merchant ships to transport troops and supplies.[72]

The next day—September 2—Roosevelt's formal reply to the shah's appeal of August 26 was delivered to the Iranian government. The note did not excuse or justify the morality of the Anglo–Soviet actions against Iran, but it did attempt to rationalize the necessity for those actions. Because Roosevelt felt compelled to defend this morally questionable but strategically necessary action, he implied an acceptance of the moral responsibility for ensuring that Anglo–Soviet promises to Iran would be observed.

Roosevelt told the shah that he was "following the course of events in Iran with close attention and [was] persuaded that this situation is entitled to the serious consideration of all free nations . . . with respect to the basic principles involved." But then he urged the monarch to "view the situation in its full perspective of present world events and development . . . arising from Hitler's ambition of world conquest." Roosevelt expressed fear that German conquests would extend "beyond Europe to Asia, Africa, and even to the Americas, unless . . . stopped by military force" and that nations desiring "to maintain their independence must engage in a great common effort if they are not to be engulfed one by one." He cited U.S. efforts to provide "material assistance to those countries . . . engaged in resisting German ambition for world domination."[73]

The president assured the shah that the U.S. government "has noted the statements to the Iranian Government by the British and Soviet Governments that they have no designs on the independence and territorial integrity of Iran." As a "long-time friend"—he said—the United States was seeking information as to Anglo–Soviet intentions in Iran, while pressuring the two Allies to restate publicly before the world their assurances to Iran.[74]

But Roosevelt's evasive communiqué was small solace to the embattled shah, who realized that the internal situation in Iran was deteriorating rapidly. Unless public order, authority, and national pride could be restored quickly, the days of his rule were numbered.

12

Can You Hold the Throne?

Churchill's patience with the shah had neared its limit by Monday, September 2. At ten that morning, he angrily telephoned Sir Alexander Cadogan, the Foreign Office's permanent under secretary, demanding to know why there had been no action on removing the Germans from Iran. Cadogan calmed him down with assurances that everything possible was being done. But Churchill—believing that the Iranians were stalling—was very close to taking matters out of their hands.[1]

Tehran on Monday morning was near chaos. The police and military were barely able to maintain order. Not enough soldiers were left to enforce martial law, while many policeman had deserted and fled the city. Travelers and refugees circulated terrifying and usually exaggerated stories of Soviet atrocities.[2]

The Iranian government formally replied to the Anglo–Soviet terms; they agreed to most points, but requested that the cities of Dizful and Khorramabad be excluded from the British zone and that the Soviets withdraw from Kazvin, Semnan, and Shahrud. The Iranians agreed to expel the Germans, but expected the Allies to arrange safe conduct. The Allies were further requested to return captured arms and ammunition, to purchase goods previously ordered by Germany, and to withdraw from Iran when the situation permitted. According to information received by U.S. Minister Dreyfus, Iranian officials feared that the Soviet forces near Tehran might seek a pretext to occupy the capital. Sir Reader Bullard told Dreyfus confidentially that he shared their concern.[3] The next day, September 3, Prime Minister Ali Foroughi collapsed from a heart attack.[4] He had been holding the government together—barely—on the strength of his integrity and reputation. His sudden incapacitation paralyzed Iran's bureaucracy at a most critical moment.

About 1,500 miles northwest of Tehran that morning, in the charred wheat fields of the Soviet Ukraine, a huge Nazi offensive rolled forward, closing its steel jaws around nearly 1 million Soviet troops trapped in the Kiev salient. To eliminate this exposed bulge, Hitler suspended his drive toward the Caucasus and Iran. The oil fields of those regions now seemed a less urgent objective, as a result of the Allied occupation of Iran and with the approaching onset of winter. The fuehrer instead desired a knockout blow against the Soviet Union. His generals persuaded him that the swift seizure of Moscow would have a crushing effect on Soviet morale. Thus, Moscow became the new focus of the German advance.[5]

From Moscow on September 2 Ambassador Cripps again cabled his concerns to London over Soviet political ambitions in Iran:

> Do you wish me to do anything about [the Soviet] demand for continued occupation of Meshed? I think this is a matter in which a very strong protest should be lodged at once, as otherwise it will be difficult to get the Soviet Government to change its attitude once we appear to have accepted their position. It is, I feel, important in this first political action together, not to let the Soviet Government get away with anything outside what we have agreed. If they feel they can jump things upon us at the last moment, we shall have infinite trouble in the future.[6]

Cripps further emphasized that Britain should make a stand now, while still in a strong position—which might not happen to be the case later.

On September 3, 1941, Tehran's security situation remained unstable. Many senior army officers had fled to the south. Soldiers sent back to their barracks could find little food, and often deserted again. Those remaining had almost no discipline. Officers and men alike looted army stores. Artillery horses were sold in the bazaar for a pittance. Many previously elite regiments were reduced to a quarter of their normal strength.[7]

However, sufficient food was finally made available to the people as fears of an imminent Soviet occupation receded. To further calm the citizenry, newspapers were ordered to print announcements that Anglo–Soviet forces would not enter Tehran.[8]

But such assurances only worsened matters with respect to the Germans, who were already upset by the lack of progress in arrangements for their safe evacuation. Ettel took advantage of the chaos to stall negotiations over the departure of his countrymen. He feigned illness, haggled over which Germans warranted diplomatic immunity, and broke agreements over technical points.[9]

Ettel's surliness was reflected among the almost 900 Germans encamped at the German legation's summer residence at Shirmran. Many threatened to resist any Allied efforts to intern them.[10] A British correspondent described the Germans as "dashing about [Tehran] in high-powered cars, hanging out the swastika, cutting a figure in Persian homes, insulting British passers-by, and spreading anti-Allied rumors."[11] Despite the jingoistic tone of this report, there was some truth to it. Journalist Alan Moorehead experienced Nazi arrogance firsthand when he arrived in Tehran late on September 2. While dining in an Iranian restaurant, he and two fellow journalists were verbally accosted by three inebriated German youths shouting Sieg Heil's. One of the Germans banged his fist on the table and glared at the Englishmen.[12]

To complicate matters, the Allies were discussing demands for the expulsion of all Axis nationals—including the Italians, Bulgarians, and Rumanians. Dreyfus apprised Washington that this decision resulted from a Turkish offer of asylum and from the "highhanded attitude" of the Germans, who now felt that they were "temporarily safe from the dreaded Russians."[13]

While walking in Tehran that day, Rev. William Miller encountered unexpected hostility from various Iranian acquaintances. They had heard—and believed—a British radio broadcast reporting Roosevelt's approval of the invasion. They felt bitter and betrayed by the United States. Their government even lodged a minor protest through the U.S. ambassador in Turkey. "Poor people!" Miller noted in his diary. "They have been disgraced and they feel they must blame somebody. So we get our share."[14]

The Iranian inaction on meeting Allied demands prompted Churchill on September 3 to instruct Bullard to use the "leverage of a possible Russian occupation of Tehran" to "get what we want by agreement with the Persian Government":

> We hope it will not be necessary, in the present phase at least, to have an Anglo–Russian occupation of Tehran, but the Persian Government will have to give us loyal and faithful help and show all proper alacrity if they wish to avoid it. . . . Although we . . . do not wish to drive them into active hostility, our requirements must somehow be met [for] the best possible route from the Persian Gulf to the Caspian [to] be developed at the utmost speed and at all costs in order to supply Russia. . . . There is no need to fear undue Russian encroachments as their one supreme wish will be to get the through route for American supplies.[15]

Churchill's view of Soviet intentions seems naive in view of Cripp's warning.

The following day—Thursday, September 4—Adolph Hitler ordered every effort possible to evacuate all Germans from Iran. Besides securing their safety, he also desired "complete freedom of action" once German troops approached Iran. Walter Hewel, a member of Ribbentrop's personal staff, explained to the fuehrer that everything possible was already being done to repatriate the colony, but that—for the moment—it was not technically feasible until arrangements could be negotiated. Turkey had complicated matters by backing away from her earlier offer and refusing to act as a "protective power."[16]

Hewel suggested that the Reich negotiate directly with the Iranians and attempt to exploit a perceived conflict between Britain and the Soviet Union. The German government could assert that the forcible internment of the German colony by the Iranians—in obedience to British pressure—infringed on Iranian sovereignty. The Iranians would then hopefully be compelled to take a firmer stand against the Allies. Hewel also offered one last possibility; If all else failed, Germany could take reprisal against British citizens living in the German-occupied Channel Islands. In any event, Hitler and Hewel both agreed that the German legation would remain in Tehran until the fate of its citizens was decided.

In Tehran at 4 P.M. that afternoon, Bullard and Smirnov discussed a proposal with Foreign Minister Soheili for the expulsion of all Axis nationals. The Allies now expected the Iranians to turn the Germans over to them directly for internment. Soheili brought this proposal to the shah at 6:15 P.M. The monarch became irate at the suggestion of foreign interference in Iran's conduct of its affairs. "We will lose face," he exclaimed to Soheili, "if we let the Allies take over the expulsion of the Germans." The shah ordered his foreign minster to convince the Allies that the Iranian government should handle the matter.[17]

Tehran's chaotic security situation worried the ruler, who was dissatisfied with the daily reports he received from the acting police chief, Colonel Eatemadi. To restore the situation, the shah telegraphed all the provinces, and ordered the immediate return of Colonel Mohktary—in whose ruthless methods he had confidence. Mokhtary was in Rafsanjan when he received these instructions; he departed for Tehran the next morning, September 5.[18]

At noon on September 5, the British and Soviet envoys presented their final demands formally to the Iranian Foreign Ministry. Both governments refused Iranian requests that they withdraw from certain occupied cities, but they offered the fullest cooperation with Iranian officials in administering those areas. They refused to pay for war damages, but noted that Iranian requests for economic assistance and the return of arms and ammunition would remain under consideration. Regarding Axis nationals, the entire German, Italian, Hungarian, Bulgarian, and Rumanian colonies were to be expelled. The legations would be repatriated, while private citizens would be sent to Ahvaz for internment in India. The Soviets included a list of named individuals who were to be turned over to them. The Allies also demanded that the Axis legations be denied the use of their codes and ciphers.[19]

Foreign Minister Soheili appealed to Sir Reader Bullard to arrange safe conduct through Turkey for the women and children returning to Germany. He also asked that the German men of military age be interned near Shiraz, under British control. The Iranian admitted candidly that, without these concessions, he doubted that his very weak government could survive the effects of Allied actions on public opinion. Bullard remained firm, however—having already been reprimanded by London for suggesting ways to prevent any Germans from falling into Soviet hands.[20]

Soheili went to the U.S. legation and warned Dreyfus that he saw no hope for his government or his people. The Allied demands would, he thought, force Foroughi's cabinet to resign—which would stimulate further chaos, and possibly invite an Allied occupation of Tehran. Dreyfus informed Washington that the Iranian government was "in a precarious position": "The Shah's prestige sinks ever lower and the tide has so turned against him that his disappearance from the scene is probable."[21]

Popular discontent was spreading rapidly through the capital that day. In one incident, several young Iranian men were passing a statue of the shah on horseback in Sepah Square. One man stopped, looked up at the imposing figure, and shouted, "You son of a burnt father! You have taken our money. You have taxed our tea and sugar. You have forced us to serve in your army. And now you have sold us out to foreigners!" The fellow then spat on the statue.[22]

Although food shortages had lessened in Tehran, the bazaars were largely closed, and larceny was widespread. Some 600 people had been jailed without trial, and the police were still having difficulty in maintaining order. Iran's foreign minister informed Ettel that the British minister was refusing to grant the Germans safe conduct to Turkey—insisting instead that the colony surrender to the British for internment in India.[23]

Meanwhile, in Kurdistan, armed rebellion broke out. The fierce, independent-minded Kurds had seized or purchased weapons from disbanded Iranian soldiers, and were attacking and looting villages. The few remaining Iranian Army detachments were driven into the major towns. General Slim rushed to Sinneh—the capital of Kurdistan—to deal with the situation, but he had at hand only the First Household Cavalry Regiment. A large Kurdish force was reportedly preparing to enter Iran from Iraq. Slim's mission was uneviable: to bring the rebellion under control without engaging the warlike tribesmen. He therefore ordered up the Warwickshire Yeomanry, with artillery as reinforcement. His main advantage lay in that the Kurds' hostility was focused solely on the Iranians.[24]

From Moscow on September 6, U.S. Ambassador Laurence Steinhardt relayed his government's hope to Vladimar Dekanosov, commissar for Near Eastern affairs, that the Soviet government would issue a public statement "to all free peoples, reiterating the assurances already given to the Government of the Shah." Dekanosov assured Steinhardt that, although the situation in Iran was "not as dangerous as before," all issues were not solved. Referring to the aborted Iranian Air Force revolt, he emphasized that Iran was "not yet peaceful enough" to permit Soviet withdrawal and that the final solution "was not simple." Though stating that it was "too soon" to reaffirm assurances of an eventual withdrawal, Dekanosov did affirm that his government would confine its occupation to an area "not so big—along the frontier," that it would not affect Iranian sovereignty, and that it would "scrupulously" observe the assurances stated in its note of August 25.[25]

Dekanosov's statement cast an ominous shadow of doubt over true Soviet intentions in Iran. Foreign Secretary Anthony Eden now perceived the developing problem—even if Churchill did not. Eden replied to Cripps on September 6 that "I agree with your views" regarding Soviet intentions in northeastern Iran, "but I do not wish you for the present to take any action . . . since British troops in Persia are also occupying places outside their line of occupation." Eden was referring to Hamadan, in particular. He added that he had learned that morning from Ambassador Maisky that the Soviets wanted to modify their zone of occupation to include the Caspian Sea and a salient leading southeasterly from the southeastern corner of that sea. Maisky had assured Eden that Soviet forces did not intend to enter Tehran. Also—the ambassador said—the Soviet Union shared Britain's view that Iran's territory and independence must be maintained.[26]

Winston Churchill himself was focusing on developing the trans-Iranian railway with U.S. cooperation. On September 6, he expressed his hope that the United States would supply urgently needed locomotives and freight cars for use on the railway. Churchill pointed out that Iran's rail system offered the best available supply route to the U.S.S.R. during the winter months.[27]

In Tehran that evening of September 6 the shah summoned U.S. Minister Louis Dreyfus to a special audience, where he expressed his sincere appreciation for the president's telegram of September 2. The monarch was particularly satisfied that Roosevelt had noted British and Soviet statements acknowledging that they had no designs on Iranian territory or independence. The shah then stated emphatically that not only did he have no sympathy for the Germans, but he had had serious difficulties with them on several occasions. He further expressed his readiness to join a common effort to resist German aggression. The British and the Soviets, he indicated, could have received what they needed in Iran through friendly negotiations.[28]

But Dreyfus was suspicious of the shah's new views, and told the monarch that much harm had resulted because foreign diplomats had been unable to obtain a direct audience with him. Reza Pahlavi disagreed, insisting that he had always been willing to receive foreign envoys. Dreyfus knew differently, but believed that the shah was trying to announce a new policy without losing face. Afterward, Dreyfus cabled his opinion to the State

Department that "if the Shah is willing to cooperate fully with the British and correct some of his more serious shortcomings which have lost him the support of both the Iranians and the British, I believe he may still be able to save his throne."[29] The shah would have been shocked, had he known that the contents of this cable had been decrypted by German intelligence and reported to Hitler personally.[30]

On September 7, Nazi Foreign Minister Joachim von Ribbentrop instructed Erwin Ettel "not to place any obstacles in the way" of evacuating the Germans to Ahvaz, "should the case arise." Berlin feared that the British might fulfill a threat by Sir Reader Bullard to turn the whole colony over to the Soviets. "An internment by the English is still to be preferred to surrendering the colony to the Bolshevists," he reminded Ettel, and added that the Reich was preparing to intern and deport several thousand British citizens from the Channel Islands unless the British facilitated safe conduct for the Germans in Iran.[31]

In Tehran that afternoon, Colonel Mohktary reached police headquarters at 3 P.M. Though fatigued after his long journey back to the capital, he was ready to tackle his mission of reimposing the shah's iron rule. His unexpected appearance surprised his deputy, Colonel Eatemadi. "Your leaving was wrong," the acting police chief admonished, "but, even worse, you returned." He advised Mohktary that the situation had changed since he left, and warned that "you might be killed by unknown people."[32]

But Mohktary brushed the admonition aside, and proceeded to demonstrate that he was again in charge of Tehran's security. That evening, the foreign radios resumed their attacks on the shah. Translated transcripts of the broadcasts were forwarded as usual by the Iranian news agencies to the police department. After reading the reports, Mohktary summoned the reporters and accused them of writing lies. "I have heard that those stations praised the Shah," he stated cynically. "You had better go and change your reports." The newsmen did as instructed—out of fear—only still to be jailed by Mohktary immediately afterward.[33]

The next day—September 8—martial authorities cracked down further on dissent. Mounted army patrols scoured the city—breaking up street meetings, and trying to prevent graffiti. They were less than effective. Legends denouncing the shah were scrawled on buildings in the southern, working-class district. Even the palace itself was painted with invectious slogans reading, "The Shah is a murderer—oust him" and "Down with the Shah."[34]

In the Majlis there was introduced a measure proposing to strip the shah of his authority as military commander in chief. No action was taken on the legislation, but the mere proposal symbolized a growing parliamentary defiance.[35]

That night Rev. William Miller heard a rumor that the shah had already abdicated and was remaining in the palace only to hold the situation together. Miller asked an Iranian friend whether or not the young crown prince should assume the throne if his father left. "Never!" the man cried. "The people are so fed up with this family, they can't endure them. In England, the Royal Family is beloved by all, but these people are hated."[36]

At 10 A.M. on September 9, Prime Minister Foroughi—appearing feeble after his heart attack—presented the final armistice terms to the Majlis for ratification. The deputies were torn by conflicting emotions. Many hated the shah, feared the Soviets, and distrusted the British. If they accepted the Allied demands, the shah would gain a reprieve, and they would infuriate the Germans. But the Wehrmacht was still far away, while the Allied armies were at the gates. They therefore approved the terms unanimously.[37]

Whether the Iranian government could enforce the expulsion demands remained to be seen, but the British were not taking any chances. General Slim ordered the Ninth Armoured Brigade at Kermanshah to be prepared to advance on Tehran at short notice. The occupation force would include the Household Cavalry and the Wiltshire Yeomanry, reinforced by the 1/5th Gurkha Rifles.[38]

The next morning, General Slim left Hamadan for Arak to discuss the possible occupation of Tehran with the military attaché, Maj. Gen. W. A. K. Fraser. Slim and his party were on the road less than an hour when his driver fell asleep and rammed the station wagon into a bridge. For several moments, the auto hung perilously on the edge of a ravine while the driver frantically maneuvered it back onto the road. Slim escaped unhurt, transferred to a second car, and pushed on to Arak. General Fraser was not there; there was a telegraph from him, saying that he was unable to leave Tehran. Fraser advised Slim to purchase some civilian clothes and enter the capital clandestinely. Slim proceeded to outfit himself and his chief of staff, Col. Ouvry Roberts, with ridiculous-looking Iranian suits and cloth hats.[39]

Meanwhile, a major crisis was brewing in Tehran. The British and Soviet legations were furious over an editorial in the morning edition of the Tehran daily, *Ettellaat*. The item described the demands on Iran as "shocking"; and it declared that, although the Axis legations in Iran were to be closed, the Iranian "legations in [Axis] countries will remain active." It even criticized the Allies for violating Iranian neutrality. The shah was praised for having created a unified nation, following years of previous misrule and chaos.[40]

The article was unsigned. In fact, its origins remain a mystery, although the wording led diplomats to suspect the crown prince. In any case, it was clearly intended to cool German anger over the closing of their legation. But its inflammatory style all but convinced Sir Reader Bullard that Tehran must be occupied. He and Ambassador Smirnov personally protested its content to Prime Minister Foroughi, who denied any foreknowledge. To placate the Allies, Foroughi ordered *Ettellatt's* offices closed for three days. This failed to satisfy the British, and Bullard issued a blunt ultimatum.

Either the Iranians deliver the Germans to the Allies within 48 hours, or Tehran would be occupied.[41]

In London that day, Foreign Secretary Anthony Eden was asked before Parliament by an opposition Labor party leader whether Britain would "take steps to kick [the Germans] out ourselves," if the Iranian government were reluctant. "You may be certain," he answered, "we have in mind the necessity of taking action ourselves. Personally, I welcome this method but have insisted to the Iranian Government that it must be expeditious."[42]

While the various governments argued its fate, the German community encamped in tents outside the German legation summer residence at Shimran—in the cool foothills of the Elburz Mountains—calmly awaited a decision. Men sat around campfires and sung marching songs, while carefree children frolicked in the grass. The scene was almost festive. But to Maj. Bertold Schulze of the Abwehr, the camp was a fool's paradise. He told his wife on September 10 that "we can not stay here. I can smell barbed wire."[43]

Driving into Tehran to find Ettel, Schulze and his wife learned from the minister's deputy, Herr Dittman, that he was at the Foreign Ministry negotiating passage for the Germans to Turkey. Schulze expressed concern that, if the evacuation really did come to pass, the Soviets might haul out of the convoy certain people whom they wanted to question. Dittman could not be sure; but he advised the major that, being an "intelligence officer," Schulze was not required to share the "dictated optimism" of the legation. Leaving the legation, Schulze discussed his options with his wife, and decided finally to try to reach Afghanistan—from where he could continue his intelligence operations in Iran. His wife insisted on going with him, rather than evacuating.[44]

Returning to the legation that evening, Schulze noticed a yellow glow behind the building. Inside, he found Ettel in the boiler room, directing the incineration of secret papers. Assisting him were the SD chiefs, Franz Mayr and Roman Gamotha. Schulze asked if there were any instructions from Berlin regarding the status of their work. Mayr replied coldly, "No, but naturally I'm staying here"—indicating that he would go underground if the Allies entered Tehran. Schulze announced his intention to reach Afghanistan, to which Ettel shouted, "This is madness! You belong to the Diplomatic Corps and will return through Turkey with us." "Your Excellency," Schulze indulged, "my post as Vice Consul is finished. I now take my orders from Abwehr I in Berlin." Ettel fumed, "We'll see about that"— and stalked off.[45]

Southwest of Tehran on September 11, General Slim and Colonel Roberts approached the first Iranian checkpoint en route to the capital. In their disguises, they apprehensively halted their auto. The guard turned out smartly and presented arms. Each succeeding post followed suit. Reaching the British legation, they conferred with Sir Reader Bullard and General

Fraser. Bullard explained that Iran had been given 48 hours to hand over the Germans; otherwise, the British and Soviet armies would roll.[46]

In Berlin the next day, Ribbentrop told Hitler that the Soviets were demanding the surrender—by name—of 50 Germans in Iran. To avoid this, Ribbentrop sent a note via Bulgaria to Moscow, in which he offered to free 194 important Soviet citizens if the U.S.S.R. would allow the Germans in Iran safe conduct to Turkey. The Soviets rejected the proposal "without examination."[47]

But Hitler had other ideas, for his real wrath was directed against the British. He directed the Foreign Ministry that "for every German deported, ten selected Englishmen [would] be deported from the Jersey Islands to the Pripet Marshes" in the western Soviet Union. Hitler directed that the world be told by press and radio of the reasons for their deportation.[48]

The Foreign Ministry immediately instructed the feldkommandantur in the Channel Islands to prepare for large-scale deportation, but stressed that the fuehrer's order was provisional. The German garrison was able to identify—with great difficulty—about 1,200 British citizens who met the proper criteria. Although Hitler himself gave the order, it was not carried out, for some reason. A full year later, someone in Berlin finally discovered the oversight, and deportations to Germany were finally carried out.[49]

Back in Tehran on September 12, Ettel protested to Foreign Minister Soheili that Iranian troops and police had surrounded the legation summer residence. Soheili lamely ascribed this measure to reports of armed men within the compound. When pressed, he promised to withdraw the machine guns aimed at the camp.[50]

Meanwhile, Schulze drove with his wife to the German legation, in the hope of receiving instructions from Berlin on his request to remain behind. The legation was closed up, and the Swastika was furled around the flagstaff. Ettel had moved his staff to Shimran the previous evening. As the couple drove on to Shimran, they found the streets deserted; at every intersection, they saw an army–police patrol pacing the sidewalk.[51] They reached Shimran after dusk, and found the compound surrounded by Iranian police. Schulze used his diplomatic pass to enter; he thereupon located Ettel and asked if he might leave for Kabul. Ettel barked that "as far as I am concerned, you can go to hell." "Am I to take from your friendly reply," Schulze asked sarcastically, "that you received confirmation from Berlin?" Ettel replied, "Yes!"—and then walked away.[52]

Schulze then sought out a German named Hirschauer, who had volunteered to join his venture. He found Hirschauer sitting around a campfire with his drinking chums; they were roasting a sheep on a spit. After saying good-bye to his friends, Hirschauer packed his luggage into Schulze's car, and they drove off. Along the road to Esfahan, they encountered other autos heading in the same direction. Many wealthy Tehranians were also fleeing south.

At 5 P.M. that afternoon, the Iranian machine guns were still in place around the German compound. Ettel—feeling betrayed—suspended a meeting that had been scheduled with Foreign Ministry and police officials to clarify the list of German nationals who were to be surrendered to the Allies. Ettel refused to continue discussions until the machine guns were withdrawn. The Iranians hastily conferred. The guns were removed; and an hour later, the meeting resumed. The checking of lists was not completed until 10 P.M.[53] The British would take 292 German men into custody, while 29 were to be turned over to the Soviets. About 100 men over 45 years of age—including Jews—would remain under the care of the Swedish legation, pending further disposition.[54]

Director General Sayah of the Foreign Ministry then announced that the listed persons would have to be at the Tehran railway station by midnight. Stunned, Ettel protested that such a demand was impossible, for it would take at least three hours for the police to notify each person. They could not depart before morning—at the earliest. Ettel's reply brought Sayah nearly to tears, for his government had made promises that it could not keep. The British minister had set 10 P.M. on September 12 as the final time limit for the departure of the Germans, he explained. Any futher delay would threatened an immediate occupation of Tehran by the Soviets and British, who would round up the colony themselves.[55]

Hurriedly telephoning Foreign Minister Soheili, Sayah heatedly asked that a time extension be sought from Bullard. Indecision resulted. No Iranian official could summon the courage to approach the British minister. At 10:45 P.M., Sayah and another Foreign Ministry official left the legation; they were trembling with fear. Though disgusted by the scene, Ettel persuaded the Swedish chargé d'affaires—who was present—to seek the necessary extension.

The Swede consulted with the British and Soviet negotiators, Mr. Greenway and Mr. Ivanov. The negotiators conferred privately, and then decided to cancel the trains scheduled for that evening and to give the Germans until 5 A.M. to board the trains—or they would be "fetched."[56]

Learning of this, Ettel convened his staff and explained that any further delays would only jeopardize the safe conduct promises given in regard to the women and children. At 11:30 P.M., the German minister entered the compound and assembled the refugees. "The men must sacrifice themselves and go willingly into British or Russian captivity," he declared, "so that the women, children and old people can be allowed to return to Germany."[57] They must not, he advised, give the Allies any excuse to act on their own. Families weeped, realizing that the moment of truth had arrived. Many men could not muster the courage to part with their families.[58]

By 8 A.M. the next morning, Ettel had mustered only 80 men at the train station. Of these, 72 were to be sent under British guard to Ahvaz, and eight with the Soviets to Kazvin.[59] British newsman Richard Dimbleby watched the Germans as they lined up in ranks on the train platform, and he described the scene as follows:

> [There were] tubby Bavarians in knickerbockers and caps, men of Prussian build and bearing, and a few . . . sleek, black-haired, bespectacled characters who make the most fanatical Nazis. They had brought mountains of luggage. . . . At half-past eight, when the business of checking was done, the eighty marched down to the departure platforms. The German Minister and several of his staff were there, including . . . the boss of the Nazi Brown House. . . . They piled into the trains, throwing their luggage through the windows. . . . The whistle blew, the south-bound locomotive hooted in reply, and the first train began to move. At that moment the [Party boss] stepped forward. He parted his legs, thrust his left hand into the top of his breeches, flung out the right in the Nazi salute, and bellowed, "Für unseren Fuehrer—drei Sieg Heil!" From every window of the train hands shot out in answering salute, and the voices chorused "Sieg Heil! Sieg Heil! Sieg Heil!"[60]

The two allied governments were not pleased by what appeared to be the lack of German cooperation, and they notified Ettel that the remaining German men should be ready to depart without fail early on Monday morning, September 15.

Later on the morning of September 13, Maj. Gen. William Slim drove to Kazvin to meet with his Soviet counterpart, Maj. Gen. Vasily Novikov. Ten miles south of Kazvin, Slim's party overtook a British column en route to meet the Soviets. A Soviet guide led them to a parade ground outside Kazvin; the place was crowded with Soviet troops and tanks. The British found a festive welcome prepared. Tables were piled with food, and kettles bubbled with broth. Rousing speeches were exchanged, extolling the bravery of each army and excoriating the Germans. Slim and his party were then taken to the hotel that served as Novikov's headquarters. There, they were given a sumptuous feast, punctuated by endless toasts of vodka. Slim—a teetotaler—became inebriated, and was finally led by his Soviet escorts to his spacious but heavily guarded hotel room.[61]

In Tehran that night, Rev. William Miller recorded that "the fur is beginning to fly in Iran." He was referring to the reactions of the people to a Persian-language broadcast from London the previous evening. It had accused the shah of raising taxes 17 times over what they were in 1921. New Delhi Radio reported that the monarch had removed the crown jewels from the country. The ruler was further castigated for illegally imprisoning Gen. Ahmad Nakjevan; and his "tyrannical rule" was compared with that of the Nazis.[62]

The Majlis convened a special session at 9 P.M. on Sunday, September 14, to investigate the report that the shah had removed the crown jewels. Prime Minister Foroughi introduced his finance minister, Hassangoli Golshaian, who read a prepared letter; it explaining that all was in order, and invited the deputies to inspect the jewels personally. The legislators scoffed at these assurances and remained unsatisfied until, indeed, they were taken to the royal treasury to lay their own eyes on the jewels.[63]

In London that day, Churchill decided that the time had come for the Allied forces to occupy Tehran. The failure of the Germans to cooperate in the deportation clearly indicated that the authority of the shah's government was completely undermined. The growing tribal unrest in the south and west of Iran only strengthened this perception. Iran appeared to be on the verge of anarchy and revolution. Even if the shah could retain control, the recent editorial in *Ettellaat*—declaring that Iran would maintain relations with the Axis after the closing of the legations—left no doubt about the shah's sympathies. Only the timely intervention of Allied forces could redress the deteriorating situation—which, ironically, had been in no small part encouraged by the British themselves.[64]

The British Chiefs of Staff informed General Wavell in Cairo on September 14 that a combined British–Soviet advance to occupy Tehran would commence as soon as coordination with the Soviets was completed. London informed Moscow of its plans, and urged the Soviets to issue similar instructions to their commander in Iran. Both governments agreed to enter Tehran simultaneously, at 3 P.M. on September 17.[65]

In Tehran, Sir Reader Bullard informed the Iranian government that the capital would soon be occupied jointly by the British and the Soviets, once the details were worked out. At the British legation, German Jews anxiously crowded the building; they were seeking exemptions from the active Iranian police roundup of Germans.[66]

Aside from the Germans, the man in Tehran most wanted by the British was Haj al-Husseini, the Grand Mufti of Jerusalem. Rashid Ali had already slipped out of Iran to Turkey. The mufti and his Iraqi collaborators, however, remained behind in the listless luxury of a mountainside tourist hotel overlooking Tehran. When the Iranian police moved in to arrest the group, the mufti obtained sanctuary in the Japanese legation.[67]

That evening, the London Persian-language broadcast accused the shah of stealing land from the people and of forcing peasants to "sweat and toil to fill his pockets with gold." A popular opponent of the shah recited a poem comparing Reza Shah to the Persian tyrant, Zohak, who was overthrown by two heros, Feridun and Kava. And the poet asked, where were such men today?[68]

Before dawn on Monday, September 15, Brig. John Tiarks's Ninth Armoured Brigade was rolling eastward from Kermanshah on the initial leg of its march to Tehran. Accompanying the brigade were armored cars of the 13th Lancers, just arrived from Ahvaz. The First Household Cavalry Regiment led the column toward Malayir—112 miles distant—their initial stop. Though the poor roads caused many breakdowns, they reached the city by evening.[69]

The Soviet high command had meanwhile transmitted orders to their forces to advance to the outskirts of Tehran on the following morning, September 16. In Kazvin, General Novikov readied elements of the 24th Cavalry Division for an advance from the west. In Askhabad, Maj. Gen. Mikhail Kazakov faced an even more formidable task in moving elements of the 53d Independent Central Asian Army from the east. The nearest units to Tehran were the 39th Cavalry Division and a regiment of the 68th Mountain Infantry Divison at Semnan, 200 miles northeast. Kazakov's staff calculated that it would take two to three days of forced marching for the cavalry to reach the city. Instead, they developed a plan to move two separate groups toward the capital. A motorized detachment would drive overland, while a full regiment of the 68th Division would proceed by railway.[70]

Back in Tehran on September 15, parliamentary deputies in the Majlis openly criticized the shah and demanded constitutional reforms. One group requested a royal audience during which—they claimed boldly—they would urge his abdication. The British legation meanwhile informed the Iranian government that their forces were moving toward the capital and would enter jointly with the Soviets on the afternoon of September 17.[71]

Most of the remaining German men had surrendered that morning—as demanded—and were shipped off. 220 to Ahvaz, and 21 under Soviet guard to Kazvin. Nearly 150 Germans whose disposition remained undetermined remained in Tehran. These actions had come too late, however, to prevent the occupation.[72]

When news of the British advance reached the shah, he knew that he must abdicate, but struggled with himself as to whether to go through with it. He told his son, Crown Prince Mohammed Reza, that, because he was known as a strong and independent monarch who always acted only in what he believed was the best interest of Iran, he could never function as the puppet ruler of an occupied nation. "Do you think that I can receive orders from some little English or Russian captain?" he asked.[73]

That afternoon, the ruler summoned the prime minister to the palace. Foroughi replied that he was not well enough to leave home. The shah therefore broke all tradition and called on Foroughi at 3 P.M. The two men met in private for an hour.[74]

Afterward, the shah convened his last cabinet meeting and informed his ministers that he was soon leaving the country. He explained that some of them had rendered him excellent service but that he had never thanked or rewarded them because he alone could perform the "role of minority," due to his own supreme rule. The secret of his success—he claimed—was that he had never consulted with anyone, but rather studied problems quietly with seeming disinterest. "But this last year I tried to change this way," he admitted bitterly, "and consulted the Higher War Council on my proposal move into Iraq. If I had not done so, I would not now find myself in this situation."[75]

A special session of the Majlis was scheduled for the following morning. The interior minister informed the deputies that evening that an important announcement would be made during the assembly, and urged all to attend.[76]

If the shah remained at all uncertain about surrendering the throne, he did not have to wait long to decide. At 3 A.M. on September 16, the Soviet 24th Tank Regiment and 54th Mechanized Regiment of the 24th Cavalry Division rumbled eastward from Kazvin—getting an early jump on the British.[77]

News of the Soviet approach was telephoned to the shah at the palace. Believing that the Soviets were coming to overthrow him, he summoned the prime minister to the palace. Foroughi carefully drafted an abdication proclamation and handed it to the monarch, whose eyes were bloodshot from the constant stress and a painful ulcer that had aged him beyond his 63 years.[78]

"I, Shah of Iran, by the Grace of God and the nation, have taken the grave decision to withdraw and abdicate in favor of my beloved son, Mohammed Reza Pahlavi," Foroughi penned.[79] The paper cited age and failing health as the major reasons for stepping down. Reza Shah read the note several times. Finally, after ten minutes, he dipped the royal pen in the inkwell, shook off the excess ink, and then rapidly signed his name. He handed the note to Foroughi, who blotted the signature with a seal.[80]

"Take my car and go read this to the Majlis," Reza Pahlavi ordered. "Meanwhile, I have some things I want to say to my son."[81] Foroughi rushed out, but—instead of going to directly the Majlis—he stopped at the British legation at 7 A.M. to pleasingly display the paper to Sir Reader Bullard.[82]

Back at the palace, an emotional Reza Pahlavi spoke for the last time with his son, Mohammed Reza. "Can you keep the throne?" he asked. Mohammed remained silent. "I didn't fail to keep the throne," he insisted, "but forces stronger than me defeated me. I kept the throne for you. Will you be able to keep it?" The prince nodded. "Pay attention, my son," his father counseled. "Don't resist. We and the whole world are facing a storm that is bigger than any of us. Bow your head till the storm passes." As the shah started to leave, he added "Get a son!"—and then walked out to his waiting Rolls Royce. Shortly after 7 A.M., he was en route to Esfahan.[83]

Rev. William Miller was preparing to mail his weekly letters—in which he had described how Tehran was quiet and normal—when a fellow missionary rushed up. "Have you been in the street?" the man asked. Miller answered, "No, why?" "They say the Russians are coming in," the other man replied. A British friend ran up the street—warning, "The Russians have passed Karaj [25 miles from Tehran] with 50 tanks and a lot of armored cars, and will be here in half an hour. Tell the Americans to stay off the streets, there may be fighting. The King and his officers will probably send out troops to delay the advance till they can escape." A short while later, Miller was told that the Soviets had halted and weren't coming any closer. "Whether they are or not," he scribed, "they gave Tehran a real thrill, and probably more than one high official has again run for his life. I confess it gives me real pleasure to see these little gods who have terrorized the poor people of this land for so long now getting a dose of their own medicine. And I hope it will be a large and effective dose before the treatment ends!"[84]

Novikov's force reached Karaj at 7 A.M., and halted. The Iranian Air Force panicked and hurriedly flew their aircraft away from the capital. The Soviets were not to enter Tehran until 3 P.M. on September 17—more than 24 hours away—in coordination with the British. No Iranian troops were deployed, but a high police official was sent to discuss terms of occupation with Novikov. The British were still more than 200 miles away. On learning of the Soviet advance, the Ninth Armoured Brigade broke camp early; its 300 vehicle convoy swept through Malayir and on to Qum at 30 miles per hour.[85]

Shortly after 11 A.M., Prime Minister Foroughi entered the Parliament, accompanied by Speaker of the Parliament Esfandiary. Ascending the speaker's platform, Foroughi removed a paper from his briefcase. The crowd was silent. He announced that the shah had abdicated, and then read the full text of the resignation. When he finished, the deputies sat stunned. Foroughi then asked for a motion to ratify the act. Again, no one moved. Several men wept openly. Many whispered feverishly to each other. Finally, Esfandiary ordered the doors closed until the abdication was ratified. The vote was completed within half an hour. Two hours later, the news was announced by radio. Newspapers were rushed into the streets, with copies of the resignation.[86]

The papers quoted the shah as having "spent his strength in the service of his country." "Spent his strength," one Iranian remarked bitterly to Rev. William Miller, "he has given us the devil!" People filled the streets—joyfully cheering the announcement. But their glee was tempered by fear of the nearby Soviet forces.[87]

As the Allies approached Tehran, Churchill cabled Stalin, and emphasized his anxiousness to formalize an alliance with Iran and establish an "intimate working arrangement" with the Soviet occupation forces. He expressed concerned about

> signs of serious disorder among tribesmen and of breakdown of Persian authority. Disorder, if it spreads, will mean wasting our divisions holding down these people, which again means burden-

ing the road and railway communications with movements and supplies of aforesaid divisions, whereas we want to keep the lines clear and improved to the utmost in order to get supplies through to you. Our object should be to make the Persians keep each other quiet while we get on with the war. Your Excellency's decisive indications in this direction will speed forward the already favourable trend of our affairs in this minor theatre.[88]

Churchill's true intent—hardly disguised—was to discourage the almost inevitable inclination by the Soviets to undermine Iranian authority, to their own ultimate advantage. By downplaying Iran's importance, Churchill hoped—vainly, as it turned out—to pressure Stalin into openly voicing his compliance with these views.

Throughout that night in Tehran, Rev. William Miller heard speeding cars in the distance and wondered if the Soviets had arrived. The next morning—September 17—no one knew what was happening. But one young Iranian provided Miller with an unusual perspective on Iran's plight.

The evil that [the Shah] did is only a fraction of the good he accomplished. He was a powerful man. No man like him can be found in the East, and they might have accomplished much in his name. But now he is gone, and all the reactionary forces will break loose. He broke the power of the mullahs, but now they are all ready to take their revenge. . . . Already women have appeared in their veils. I was much displeased by the speeches which members of parliament made about the Shah, for they showed a lack of appreciation for what he accomplished. This just shows how very evil we are! It has been a great mistake.[89]

Seldom had Miller seen Iranians express gratitude and appreciation. The young man's sincerity touched him deeply.

Meanwhile, the Soviets were methodically encircling the city. By 6 A.M., they had established checkpoints and patrols along all the major exits. Tanks and armored cars lined the runway of the deserted Mehrabad Airport, on the western outskirts. On the eastern side, a detachment from the 53d Army arrived during the night at the train station nearest Tehran. In their enthusiasm, the small group prematurely entered the city at 10 A.M.— five hours ahead of schedule—to the complaint of the British. Shortly after 8 A.M., a British armored column drove through Qum en route to Tehran; it passed numerous cars hurrying in the opposite direction.[90]

At the Saadabad Palace, Crown Prince Mohammed Reza was pale with fear as he prepared for his trip to the Majlis to take the oath of office. He had no idea whether the people—who detested his father—would accept him as their new king, whether the army would remain loyal, and whether the

Allies might interfere with his coronation. His family had gone, leaving him to face an uncertain future alone. The security situation was chaotic, and the police disorganized. Many people opposed the monarchy. There were even rumors that the British favored crowning a Qajar prince who was serving in the Royal Navy. The climate seemed ripe for a revolution.[91]

In a northern suburb of Tehran that day, U.S. Consul James S. Moose cautiously watched events unfold. That afternoon, an Iranian friend told him that the only reliable troops remaining in the city were at the Bushanteteh barracks. A commander had been found for these troops—a general known to be a strict disciplinarian. The best thing about him, the friend added, was that he could not be bribed, for he had been awarded a small fortune by Reza Shah for suppressing the Lurs tribe. The general was Amir Ahmadi, who—though only recently released from the shah's prison—began restoring a sense of order to the garrison.[92]

That afternoon, the First Household Cavalry Regiment reached a bridge across a railway leading into Tehran, only to encounter Soviet pickets. Finding every road into the city blocked by Soviet checkpoints, the regiment pitched camp near the outlying town of Rei, and decided to delay their entrance until the next day.[93]

Tehran hardly looked like a city preparing to receive a new monarch, that afternoon. The streets were nearly vacant. People hid their automobiles, in fear that they would be stolen by the occupiers. No flags or decorations were displayed along the route of march for the crown prince. Rev. William Miller arrived an hour ahead of time to watch the procession. Police and soldiers were stationed every 50 yards, but the crowd was small and scattered. Passing the German legation, he noticed that the Swedish flag had replaced the Swastika. Near the parade route, he spoke with an embittered Iranian bank employee. "The new Shah!" the man growled. "It is ridiculous. No one wants him to be king! He is just like his father, and people are fed up with them both."[94]

As the hour approached, more people lined the street. But their attitude remained indifferent. Finally, the crowd heard the clopping of hoofs in the distance. A regiment of cavalry marched unsteadily down the avenue. Miller watched—feeling sorry for the horses, who had great difficulty walking on the slippery cobblestones. Several fell, and the embarrassed riders struggled to their feet to remount the steeds as best they could. In the midst of the horsemen came the royal car, moving slowly down the street. The crown prince sat in the backseat. As the car approached, Miller heard the crowd begin to clap. Their reaction surprised him, until he saw the reason. The young monarch was graciously bowing and smiling, as if saying that now he was their servant. Miller suddenly found himself caring about this young man's success. Miller turned to an Iranian near him. "What do you think of the change?" he asked. The man was skeptical, but encouraged. "Let's see what this one does," he answered.[95]

In his carriage, young Mohammed Reza drew confidence from the crowd's reaction, and a determination to retain the crown.[96] At the Parliament building, ministers in morning coats and generals in parade uniforms waited in the entrance hall. A Guards company and military band stood outside. Most of the dignitaries seemed gloomy or subdued. The British and Soviet ambassadors were conspicuously absent. The only diplomat present was the Japanese minister. Outside, the band struck up the national anthem as the crown prince arrived, at 4 P.M. The Guards shouted "Javid-bad-Ala-Hazrat"—the greeting for a new monarch. In parade uniform, Mohammed Reza entered the hallway—looking ashen, but composed.[97]

The senior Iranian general commanded, "Attention!" The civilians bowed courteously. All eyes followed the young monarch as he ascended the podium. Holding the Koran, he pledged to rule according to the constitution, and to ensure justice for all. The ceremony was brief, but solemn, and his well-delivered speech was soundly applauded. The new shah then left the assembly. Outside, a large crowd cheered loudly when he and Prime Minister Foroughi emerged. In Esfahan, his family listened intently to the ceremony on the radio. Hearing the cheering and applause, the old shah felt hope for his son at this turbulent hour.[98]

The former monarch was soon to leave Iran. On September 27, 1941, he and his family, boarded a British steamer at Bushire. They were taken to Bombay, and—escorted by a British political officer—then transferred to a second ship and sent to the island of Mauritius. Reza Pahlavi was not allowed to go to South America, as he had hoped. Instead, he and his family were moved several months later to Johannesburg, South Africa, where he died in 1944.[99]

Shortly after the coronation ceremony, the new shah issued several orders. He immediately dismissed Tehran's hated chief of police, Colonel Mohktary. He summoned Gen. Hassan Arfa to the palace, appointed him liaison officer to the British Army, and directed that he make contact with the English forces outside Tehran to arrange their billeting in the city.[100]

Driving to the British legation, General Arfa picked up the military attaché, Maj. Gen. W. A. K. Fraser, and an English lieutenant colonel. On Ferdowsi Street, they saw numerous cars and buses lined up in front of the German legation. Hundreds of tragic-looking German women and children were boarding vehicles for their passage through the Soviet lines. Arfa watched them sadly. The English colonel, however, joked that it was too bad the women were not being sent through the British zone. His vulgar humor infuriated Arfa, who replied, "I wonder in accordance with what law or treaty the nationals of a country friendly to an independent and neutral state are subjected to these indignities in the name of a struggle for freedom and justice?"[101]

Ettel and his wards met their Soviet escort on the eastern edge of Tehran late that afternoon. The women all wept uncontrollably. One mother begged an Iranian woman to give her some water for her crying baby. The Iranian woman refused, barking, "No! You are an infidel."[102]

Generals Arfa and Fraser were nearing Kahrizak when they spotted the armored cars and lorries of the Household Cavalry. Fraser introduced Arfa to Brigadier Aizelwood. At the same moment, a Soviet liaison officer arrived from General Novikov's column. The Soviet pulled out a map, and explained his army's marching dispositions. For that night—the group of officers agreed—the British would remain at Rei, and the Soviets at Mehrabad. They would enter Tehran together on the next day, September 18. The Soviets would be quartered at the Baghe-shah barracks, while the British would occupy the Skoda machine-gun factory east of Tehran.[103]

The next morning—September 18—the Soviets allowed the British to pass into Tehran.[104] The Italian legation grabbed this opening to sprint to the safety of the British zone. The British had reached the outskirts of the city when several luggage-laden autos bearing the Italian minister and several families pulled up to their lines. The Italians—who had diplomatic immunity—were permitted to pass on to Baghdad, and hence to Turkey.[105] In the process, the British failed to recognize the small, Semitic-looking man serving as the Italian minister's footman. The Grand Mufti of Jerusalem again slipped through British hands—and eventually continued on to Germany.[106]

General Slim learned that a number of German men, women, and children were still holed up in the German legation, and were refusing to leave. Many of them were wanted by the Allies, and there were rumors that they might resist arrest. Slim's Soviet liaison officer believed that the British would be reluctant to fire on the legation. "The Germans bombed my ninety-year old mother," Slim replied coldly, "and my children at school. If they refuse to come out, I should have few scruples about returning the compliment." To demonstrate his earnest, he ordered up several howitzers. But the remaining Germans—about 130—soon lost their nerve and rushed to the British lines. Among them were 30 men sought by the Soviets. Slim handed them over to Novikov's troops. A Soviet staff officer checked the list, and then thanked Slim for his help. "If there is anything you wish to know about these Germans—where they have been, what they have been doing, their contacts, or anything at all—just let us know and we'll tell you," he added.[107]

Slim asked how they would obtain this information, and the Soviet officer answered, "We shall interrogate them severely." Slim shuddered. As he wrote later, "War is war, but a 'severe' interrogation by our Allies was quite another thing!" Having no other choice, he reconciled himself by thinking that the Nazis were only getting a "dose of their own medicine."[108]

The two armies finally entered Tehran. They skirted the city center, to avoid the downtown boulevards. The British marched down one side of a street, and the Soviets down the other. The contrast between them was striking. The English were in their light summer khaki shorts, while the Soviets were clad in warmer, gray-green woolen uniforms. The sidewalk crowds of sullen, shabby-looking Iranians displayed little interest in either army.[109]

At the palace on September 17, the new shah had announced several decrees intended to repair the damage of his father's rule. He bequeathed his father's lands and riches as a "gift" to the nation. Much of the money was used immediately to pay government salaries. The shah also announced programs to reduce taxes, trim government spending, and rescind the practice of selling government land to individuals. A general amnesty for all political prisoners was also announced, and several troublesome tribal leaders were released from house arrest to return to their tribes.[110]

The next day—September 18—Erwin Ettel and his legation staff—together with 58 men, 274 women, and 136 children—reached the Iranian–Turkish border. Before they were allowed to pass the Soviet checkpoint, Soviet women sentries ransacked and plundered their baggage. One man who had diplomatic privilege was pulled off the bus and arrested.[111]

Great Britain and the U.S.S.R. formally recognized the government of the new shah on September 19.[112] In Tehran that day, Soviet soldiers rushed to the bazaar and busily bought up the consumer items that they had been longing for. British and Indian soldiers sought liquor—which outraged the abstentious Iranian Moslems.[113]

Elsewhere in Tehran, Rev. William Miller spoke with the patriotic young Iranian who had sympathized with the old shah. Miller asked him what he thought of things now. The man replied frankly.

> The British have made a great mistake. They have put our civilization back 25 years. The reforms brought about by Reza Shah with such difficulty are all being abolished. The new Shah in his oath promised to strive for the advancement of the Shiite religion, and all the mullahs and seyyids who had become grocers are now coming out of hiding. The Shah curbed the power of the local rulers, who were petty tyrants oppressing the people and killing whom they would. And now the authority will go back to them again. They say the Shah took people's property. It was from evil men like this that he took it, and developed it, and put it to good use. Yes, the progress of our civilization has been put back 25 years, and Tehran is now in a state of siege.[114]

Miller was again moved by the lad's intensity. "These are the opinions of an unusually thoughtful and sincere young man," he recorded, "but it seems that the great majority of the people think otherwise, or don't think at all."[115]

The British were already beginning to realize one mistake that they had made, in placing too much faith in the promises of their Soviet allies. That same day—September 19—Consul Cook in Tabriz warned that the Soviets were deliberately encouraging separatist tendencies in Azerbaijan. Before the end of September, the Soviets were calling for local elections in their zone; and in Tabriz, they distributed a propaganda newspaper—written in Farsi—that criticized the central government and encouraged the people to revolt against their "impoverished life." British Foreign Secretary Eden finally had to warn the Soviets against the "harmful" effects of "undue interference in Iranian affairs or sympathy towards separatist movements."[116] The invasion of Iran had eliminated one set of problems, only to create a set of new ones.

Abadan Refinery, Iran, from over the Shatt-al-Arab River. *Photograph by British Petroleum.*

Rajputanas March into Abadan Refinery Following Its Capture. *Photograph by British Petroleum.*

Axis Merchantman on Fire, Sunrise, August 25, 1941. *Photo Courtesy of the Imperial War Museum.*

Gen. A. P. Wavell, Commander in Chief, India (left), and Lt. Gen. E. P. Quinan, General Officer Commanding, Iraq (right). *Photo Courtesy of the Imperial War Museum.*

Iranian Sloop *Babr* after Being Shelled by HMAS *Yarra*. *Photo Courtesy of the Imperial War Museum.*

Major Abdullah Massoud of Iranian Cavalry (center) Discusses Cease-fire Terms with British Officers. *Photo Courtesy of Imperial War Museum.*

Iranian Troops near Zibiri Following Cease-fire. *Photo courtesy of Imperial War Museum.*

British Forces Enter Kermanshah, August 30, 1941. *Photo Courtesy of Imperial War Museum.*

British and Soviet Forces Meet South of Kazvin, August 31, 1941. *Photo Courtesy of Imperial War Museum.*

Maj. Gen. William Slim, Maj. Gen. Vasily Novikov, and Brig. James Aizelwood at Banquet in Kazvin. *Photo Courtesy of Imperial War Museum.*

Crown Prince Mohammed Reza Pahlavi at His Coronation Ceremony,
September 17, 1941. *Photo Courtesy of Imperial War Museum.*

Epilogue

The occupation of Iran and the ousting of the old shah was barely completed before the illusion of Anglo–Soviet cooperation began to break down. On October 3, 1941, Sir Reader Bullard warned London that he was "disturbed by signs that Soviet authorities here are suspicious of us," and noted that "the evidence suggests that the Soviet Government wishes to convert northern Persia to the Soviet idea before they leave, if they ever do leave." His advice was simple; "although our policy is directed towards increasing supplies to Russia . . . it is opposed to what must be the ultimate policy of Soviet Russia, namely the absorption of Persia."[1]

In the wake of the freedom that immediately followed the shah's downfall, many Iranian communists were released from prison. With Soviet backing, they quickly formed the Tudeh (Masses) party, and—through their de facto political control of the Soviet zone—soon became one of the predominant political parties.[2] In their haste to take over Iran, Soviet agents even approached the Iranian minister of war in October, and asked him to lead a pro-Soviet revolution.[3] Since the Soviet government was ignoring British advice on noninterference in Iranian affairs, Bullard pressed for the withdrawal of all Allied forces from Tehran in order to facilitate concluding a peace treaty between Britain, the U.S.S.R., and Iran. Ambassador Smirnov, however, opposed removing Soviet troops from Tehran "until everything is running smoothly."[4]

But events elsewhere suddenly changed Soviet policy on this matter. On September 26, 1941, the Germans captured Kiev—and with it, some 600,000 Soviet troops. The Nazi offensive against Moscow commenced on October 2; it surrounded three Soviet armies in the first five days. Stalin suddenly became so desperate for forces that he urged Churchill to dispatch 25–30 British divisions to reinforce the Red Army. Churchill termed this request "fantastic," and replied to Stalin that "our only interest in Persia are first, as a barrier against German penetration eastward, and secondly, as through route for supplies to the Caspian basin." However, Churchill shrewdly perceived an opportunity to remove the Soviets from Iran, and proposed that Stalin "withdraw the five or six Russian divisions [in Iran] for use on the battlefront." He added that Britain would take over internal security in Iran, and promised "not seek any advantage for ourselves at the expense of any rightful Russian interest." Stalin rebuffed the offer.[5]

The Iranian government—after much debate—acceded to the proposed terms for a Tripartite Treaty in December 1941.[6] But the young shah, who trusted neither the British nor the Soviets, needed to find a strong third power who would support Iranian interests. For him, Nazi Germany was not an option—although some of his generals were secretly involving themselves with Nazi agents—particularly Franz Mayr, who had remained behind in Iran and formed an underground organization that included General Zahidi, commander of the Esfahan garrison. Together, Mayr and Zahidi prepared plans for the Iranian Army to assist an eventual German invasion. Maj. Bertold Schulze eventually became the military advisor to Nasr Khan, the anti-British leader of the powerful Qashqai tribe in southern Iran.[7]

The new shah, however, looked toward the United States for support, especially with technicians and advisors. As Louis Dreyfus explained to Washington on November 5, 1941; "Iran is looking more and more to the United States for assistance and guidance, and we should not, I feel, miss the opportunity to improve our position."[8] The shah also sought direct U.S. participation in the Tripartite Treaty. Although Roosevelt declined, he told the shah that he was "gratified to observe among [the treaty's] provisions an undertaking by the Allied Powers to respect the territorial integrity, the sovereignty and the political independence of Iran."[9]

Stalin, who desperately needed Allied assistance to stem the German tide, finally agreed to the terms of the treaty proposed by Britain. On January 31, 1942, the three nations concluded the treaty in Tehran. A key provision called for all Allied powers to withdraw from Iran no later than six months after the war ended.[10]

In the meantime, in December 1941, the Red Army repulsed the Wehrmacht on the outskirts of Moscow. Hitler—in trying to seize the oil fields and save Iran from the Allies, and by waiting too late to advance on Moscow—had failed in his gamble, with apparent decisive and disastrous results for Germany. As former German General Staff officer, Maj. Gen. F. W. von Mellenthin explains,

> It will always be a question whether a different strategy on Hitler's part would have enabled us to force a decision in the critical year of 1941. The drive on Moscow, favored by [General Hans] Guderian, and temporarily abandoned in August in favor of the conquest of

the Ukraine, might have yielded decisive results if it had been ruthlessly pursued.[11]

Despite their local victory, however, the Soviets girded for the powerful Nazi offensive expected in the spring of 1942. To meet it, they urgently needed U.S. war supplies.

To expedite the transport of supplies to the Soviet Union, U.S. technicians and equipment began pouring into Iran in early 1942. By July, truck and aircraft assembly plants were in full operation, with large shipments being sent north over the Iranian railway.[12] At Iran's request, U.S. advisors were loaned to the Iranian government. Dr. Arthur C. Millspaugh returned with a team of financial advisors to reorganize the Finance Ministry. U.S. military officers advised and directed the Iranian Army and Gendarmerie. As Wallace Murray proudly admitted to Under Secretary of State Sumner Welles on August 3, 1942; "We shall soon be in the position of actually 'running' Iran."[13]

Hitler was determined to finish what he had begun the previous year. On April 5, 1942, he directed that "all available forces are to be combined for the main operations in the southern sector . . . in order to gain the oil region in the Caucasian area and to cross the Caucasus Mountains."[14] The offensive against the Caucasus opened on June 25. The Soviet line crumbled; and Rostov—the key to the Caucasus—fell on July 23. German forces poured south, reaching the northern foothills of the Caucasus and capturing the Maikop oil fields on August 9. In Africa, meanwhile, Gen. Erwin Rommel's Afrika Korps pressed the British Eighth Army back to El Alamein, and threatened to break through to the Suez Canal and beyond.

Churchill—desperately worried about the looming Nazi threat to the Baku and Iranian oil fields—flew to the Soviet Union on August 12 to confer with Stalin, and even offered Anglo–American air forces to assist the beleaguered Red Army. Stalin confidently assured him that "we shall stop them. They shall not cross the mountains." But he did admit that his army was critically short of trucks.[15]

Without sufficient trucks to transport troops and supplies, the Soviets could neither mount nor sustain a major counteroffensive. Also, Stalin had secretly stripped all available Soviet forces in Iran to reinforce the Caucasus defenses, leaving only token units behind.[16]

The German offensive into the Caucasus pressed forward, but was weakened because Hitler demanded a simultaneous advance on the vital industrial city of Stalingrad. Even so, three key passes through the Caucasus were captured on August 18, and a German climbing party scaled Mount Elbrus—the highest peak in the range—on August 21.[17] The Soviet government declared a "state of emergency" in the Transcaucasus on August 24. The next day, German forces captured Mozdok, but stalled on the Terek River.[18] The Nazi wave of conquest had crested.

In the meantime, U.S. aid was reaching the Red Army in increasing quantities. Churchill had discovered that the British-run trans-Iranian railway was working at only half capacity. He therefore accepted a U.S. offer to take over management of the railway. When one British general objected that this would leave the British dependent on the Americans for supplies, Churchill snapped, "In whose hands could we be better dependent?"[19] Little did he realize that this decision effectively eschewed Britain's role in Iran, in favor of the United States.

To better manage the Soviet aid program, the U.S. Army formed the Persian Gulf Command, and soon poured 30,000 logistics troops into Iran. By November 1942, the United States had shipped more than 400,000 trucks, 27,000 aircraft, and 28,000 tanks and half-tracks to the U.S.S.R. through the Persian Gulf.[20]

Infused with new vigor by U.S. aid, the Soviet forces around Stalingrad methodically prepared for their coming attack. Gen. Georgi K. Zhukov, who led these forces, wrote; "To prepare for the counteroffensive, stupendous movements of troops and material were affected for all the fronts especially the newly organized Southwest Front. . . . A total of 27,000 vehicles were employed to transport troops and freight. . . . There can be no denial that [U.S.] supplies . . . were of certain help." Soviet motor transport moved 2,700,000 men and 12.3 million tons of cargo during 1942.[21]

The massive Soviet offensive commenced on November 19 and made immediate gains. Stalingrad was quickly surrounded, and the entire German Sixth Army was forced to surrender on February 2, 1943. The Germans hurriedly withdrew their forces from the Caucasus before they were cut off. Iran was out of danger. But without the Allied occupation—which enabled the flow of U.S. supplies—the outcome might well have been different.

The tide turned decisively against Germany in 1943. The British Eighth Army routed Rommel at El Alamein; and an Anglo–American army landed in French North Africa, and drove the Germans and Italians into a small pocket in Tunisia. In Iran that year, the British finally captured Mayr and Schulze—which ended Nazi intrigues there.

The Soviets, however—with victory in sight—intensified their subversive activities in Iran. But the situation had changed, for now the United States was effectively a full player. British and U.S. officials agreed on January 8, 1943, to "coordinate their policies and stand together in Iran." The State Department pressed for strengthening Iran internally in order to "remove any excuse for a post-war occupation, partition or tutelage of Iran." The department noted that "Iran constitutes a test case for the good faith of the United Nations" and that "nowhere else in the Middle East is there to be found so clear-cut a conflict of interests between two of the United Nations."[22]

In preparing Roosevelt for his famous "Big Three" conference in Tehran, Secretary of State Hull warned that,

> if events are allowed to run their course unchecked, it seems likely that either Russia or Britain, or both, will be led to take action which will seriously abridge, if not destroy, effective Iranian independence. . . . From a more directly selfish point of view, it is to our interest that no great power be established on the Persian Gulf opposite the important American petrolem development in Saudi Arabia.[23]

When Roosevelt met with Churchill and Stalin in Tehran in November 1943, he persuaded the other two to sign a three-party declaration respecting Iran's desire to maintain her "independence, sovereignty, and territorial integrity."[24]

But the Soviets continued to undermine the Allies and the central government in Iran. No political parties other than the Tudeh were permitted in the Soviet zone.[25] The Soviets banned Western reporters from their zone, and their censors on the three-power censor board allowed no negative coverage of Soviet activities. In fact, the Soviets were even willing to bite the hand that was feeding them: On November 4, 1944, *Isvestia* criticized the presence of U.S. service troops in Iran.[26]

A major crisis erupted between Iran and her northern neighbor in September 1944 when the U.S.S.R. demanded an oil concession in northern Iran. To back their demands, 40,000 Soviet reinforcements poured into their zone. The Iranian government and the Majlis refused the demands, and Tudeh-inspired riots resulted. The Iranian government stood fast, but changes in its cabinet resulted.[27]

Harry S. Truman succeeded to the U.S. presidency after the death of Franklin Roosevelt on April 12, 1945. In preparing for the Potsdam conference, Truman received briefing papers from the State Department, warning that "the Near East is rapidly developing into one of the vital danger spots in world relationships."[28] At Potsdam, Truman proposed—without success—the early withdrawal of all Allied troops from Iran.

Iran was indeed rapidly becoming the focus of postwar friction, as instances of Soviet interference mounted. The Iranian government discovered pro-Soviet plotters in its Meshed garrison, and also Soviet-inspired plans for an independent Kurdistan.[29] U.S. Ambassador Wallace Murray—Dreyfus's successor—warned Washington on September 25, 1945, that he regarded the situation in Iran with

> grave concern. . . . Ultimate Russian objectives may include access to Persian Gulf and penetration into other regions of the Near East. . . . Soviet dominance of Iran Government would be defi-

nitely harmful to American interest. . . . I am strongly of the opinion [that the] time has come for us to take positive stand against . . . present Soviet activities.[30]

Anglo–American appeals to the U.S.S.R. for the early withdrawal of forces from Iran were rebuffed. The last U.S. troops left Iran on December 31, 1945—with the British Army pulling out the next day. Some 70,000 Soviet troops remained in northern Iran.[31]

The situation deteriorated in November and December 1945, with a full-scale communist uprising in Azerbaijan. The Soviets aided the Azerbaijani rebels—who were led by Tudeh leader Jivad Pishevari—and prevented the Iranian Army from dispatching troops to quell the insurrection. Isolated Iranian garrisons in the Soviet sector fell, one after the next.[32] On December 15, Murray cabled Washington that the "feeling is widespread that [the] only hope for Iranians is American assistance. Impression is growing that British are not particularly interested."[33]

The British government under the Labor party of Clement Atlee took a different view of Iran from that of its predecessor. The first priority became postwar reconstruction, while the slow process of dismembering the overseas empire was begun. Britain's only real objective in Iran was to protect her interests in the oil field region of Khuzistan. The British seemed quite content to leave the growing crisis for the Americans to handle.

The Iranian government realized this. Ambassador Hussein Ala appealed directly to Truman for support on September 28, 1945:

> In this critical situation, I earnestly beg you . . . to continue to stand up for the rights of Iran. . . . Your country alone can save us, for you have always defended moral ideas and principles and your hands are clean.[34]

In response, Secretary of State James Byrnes flew to Moscow in mid-December; he explained to Stalin the U.S. desire to withdraw all troops from Iran in accordance with the 1942 Tripartite Treaty. Stalin replied that he had no confidence in the Iranian government, and intended to keep his forces in Iran until March 15, 1946, in order to protect the Baku oil fields from "saboteurs." Byrnes reminded him that March 2—not March 15—was the final deadline for withdrawal, and urged Stalin to take no action in Iran that would cause a rift in the U.S.–Soviet alliance.[35] Afterward, Byrnes remarked privately that he expected "real trouble over Iran."[36]

In January 1946, the Soviets engineered a change in the Iranian government, which made the frail and aging Qavam-es-Saltaneh the prime minister. Moscow expected Qavam to prove malleable to their will. The new prime minister immediately announced that he intended to visit Moscow and negotiate with Stalin directly. He was cordially received on February

19, and spent the next three weeks in secret negotiations. However, Qavam proved less pliable than expected, and told Molotov that the Majlis would never accept an autonomous Azerbaijani government.[37]

Stalin told Qavam that he would not withdraw his forces, and cited the 1921 treaty as justification for their retention. When Qavam quoted the treaty and noted that it did not apply, Stalin responded that "Soviet honor was involved" and that Soviet "interests" required the continued presence of its forces in Iran.[38]

On March 28, 1946—two days before the final deadline—Secretary Byrnes publicly warned that the U.S. government had a "responsibility to use our influence to see that other powers live up to their convenant. . . . We must make it clear in advance that we do intend to act to prevent aggression, making it clear at the same time that we will not use force for any other purpose."[39] The timing of Byrnes's warning implied that it referred to Soviet actions in Iran. It further implied that the United States would revert to the use of armed force to thwart Soviet military action, if all peaceful means failed.

When the deadline for withdrawal of forces arrived, Moscow merely announced that only Soviet forces in northeastern Iran would be withdrawn—and, "as regards Soviet troops in other districts of Iran, they will remain pending examination of the situation."[40] The next night, the U.S. consul in Tabriz, Robert Rossow, reported that Soviet forces there were moving out in the direction of Tehran. Soviet movements continued for the next two days. Red Army units reached Karaj, outside Tehran.[41] On March 5, the U.S. and British governments presented notes to the U.S.S.R., in which they protested the continued presence of Soviet military forces in Iran.[42]

A map displaying the Soviet movements in Iran was shown to Secretary Byrnes on March 6. After studying the map, he slammed his fist into his hand, and exclaimed, "Now we'll give to them with both barrels." The next morning, a cable from Consul Rossow in Tabriz noted the arrival of fresh Soviet units: "Soviet troop reinforcements continue arriving night and day by truck and rail from the Soviet frontier, and are constantly being redeployed here." Rossow added that they were "ready for combat."[43]

In response, the U.S. Navy announced on March 8 that the USS *Missouri* was being dispatched to Istanbul to deliver the body of the deceased Turkish ambassador.[44] This move had been considered as a means of displaying U.S. resolve in the Middle East. Secretary of State Byrnes even weighed dispatching a full naval task force to the area.[45]

Qavam returned to Tehran on March 10—to a cheering crowd—and immediately briefed the young shah on his trip. He also announced that he would keep the Iranian issue on the agenda of the UN Security Council. The Soviet chargé d'affaires in Tehran warned Qavam that the planned Iranian complaint would be viewed as an "unfriendly and hostile act." The plea for withdrawal of Soviet forces was submitted to the United Nations two days later by Iranian Ambassador Hussein Ala, who accused the U.S.S.R. of "continuing to interfere in the internal affairs of Iran."[46]

Soviet Ambassador Andrei Gromyko pressed for postponing a hearing on the issue until April 10.[47] It became clear that, should Iran or the United States yield on this point, the whole issue would be lost—for the Soviets would have time to engineer the downfall of the Iranian government. The U.S. chargé in Moscow, George Kennon, provided his view on March 17 that the "Soviets must make some effort in immediate future to bring into power in Iran a regime prepared to accede to Soviet demands." He noted that the Soviet Union had "no intention of withdrawing its troops from Iran." "They are doubtless prepared to face very serious diplomatic and political difficulties," he asserted, "but to attain their objectives they will try to gauge their action, if our hypothesis is correct, in such a way as to stop just short of the decisive point. It is not like the Kremlin to blunder casually into situations, implications of which it has not thought through."[48]

Buoyed by this assessment, Truman met with Byrnes and Adm. William D. Leahy, chairman of the Joint Chiefs of Staff, to discuss the crisis. As Truman saw it, three major issues were involved: (1) the security of Turkey, which was also under Soviet pressure to grant rights and concessions; (2) the threat of the Soviets gaining control over the vast Iranian oil reserves and being in a position to threaten the U.S. position in the Persian Gulf; and (3) the belief that international cooperation would be impossible if the Soviet Union could ignore solemn promises, bypass the United Nations, and trample on the rights of small nations.[49]

Truman had one important trump card—and Stalin was well aware of it. The United States held a monopoly on atomic weapons; and, by bombing Hiroshima and Nagasaki several months earlier, Truman had displayed a willingness to use these horrifying weapons, if required. Truman therefore directed Byrnes to send a highly secret—but pointed—note to Stalin, demanding that the Soviet forces be withdrawn.[50] He then held a press conference on March 21 at which he stated that the U.S. government would not agree to the Soviet request for a postponement. Instead, it would insist on an immediate consideration of Iran's case.[51]

Afterward, Truman summoned W. Averell Harriman to the White House. He appointed him envoy to Britain, and warned Harriman that "there's a very dangerous situation developing in Iran. The Russians are refusing to take out their troops . . . and this may lead to war."[52]

In the face of U.S. strength and steadfastness, Stalin crumbled. On March 25, TASS announced that all Soviet forces would be withdrawn within five to six weeks.[53] The last Red Army units left Iran in early May—leaving behind the Tudeh-controlled government of Azerbaijan and an independent Kurdistan.[54]

The Iranian government now concentrated on regaining control of these provinces. Support from the United States became increasingly firm. The Joint Chiefs of Staff favored strengthening Iran with military hardware. A new State Department policy stated on October 18, 1946, that "The Iranian question . . . involves the defense of our military interests in the entire Near and Middle Eastern area." Ambassador Allen was directed to tell the shah and Prime Minister Qavam that, so long as Iran was willing to stand up against "external pressure," the United States would support Iranian independence—"not only by words but by appropriate acts."[55]

Buoyed by this commitment, the Iranians dispatched three army columns into Azerbaijan and Kurdistan in early December. The Soviets made threatening noises, but did not directly interfere. The Azerbaijani army made a brief but futile stand outside Mianeh on December 10, but was soundly defeated. Pishevari and the other Tudeh leaders in Tabriz panicked and fled to the Soviet border. The people of Tabriz rose in rebellion—murdering hundreds of communists before the Iranian Army arrived on December 13 and restored order. Throngs cheered its entrance into the city.[56]

From Tabriz on the day the communist government collapsed, U.S. Consul Lester Sutton telegraphed Tehran that

> The pall has lifted. Just a year and a day after it was founded, the Democratic regime of Azerbaijan crumbled in a few hours yesterday. . . . It was evident that the people had no wish to fight and that [the] leaders could count on little or no support. Today it is as if we live in a different city. . . . I have never seen so many smiling faces since I came to Azerbaijan. They are relieved and happy.[57]

At this, the last vestige of the 1941 British and Soviet invasion was removed. But the question of the legality and morality of their initial action persists—for which there is no simple answer. That both powers committed aggression in attacking Iran without warning is beyond question. But that control of Iran and its vital railway and oil resources was essential to the prosecution and ultimate outcome of the war is also almost without argument. Therefore, the question focuses on the means, rather than the ends.

Shah Reza Pahlavi—though not specifically pro-Nazi—nevertheless wanted Germany to defeat the Soviet Union, and was not (probably under any circumstances) likely to submit to a formal alliance with the Allies, especially with Germany still victorious. Even so, it can be argued that Britain's policy lacked honesty of purpose, and should have been straightforward. The primary factor mitigating against this was the British belief that the shah would remain stubborn and, therefore, an ultimatum would be required. This would have jeopardized the vital element of surprise—so absolutely essential to safely securing the vulnerable and strategically vital Abadan oil refinery. Therefore, the British felt compelled—with some justification—to attack without warning.

The U.S. government was also not blameless. It could have—and probably should have—done more to support Iran's position. But Roosevelt had already agreed to the Anglo–Soviet action, even though he did not at the time fully understand its implications. This agreement seems to have resulted in some American guilt over the U.S. role in the affair; and this led ultimately to the U.S. guarantee to ensure respect for those Iranian rights that Roosevelt had so casually disregarded in his August 1941 meeting with Churchill. This, in turn, developed into full-scale U.S. involvement in Iran, and to the United States displacing Britain as the main anti-Soviet counterweight.

Lastly, the Soviet Union's intentions in Iran were—from the beginning—more extensive and insidious than those of Britain or the United States. The Soviet desire to control Iran was driven by both strategic and ideological reasons. Iran could provide vast oil resources and an outlet to the open oceans. Control of Iran could also better protect the Soviet Union's vital but vulnerable southern border. Furthermore, Iran provided an excellent base for communist infiltration of the Middle East.

The dictatorial and expansionist history of the Soviet system—particularly under Stalin—is well known; and its actions and intentions in Iran must be judged in that light, and not by the same standards applied to the West. In this regard, perhaps the most interesting aspect of Soviet involvement in the Allied scheme against Iran was the incredible naiveté of the British belief that the Soviets would adhere to their pledges—no matter how solemnly those pledges may have been given. For, in the light of history, it is impossible to imagine that the Soviet's would have compliantly withdrawn from an established position in Iran without first requiring the most determined political and military pressure, such as occurred in early 1946.

The result was a showdown between the Soviet Union and the United States—so serious that it threatened a third world war. Had the United States not accurately gauged Stalin's reaction, it could have been forced to proceed to military measures. What measures these might have been are a matter of speculation. It seems unlikely that Truman would have immediately dropped an atomic bomb on Baku or some other strategic Soviet target. Certainly, there were no U.S. forces in the area immediately capable of threatening Soviet forces in Iran. For that matter, the state of U.S. military readiness at that point was abysmal. But—regardless—Stalin was shrewd and cautious enough to realize that Truman meant business and had the fortitude to follow through with his threats.

In the end, the issue of the rightness of the Anglo–Soviet invasion of Iran remains a perplexingly elusive question. The fundamental issue for Britain and the United States was whether strategic necessity—which ultimately involved the fate of all free (democratic) nations—morally or legally permitted unprovoked and unannounced violent aggression. Unfortunately, in the case of Iran, the answer must be in the affirmative. As has been explored and explained above, no way existed for the Allies to gain the control that they required over Iran's vital communications system and mineral wealth without resort to force. The shah would never have acquiesced to Allied requirements so long as Germany appeared triumphant. What purpose would have been served had Britain scrupulously observed international law—no matter how moral the basis of that convention—if the result were to ultimately lose a mammoth struggle for freedom versus certain tyranny?

This ultimate conclusion (which is not beyond unending dispute) does in no way dismiss many of the expedient and questionable political and military actions either undertaken or proposed by the British against Iran, prior to the invasion. The British must also be faulted for not later strongly supporting Iran against Soviet intrigues and ambitions, since it was the British who had placed the Iranians in that precarious situation. The fact that Britain was governed by a different political party—with a different agenda and policies—in no way changes the moral burden undertaken initially and then confirmed in subsequent promises to guarantee Iranian sovereignty and independence. Therefore, the invasion of Iran provides a classic example of the type of moral dilemma posed to democratic nations who are struggling to survive against regimes determined on their destruction.

Notes

See the Bibliography for translations of the foreign-language titles. Also, the following abbreviations are used in these notes, for the purpose of brevity:

DGFP U.S. Department of State, *Documents on German Foreign Policy*, Series D, vol. 9–13 (Washington, D.C.: Government Printing Office, 1956–64).

FRUS U.S. Department of State, *Foreign Relations of the United States, 1940–1946* (Washington, D.C.: Government Printing Office, 1958–69).

PRO Her Majesty's Public Records Office, various files.

INTRODUCTION

1. Winston S. Churchill, *The Second World War: The Grand Alliance* (Boston: Houghton Mifflin, 1950), p. 477.

2. Winston S. Churchill, *The Second World War: The Gathering Storm* (Boston: Houghton Mifflin, 1948), p. 547. The relevant passage is quoted below in the text, at the end of the Introduction.

3. Sir Reader Bullard, *The Camels Must Go* (London: Faber and Faber, 1961), p. 227.

4. Churchill, *Gathering Storm*, p. 547.

CHAPTER 1

1. George N. Curzon, *Persia and the Persian Question*, vol. 1 (London: Longmans, Green and Company, 1892), pp. 3–4.

2. For this period of Iranian history, see David Marshall Lang, *The Last Years of the Georgian Monarchy, 1658–1832* (New York: Columbia University Press, 1957), pp. 111–16, and 220–23; J. B. Kelly, *Britain and the Persian Gulf, 1795–1880* (Oxford: Oxford University Press, 1968), pp. 63–72; and Firuz Kazemzadeh, *Russia and Britain in Persia, 1864–1914* (New Haven, Conn.: Yale University Press, 1968), pp. 8–9.

3. PRO, FO65-1202.

4. Minute by Commander in Chief Napier of Magdala (Government of India, Foreign Department, No. 123 of 1875; India Office Records: four, Letters from India, 1875).

5. The following sources cover the period of Iranian history leading to the 1907 Convention of Leningrad: Sir Percy Sykes, *A History of Persia,* vol 2 (London: Macmillan and Company, 1951), pp. 369–70; and Nasrollah S. Fatemi, *Oil Diplomacy: Powderkeg in Iran* (New York: Whittier Books, 1954), pp. 8, and 18–24.

6. For text of convention clauses dealing with Persia, see J. C. Hurewitz, *Diplomacy in the Near and Middle East,* vol. 1 (Princeton, N.J.: Princeton University Press, 1956), pp. 266–67.

7. The following sources cover the period of Iranian history leading to the 1921 coup d'état: Mohammed Reza Shah Pahlavi, *Mission for my Country* (New York: McGraw-Hill, 1961), pp. 36–38; George Lenczowski, *Russia and the West in Iran, 1918–1948* (Ithaca, N.J.: Cornell University Press, 1949), pp. 15–17, 45–46, and 52; and Donald N. Wilber, *Riza Shah Pahlavi* (Hicksville, N.Y.: Exposition Press, 1975), pp. 9–15, and 40–43.

8. Pahlavi, *Mission,* pp. 45–46; Peter Avery, *Modern Iran* (London: Ernest Benn, 1965), pp. 246–49; and Lenczowski, *Russia and West,* pp 70–71, and 317. For complete text of the 1921 treaty, see Faramarz S. Fatemi, *The U.S.S.R. in Iran* (London: A. S. Barnes and Company, 1980), pp. 192–94.

9. The following sources cover Reza Shah's consolidation of power: Lenczowski, *Russia and West,* pp. 59–60; and Wilber, *Riza Shah,* pp. 73, 98–99, 106–7, 114–15, 166–67, 254–55, and 260–63.

10. Arthur C. Millspaugh, *Americans in Persia* (Washington, D.C.: Brookings Institution, 1946), pp. 22–24, and 25fn.

11. Ibid., p. 26fn.

12. Wilber, *Riza Shah,* pp. 123–24, 169–70, and 175; and Fatemi, *Oil Diplomacy,* pp. 104–37.

13. The following sources cover German involvement in Iran up to World War II: L. P. Elwell-Sutton, *Modern Iran* (London: George Rutledge and Sons, 1941), pp. 164–65; DGFP, vol. 8, p. 335; R. K. Karanjia, *The Mind of a Monarch* (London: George Allen and Unwin, 1977), p. 41; Lenczowski, *Russia and West,* pp. 153 and 161; Wilber, *Riza Shah,* p. 147, and 162–63; and Pahlavi, *Mission,* pp. 66–67.

14. Wilber, *Riza Shah,* p. 182.

15. Millspaugh, *Americans,* pp. 24–25.

16. The following sources cover the development of the shah's military: Gen. Hassan Arfa, *Under Five Shahs* (London: John Murray, 1964), p. 325; U.S. National Archives, "History, Traditions, and Mission of the Iranian Army," Attaché Report R-26-45, RG 226, pp. 5–6; and George Lenczowski (ed.), *Iran under the Pahlavis* (Stanford, Calif.: Stanford University Press, 1978), p. 393.

17. U.S. National Archives, MID-233737, June 20, 1940, RG 165.

18. Wilber, *Riza Shah,* p. 175.

19. For a complete text of the treaty, see Raymond James Sontag and James Stuart Beddies (eds.), *Nazi–Soviet Relations, 1939–1941* (Washington, D.C.: Government Printing Office, 1948), pp. 76–78.

CHAPTER 2

1. Ashraf Pahlavi, *Faces in the Mirror* (Englewood Cliffs, N.J.: Prentice-Hall, 1980), p. 39.
2. Wilber, *Riza Shah*, pp. 192–93; FRUS, *1940*, vol. 3, p. 633; and DGFP, vol. 8, p. 353.
3. FRUS, *1940*, vol. 3, p. 621.
4. Ibid.; Wilber, *Riza Shah*, p. 193.
5. DGFP, vol. 8, p. 355.
6. FRUS, *1940*, vol. 1, p. 449.
7. Sir Llewellyen Woodward, *British Foreign Policy in the Second World War*, vol 1. (London: Her Majesty's Stationery Office, 1970), p. 27.
8. David J. Dallin, *Soviet Russia's Foreign Policy, 1939–1942* (New Haven, Conn.: Yale University Press, 1942), p. 111.
9. FRUS, *1940*, vol. 3, p. 626.
10. DGFP, vol. 8, p. 419.
11. FRUS, *1940*, vol. 3, p. 625.
12. Ibid., p. 626.
13. PRO, Chiefs of Staff Report, Febuary 23, 1940, War Cabinet Minutes, CAB 66, vol. 5, W.P. (40) 18.
14. Woodward, *British Foreign Policy*, vol. 1, pp. 10–12.
15. PRO, Appreciation by Chiefs of Staff Committee, October 6, 1939, War Cabinet Minutes, CAB 66, vol. 2, W.P.(39) 73.
16. Bisheshwar Prasad (ed.), *Official History of the Indian Armed Forces in the Second World War, 1939–1945: The Campaign in Western Asia* (Calcutta: Sree Sarawata Press, 1957), p. 32.
17. Ibid., pp. 33–34.
18. PRO, Review of Military Policy in the Middle East, December 1939, War Cabinet Minutes, CAB 66, W.P.(39) 148.
19. PRO, Military Policy in the Middle East, January 13, 1940, War Cabinet Minutes, CAB 66, W.P.(40) 18. See also Maj. Gen. I. S. O. Playfair, *The Mediterranean and the Middle East*, vol. 1 (London: Her Majesty's Stationery Office, 1954), p. 62.
20. PRO, Chiefs of Staff Report, February 23, 1940, War Cabinet Minutes, CAB 66, W.P. (40) 66.
21. PRO, FO371-24855-4368.
22. See Prasad, *Campaign in Western Asia*, pp. 34–37, and 43–45, for TROUT planning and Lane study.
23. Woodward, *British Foreign Policy*, vol. 1, pp. 71–76.
24. *Die Geheimakten des Franzoesischen Generalstabes*, vol. 6 (Berlin: Reich Foreign Minstry, 1941), docs. 19 and 22.
25. PRO, Chiefs of Staff Report, March 8, 1940: Military Implications of Hostilities with Russia in 1940, War Cabinet Minutes, CAB 66, W.P. (40) 91.
26. Woodward, *British Foreign Policy*, vol. 1, p. 109.
27. *Geheimakten*, doc. 26.
28. Woodward, *British Foreign Policy*, vol. 1, p. 110.
29. Churchill, *Gathering Storm*, p. 547.
30. Woodward, *British Foreign Policy*, vol. 1, pp. 110–12.

31. Francis H. Hinsley, *British Intelligence in the Second World War,* vol. 1 (New York: Cambridge University Press, 1979), pp. 198–99; and J. Weygand (trans. J. H. F. McEwen), *The Role of General Weygand* (London: Eyre and Spottiswoode, 1948), p. 37.

32. New York *Times,* March 30, 1940.

33. Data on Soviet reinforcement of the Transcaucasus and drawn from the following sources: *Krasnoznamennyi Zakavkavskii* (Moscow: Military Publishing House, 1969), pp. 146–47; *Sovetskaia Voennaia Entsiklopediia,* vol. 3 (Moscow: Military Publishing House, 1976–81), p. 370; (Mar.) Andrei Grechko, *Bitva za Kavkaz* (Moscow: Military Publishing House, 1971), p. 28; and P. W. Fabry, *Iran, Die Sowjet Union und das Kriegfuehrende Deutschland im Sommer und Herbst 1940* (Gottingen: Muster-Schmidt Verlag, 1980), p. 11. Numbers of Soviet troops and tanks are based on standard unit strengths during that period. See John Erickson, *The Soviet High Command: A Political History, 1918–1941* (New York: Macmillan, 1962), pp. 507 and 585fn.

34. U.S. Army, *History of the Great Patriotic War,* vol. 1, unedited trans. distributed by the Office of the Chief of Military History, U.S. Army (Moscow: Military Publishing House, 1961), pp. 284 and 374; and *Entsiklopediia,* vol. 3, p. 370.

35. *Krasnoznamennyi Turkestanskii* (Moscow: Military Publishing House, 1976), pp. 133–37.

36. *Geheimakten,* doc. 34.

37. Gen. Maxime Wevgand (trans. E. W. Dickes), *Recalled to Service* (Garden City, N.Y.: Doubleday, 1952), pp. 40–41; and *Geheimakten,* doc. 38.

38. FRUS, *1940,* vol. 3, p. 631.

39. DGFP, vol. 9, p. 384.

40. Playfair, *Mediterranean,* vol. 1, pp. 89–90.

41. Gen. André Beufre (trans. Desmond Flowe), *1940: The Fall of France* (London: Cassell and Company, 1965), p. 172fn; and Dallin, *Soviet Foreign Policy,* p. 166fn.

42. PRO, FO371-24583-2058.

43. Prasad, *Campaign in Western Asia,* pp. 39–41.

44. PRO, Secretary of State for India Report, 29 June 41, War Cabinet Minutes, CAB 66, vol. 10, W.P.(40) 291.

45. DGFP, vol. 9, p. 95.

46. Ibid. p. 170; Wilber, *Riza Shah,* pp. 196–98; and Bullard, *Camels Must Go,* p. 221.

47. Jane Degras (ed.), *Soviet Documents on Foreign Policy,* vol. 3 (London: Oxford University Press, 1953), p. 458.

48. DGFP, vol. 10 pp. 77–78.

49. Playfair, *Mediterranean,* vol. 1, pp. 129 and 187.

50. DGFP, vol. 10, pp. 124fn and 196; and FRUS, *1940,* vol. 3, p. 634.

51. FRUS, *1940,* vol. 3, p. 634; German Air Attaché, Sofia, Bulgaria to the Reichs Air Minister, August 8, 1940, German Political Archives, Acting State Secretary Iran 1, cited in Fabry, *Iran,* p. 30.

52. DGFP, vol. 10, p. 170.

53. Sontag and Beddies, *Nazi–Soviet,* pp. 164–65.

54. DGFP, vol. 10, pp. 231, and 280–81.

55. Ibid., p. 231.

56. Fabry, *Iran*, p. 23.

57. DGFP, vol. 10, p. 170fn.

58. On the Foreign Office memo, see Woodward, *British Foreign Policy*, vol. 1, p. 473. On the dispatch of the Ninth Indian Brigade, see Henry Maule, *Spearhead General: The Epic Story of General Sir Frank Messervy and His Men in Eritrea, North Africa and Burma* (London: Odhams Press, 1961), p. 21. On the convoy of the Ninth Brigade, see Jack S. Harker, *Well Done Leander* (Auckland, N.Z.: Collins Bros., 1971), pp. 71–72. See also Playfair, *Mediterranean*, vol. I, pp. 175 and 187.

59. For full text of speech, see Degras, *Soviet Documents*, p. 463.

60. PRO, FO371-24849-6107.

61. Playfair, *Mediterranean*, vol. 1, pp. 171, 175, and 187.

62. FRUS, *1940*, vol. 3, p. 635.

63. Woodward, *British Foreign Policy*, vol. 1, p. 487.

64. FRUS, *1940*, vol. 1, pp. 498–99.

65. William L. Shirer, *The Rise and Fall of the Third Reich* (New York: Simon and Schuster, 1959), p. 1048.

66. Gen. Sergei M. Shtemenko (trans. Robert Daglish), *The Soviet General Staff at War, 1941–1945* (Moscow: Progress Publishers, 1970), p. 24. Shtemenko refers to this study, which was captured by the invading German Army, translated verbatim into German, and the German version later recovered by the U.S. Army and retained on microfilm in the National Archives. For an English translation, see Dr. Gerold Guensberg (ed.), *Soviet Command Study of Iran and Brief Analysis* (McLean, Va.: SRI International; 1980).

67. (Gen.) Walter Warliamont (trans. R. H. Barry), *Inside Hitler's Headquarters: 1939–1945* (New York: Praeger Publishers, 1964), p. 135.

68. *Trial of the Major War Criminals before the International Military Tribunal, Nuremburg, 14 November 1945–1 October 1946* (Nuremberg: Secretariat of the Tribunal, 1947–49), doc. 066-C.

69. Sontag and Beddies, *Nazi–Soviet*, pp. 214–16.

70. Woodward, *British Foreign Policy*, vol. 1, pp. 491–95.

71. Sontag and Beddies, *Nazi–Soviet* pp. 221–25.

72. Ibid., pp. 226–46, 247, and 253–57.

73. FRUS, *1940*, vol. 3, p. 636.

74. DGFP, vol. 10, p. 597.

75. Ibid., pp. 632 and 632fn.

76. Sontag and Beddies, *Nazi–Soviet*, pp. 258–59.

77. Ismail Akhmedov, *In and Out of Stalin's Gru* (Frederick, Md.: University Publications of America, 1984), p. 133.

78. Sontag and Beddies, *Nazi–Soviet*, p. 260.

79. DGFP, vol. 11, p. 270.

80. Prasad, *Campaign in Western Asia*, pp. 46–50 and 54.

81. Arfa, *Five Shahs*, pp. 272–73, discusses both his and Razmara's plans.

82. Guensberg, *Soviet Command Study*, pp. 109–10.

83. Shtemenko, *Soviet General Staff*, p. 24. See Guensberg, *Soviet Command Study*, pp. 116, 126, 159, 193, and 211.

84. Guensberg, *Soviet Command Study*, pp. 125 and 144.

85. Ibid., pp. 240–41.

86. Shtemenko, *Soviet General Staff*, p. 24.

87. See Prasad, *Campaign in Western Asia*, pp. 50–54, for details of the Plan SABINE conference.

CHAPTER 3

1. The following sources refer to the background of the pro-Nazi coup in Iraq: Stephen Hemsley Longrigg, *Iraq, 1900 to 1950* (London: Oxford University Press, 1953), pp. 287–88; Majid Khadduri, *Independent Iraq, 1932–1958: A Study in Iraqi Politics* (London: Oxford University Press, 1960), pp. 146–47, 162–63, 215, and 287; Freya Stark, *The Arab Island: The Middle East, 1939–1943* (New York: Alfred A. Knopf, 1945), pp. 150 and 155; FRUS, *1941*, vol. 3, pp. 491–92; DGFP, vol. 12, pp. 18–19; Woodward, *British Foreign Policy*, vol. I, p. 57; and Hirszowicz Lukasz, *The Third Reich and the Arab East* (London: Rutledge and Kegan Paul, 1966), pp. 134–35.

2. Freya Stark, *Dust in the Lion's Paw* (New York: Harcourt, Brace and World, 1962), p. 77.

3. Churchill, *Grand Alliance*, pp. 254 and 257; and Prasad, *Campaign in Western Asia*, pp. 63–64.

4. John Connell, *Wavell: Scholar and Soldier* (London: Collins Brothers and Company, 1964), p. 432.

5. Khadduri, *Independent Iraq*, p. 219.

6. A. F. Parry, *H.M.A.S. Yarra: The Story of a Gallant Ship* (Sydney: Angus and Robertson, 1944), pp. 60–61.

7. DGFP, vol. 12, p. 591.

8. Churchill, *Grand Alliance*, pp. 254–55.

9. DGFP, vol. 12, pp. 592–94.

10. Ibid., pp. 653 and 655–56.

11. Khadduri, *Independent Iraq*, pp. 220–22.

12. The following describe the RAF Habbaniya Air Station and events leading up to the hostilities: Capt. A. Graham, "The Iraq Levies at Habbaniya," *Army Quarterly*, 44,7 (1947): 250; Denis Richards, *The Royal Air Force: 1939–1945*, vol. 1: *The Fight at Odds* (London: Her Majesty's Stationery Office, 1974), pp. 313–15; Christopher Buckley, *Five Ventures* (London: Her Majesty's Stationery Office, 1954), p. 7; *PAIFORCE: The Official History of the Persia and Iraq Command, 1941–1946* (London: His Majesty's Stationery Office, 1948), pp. 22 and 29; Longrigg, *Iraq*, p. 290; and Prasad, *Campaign in Western Asia*, pp. 73–74.

13. Richards, *Royal Air Force*, p. 316; and *PAIFORCE*, p. 23.

14. DGFP, vol. 12, pp. 686 and 686fn.

15. Connell, *Scholar and Soldier*, p. 434.

16. Churchill, *Grand Alliance*, p. 256. See also Connell, *Scholar and Soldier*, p. 435, on this incident.

17. Richards, *Royal Air Force*, p. 317.

18. DGFP, vol. 12, pp. 688–90.

19. *PAIFORCE*, p. 25; and Richards, *Royal Air Force*, p. 318.

20. Connell, *Scholar and Soldier*, p. 437.

21. Churchill, *Grand Alliance*, pp. 257–58.

22. Parry, *H.M.A.S. Yarra*, pp. 64–65.

23. *PAIFORCE*, pp. 26–27; Prasad, *Campaign in Western Asia*, p. 80; and Richards, *Royal Air Force*, p. 319.

24. DGFP, vol. 12, pp. 689–90.
25. Ibid., p. 727.
26. Wilber, *Riza Shah*, p. 200.
27. DGFP, vol. 12, pp. 737–38.
28. Churchill, *Grand Alliance*, pp. 260–61.
29. DGFP, vol. 12, p. 775, and vol. 13, pp. 238–41. See also Khadduri, *Independent Iraq*, p. 231, for Grobba's meeting with the Iraqis.
30. Longrigg, *Iraq*, p. 294; and Stark, *Dust*, p. 104.
31. PRO, FO371-27202-E2205.
32. Ibid.
33. Churchill, *Grand Alliance*, p. 261.
34. DGFP, vol. 13, p. 244.
35. DGFP, vol. 12, p. 835; and Richards, *Royal Air Force*, p. 321.
36. DGFP, vol. 12, p. 835.
37. *PAIFORCE*, pp. 29–30; and Buckley, *Ventures*, pp. 25–26.
38. DGFP, vol. 12, pp. 836–37.
39. PRO, FO371-27149-E2752 and E2412.
40. See the following for German plans and operations against Crete and subsequent objectives: Gavin Long, *Australia in the War of 1939–1945*, vol. 2: *Greece, Crete and Syria* (Canberra: Australian War Memorial, 1953), pp. 221–34; and D. M. David, *Official History of New Zealand in the Second World War, 1939–1945: Crete* (London: Oxford University Press, 1955), p. 80.
41. PRO, FO371-27202-E195.
42. Buckley, *Ventures*, p. 27; Graham, "Iraq Levies," p. 254; and Richards, *Royal Air Force*, p. 322.
43. Long, *Australia in the War*, pp. 233–37, and 317–18; and Davin, *New Zealand in the War*, pp. 80–81.
44. DGFP, vol. 12, pp. 853–54 and 877–78.
45. Ibid.
46. Ibid., pp. 862–64.
47. Ibid., pp. 890–91.
48. Buckley, *Ventures*, pp. 31–33; DGFP, vol. 12, p. 917; Longrigg, *Iraq*, p. 296; and Stark, *Dust*, p. 111.
49. Hinsley, *British Intelligence*, vol. 1, p. 414; and DGFP, vol. 12, p. 932 and 932fn.
50. Connell, *Scholar and Soldier*, p. 446.
51. Col. Humphrey Wyndham, *The Household Cavalry at War: First Household Cavalry Regiment* (Aldershot, U.K.: Gale and Polden, 1952), p. 32.
52. David Dilks (ed.), *The Diaries of Sir Alexander Cadogan* (New York: G. P. Putnam's Sons, 1972), p. 382.
53. *Pravda*, June 14, 1941.
54. Churchill, *Grand Alliance*, p. 367.
55. DGFP, vol. 12, p. 531.
56. PRO, FO371-27149-E1990.
57. Shtemenko, *Soviet General Staff*, p. 25.
58. *Entsiklopediia*, vol. 4, p. 228.
59. Shtemenko, *Soviet General Staff*, p. 25, discusses designating the front. *Entsiklopediia*, vol. 7, p. 449, references the 28th Mechanized Corps.

60. Shtemenko, *Soviet General Staff*, p. 25, mentions Kozlov's hasty summons to Moscow. See (Gen.) Mikhail Illich Kazakov, *Nad Kartoi Bylykh Svazhenii* (Moscow: Military Publishing House, 1971), pp. 63–64, for reasons behind recall.

61. Maj. Gen. A. A. Lobachev, *Trudymi Dorogami* (Moscow: Military Publishing House, 1960), pp. 110–13.

62. Shtemenko, *Soviet General Staff*, p. 25, and Kazakov, *Kartoi*, p. 63, describe the arrival of the General Staff and go into the details of these exercises.

63. Shtemenko, *Soviet General Staff*, p. 26.

64. Kazakov, *Kartoi*, pp. 63–64.

65. Anthony Eden, *The Reckoning* (Boston: Houghton Mifflin, 1965), pp. 308–10. Eden describes his meeting with Maisky. For more details, see Woodward, *British Foreign Policy*, vol. 1, pp. 616–17.

66. Eden, *Reckoning*, pp. 308–9.

67. Ibid., p. 310.

68. Ibid., p. 310; and Woodward, *British Foreign Policy*, vol. 1, pp. 619–21.

69. Kazakov, *Kartoi*, pp. 63–64.

70. Mar. Georgi K. Zhukov, *The Memoirs of Marshal Zhukov*. (New York: Delacorte Press, 1971), pp. 220–21; and Lobachev, *Dorogami*, pp. 110–13.

71. Zhukov, *Memoirs*, pp. 218 and 220–21.

72. Kazakov, *Kartoi*, p. 64.

73. Zhukov, *Memoirs*, p. 230.

74. *Pravda*, June 14, 1941.

75. Kazakov, *Kartoi*, p. 64.

76. Somerset De Chair, *The Golden Carpet* (London: Faber and Faber, 1962), pp. 153–54 and 166.

77. PRO, FO371-27192-433.

78. Churchill, *Grand Alliance*, pp. 340–42; and Connell, *Scholar and Soldier*, pp. 496–501.

79. Maj. Gen. Sir John Kennedy, *The Business of War* (London: Hutchinson, 1957), p. 133. U.S. envoy Averell Harriman observed the poor morale and hasty evacuation planning in Cairo. See W. Averell Harriman and Elie Abel, *Special Envoy to Churchill and Stalin, 1941–1946* (New York: Random House, 1975), p. 67.

80. DGFP, vol. 12, pp. 1012–14 and 1012fn.

81. Kazakov, *Kartoi*, pp. 64–65.

82. Shtemenko, *Soviet General Staff*, p. 25.

83. The following sources describe events on the eve and morning of the German invasion: John Erickson, *The Soviet High Command: A Political History, 1918–1941* (New York: Macmillan, 1962), pp. 586–87; (Gen.) Franz Halder, *The Halder Diaries*, vol. 6 (Washington, D.C.: Infantry Journal Press, 1950), p. 161; and Zhukov, *Memoirs*, pp. 231–33.

84. Churchill, *Grand Alliance*, pp. 345–46. Delivery of the message by Smith is described in Bernard Ferguson, *Wavell: Portrait of a Soldier* (London: Collins, 1961), p. 59.

85. Churchill, *Grand Alliance*, pp. 371–72.

CHAPTER 4

1. (Bertold) Schulze-Holthus, (trans. Mervyn Savill), *Daybreak in Iran* (London: Staples Press, 1954), pp. 31–32, 37–45, and 49–51, describes Schulze's mission, actions in Tabriz, and meeting with Nasarow.

2. David Kahn, *Hitler's Spies: German Military Intelligence in World War II* (New York: Macmillan, 1978), pp. 56–61, 126, 234–35, and 267–69.

3. Schulze-Holthus, *Daybreak*, pp. 45–46.

4. Ibid., p. 52.

5. Ibid., pp. 53–54.

6. Fatemi, *Oil Diplomacy*, p. 191fn. No precise figures are available on the number of Germans then in Iran. The Allies interned 434 adult males. Some 60 left just prior to the invasion. Another 11—mainly older Jews—were permitted to remain. See Schulze-Holthus, *Daybreak*, p. 85. The German legation staff of 58 men together with 274 women, 126 children, and 10 sick men were allowed to depart for Germany. See U.S. National Archives, German Foreign Ministry microfilm records, serial 913, 294979. There were also some 60 German seamen at Bander-i Shahpur. See Col. W. E. Maxwell, *Capitol Campaigners* (Aldershot, U.K.: Gale and Polden, 1948), p. 97.

7. FRUS, *1941*, vol. 3, p. 383; Kahn, *Hitler's Spies*, p. 67; and Schulze-Holthus, *Daybreak*, p. 13.

8. Ahmad Namdar, "The German Fifth Column in Iran" (translated title), *Khandaniha* (Seventh Year) 4: 12ff; Schulze-Holthus, *Daybreak*, p. 66; and U.S. National Archives, German Foreign Ministry microfilm records, serial 917, 294893–294991.

9. U.S. National Archives, German Foreign Ministry microfilm records, serial 913, 294751, 294755, and 294757–294762.

10. (Gen.) Walter Warliamont, "German Exploitation of Arab Nationalist Movements in World War II, Part Two," in Donald S. Detwiler, Charles S. Burdick, and Jurgen Rowher (ed.), *World War II: German Military Studies*, vol. 13 (New York: Garland Publishing, 1979), pp. 56–57.

11. Wilber, *Riza Shah*, p. 200.

12. Elwell-Sutton, *Modern Iran*, p. 186.

13. FRUS, *1941*, vol. 3, p. 383–84.

14. Elwell-Sutton, *Modern Iran*, p. 186.

15. PRO, FO371-27150-E3383.

16. Arfa, *Five Shahs*, p. 272.

17. DGFP, vol. 12, pp. 1012–13fn.

18. PRO, FO371-27150-E3514, details the Eden–Moggadam meeting.

19. Gen. A. P. Wavell, "Despatch on Operations in Iraq, East Syria and Iran, from 10th April, 1941 to 12th January, 1942," suppl. to The London *Gazette*, August 13, 1946, p. 4097; and Prasad, *Campaign in Western Asia*, p. 122.

20. Prasad, *Campaign in Western Asia*, pp. 125–26.

21. DGFP, vol. 12, p. 727, and vol. 13, pp. 77–78.

22. Mohammed Reza Shah Pahlavi, *Answer to History* (New York: Stein and Day, 1980), p. 67.

23. DGFP, vol. 13, pp. 77–78.

24. John Connell, *Wavell: Supreme Commander* (London: Collins Brothers and Company, 1969), pp. 23–24.

25. PRO, FO371-27230-E3444.

26. Prasad, *Campaign in Western Asia*, pp. 125–26.

27. The following sources describe British and U.S. military attitudes toward the Soviet resistance, and Roosevelt's opinion: Harriman and Abel, *Special Envoy*, p. 66; Robert E. Sherwood, *Roosevelt and Hopkins: An Intimate History* (New York: Harper and Brothers Publishers, 1950), pp. 303–4; and Herbert Feis, *Churchill, Roosevelt,*

Stalin: The War They Waged and the Peace They Sought (Princeton, N.J.: Princeton University Press, 1957), p. 10fn.

28. PRO, FO371-27230-E3444.
29. Prasad, *Campaign in Western Asia*, pp. 301–2.
30. Woodward, *British Foreign Policy*, vol. 2, p. 11, for meeting with Stalin. See PRO, FO371-27230-E3707, for Cripps's cable to Eden.
31. DGFP, vol. 13, pp. 103–4.
32. Churchill, *Grand Alliance*, p. 477.
33. Prasad, *Campaign in Western Asia*, pp. 126–28.
34. PRO, FO371-27230-E3707.
35. Churchill, *Grand Alliance*, p. 477.
36. PRO, FO371-27151-E3840.
37. PRO, FO371-27240-E3820 and E5339.
38. PRO, FO371-27230-E3844.
39. Ibid.
40. PRO, FO371-27230-E3856.
41. Prasad, *Campaign in Western Asia*, p. 302.
42. Schulze-Holthus, *Daybreak*, pp. 54 and 57.
43. U.S. National Archives, German Foreign Ministry microfilm records, serial 913, 294751.
44. PRO, FO371-27230-E4065.
45. PRO, FO371-27231-E4141.
46. PRO, FO371-27230-E3055.
47. PRO, FO371-27231-E4141.
48. Woodward, *British Foreign Policy*, vol. 2, pp. 24–25.
49. PRO, FO371-27231-E4006, E4036, and E4135; and Woodward, *British Foreign Policy*, vol. 2, p. 25.
50. PRO, FO371-27231-E3995.
51. PRO, FO3671-27231-E4036.
52. Churchill, *Grand Alliance*, p. 477.
53. Ibid., p. 478.
54. PRO, FO371-27230-E4056; and Prasad, *Campaign in Western Asia*, pp. 304–5.
55. *PAIFORCE*, p. 32.
56. PRO, ADM199-410 (War Diary of Persian Gulf Squadron); and Prasad, *Campaign in Western Asia*, p. 340.
57. PRO, FO371-27230-E4056.
58. PRO, FO371-27200-E4779.
59. PRO, ADM199-410 (War Diary of Persian Gulf Squadron). For details of Plan DOVER, see Bisheshwar Prasad (ed.), *Official History of the Indian Armed Forces in the Second World War, 1939–1945: The Royal Indian Navy* (Agra, India: Agra University Press, 1964), pp. 92–94.
60. PRO, FO371-27231-E4141.
61. Ibid.
62. PRO, FO371-27151-4244.
63. In a speech to his generals, the shah expressed the view that Britain would not allow the Soviets to invade. See Tehran *Mosavar*, October 6, 1953, cited in Fatemi, *Oil Diplomacy*, p. 191. See also Arfa, *Five Shahs*, p. 277. For details on Iranian troop deployments, see Fld. Mar. Sir William Slim, *Unofficial History* (London: Cassell and

Company, 1959), pp. 194–95; Daoud Mo'eyd Amini, *Az Sevvom ta Bist-o-Panjum-E-Shahrivar 1320* (Tehran: n.p., 1942), p. 94; Arfa, *Five Shahs,* p. 298; and Prasad, *Campaign in Western Asia,* pp. 293, 344, and 352.

64. Woodward, *British Foreign Policy,* vol. 2, p. 25.

65. PRO, FO371-27199-E4179.

66. PRO, FO371-27200-E4179.

67. Prasad, *Campaign in Western Asia,* p. 313. For incident in the Second Gurkhas, see Lt. Col. G. R. Stevens, *History of the 2nd King Edward VII's Own Goorkha Rifles,* vol. 3: *1921–1948* (Aldershot, U.K.: Gale and Polden, 1952), p. 49.

68. FRUS, *1941,* vol. 3, p. 384.

69. Ibid., pp. 364–65.

70. Ibid.

71. Ibid., pp. 383–84.

72. PRO, ADM199-410 (War Diary of Persian Gulf Squadron).

73. Hinsley, *British Intelligence,* vol. 2, p. 82.

74. Pavel Grigorievich Kuznetsov, *Marshal Tolbukhin* (Moscow: Military Publishing House, 1966), p. 45. See also Schulze-Holthus, *Daybreak,* pp. 39, 49, and 53–54.

75. *Entsiklopediia,* vol. 7, p. 370.

76. Churchill, *Grand Alliance,* pp. 478–79.

77. PRO, ADM199-410 (War Diary of Persian Gulf Squadron).

78. Hinsley, *British Intelligence,* vol. 2, p. 82.

79. FRUS, *1941,* vol. 3, p. 387.

80. PRO, FO371-27232-E4478.

81. PRO, FO371-27232-E4423.

82. Prasad, *Campaign in Western Asia,* p. 313; PRO, ADM199-410 (War Diary of Persian Gulf Squadron); and G. Hermongle, *Australia in the war of 1939–1945: Royal Australian Navy, 1939–1942* (Canberra: Australian War Memorial, 1957), p. 384fn.

83. Churchill, *Grand Alliance,* p. 428.

84. Sherwood, *Roosevelt and Hopkins,* pp. 327–344, covers Hopkins's conference with Stalin.

CHAPTER 5

1. PRO, FO371-27305-E4435.

2. PRO, FO371-27201-E4375.

3. Ibid.

4. PRO, FO371-27232-E4524.

5. Ibid.

6. PRO, FO371-27201-E4375.

7. PRO, FO371-27205-E4526.

8. FRUS, *1941,* vol. 3, pp. 388–90.

9. Ibid.

10. PRO, FO371-27201-E4558.

11. PRO, FO371-27201-E4541.

12. Hinsley, *British Intelligence,* vol. 2, p. 82.

13. Prasad, *Campaign in Western Asia,* p. 303.

14. For discussions between Churchill and Roosevelt on the Atlantic Charter and strategic concerns, see Churchill, *Grand Alliance*, pp. 433–38 and 443–44.

15. PRO, Prime Minister to Foreign Secretary Cable, August 15, 1941, War Cabinet Minutes, CAB 66, vol. 18, W.P. (41), 203. See also PRO, War Cabinet Minutes, CAB 66, vol. 18, W.P. (41), 202, which indicate that the discussion on Iran must have occurred on August 11, 1941.

16. FRUS, *1941,* vol. 3, pp. 393–94.

17. PRO, FO371-27201-E4659.

18. PRO, FO371-27205-E4538.

19. PRO, ADM199-410 (War Diary of the Persian Gulf Squadron).

20. PRO, FO371-27201-E4716.

21. PRO, FO371-27232-E4662 and 27201-E4597.

22. PRO, FO371-27201-E4624.

23. Prasad, *Campaign in Western Asia*, p. 313.

24. W. S. Thatcher, *The Tenth Baluch Regiment in the Second World War* (Abbotabad, India: Baluch Center Press, 1980), p. 6; and Prasad, *Campaign in Western Asia,* pp. 313–14, and 534–35.

25. PRO, WO169-3433 (War Diary of the 2/6 Rajputana Rifles, May–December 1941).

26. Parry, *H.M.A.S. Yarra,* p. 92.

27. Prasad, *Royal Indian Navy,* pp. 79–80.

28. T. M. Jones and Jon L. Idriess (eds.), *Silent Service: Action Stories of the Anzac Navy,* 2d ed. (Sydney: Angus and Robertson, 1952), pp. 200–201; and Hermongle, *Royal Australian Navy,* p. 385.

29. Prasad, *Royal Indian Navy,* pp. 85–86, details the German and Italian scuttling preparations.

30. Jones and Idriess, *Silent Service,* pp. 196 and 200.

31. Wilber, *Riza Shah,* pp. 202–3. Details are supplemented by information from Dr. Donald N. Wilber's letter to the author, July 6, 1982.

32. Mohammed Khalili A'raqi, *Vaqay'A-I Shahrivar* (Tehran: Zarbaksh, 1944), pp. 284–85.

33. PRO, FO371-27205-E4939 and E4544, and 27206-E5023; and Prasad, *Campaign in Western Asia,* pp. 291–95.

34. A'raqi, *Shahrivar,* pp. 61, 92–110, and 117.

35. The following sources detail the makeup of Bayendor's forces: *Jane's Fighting Ships, 1941* (London: Macmillan and Company, 1942); PRO, ADM199-410 (War Diary of Persian Gulf Squadron); Stevens, *History of the 2nd Goorkha Rifles* pp. 49–50; and Prasad, *Campaign in Western Asia,* p. 60.

36. Prasad, *Campaign in Western Asia,* pp. 317 and 325–26; and PRO, ADM199-410 (War Diary of the Persian Gulf Squadron). Both sources provide details on the river and refinery defenses.

37. PRO, FO371-27201-E4716.

38. Kuznetsov, *Tolbukhin,* p. 45; and Schulze-Holthus, *Daybreak,* p. 57. Kuznetsov notes the secrecy of the Soviet buildup. Schulze-Holthus indicates that the buildup was away from the border.

39. Schulze-Holthus, *Daybreak,* p. 57. See also footnote 38, above.

40. Ibid., p. 56.

41. Sergei Frantsevich Edlinskii, *Kapiiskii Transportnyi Flot v Velikoi Otechestven-*

noi Voine Sovetskogo Souiza 1941–1945 (Moscow: Mor. Transport, 1963), p. 20; Jurg Meister (ed.), *Soviet Warships of the Second World War* (New York: Arco Publishing, 1977), pp. 334–39. Meister gives details on the ships of the flotilla.

42. A. A. Makovskii and B. M. Radchenko, *Kapiiskaia Krasnoznamennaia* (Moscow: Military Publishing House, 1961), pp. 147–48.

43. Edlinskii, *Kapiiskii Transportnyi Flot,* p. 20.

44. N. T. Baghyrov, *77 Simferopolskaia: Kratkaia Istoriia* (Baku: Azerbaidzhanskoe gos. izd-vo, 1981), p. 43. See also A'raqi, *Shahrivar,* pp. 36 and 40; and Schulze-Holthus, *Daybreak,* p. 56.

45. Details on the organization of the Operational Group are drawn from Kuznetsov, *Tolbukhin,* p. 45; Shtemenko, *Soviet General Staff,* pp. 50–51; and *Entsiklopediia,* vol. 3, p. 370.

46. Kuznetsov, *Tolbukhin,* p. 45.

47. Details on composition of the 47th Army are from the following sources: *Entsiklopediia,* vol. 7, p. 449; Kazakov, *Kartoi,* p. 78. Figures are based on average Soviet unit strengths for that period. Stalin told Harry Hopkins in July 1941 that a Soviet tank division had from 350–400 tanks, while each infantry division had 50 tanks. Sherwood, *Roosevelt and Hopkins,* p. 335. See also John Erickson, *The Road to Stalingrad* (London: Weidenfeld and Nicolson, 1975), pp. 63, 501, and 503. For data on Iranian forces, see PRO, FO371-27234-E4846.

48. Description and background of Novikov are provided by the following sources: Slim, *Unofficial,* pp. 221–28; Zhukov, *Memoirs,* p. 127; and *Entsiklopediia,* vol. 7, p. 449.

49. *Entsiklopediia,* vol. 7, p. 449. All pertinent sources indicate that the major portion of the 47th Army was committed on the Julfa–Tabriz–Tehran axis. See Prasad, *Campaign in Western Asia,* p. 311; and Kazakov, *Kartoi,* p. 78. Most Soviet soldiers who occupied Tabriz were Armenian, according to an interview by the author with former Iranian Cpl. Tomic Romson on October 27, 1982—who was captured by Soviet-Armenian troops—and also according to the diary of former Presbyterian missionary, Rev. William Miller. See William M. Miller, *The Diary of Reverend William Miller,* (unpublished) (Philadelphia: Presbyterian Historical Society Collection, 1941). Also, former U.S. Consul James Moose, who visited Rezeiyeh immediately after the invasion, told the author in an interview on October 10, 1982, that the Soviet forces there were primarily Georgian and Circassian.

50. (Mar.) Andrei Grechko, *Bitva za Kavkaz* (Moscow: Military Publishing House, 1971), pp. 29–30.

51. *Turkestanskii,* pp. 177–78. See also Kazakov, *Kartoi,* pp. 71–77.

52. William L. Langer and S. Everett Gleason, *The Undeclared War, 1940–1941* (New York: Harper and Brothers Publishers, 1953), p. 804fn.

53. PRO, FO371-27201-E4717.

54. FRUS, *1941,* vol. 3, pp. 397–98.

55. Langer, and Gleason, *Undeclared War,* pp. 803–4; FRUS, *1941,* vol. 3, p. 398.

56. FRUS, *1941,* vol. 3, pp. 391–96.

57. PRO, FO371-27201-E4712–E4720.

58. Ibid.

59. Former Iranian Army Deputy Chief of Staff and onetime official historian, Lt. Gen. Karim Varahram told the author in an interview on July 14, 1982, of the shah's order restricting the northern garrisons to their barracks.

60. Pahlavi, *Mission,* p. 70.

61. Sir Reader Bullard, *Britain and the Middle East* (London: Hutchinson, 1964), p. 133.

62. Tehran *Mosavar,* October 6, 1953, cited in Fatemi, *Oil Diplomacy,* p. 191.

63. The following sources provide clues to the shah's reasoning in response to the Allied demands: Fatemi, *Oil Diplomacy,* p. 191; Arfa, *Under Five Shahs,* pp. 277–78; FRUS, *1941,* vol. 3, p. 404; and DGFP, vol. 13, pp. 335–38.

64. David Irving, *Hitler's War* (New York: Viking Press, 1977), pp. 303 and 305–6.

65. PRO, FO371-27233-E4791. Leatham's warning is noted in PRO, ADM199-410 (War Diary of the Persian Gulf Squadron).

66. PRO, FO371-27205-E4812.

67. FRUS, *1941,* vol. 3, pp. 413–14.

68. Prasad, *Campaign in Western Asia,* p. 307. See also FRUS, *1941,* vol. 3, p. 400.

69. FRUS, *1941,* vol. 3, pp. 399–400.

70. Ibid., pp. 404–6.

71. Churchill, *Grand Alliance,* p. 480.

72. PRO, FO371-27205-E4830.

73. DGFP, vol. 13, pp. 336–38.

74. Ibid.

75. A'raqi, *Shahrivar,* pp. 7–10.

76. FRUS, *1941,* vol. 2, p. 400. See also the *Times of London,* August 21, 1941.

77. PRO, FO371-27234-E4897 and E4899.

78. PRO, FO371-27201-E4860.

79. PRO, FO371-27201-E4717.

80. PRO, FO371-27205-E4892.

81. PRO, ADM199-410 (War Diary of Persian Gulf Squadron); and A'raqi, *Shahrivar,* p. 54. The Fourth Air Regiment is cited in Leonard Bridgeman (ed.), *Jane's All The World's Aircraft, 1941* (London: Macmillan and Company, 1942), p. 45a. (Lt. Gen. Karim Varahram told the author on July 14, 1982, that Colonel Gilanshah commanded the air regiment at Ahvaz.

82. A'raqi, *Shahrivar,* pp. 50–55 and 313; and Prasad, *Campaign in Western Asia,* pp. 291–92.

83. PRO, ADM199-410 (War Diary of the Persian Gulf Squadron); and Prasad, *Campaign in Western Asia,* p. 31.

84. PRO, FO371-27233-E4846.

85. PRO, FO371-27234-E4984; and Prasad, *Campaign in Western Asia,* p. 315.

86. FRUS, *1941,* vol. 3, p. 403.

87. Ibid.

88. Prasad, *Campaign in Western Asia,* p. 308.

89. PRO, FO371-27234-E4984, E4897 and E4899.

90. PRO, FO371-27201-E4983.

CHAPTER 6

1. New York *Times,* August 22, 1941.

2. *The Complete Presidential Press Conferences of Franklin D. Roosevelt,* vol. 18: *1941* (New York: Da Capo Press, 1972), pp. 101–2.

3. New York *Times,* August 23, 1941.

4. FRUS, *1941,* vol. 3, pp. 406–7.

5. Ibid., p. 407.

6. Ibid., p. 414.

7. Fatemi, *Oil Diplomacy,* p. 188.

8. FRUS, *1941,* vol. 3, p. 411.

9. Ibid.

10. PRO, ADM199-410 (War Diary of Persian Gulf Squadron).

11. Jones and Idriess, *Silent Service,* p. 200.

12. Edlinskii, *Kapiiskii Transportnyi Flot,* p. 25.

13. PRO, WO169-3326 (War Diary of the Tenth Indian Division, April–December 1941). See also Prasad, *Campaign in Western Asia,* p. 342; and Capt. C. G. M. Gordon, "First Household Cavalry Regiment," *War Illustrated* 10, 240 (August 30, 1945); 299.

14. Prasad, *Campaign in Western Asia,* pp. 340–42. For a report on these movements that was sent to London by the British military attaché, Maj. Gen. W. A. K. Fraser, see PRO, FO371-27206-E5023.

15. A'raqi, *Shahrivar,* pp. 55–56.

16. PRO, FO371-27206-E5023.

17. PRO, FO371-27234-E4896.

18. For Soviet strength, see Chapter 5, footnotes 47 and 51 above. Figures for Iranian strength along the Soviet border are based on Third, Fourth, Ninth, Tenth, 11th, 15th, and 17th Divisions; along Iraqi border based on Fifth, Sixth, 12th, 16th, and reinforcing elements of the Tehran garrison. See PRO, FO371-27234-E4846. For British strengths, see T. H. Vail Motter, *The United States Army in World War II: The Persian Corridor and Aid to Russia* (Washington, D.C.: Government Printing Office, 1956), p. 10.

19. PRO, FO371-27208-E4537.

20. *Entsiklopediia,* vol. 3, p. 370.

21. PRO, FO371-27201-E4563. When Sir Hughe Knatchbull-Hugessen used the figure 3,000, Bullard corrected him, and insisted that there were no more than 2,000. See PRO, FO371-27205-E4483.

22. PRO, FO371-27206-E4960.

23. FRUS, *1941,* vol. 3, pp. 407–8.

24. Ibid., pp. 409–11.

25. DGFP, vol. 13, pp. 358–359 and 359fn.

26. PRO, FO371-27205-E4812.

27. Makovskii and Radchenko, *Kapiiskaia,* p. 147; and Edlinskii, *Kapiiskii Transportnyi Flot,* p. 25.

28. Jones and Idriess, *Silent Service,* pp. 199–200.

29. Parry, *H.M.A.S. Yarra,* p. 101.

30. Ibid., pp. 101–2; and PRO, ADM199-410 (War Diary of the Persian Gulf Squadron).

31. Details of the assembly and departure of the British amphibious flotilla from Basra are based on the following sources: PRO, ADM199-410 (War Diary of the Persian Gulf Squadron); *PAIFORCE,* p. 64; PRO, WO168-3433 (War Diary of the 2/6 Rajputana Rifles, May–December 1941); Prasad, *Royal Indian Navy,* pp. 76 and 86–87; Parry, *H.M.A.S. Yarra,* p. 102; and Brig. P. M. Kent's letter to the author, April 1, 1984.

32. Interview with Mr. George Wheeler on September 4, 1983.

33. Slim, *Unofficial*, pp. 181–82.

34. Aizelwood's plan is outlined in Prasad, *Campaign in Western Asia*, pp. 340–42. Aizelwood's feelings on being relieved are noted in Maj. Gen. J. A. Aizelwood's letter to the author, October 25, 1982. See also Slim, *Unofficial*, p. 182.

35. The organization and movement of Rapier Force are described in Prasad, *Campaign in Western Asia*, pp. 326–27.

36. Ibid., pp. 327–28. The description of Lieutenant Humphries' actions was provided during an interview with Maj. J. W. Humphries on September 4, 1983.

37. FRUS, *1941*, vol. 3, p. 414.

38. Bullard, *Camels Must Go*, p. 227.

39. A'raqi, *Shahrivar*, p. 58.

40. A'raqi, *Shahrivar*, pp. 42–43. The barracks location is from a reproduced Soviet map of Bander-i Pahlavi, contained in an enclosure to Guensberg, *Soviet Command Study*.

41. Edlinskii, *Kapiiskii Transportnyi Flot*, p. 25; Makovskii and Radchenko, *Kapiiskaia*, p. 147.

42. See Chapter 5, footnote 47, above. See also A'raqi, *Shahrivar*, p. 36; *Entsiklopediia*, vol. 7, pp. 449 and 451; and Baghyrov, *77 Simferopol skaia*, p. 45. Details of the Soviet border crossing were also provided during an interview with Lt. Gen. Karim Varahram on July 14, 1982.

43. Henry C. Cassidy, *Moscow Dateline* (Boston: Houghton Mifflin, 1943), pp. 200–201.

44. Prasad, *Campaign in Western Asia*, pp. 327 and 330; and interview with Maj. J. W. Humphries on September 4, 1983. Details on 18th Brigade were provided in Lt. Col. C. H. McVean's letter to the author, October 14, 1983.

45. Details on RAF actions in Prasad, *Campaign in Western Asia*, p. 336. Details on Baluchi airlift operation in Thatcher, *Tenth Baluch Regiment*, pp. 13–14.

46. PRO, ADM199-410 (War Diary of the Persian Gulf Squadron).

47. Movement to Bander-i Shahpur described in Jones and Idriess, *Silent Service*, p. 201; and Hermongle, *Royal Australian Navy*, p. 388.

48. Movement of flotilla to Abadan and Khorramshahr described in PRO, ADM199-410 (War Diary of the Persian Gulf Squadron); Hermongle, *Royal Australian Navy*, pp. 384 and 387; and Parry, *H.M.A.S. Yarra*, 103–4.

49. PRO, ADM199-410 (War Diary of the Persian Gulf Squadron).

50. The sinking of the *Palang* is described in A'raqi, *Shahrivar*, pp. 162–72 and 329; and in an interview with Adm. Shamseddin Safavi on March 5, 1984.

51. Details on the delivery of the diplomatic notes are described in Amini, *Shahriver 1320*, pp. 1–2; A'raqi, *Shahrivar*, p. 21; and Bullard, *Camels Must Go*, p. 227.

CHAPTER 7

1. Details of the British capture of Bander-i Shahpur are based on the following sources: PRO, ADM199-419 (War Diary of the Persian Gulf Squadron); Prasad, *Royal Indian Navy*, pp. 80, 83, and 89–91; Hermongle, *Royal Australian Navy*, pp. 385 and 388; Maxwell, *Campaigners*, pp. 98–99; Thatcher, *Tenth Baluch Regiment*,

pp. 8–10; Jones and Idriess, *Silent Service,* pp. 200–203; and interview with Capt. Jafar Fosuni on March 31, 1984.

2. Jones and Idriess, *Silent Service,* p. 201.

3. Ibid., p. 202.

4. The seizure of the Abadan oil refinery is based on the following sources: PRO, WO169-3368 (War Diary of the 24th Indian Brigade, June–December 1941), 3433 (War Diary of the 2/6 Rajputana Rifles, May–December 1941), 3472 (War Diary of 1st Kumaon Rifles, April–December 1941), and ADM199-410 (War Diary of the Persian Gulf Squadron); Prasad, *Campaign in Western Asia,* pp. 319–21; *PAIFORCE,* pp. 64–65; Maj. M. G. Abhyankar, *The Rajputana Rifles, 1775–1947* (Bombay: Orient Longmans, 1961), pp. 281–83; Brig. Patrick M. Kent's letter to the author, April 1, 1984; interview with Mr. George Wheeler on September 4, 1983; and the Iranian version described in A'raqi, *Shahrivar,* pp. 59–62 and 66–68.

5. Alan Moorehead, *Don't Blame the Generals* (New York: Harper and Brothers Publishers, (1943), p. 29.

6. Details on the sinking of the *Babr* and the capture of the Iranian warships and port of Khorramshahr are based on the following sources: PRO, ADM199-410 (War Diary of the Persian Gulf Squadron), and WO169-3441 (War Diary of the 3/10 Baluch, August–December 41); Prasad, *Campaign in Western Asia,* pp. 326–27; Prasad, *Royal Indian Navy,* pp. 87–88; Parry, *H.M.A.S. Yarra,* pp. 104–10; A'raqi, *Shahrivar,* pp. 121–27; and interview with Adm. Shamsedden Safavi on March 5, 1984.

7. Interview with Adm. Shamsedden Safavi on March 5, 1984.

8. Ibid.

9. PRO, WO169-3431 (War Diary of the 5/5 Mahratta Light Infantry); Prasad, *Campaign in Western Asia,* pp. 327–28; and interview with Maj. John W. Humphries on September 4, 1983.

10. Seizure of the Iranian gunboats and tug is detailed in Prasad, *Royal Indian Navy,* pp. 87–88; and Parry, *H.M.A.S. Yarra,* pp. 107–8.

11. Interview with Adm. Shamsedden Safavi on March 5, 1984.

12. Prasad, *Royal Indian Navy,* p. 88.

13. The actions of Bayendor and Nejad are described in A'raqi, *Shahrivar,* pp. 121–27.

14. The seizure of the defenses around the wireless station is described in the following sources: PRO, WO169-3431 (War Diary of the 5/5 Mahratta Light Infantry); Prasad, *Campaign in Western Asia,* pp. 326–28; Maj. John W. Humphries' letter to the author, November 2, 1982; and interview with Major Humphries on September 4, 1983.

15. Accounts of the circumstances surrounding Bayendor's death have been conflicting. The A'raqi account (*Shahrivar,* pp. 121–27), which is based on the recollection of Bayendor's driver, indicates that Bayendor and Nejad were pursued from the wireless station, and left the car when they were shot. Nejad was killed, while Bayendor lay mortally wounded. Major John W. Humphries told the author (interview on September 4, 1983) that he found Bayendor dead in the backseat of the car, and did not notice Nejad. Adm. Shamsedden Safavi (interview on March 5, 1984) confirms the A'raqi account.

16. The capture of Khorramshahr by the two Gurkha battalions is described in the following sources: PRO, WO169-3458 (War Diary of the 1/2 Gurkha Rifles,

April–December 1941), and 3459 (War Diary of the 2/3 Gurkha Rifles, July–December 1941); Stevens, *History of the 2nd Goorkha Rifles*, pp. 50–51; Prasad, *Campaign in Western Asia*, p. 328; Lt. Col. Donald Ramsey-Brown's letter to the author, June 27, 1984; Mr. A. D. R. Geddes' letter to the author, May 7, 1984; and interview with Mr. Neal Ford on September 4, 1982.

17. Prasad, *Campaign in Western Asia*, pp. 291 and 335–36.

18. *PAIFORCE*, p. 67.

19. The air landing at and seizure of Haft Khel are described in the following sources: Maxwell, *Campaigners*, pp. 100–1; Thatcher, *Tenth Baluch Regiment*, pp. 14–15; and Col. J. M. Forster's letter to the author, November 3, 1982.

20. The securing of the refinery, ferry crossing, and Marid is described in Prasad, *Campaign in Western Asia*, pp. 322–23 and 329.

21. Dehtaziyani's situation was described to the author in an interview with Adm. Shamsedden Safavi on March 5, 1984. Description of Qasr Shiekh fort and defenders is based on an interview with Maj. Robert J. Henderson on September 4, 1983; and a letter from Lt. Col. Colin H. McVean, October 14, 1983.

22. The advance toward and attack on Qasr Shiekh are described in the following sources: PRO, WO169-3356 (War Diary of the 18th Indian Brigade, June–December 1941), and 3443 (War Diary of the 2/11 Sikh, March–December 1941); Col. J. T. Birdwood, *The Sikh Regiment in the Second World War* (Norwich: Jarrold and Sons, n.d.), pp. 52–54; Lt. Col. Colin H. McVean's letter to the author, October 14, 1983; interview with Maj. Robert J. Henderson on September 4, 1983; and interview with Adm. Shamsedden Safavi on March 5, 1984.

23. The advance of the Tenth Indian Division toward Gilan and the Paitak Pass is described in the following sources: PRO, WO169-3326 (War Diary of the 10th Indian Division, April–December 1941), 3337 (War Diary of the 2nd Armoured Brigade, September 1940–November 1941), and 3462 (War Diary of the 1/5 Gurkha Rifles); Buckley, *Ventures*, pp. 154–55; Brig. J. R. Platt, *The Royal Wiltshire Yeomanry (Prince of Wales Own), 1907–1967* (London: Garnstone Press, 1972), p. 111; *Yeoman, Yeoman: The Warwickshire Yeomanry: 1920–1956* (Birmingham, U.K.: Silk and Terry, 1971), p. 34; Prasad, *Campaign in Western Asia*, pp. 345–46; *Times of London*, August 31, 1941; *New York Times*, September 1, 1941; Lt. Col. G. M. Nightingale's letter to the author, April 28, 1984; Lt. Col. R. M. Maxwell's letter to the author, June 19, 1984; and Mr. John M. Day's letter to the author, January 26, 1983.

24. A'raqi, *Shahrivar*, pp. 47–48.

25. Slim, *Unofficial*, p. 185.

CHAPTER 8

1. A'raqi, *Shahrivar*, pp. 205–6 and 229.

2. Ibid., p. 229. Maku is described in Guensberg, *Soviet Command Study*, p. 123. The Soviet motorized advance to and attack on Maku were described to the author by Lt. Gen. Karim Varahram on July 14, 1982.

3. A'raqi, *Shahrivar*, pp. 83–90, 173–76, and 204, describes Iranian reactions to the attack on Maku.

4. *Entsiklopediia*, vol. 7, p. 451. See also Guensberg, *Soviet Command Study*, p. 123. Former U.S. Consul James Moose, who visited Rezeiyeh immediately after the

invasion, told the author on October 10, 1982, that the Soviet troops there were primarily Georgian.

5. PRO, FO371-27233-E4896; *Times of London,* September 6, 1941; and A'raqi, *Shahrivar,* pp. 208–20.

6. A'raqi, *Shahrivar,* pp. 208–10 and 263–64.

7. *Entsiklopediia,* vol. 7, p. 449; and *Times of London,* August 26, 1941. Julfa is described in Charles Thayer, *Bears in the Caviar* (London: Michael Joseph, 1952), pp. 199–200. In an interview with the author on October 27, 1982, former Iranian Cp. Tomic Romson indicated that the Soviet troops that occupied Tabriz were mainly Armenian. This is supported by Miller, *Diary.* The 63d Mountain Infantry Division was the only Armenian division in the 47th Army. The presence of the 24th Cavalry Division is noted in Kazakov, *Kartoi,* p. 78; and by a photo in the *Illustrated London News,* October 4, 1941, p. 437, showing Soviet cavalry entering Tabriz.

8. Former Iranian Cpl. Tomic Romson in an interview on October 27, 1982; and A'raqi, *Shahrivar,* p. 229.

9. Schulze-Holthus, *Daybreak,* p. 57.

10. Dr. Charles Lamme, "The Occupation of Tabriz, August 1941," typed memo dated October 27, 1941 (provided to the author by the Rev. Hugo Muller).

11. A'raqi, *Shahrivar,* pp. 368–69.

12. Ibid., p. 370. The use of civilian trucks and the presence of pom-pom guns in the Soviet column is noted in Moorehead, *Don't Blame,* pp. 34–35. Daradis Gorge is described in Guensberg, *Soviet Command Study,* pp. 127–28.

13. That the Yam Pass was the initial objective is apparent from several sources. See the Soviet military dispatch on August 25, 1941, in the New York *Times,* August 26, 1941. Arfa, *Five Shahs,* p. 298, notes that the Soviet advance on the first day reached only Sofian, just beyond the Yam Pass. Also Guensberg, *Soviet Command Study,* pp. 110–11, and Lt. Gen. Karim Varahram in interview on July 14, 1982, indicate that the Iranian Army fortified the pass.

14. A'raqi, *Shahrivar,* p. 370. General Matbooi's reasoning and actions are indicated by information derived from the author's interview with Lt. Gen. Karim Varahram on July 14, 1982, and with former Iranian Cpl. Tomic Romson on October 27, 1982; and from Schulze-Holthus, *Daybreak,* p. 61. Fortifications of Shibli Pass are described in Guensberg, *Soviet Command Study,* pp. 109–10 and 135–36.

15. A'raqi, *Shahrivar,* pp. 36 and 40, describes the Soviet border crossing. The 44th Army order of battle is in *Entsiklopediia,* vol. 7, p. 451. The 77th Division advance is described in Makovskii and Radchenko, *Kapiiskaia,* p. 148. The Soviet route through the mountains and Namin is described in Guensberg, *Soviet Command Study,* pp. 151–55.

16. New York *Times,* August 26, 1941—mistakenly refers to a Soviet advance toward Astarabad (Gorgan), which had not yet occurred—apparently confusing the spelling with Astara. See also Makovskii and Radchenko, *Kapiiskaia,* p. 148.

17. Amini, *Shahrivar 1320,* pp. 95–99; and A'raqi, *Shahrivar,* pp. 39–41.

18. A'raqi, *Shahrivar,* p. 263. The number of trucks is described in Guensberg, *Soviet Command Study,* p. 156.

19. Edlinskii, *Kapiiskii Transportnyi Flot,* p. 25. See also Makovskii and Radchenko, *Kapiiskaia,* pp. 147–48; and *Entsiklopediia,* vol. 4, p. 228.

20. Edlinskii, *Kapiiskii Transportnyi Flot,* p. 25. *Times of London,* August 30, 1941,

reports a Soviet landing at Hevikon—a village apparently identical with Haviq, which shows on a 1:250,000 map of the same vicinity, and in the same location as that of Khevi, which is described in Guensberg, *Soviet Command Study*, p. 164.

21. Events at Bander-i Pahlavi are described in A'raqi, *Shahrivar*, pp. 42–44.

22. A'raqi, *Shahrivar*, pp. 43–45 and 362. This incident was also described during an interview with Rear Adm. Morteza Daftary on February 25, 1983.

23. Amini, *Shahrivar 1320*, pp. 2–3; and A'raqi, *Shahrivar*, pp. 21–22.

24. Amini, *Shahrivar 1320*, p. 3.

25. Fatemi, *Oil Diplomacy*, pp. 192–93.

26. The council meeting is described by Amini, *Shahrivar 1320*, p. 4; DGFP, vol. 13, p. 380; and A'raqi, *Shahrivar*, p. 35.

27. FRUS, *1941*, vol. 3, p. 417.

28. PRO, FO371-27206-E5005.

29. Prasad, *Campaign in Western Asia*, p. 310.

30. Cassidy, *Moscow*, pp. 200–3.

31. FRUS, *1941*, vol. 3, p. 441.

32. PRO, FO371-27206-E5016.

33. PRO, FO371-27201-E4983.

34. FRUS, *1941*, vol. 3, pp. 415–16.

35. Ibid.

36. Lamme, "Occupation of Tabriz" and "First Chronicles," a typewritten Presbyterian missionary chronology of the invasion (both documents provided to the author by the Rev. Hugo Muller); and Miller, *Diary*. Also relating is a letter to the author from Dr. Joseph Cochrane, dated October 22, 1982.

37. The retreat of the Third Division was described in an interview with former Iranian Cpl. Tomic Romson on October 27, 1982. The desertion of General Matbooi is described in Amini, *Shahrivar 1320*, p. 104; and A'raqi, *Shahrivar*, p. 370.

38. See the Soviet dispatch printed in the New York *Times*, August 26, 1941.

39. Schulze-Holthus, *Daybreak*, pp. 57–59.

40. Ibid., pp. 59–60.

41. Ibid., pp. 60–61.

42. Ibid., pp. 61–62.

43. Amini, *Shahrivar 1320*, p. 4; and A'raqi, *Shahrivar*, p. 22.

44. Pahlavi, *Faces*, pp. 40–41. For Mansur's failure to relay warnings, see Pahlavi, *Mission*, p. 70.

45. A'raqi, *Shahrivar*, pp. 44–46. Coastal fortifications and the coastal gun situation are described in Guensberg, *Soviet Command Study*, p. 109; and during an interview with Rear Adm. Morteza Daftary on December 3, 1982.

46. Interview with Rear Adm. Morteza Daftary on December 3, 1982.

47. Reaction fo the leaflets is described in Amini, *Shahrivar 1320*, p. 4. Contents of the leaflets are detailed in Prasad, *Campaign in Western Asia*, p. 543.

48. Amini, *Shahrivar 1320*, p. 4; Miller, *Diary*.

49. Amini, *Shahrivar 1320*, pp. 5–8.

50. The situation in the city is described in Miller, *Diary*. The situation at the barracks is described in A'raqi, *Shahrivar*, pp. 25–26.

51. Pahlavi, *Faces*, p. 41.

52. Wilber, *Riza Shah*, p. 205.

53. DGFP, vol. 13, pp. 379–81.

54. Amini, *Shahrivar 1320*, p. 8.
55. A'raqi, *Shahrivar*, pp. 24–27.
56. Interview with former U.S. Consul James S. Moose on October 10, 1982.
57. FRUS, *1941*, vol. 3, pp. 418–19.
58. A'raqi, *Shahrivar*, p. 41.
59. Description of the occupation of Astara is based collectively on A'raqi, *Shahrivar*, p. 40; New York *Times*, August 26, 1941; and Guensberg, *Soviet Command Study*, pp. 12–13 and 150–52.
60. The occupation of Sofian is noted in Arfa, *Five Shahs*, p. 298.
61. Interview with former Iranian Cpl. Tomic Romson on October 27, 1982.
62. A'raqi, *Shahrivar*, pp. 370–72.
63. The fighting outside Maku is described in A'raqi, *Shahrivar*, pp. 174–78 and 204.
64. Ibid., p. 204.
65. Prasad, *Campaign in Western Asia*, p. 346; Slim, *Unofficial*, pp. 182–83; and *Times of London*, September 2, 1941.
66. The fighting at Gilan is detailed in Platt, *Wiltshire Yeomanry*, p. 111; Prasad, *Campaign in Western Asia*, p. 347; and the *Times of London*, September 1, 1941.
67. Slim, *Unofficial*, p. 184; and Prasad, *Campaign in Western Asia*, pp. 346–49.
68. Prasad, *Campaign in Western Asia*, pp. 320 and 323. The prisoners and captured material are noted in the New York *Times*, August 28, 1941.
69. The Soviet landing attempt at Bander-i Pahlavi is described in A'raqi, *Shahrivar*, pp. 45–46; Edlinskii, *Kapiiskii Transportnyi Flot*, p. 25; and by Rear Adm. Morteza Daftary in an interview on December 3, 1982.
70. Lamme, "Occupation of Tabriz."
71. Miller, *Diary*.
72. Amini, *Shahrivar 1320*, p. 9.

CHAPTER 9

1. A'raqi, *Shahrivar*, pp. 372–73.
2. The bombing of Kazvin is noted in FRUS, *1941*, vol. 3, p. 426.
3. Amini, *Shahrivar 1320*, p. 99; and A'raqi, *Shahrivar*, pp. 259–62.
4. The advance of the 44th Army is noted in the *Times of London*, August 28, 1941; and Makovskii and Radchenko, *Kapiiskaia*, p. 148. See also *Entsiklopediia*, vol. 7, p. 451. For a description of the Caspian highway, see Guensberg, *Soviet Command Study*, p. 94.
5. The landing of the 105th Regiment is noted in Makovskii and Radchenko, *Kapiiskaia*, p. 147. A description of the roadstead and the meaning of "Gilan" is noted in Guensberg, *Soviet Command Study*, pp. 161–64. The advance to Lissar is noted in the *Times of London*, August 28, 1941. Rear Adm. Morteza Daftary told the author on December 3, 1982, that he personally observed the Red Army's heavy road construction equipment.
6. A'raqi, *Shahrivar*, pp. 280–91 and 297; and interview with Rear Adm. Morteza Daftary on December 3, 1982.
7. Lamme, "Occupation of Tabriz."
8. Miller, *Diary*.

9. The Soviet entry into Tabriz and actions at the American hospital are described in Lamme, "Occupation of Tabriz"; and in Dr. Joseph Cochrane's letter to the author, October 22, 1982.

10. Schulze-Holthus, *Daybreak,* p. 87.

11. Interview with former Iranian Cpl. Tomic Romson on October 27, 1982.

12. Amini, *Shahrivar 1320,* p. 104; and A'raqi, *Shahrivar,* pp. 263–64.

13. New York *Times,* August 28, 1941.

14. Prasad, *Campaign in Western Asia,* pp. 333 and 336.

15. Ibid., pp. 319–22.

16. Buckley, *Ventures,* p. 150; and interview with Adm. Shamseddin Safavi on March 5, 1984.

17. Prasad, *Campaign in Western Asia,* p. 327.

18. Prasad, *Royal Indian Navy,* pp. 81 and 84–85.

19. Maxwell, *Campaigners,* p. 101; and Thatcher, *Tenth Baluch Regiment,* p. 15.

20. The effect of Forster's patrol on the Iranians is noted in Arfa, *Five Shahs,* p. 298; Maxwell, *Campaigners,* p. 101; and Prasad, *Campaign in Western Asia,* p. 348.

21. A'raqi, *Shahrivar,* pp. 313–16.

22. The Koh-i Wazhlan actions are described in the *Times of London,* September 1, 1941; A'raqi, *Shahrivar,* p. 296; and Prasad, *Campaign in Western Asia,* p. 348.

23. Yeoman, *Yeoman* pp. 34–35; and Lt. Col. John Lakin's letter to the author, February 17, 1983.

24. See footnote 22, above.

25. Slim, *Unofficial,* p. 183. See also Prasad, *Campaign in Western Asia,* p. 349.

26. John Masters, *The Road past Mandalay* (New York: Harper and Brothers, 1961), pp. 55–56.

27. Ibid.

28. The War Council meeting, and the war situation are described in the following sources: Amini, *Shahrivar 1320,* p. 13, A'raqi, *Shahrivar,* pp. 27, 228, and 230; and Arfa, *Five Shahs,* p. 298.

29. The situation in Tehran is noted in A'raqi, *Shahrivar,* p. 230; and "First Chronicles." The truck driver incident is noted in Amini, *Shahrivar 1320,* pp. 14–15.

30. Miller, *Diary.*

31. FRUS, *1941,* vol. 3, p. 423.

32. Ibid.

33. Pahlavi, *Faces,* p. 41.

34. Amini, *Shahrivar 1320,* p. 6.

35. FRUS, *1941,* vol. 3, pp. 424–25.

36. Ibid., pp. 419–20.

37. Ibid., p. 420.

38. Ibid.

39. Ibid., pp. 421–22.

40. New York *Times,* August 26, 1941.

41. Ibid.

42. Prasad, *Campaign in Western Asia,* p. 333.

43. A'raqi, *Shahrivar,* pp. 319–23; and Prasad, *Campaign in Western Asia,* pp. 324–25.

44. The advance of HAZELFORCE is described in the following sources: *Times*

of London, September 2, 1941; Lt. Col. R. M. Maxwell's letter to the author, June 19, 1984; and Prasad, *Campaign in Western Asia*, p. 348.

45. The Soviet entry into Sarakhs was described to the author during an interview with Mr. Hassan Soburi on September 15, 1981.

46. Interview with Mr. Hassan Soburi on September 15, 1981; and *Turkestanskii*, p. 178.

47. *Turkestanskii*, p. 178; and Clairmont Skrine, *World War in Iran* (London: Constable and Company, 1962), p. 106.

48. The actions of General Mohtashami and the dispatch of columns toward Sarakhs and Quchan are described in Amini, *Shahrivar 1320*, pp. 109–10. The location of the Ninth Division barracks is noted in Guensberg, *Soviet Command Study*, p. 228. Skrine, *World War*, pp. 103–4, describes the false hopes raised by the war communiqué.

49. The Soviet air attacks and the movement of Iranian troops out of Meshed are described in the following sources: "First Chronicles"; Miller, *Diary*; Amini, *Shahrivar 1320*, p. 111; and Skrine, *World War*, pp. 103–4.

50. "First Chronicles"; and Skrine, *World War*, p. 104. The Iranian Third Air Regiment is noted in Bridgeman, *Jane's Aircraft, 1941*, p. 48a.

51. Amini, *Shahrivar 1320*, pp. 94 and 101; and A'raqi, *Shahrivar*, p. 265.

52. Kazakov, *Kartoi*, pp. 71–72, 75, and 78; and Amini, *Shahrivar 1320*, p. 101.

53. Slim, *Unofficial*, p. 185.

54. Prasad, *Campaign in Western Asia*, p. 348; *Times of London*, September 1, 1941; and Mr. John M. Day's letter to the author, January 26, 1983.

55. Prasad, *Campaign in Western Asia*, p. 348; and Slim, *Unofficial*, p. 185.

56. Mr. John M. Day's letter to the author, January 26, 1983; Prasad, *Campaign in Western Asia*, pp. 343 and 350; and the *Times of London*, September 2, 1941.

57. Prasad, *Campaign in Western Asia*, p. 345; and *Times of London*, September 2, 1941.

58. Brig. Patrick M. Kent's letter to the author, April 1, 1984; and Prasad, *Campaign in Western Asia*, p. 324;

59. Moorehead, *Don't Blame*, p. 30.

60. A'raqi, *Shahrivar*, p. 323.

61. Interview with Maj. Allan Johnstone on September 4, 1983. See also Prasad, *Campaign in Western Asia*, p. 333.

62. Amini, *Shahrivar 1320*, p. 18.

63. Ibid., p. 112; and A'raqi, *Shahrivar*, p. 285.

64. "First Chronicles"; and Miller, *Diary*.

65. Makovskii and Radchenko, *Kapiiskaia*, p. 148; and the New York *Times*, August 29, 1941.

66. New York *Times*, August 28, 1941; and Amini, *Shahrivar 1320*, p. 99. The 20th Division was the only infantry division in the 44th Army, aside from the 77th. See *Entsiklopediia*, vol. 7, p. 451. The official history of the 20th Division intimates that the division was involved in operations in Iran. See Victor Nikolaevich Davidich, *Raizni Svoei Neshchadya* (Moscow: Military Publishing House, 1981), pp. 56–57.

67. New York *Times*, August 29, 1941; and Kazakov, *Kartoi*, p. 78. The follow-

ing sources describe the Soviet requisitioning of civilian vehicles in Tabriz: George Rodger, *Desert Journey* (London: Cresset Press, 1946), p. 124; and Miller, *Diary*.

68. *Times of London*, August 29, 1941; Amini, *Shahrivar 1320*, p. 104; and interview with former Iranian Cpl. Tomic Romson on October 27, 1982.

69. Skrine, *World War*, p. 104.

70. Amini, *Shahrivar 1320*, p. 111. See also Skrine, *World War*, p. 105; and Kazakov, *Kartoi*, pp. 62 and 75.

71. Amini, *Shahrivar 1320*, p. 112.

72. FRUS, *1941*, vol. 3, pp. 431–33.

73. Ibid., pp. 433–35.

74. Bullard, *Camels Must Go*, p. 227; and Amini, *Shahrivar 1320*, p. 19.

75. Prasad, *Campaign in Western Asia*, p. 334.

76. Interview with Maj. Robert J. Henderson on September 4, 1982.

77. Prasad, *Campaign in Western Asia*, pp. 329 and 336.

78. A'raqi, *Shahrivar*, p. 323.

79. Mr. Sam Croft's letter to the author, January 26, 1984.

80. Prasad, *Campaign in Western Asia*, pp. 350–51; and the *Times of London*, September 2, 1941.

81. Amini, *Shahrivar 1320*, p. 19.

82. Events in Meshed are described in the following sources: Skrine, *World War*, pp. 104–5; Amini, *Shahrivar 1320*, pp. 112–13; and Miller, *Diary*.

83. Interview with Col. Ali Farivari on July 9, 1982.

CHAPTER 10

1. Description of the advance on Ahvaz is based on the following sources: PRO, WO169-3356 (War Diary of the 18th Indian Brigade, June–December 1941), 3371 (War Diary of the 25th Indian Brigade, April–December 1941), 3458 (War Diary of the 1/2 Gurkha Rifles, April–December 1941), 3459 (War Diary of the 2/3 Gurkha Rifles, July–December 1941), 3428 (War Diary of the 1/5 Mahrattas, May–December 1941); Prasad, *Campaign in Western Asia*, pp. 335–37; Stevens, *History of the 2nd Goorkha Rifles*, p. 51; C. N. Barclay, *The Regimental History of the 3rd Queen Alexandra's Own Gurkha Rifles*, vol. 2: *1927–1947* London: William Clowes and Sons, 1953), p. 102; interview with Maj. Allan Johnstone on September 5, 1983; and interview with Col. Edward N. Mumford on September 4, 1983.

2. Moorehead, *Don't Blame*, p. 334.

3. PRO, WO169-3326 (War Diary of the 10th Indian Division, April–December 1941); Platt, *Wiltshire Yeomanry*, p. 350; and Prasad, *Campaign in Western Asia*, p. 350.

4. Slim, *Unofficial*, pp. 185–87. The *Times of London*, August 30, 1941 refers to the presence of German advisors. Colonel Piruzan's actions are described in A'raqi, *Shahrivar*, p. 283.

5. Slim, *Unofficial*, p. 187; and the *Times of London*, September 2, 1941.

6. Lt. Col. R. M. Maxwell's letter to the author, June 19, 1984; and Slim, *Unofficial*, p. 189.

7. Arfa, *Five Shahs*, p. 229.

8. Amini, *Shahrivar 1320*, p. 20.

9. Ibid., pp. 99, 102–3, and 113.

10. Interview with Gen. Karim Varahram on July 14, 1982. Shahbakhti was Varahram's father-in-law. General Varahram retained a copy of his father-in-law's famous telegram for many years.

11. A'raqi, *Shahrivar*, pp. 313–18; and Prasad, *Campaign in Western Asia*, pp. 334–39. A September 5, 1983, interview with Maj. Allan Johnstone, commander of the attack west of Ahvaz, provided details on Iranian strength.

12. Prasad, *Campaign in Western Asia*, pp. 337–39; and Maj. Allan Johnstone interview on September 5, 1983.

13. Barclay, *History of the 3rd Gurkha Rifles*, p. 102; interview with Mr. Neal Ford on September 4, 1982; and interview with Col. E. N. Mumford on September 4, 1983.

14. Moorehead, *Don't Blame*, p. 31; and Prasad, *Campaign in Western Asia*, p. 337.

15. Prasad, *Campaign in Western Asia*, p. 338.

16. Ibid., pp. 338–39.

17. Ibid.; and Mr. A. D. R. Geddes' letter to the author, May 7, 1984.

18. Maxwell, *Campaigners*, p. 101; Thatcher, *Tenth Baluch Regiment*, pp. 15–16; and Col. J. M. Forster's letter to the author, September 12, 1984.

19. Prasad, *Campaign in Western Asia*, p. 350. There are 16 tanks in a troop. Massoud being escorted to meet Slim is described in Slim, *Unofficial*, p. 187; and the *Times of London*, September 2, 1941.

20. Parley between Slim and Massoud is described in Slim, *Unofficial*, pp. 187–88. The Iranian surrender is also described in Lt. Col. John Lakin's letter to the author, March 9, 1983; and Col. Joseph Baker's letter to the author, July 8, 1982.

21. Slim, *Unofficial*, p. 190.

22. Ibid.

23. Ibid.; and the *Times of London*, September 2, 1941. The general mentioned in the news article must be Puria. The only other Iranian general in the area—Moggadam—was in Kermanshah.

24. *PAIFORCE*, p. 69.

25. Slim, *Unofficial*, pp. 191–92.

26. Ibid.; and Prasad, *Campaign in Western Asia*, p. 350.

27. Wyndham, *First Household Cavalry*, p. 47.

28. Slim, *Unofficial*, pp. 192–94; and Prasad, *Campaign in Western Asia*, p. 295.

29. Slim's meeting with Moggadam and the arrest of Dr. Fuchs are described in Slim, *Unofficial*, pp. 193–94; and the *Times of London*, September 2, 1941.

30. The advance of the Soviet Army is described in the New York *Times*, August 30, 1941. The retreat of the Third Division is based on an interview with former Iranian Cpl. Tomic Romson on October 17, 1982.

31. Amini, *Shahrivar 1320*, p. 99.

32. The events in Rasht are based on Miller, *Diary;* and "First Chronicles."

33. The Soviet advance into Gilan is described in Makovskii and Radchenko, *Kapiiskaia*, p. 148. Cossacks in the city are referred to in Moorehead, *Don't Blame*, p. 44.

34. Interview with Adm. Morteza Daftary on December 3, 1982.

35. Amini, *Shahrivar 1320*, p. 102.

36. Interview with Col. Ali Farivari on July 9, 1982.

37. Events in Meshed are described in the following sources: Skrine, *World War*, pp. 105–6; Amini, *Shahrivar 1320*, p. 113; and "First Chronicles."

38. FRUS, *1941*, vol. 3, p. 438.
39. Miller, *Diary*.

CHAPTER 11

1. Amini, *Shahrivar 1320*, p. 22.
2. FRUS, *1941*, vol. 3, pp. 436–38.
3. The linkup agreement is noted in PRO, FO371-27233-E5201. The bombing of Kazvin is referred to in PRO, FO371-27708-E5177; FRUS, *1941*, vol. 3, p. 421; and the New York *Times*, September 3, 1941.
4. "First Chronicles." See also the New York *Times*, September 3, 1941.
5. The New York *Times*, August 4, 1941, refers to capture of Miandoab. The capture of the Iranian force was described during an interview by the author with former Iranian Cpl. Tomic Romson on October 27, 1982.
6. Kazakov, *Kartoi*, pp. 72 and 75–76. For the capture of Sabsevar, see the *Times of London*, September 2, 1941.
7. Skrine, *World War*, p. 106.
8. Interview with Col. Ali Farivari on July 9, 1982. Shopkeepers fleeing is noted in Miller, *Diary*.
9. The flight of the shah's family is noted in Amini, *Shahrivar 1320*, pp. 23–24; and Pahlavi, *Answer*, p. 67. Ghavam's meeting with Bullard is noted in FRUS, *1941*, vol. 3, p. 442.
10. Amini, *Shahrivar 1320*, p. 25; and Miller, *Diary*.
11. Churchill, *Grand Alliance*, pp. 454–55.
12. The Iranian situation in Kermanshah is described variously in Buckley, *Ventures*, p. 156; Prasad, *Campaign in Western Asia*, pp. 293 and 352; the *Times of London*, September 2, 1941; and Amini, *Shahrivar 1320*, pp. 103–5.
13. British preparations for parade are mentioned in Lt. Col. R. M. Maxwell's letter to the author, June 19, 1984. A detachment securing the refinery is referred to in Prasad, *Campaign in Western Asia*, p. 352. See Slim, *Unofficial*, pp. 213–15, for the general's reaction to Soviet moves.
14. Slim, *Unofficial*, pp. 213–15; and Buckley, *Ventures*, p. 156.
15. The radio attacks and their effects are described in Amini, *Shahrivar 1320*, p. 27; Bullard, *Camels Must Go*, p. 229; and Miller, *Diary*.
16. Miller, *Diary*.
17. Wilber, *Riza Shah*, p. 205; Amini, *Shahrivar 1320*, p. 27 and 35; and Bullard, *Camels Must Go*, p. 229.
18. Miller, *Diary*. See also Amini, *Shahrivar 1320*, p. 31.
19. The revolt of the Iranian pilots is described in Amini, *Shahrivar 1320*, p. 31; Buckley, *Ventures*, p. 159; New York *Times*, August 31 and September 2–3, 1941; and FRUS, *1941*, vol. 3, pp. 445fn and 453.
20. Amini, *Shahrivar 1320*, pp. 29–32. For details of the bombing, see also Buckley, *Ventures*, p. 159; and the New York *Times*, August 31 and September 1, 1941.
21. Amini, *Shahrivar 1320*, pp. 33–35. See also Miller, *Diary;* and "First Chronicles"—which refer to the declaration of martial law.
22. The British entry into Kermanshah is described in the *Times of London*, September 6, 1941; Prasad, *Campaign in Western Asia*, pp. 352–53; and Lt. Col. R. M. Maxwell's letter to the author, June 19, 1984.

23. Preparations of Pocock's column are described in Wyndham, *First Household Cavalry*, p. 47; Prasad, *Campaign in Western Asia*, p. 353; Buckley, *Ventures*, p. 156; and Lt. Col. R. M. Maxwell's letter to the author, June 19, 1984.

24. Amini, *Shahrivar 1320*, p. 104. See also *Yeoman, Yeoman*, p. 35, for a description of the capture of Moggadam and his regiment at Ravansur.

25. Buckley, *Ventures*, p. 157.

26. *Times of London*, September 6, 1941.

27. Slim, *Unofficial*, p. 216.

28. The advance of the 44th and 47th Armies, and the entry into Kazvin, are mentioned in: *Times of London*, September 1, 1941; New York *Times*, September 2, 3, and 5, 1941; Shtemenko, *Soviet General Staff*, pp. 50–51; and Moorehead, *Don't Blame*, p. 35.

29. Kazakov, *Kartoi*, p. 78. Maj. Gen. J. A. Aizelwood, who personally observed the Soviet forces at Kazvin, provided this estimate to the author in a letter dated October 25, 1982. The New York *Times*, September 5, 1941, reported that the "majority of [Soviet forces] are concentrated in Tabriz, Kazvin, Resht, Zinjan and the territory . . . bordering on the Turkish frontier."

30. The British entry into Hamadan is described in Rodger, *Journey*, pp. 121–22; "First Chronicles"; Miller, *Diary;* the *Times of London*, September 6, 1941; and Slim, *Unofficial*, p. 217.

31. FRUS, *1941*, vol. 3, p. 444.

32. PRO, FO371-27234-E4984.

33. Ibid.

34. FRUS, *1941*, vol. 3, pp. 443–44. See Amini, *Shahrivar 1320*, pp. 36–37, for complete text of the British and Soviet notes.

35. Ibid.

36. PRO, FO371-27233-E5201.

37. Amini, *Shahrivar 1320*, pp. 24, 38, and 44.

38. FRUS, *1941*, vol. 3, p. 443. Cordell Hull, *The Memoirs of Cordell Hull*, vol. 2. (New York: Macmillan, 1948), p. 1502.

39. Amini, *Shahrivar 1320*, p. 39. Arfa, *Five Shahs*, pp. 299–300, outlines the apparent reasons for General Nakjevan's order to release the conscripts.

40. Amini, *Shahrivar 1320*, pp. 39–40; and Arfa, *Five Shahs*, p. 299.

41. Amini, *Shahrivar 1320*, pp. 116–17.

42. Ibid., p. 105.

43. The meeting with the Soviets is described in Buckley, *Ventures*, p. 157; and in Lt. Col. R. M. Maxwell's letter to the author, June 19, 1984.

44. Lt. Col. G. M. Nightingale's letter to author, April 28, 1984.

45. Slim's orders to occupy Avej Pass, and the movement of the Gurkhas to Avej, are described in Slim, *Unofficial*, pp. 217–20; "First Chronicles"; and the *Times of London*, September 6, 1941.

46. Buckley, *Ventures*, p. 157.

47. Miller, *Diary*.

48. Amini, *Shahrivar 1320*, p. 44.

49. New York *Times*, September 1–2, 1941; and FRUS, *1941*, vol. 3, p. 444.

50. The Soviet entry into Meshed is described in Skrine, *World War*, p. 107, the New York *Times*, September 2, 1941; and Miller, *Diary*.

51. Kazakov, *Kartoi*, p. 75; and the New York *Times*, September 2, 1941.

52. Miller, *Diary*.
53. New York *Times*, September 3, 1941; and Amini, *Shahrivar 1320*, pp. 45–46.
54. The shah's arrest of the generals is described in Amini, *Shahrivar 1320*, pp. 45–46; Arfa, *Five Shahs*, p. 300; and Wilber, *Riza Shah*, p. 206. Some accounts claim that the shah beat his generals with his sword hilt. The appointment of Nakjevan is referred to in the New York *Times*, September 3, 1941; and Arfa, *Five Shahs*, p. 299.
55. The meeting with Soviets near Kazvin is described in Rodger, *Journey*, p. 123; and the *Times of London*, September 6, 1941. The British party being escorted to Kazvin is described in Moorehead, *Don't Blame*, pp. 34–35; *Times of London*, September 6, 1941; and the New York *Times*, September 3, 1941.
56. *Times of London*, September 6, 1941.
57. Slim, *Unofficial*, pp. 220–21.
58. FRUS, *1941*, vol. 3, pp. 444–45. See also DGFP, vol. 13, pp. 419–20; and Amini, *Shahrivar 1320*, p. 47.
59. Amini, *Shahrivar 1320*, pp. 52–55; and Wilber, *Riza Shah*, p. 206.
60. FRUS, *1941*, vol. 3, pp. 445–46.
61. Skrine, *World War*, p. 107; and Miller, *Diary*.
62. Interview with former Iranian Cpl. Tomic Romson on October 27, 1982.
63. FRUS, *1941*, vol. 3, p. 468.
64. Miller, *Diary*.
65. DGFP, vol. 13, pp. 419–20 and 420fn.
66. Ibid.
67. Miller, *Diary*.
68. Ibid.
69. Ibid.
70. Amini, *Shahrivar 1320*, p. 56.
71. Miller, *Diary*.
72. Churchill, *Grand Alliance*, pp. 492–93.
73. FRUS, *1941*, vol. 3, pp. 446–47.
74. Ibid.

CHAPTER 12

1. Dilks, *Diaries of Cadogan*, p. 403.
2. The situation in Tehran is described in Amini, *Shahrivar 1320*, pp. 60–62; and Miller, *Diary*.
3. FRUS, *1941*, vol. 3, p. 448.
4. New York *Times*, September 5, 1941. See also Amini, *Shahrivar 1320*, p. 62.
5. H. A. Jacobsen and Cyril Falls (eds.), *Decisive Battles of World War II: The German View* (New York: G. P. Putnam's Sons, 1965), p. 142.
6. PRO, FO371-27235-E5283.
7. Miller, *Diary*.
8. Amini, *Shahrivar 1320*, pp. 92–93; and the New York *Times*, September 5, 1941.
9. Moorehead, *Don't Blame*, p. 39.
10. New York *Times*, September 5, 1941.
11. Skrine, *World War*, p. 81.
12. Moorehead, *Don't Blame*, p. 40.

13. FRUS, *1941*, vol. 3, pp. 448–49.

14. Miller, *Diary*. On the Iranian diplomatic note through the U.S. ambassador in Turkey, see FRUS, *1941*, vol. 3, pp. 457–58.

15. Churchill, *Grand Alliance*, p. 484.

16. DGFP, vol. 13, pp. 452–53.

17. Amini, *Shahrivar 1320*, p. 115.

18. Ibid., pp. 116–17.

19. Ibid., pp. 117–24; and FRUS, *1941*, vol. 3, p. 452.

20. FRUS, *1941*, vol. 3, p. 452.

21. Ibid.

22. Miller, *Diary*.

23. The food shortage is described in ibid. The jailing of 600 without trial is noted in Amini, *Shahrivar 1320*, pp. 61–62. The foreign minister's meeting with Ettel is noted in DGFP, vol. 13, p. 461fn.

24. The Kurdish rebellion is described in: Slim, *Unofficial*, pp. 194–96; the New York *Times*, September 11, 1941; Wyndham, *First Household Cavalry*, p. 47; and Capt. William Storey, "Memoirs of the Aide-de-Camp to Maj. Gen. William J. Slim," unpublished (provided to the author by Gen. Sir Ouvry L. Roberts).

25. FRUS, *1941*, vol. 3, pp. 451–54.

26. PRO, FO371-27235-E5283 and E5364.

27. Motter, *United States Army*, p. 15.

28. FRUS, *1941*, vol. 3, pp. 454–55.

29. Ibid.

30. Kahn, *Hitler's Spies*, p. 186.

31. DGFP, vol. 13, pp. 461–62.

32. Amini, *Shahrivar 1320*, pp. 126–27.

33. Ibid., pp. 127–28.

34. New York *Times*, September 11, 1941.

35. Wilber, *Riza Shah*, p. 207.

36. Miller, *Diary*.

37. New York *Times*, September 10, 1941.

38. Wavell, "Despatch on Operations," p. 4100; and Maj. W. J. Armstrong, "The Tenth Army in Iran," *Army Quarterly* 52,2, (July 1946): 232.

39. Slim's journey is described in Storey, "Memoirs"; and Slim, *Unofficial*, p. 205.

40. Amini, *Shahrivar 1320*, pp. 130–31. For a discussion of the editorial and surrounding controversy, see also the *Times of London*, September 13, 1941; Bullard, *Camels Must Go*, p. 228; and Fatemi, *Oil Diplomacy*, p. 195. Shah Mohammed Reza Pahlavi later denied that he authored this key article. See Karanjia, *Mind of Monarch*, pp. 61–62.

41. Bullard, *Camels Must Go*, p. 228; and Slim, *Unofficial*, p. 236.

42. New York *Times*, September 11, 1941.

43. Schulze-Holthus, *Daybreak*, p. 63.

44. Ibid., pp. 63–64.

45. Ibid., pp. 66–67.

46. Slim, *Unofficial*, pp. 205–6 and 236.

47. DGFP, vol. 13, pp. 482–83.

48. Ibid.

49. Charles Cruickshank, *The German Occupation of the Channel Islands* (London: Oxford University Press, 1975), pp. 206–13.

50. DGFP, vol. 13, p. 494 and 494fn.

51. Schulze-Holthus, *Daybreak*, pp. 69–70.

52. Ibid., pp. 70–72, also describes Schulze's flight from Tehran.

53. DGFP, vol. 13, p. 494.

54. DGFP, vol. 13, p. 496fn; and the U.S. National Archives, Microfilm Records of the German Foreign Ministry, serial 913-294970 and 294979.

55. DGFP, vol. 13, pp. 494–95.

56. Richard Dimbleby, *The Frontiers are Green* (London: Hodder and Stoughton, 1943), pp. 220–21.

57. Schulze-Holthus, *Daybreak*, p. 88.

58. Ettel's meeting with the refugees is described in DGFP, vol. 13, pp. 494–95.

59. FRUS, *1941*, vol. 3, p. 460; and the U.S. National Archives, Microfilm Records of the German Foreign Ministry, serial 913-294970.

60. Dimbleby, *Frontiers*, pp. 221–22.

61. Slim, *Unofficial*, pp. 233–34; and Storey, "Memoirs." Slim's sequence of events differs slightly from Captain Storey's, whose version seems the more accurate.

62. Miller, *Diary*.

63. Amini, *Shahrivar 1320*, p. 132; and the New York *Times*, September 15, 1941.

64. Fatemi, *Oil Diplomacy*, p. 195.

65. Wavell, "Despatch on Operations," p. 4100.

66. The Bullard note to Iranian government is referenced in Fatemi, *Oil Diplomacy*, p. 195. German Jews at the British legation are noted in the New York *Times*, September 15, 1941.

67. New York *Times*, September 17, 1941, notes the mufti as the most wanted man in Tehran. Mufti's sanctuary is described in Moorehead, *Don't Blame*, p. 40.

68. Wilber, *Riza Shah*, p. 207.

69. Wavell, "Despatch on Operations," p. 4100; Platt, *Wiltshire Yeomanry*, p. 112; and Wyndam, *First Household Cavalry*, p. 48.

70. Kazakov, *Kartoi*, p. 78.

71. See Bullard, *Camels Must Go*, p. 230, for Majlis request for an audience with the shah. The British note is referred to in the New York *Times*, September 17, 1941; and Pahlavi, *Mission*, p. 71.

72. Numbers for the Germans are based on the U.S. National Archives, Microfilm Records of the German Foreign Minister, serial 913-294979; and the New York *Times*, September 16, 1941.

73. Pahlavi, *Answer*, p. 67.

74. Gérard de Villiers (trans. June P. Wilson and Walker B. Michaels), *The Imperial Shah: An Informal Biography* (Boston: Little, Brown and Company, 1976), pp. 88–89; and Wilber, *Riza Shah*, p. 207.

75. Wilber, *Riza Shah*, pp. 207–8.

76. Villiers, *Imperial Shah*, p. 90.

77. Kazakov, *Kartoi*, p. 78; and the New York *Times*, September 17, 1941.

78. Description of the shah's resignation is based on the following sources: Bullard, *Camels Must Go*, p. 230; Amini, *Shahrivar 1320*, p. 132; Villiers, *Imperial Shah*,

pp. 86 and 89; and Pahlavi, *Faces,* p. 42. Accounts differ on whether the shah or Foroughi first drafted the decree.

79. Pahlavi, *Answer,* p. 68.

80. Amini, *Shahrivar 1320,* p. 133; and Villiers, *Imperial Shah,* p. 90.

81. Villiers, *Imperial Shah,* p. 90.

82. Bullard, *Camels Must Go,* p. 230.

83. Mohammed Heikal, *Iran: The Untold Story* (New York: Pantheon Books, 1982), pp. 34–35. See also Arfa, *Five Shahs,* p. 302; and Amini, *Shahrivar 1320,* p. 133.

84. Miller, *Diary.*

85. The movement of the British and the Soviets is described in: New York *Times,* September 17, 1941; Kazakov, *Kartoi,* p. 78; and Rev. Hugo Muller's letter to "Endy," dated September 23, 1941. Muller followed the British in his auto.

86. Foroughi's speech is described in Amini, *Shahrivar 1320,* p. 133; Villiers, "Despatch on Operations," pp. 90–91; and Miller, *Diary.*

87. Miller, *Diary.*

88. Churchill, *Grand Alliance,* p. 484.

89. Miller, *Diary.*

90. The Soviet movement into/around Tehran is described in Kazakov, *Kartoi,* p. 78; Wyndham, *First Household Cavalry,* p. 48; and the New York *Times,* September 20, 1941. The British move is described in Rev. Hugo Muller's letter to "Endy," dated September 23, 1941.

91. The shah's appearance and attitude are described in Arfa, *Five Shahs,* pp. 302–3; and Pahlavi, *Answer,* p. 68.

92. Interview with former U.S. Consul James S. Moose on October 10, 1982. Wilber, *Riza Shah,* pp. 127 and 135, notes that Ahmadi was personally appointed by the shah to quell the Lurs, which he did with great success.

93. Wyndham, *First Household Cavalry,* p. 48.

94. Miller, *Diary.*

95. Ibid.

96. Pahlavi, *Answer,* p. 68; and Karanjia, *Mind of Monarch,* p. 62.

97. Arfa, *Five Shahs,* p. 303.

98. Ibid. Portions of the new shah's speech are quoted in Miller, *Diary.* The old shah's reaction is described in Pahlavi, *Faces,* p. 43.

99. The fate of the old shah and his family is described in Pahlavi, *Answer,* p. 69; and Wilber, *Riza Shah,* pp. 217–20.

100. *Times of London,* August 18, 1941; Arfa, *Five Shahs,* p. 304.

101. Arfa, *Five Shahs,* p. 304.

102. Miller, *Diary.*

103. Arfa, *Five Shahs,* pp. 304–05; and the New York *Times,* September 20, 1941.

104. Wyndham, *First Household Cavalry,* p. 48.

105. New York *Times,* September 19, 1941; and Slim, *Unofficial,* p. 237.

106. Paul Leverkuehn (trans. R. H. Stevens), *German Military Intelligence* (London: Weidenfeld and Nicolson, 1954), pp.16–17.

107. Slim, *Unofficial,* p. 237. See also the New York *Times,* September 19, 1941.

108. Slim, *Unofficial,* pp. 237–38.

109. The entrance of the British and Soviet armies is described in Slim, *Unofficial*, p. 238; Kazakov, *Kartoi*, pp. 76–77; and the New York *Times*, September 20, 1941.

110. New York *Times*, September 19, 1941; and Arfa, *Five Shahs*, p. 308.

111. U.S. National Archives, Microfilm Records of Germany Foreign Ministry, serial 913-294969. See also Schulze-Holthus, *Daybreak*, p. 91 and 93.

112. FRUS, *1941*, vol. 3, p. 461.

113. The actions of the British and Soviet soldiers in Tehran were described in an interview with former U.S. Consul James S. Moose on October 10, 1982; and in Miller, *Diary*.

114. Miller, *Diary*.

115. Ibid.

116. FRUS, *1941*, vol. 3, pp. 461–65.

EPILOGUE

1. PRO, FO371-27235-E6355.

2. Fatemi, *Oil Diplomacy*, pp. 204–5.

3. PRO, FO371-27235-E6392.

4. PRO, FO371-27233-E6283 and E6346.

5. Churchill, *Grand Alliance*, pp. 462, 464, 473, and 485.

6. PRO, FO371-27236-E7551.

7. PRO, FO371-35077; U.S. National Archives, "Axis Agents in Iran—to August 15, 1943," USA Forces in the Middle East, G-2 Regional, RG 165; Lenczowski, *Russia and the West*, p. 163.

8. FRUS, *1941*, vol. 3, pp. 475–76.

9. FRUS, *1942*, vol. 6, p. 269.

10. PRO, FO371-27236-E7551.

11. Maj. Gen. F. W. von Mellinthin (trans. H. Betzler), *Panzer Battles* (London: Cassel and Company, 1955), p. 185.

12. Motter, *United States Army*, p. 496.

13. FRUS, *1942*, vol. 4, pp. 238–39 and 539.

14. U.S. Department of War, *Fuehrer Directives and Other Top-level Directives of the German Armed Forces, 1942–1945* (Washington, D.C.: U.S. Department of War, n.d.), p. 163.

15. Winston S. Churchill, *The Second World War: The Hinge of Fate* (Boston: Houghton Mifflin, 1950), pp. 474–75, 483, 495–96, and 501.

16. Shtemenko, *Soviet General Staff*, p. 61.

17. U.S. Army, *Great Patriotic War*, vol. 2, p. 461; James Lucas, *Alpine Elite: German Mountain Troops of World War II* (London: Janes, 1980), p. 133.

18. Shtemenko, *Soviet General Staff*, p. 62. See also *Great Patriotic War*, vol. 2, p. 464.

19. Harriman and Abel, *Special Envoy*, p. 166.

20. Motter, *United States Army*, pp. 213–14 and 484.

21. Zhukov, *Memoirs*, pp. 393 and 402.

22. FRUS, *1943*, vol. 4, pp. 321 and 331–35.

23. Ibid., p. 378.

24. Ibid., p. 414.

25. Lenczowski, *Russia and the West* p. 227; and Fatemi, *Oil Diplomacy*, p. 206.

26. Lenczowski, *Russia and the West,* pp. 206–10 and 221.

27. Fatemi, *Oil Diplomacy,* pp. 235–36, 238–40, and 247–48. Soviet reinforcements are noted in U.S. National Archives, OSS Report 110650, RG 226.

28. Charles L. Mee, Jr., *Meeting at Potsdam* (New York: Dell Publishing, 1975), p. 177.

29. Arfa, *Five Shahs,* pp. 342–43; and FRUS, *1945,* vol. 8, p. 400.

30. FRUS, *1945,* vol. 8, pp. 417–19.

31. U.S. appeals rebuffed by the Soviet Union are noted in FRUS, *1945,* vol. 8, pp. 448–50 and 510–11. The departure of the last U.S. troops is described in Motter, *United States Army,* pp. 424–26. FRUS, *1945,* vol. 8, p. 482, reports on the 70,000 Soviet troops remaining in Iran.

32. Arfa, *Five Shahs,* pp. 347–48; and FRUS, *1945,* vol. 8, pp. 432–38 and 494.

33. FRUS, *1945,* vol. 8, p. 497.

34. Ibid., p. 461.

35. James F. Byrnes, *Speaking Frankly* (New York: Harper and Brothers Publishers, 1947), pp. 119–20.

36. Charles E. Bohlen, *Witness to History: 1929–1969* (New York: W. W. Norton and Company, 1973), p. 249.

37. Fatemi, *Oil Diplomacy,* pp. 293–95.

38. FRUS, *1946,* vol. 7, pp. 351–52.

39. New York *Times,* March 1, 1946.

40. FRUS, *1946,* vol. 7, p. 335.

41. Robert Rossow, Jr., "The Battle of Azerbaijan," *Middle East Journal* 10,1 (1956): 20; and FRUS, *1946,* vol. 7, p. 340.

42. New York *Times,* March 8, 1946.

43. FRUS, *1946,* vol. 7, pp. 342–44 and 346–47.

44. New York *Times,* March 8, 1946; and Rossow, "Battle of Azerbaijan," p. 22.

45. Walter Millis, *The Forrestal Diaries* (New York: Viking Press, 1951), pp. 141 and 144.

46. FRUS, *1946,* vol. 7, pp. 350–53, 357, and 365.

47. Ibid., pp. 366–67.

48. Ibid., pp. 362–64.

49. Harry S. Truman, *Memoirs,* vol. 2: *Year of Trial and Hope* (Garden City, N.Y.: Doubleday and Company, 1955), p. 95. See also Fatemi, *Oil Diplomacy,* pp. 304–6.

50. Truman, *Memoirs,* p. 95.

51. New York *Times,* March 22, 1946.

52. Harriman and Abel, *Special Envoy,* p. 550.

53. FRUS, *1946,* vol. 7, pp. 378–79.

54. Rossow, "Battle of Azerbaijan," p. 24.

55. FRUS, *1946,* vol. 7, pp. 529–32 and 535–36.

56. The collapse of the rebels and the Soviet reaction are described in the following: FRUS, *1946,* vol. 7, pp. 547 and 560; Rossow, "Battle of Azerbaijan," pp. 29–31; and Ramesh Sanghvi, *The Shah of Iran* (New York: Stein and Day Publishers, 1969), p. 133.

57. FRUS, *1946,* vol. 7, p. 561.

Bibliography

INTERVIEWS AND CORRESPONDENCE

Most of the people interviewed for this book are retired or no longer living. They are listed below with their latest rank or title, and then by their role with respect to the subject of the book.

Maj. Gen. John A. Aizelwood	brigadier, officer commanding, Second Indian Armoured Brigade
Col. Joseph K. Baker, U.S.A. (Ret.)	major, U.S. observer to British forces, Iraq, 1941
Maj. H. N. Clemas	lieutenant, 2/6th Rajputana Rifles
Dr. Joseph P. Cochrane	Presbyterian doctor, Tabriz
Mr. Sam Croft	trooper, Warwickshire Yeomanry
Maj. Malcolm L. Cruickshank	captain, 1/2d Gurkha Rifles
Rear Adm. Morteza Daftary	captain, commander of naval station, Bander-i Pahlavi
Mr. John M. Day	trooper, Warwickshire Yeomanry
Hon. Cornelius Van Engert	chargé d'affaires, U.S. Legation, Iran, 1936–40
Col. Ali Farivari	lieutenant, 23d Iranian Cavalry Regiment
Mr. Neal Ford	captain, 2/3d Gurkha Rifles
Col. J. Michael Forster	captain, 3/10th Baluch Regiment

Capt. Jafar Fosuni lieutenant, commander of gunboat *Karkas*

Mr. A. D. R. Geddis second lieutenant, 1/2d Gurkha Rifles

Hon. W. Averell Harriman personal envoy to Churchill; ambassador to the Soviet Union

Maj. Robert J. Henderson captain, 2/11th Sikh Regiment

Maj. John W. Humphries second lieutenant, A Squadron, Guides Cavalry

Maj. Allan J. F. Johnston major, 1/5th Mahratta Regiment

Mr. Malcolm L. Karam employee, Abadan oil refinery

Brig. Gen. Patrick M. Kent captain, 2/6th Rajputana Rifles

Col. John Lakin major, Warwickshire Yeomanry

Lt. Col. L. C. J. Loch major, First Kumaon Rifles

Lt. Col. Colin H. McVean major, 2/11th Sikh Regiment

Lt. Col. Robert M. Maxwell captain, 1/5th Gurkha Rifles

Rev. William M. Miller Presbyterian minister, Tehran

Hon. James S. Moose, Jr. U.S. consul in Iran, 1940–41

Rev. Hugo Muller Presbyterian minister, Hamadan

Lt. Col. Edward N. Mumford captain, 2/3d Gurkha Rifles

Lt. Col. George M. Nightingale captain, 1/5th Gurkha Rifles

Maj. Gen. Robert B. Penfold captain, 2/11th Sikh Regiment

Lt. Col. Donald Ramsey-Brown captain, 1/2d Gurkha Rifles

Gen. Sir Ouvry L. Roberts chief of staff, Tenth Indian Division

Mr. Tomic Romson corporal, Iranian Third Division

Adm. Shamseddin Safavi lieutenant, commander of gunboat *Shahrokh*

Mr. Hassan Soburi resident in Sarakhs, Iran

Maj. Gerald H. van Loo captain, 3/10th Baluch Regiment

Lt. Gen. Karim Varahram former deputy chief of staff, historian, Imperial Iranian Army

Mr. Edwin M. Wright missionary in Iran, 1941; State Department advisor on Iran, 1946

UNPUBLISHED DOCUMENTS AND MANUSCRIPTS

"First Chronicles." A type written Presbyterian missionary chronology of the 1941 invason of Iran. Provided by the Rev. Hugo Muller.

Guensberg, Dr. Gerold., ed. *Soviet Command Study of Iran and Brief Analysis.* Draft translation. McLean, Va.: SRI International, 1980. A translation of the document *Darstellung Irans: Verfasst Vom Generalstab der Sowjetrussischen Armee, Moskau, 1941* (Description of Iran: Composed by the General Staff of the Soviet Russian Army, Moscow, 1941). A Soviet invasion study of Iran undertaken in 1940–41, and recovered by invading German forces. Translated verbatim into German and kept in the files of the Wehrmacht Military Intelligence Branch, and then captured by the U.S. Army. A microfilmed copy is in the National Archives.

Lamme, Dr. Charles. "The Occupation of Tabriz, August 1941." A typewritten account dated October 27, 1941. Provided by Reverend Hugo Muller.

Miller, William M. *The Diary of Reverend William Miller.* Philadelphia: Presbyterian Historical Society Collection, 425 Lombard St., Philadelphia, Pa., 1941. Provided by the Reverend Miller. The diary is a day-by-day journal written to the minister's mother.

Muller, Rev. Hugo. Handwritten letter to "Endy." Dated September 23, 1941.

Roberts, Gen. Sir Ouvry L. "Memoirs." Provided by General Roberts.

Storey, Capt. William. "Memoirs of the Aide-de-Camp to Maj. Gen. William J. Slim." Provided by Gen. Sir Ouvry L. Roberts.

Yeaton, Col. Ivan D., U.S.A. (Ret.). "Memoirs of the U.S. military Attaché to the U.S.S.R., 1940–41." Hoover Institution, Stanford University.

OFFICIAL DOCUMENTS

Die Geheimakten des Franzoesischen Generalstabes (The Secrets of the French General Staff). Vol. 6. Berlin: Reich Foreign Ministry, 1941.

Her Majesty's Public Records Office: War Cabinet (CAB 66), Foreign Office (FO371), War Office (WO169), and Admiralty (ADM199).

His Majesty's Naval Intelligence Division. *Persia: Geographical Handbook Series.* September 1945.

India Office Records: Letters from India, 1875.

Sontag, Raymond James, and Beddie, James Stuart, eds. *Nazi–Soviet Relations, 1939–1941: Documents from the Archives of the German Foreign Office.* Washington, D.C.: U.S. Department of State, Government Printing Office, 1948.

Trial of the Major War Criminals before the International Military Tribunal, Nuremberg, 14 November 1945–1 October 1946. 42 volumes. Nuremberg: Secretariat of the Tribunal, 1947–49.

U.S. Army, *History of the Great Patriotic War.* Vols. 1 and 2. Unedited translation distributed by the Office of the Chief of Military History, U.S. Army. Moscow: Military Publishing House, 1961.

U.S. Department of State. *Documents on German Foreign Policy.* Series D. Vol. 9–13. Washington, D.C.: Government Printing Office, 1956–64.

————. *Foreign Relations of the United States, 1940–1946.* Washington, D.C.: Government Printing Office, 1958–69.

U.S. Department of War. *Fuehrer Directives and Other Top-level Directives of the German Armed Forces, 1942–1945.* Washington, D.C.: U.S. Department of War.

U.S. National Archives: Record Groups (RG) 165, 226, and 242.

NEWSPAPERS AND JOURNALS

Journal de Tehran
New York *Times*
Illustrated London News
Times of London
Armstrong, Maj. W. J. "The Tenth Army in Iran." *Army Quarterly* 52,2 (July 1946): 232.
Gordon, Capt. C. G. M. "First Household Cavalry Regiment." *War Illustrated* 10,240 (August 30, 1945): 299.
Graham, Capt. A. "The Iraq Levies at Habbaniya." *Army Quarterly* 44,7 (1947): 250.
Namdar, Ahmad. "The German Fifth Column in Iran" (translated title). *Khandaniha* (Seventh Year) 4;12–15 and 20; 5;10–11 and 20–21; 9;18–20; 13;7–10; 16;7–8; 19;10 and 20; 21;10–11; 23;14–15.
Rossow, Robert Jr. "The Battle of Azerbaijan." *Middle East Journal* 10,1 (1956): 20.
Wavell, Gen. A. P. "Despatch on Operations in Iraq, East Syria and Iran, from 10th April, 1941 to 12th January, 1942." Supplement to the London *Gazette,* August 13, 1946, p. 4097.
Wilson, Gen. Sir H. Maitland. "Despatch on the Persia and Iraq Command Covering the Period 21st August, 1942 to 17th February, 1943." Supplement to the London *Gazette,* August 27, 1946, pp. 4333–40.

BOOKS

Abhyankar, Maj. M. G. *The Rajputana Rifles, 1775–1947.* Bombay: Orient Longmans, 1961.
Akhmedov, Ismail. *In and Out of Stalin's Gru: A Tatar's Escape from Red Army Intelligence.* Frederick, Md.: University Publications of America, 1984.
Amini, Daoud Mo'eyd. *Az Sevvom ta Bist-o-panjum-e-Shahrivar 1320* (From August 25 to September 16, 1941). Tehran: n.p., 1942.
A'raqi, Mohammed Khalili. *Vaqay'a-i Shahrivar* (The Events of August and September). Tehran: Zarbaksh, 1944.
Arfa, Gen. Hassan. *Under Five Shahs.* London: John Murray, 1964.
Avery, Peter. *Modern Iran.* London: Ernest Benn, 1965.
Baghyrov, N. T. *77 Simferopolskaia: Kratkaia Istoriia* (Regimental History of the 77th Simferopol Division). Baku: Azerbaidzhanskoe gos. izd-vo, 1981.
Barclay, C. N. *The Regimental History of the 3rd Queen Alexandra's Own Gurkha Rifles.* Vol. 2: *1927–1947.* London: William Clowes and Sons, 1953.
Beufre, Gen. André. Translated by Desmond Flowe. *1940: The Fall of France.* London: Cassel and Company, 1965.

Bialer, Serweryn, ed. *Stalin and His Generals: Soviet Military Memoirs of World War II.* New York: Pegasus Press, 1969.

Birdwood, Col. J. T. *The Sikh Regiment in the Second World War.* Norwich, U.K.: Jarrold and Sons, n.d.

Bohlen, Charles E. *Witness to History: 1929–1969.* New York: W. W. Norton and Company, 1973.

Bridgeman, Leonard, ed. *Jane's All the World's Aircraft, 1941.* London: Macmillan and Company, 1942.

Buckley, Christopher. *Five Ventures.* London: Her Majesty's Stationery Office, 1954.

Bullard, Sir Reader. *Britain and the Middle East.* London: Hutchinson, 1964.

———. *The Camels Must Go.* London: Faber and Faber, 1961.

Butler, J. R. M. *Grand Strategy.* Vol. 2: *September 1939–June 1941.* London: Her Majesty's Stationery Office, 1957.

Byrnes, James F. *Speaking Frankly.* New York: Harper and Brothers Publishers, 1947.

Cassidy, Henry C. *Moscow Dateline.* Boston: Houghton Mifflin, 1943.

Churchill, Winston S. *The Second World War: The Gathering Storm.* Boston: Houghton Mifflin, 1948.

———. *The Second World War: The Grand Alliance.* Boston: Houghton Mifflin, 1950.

———. *The Second World War: The Hinge of Fate.* Boston: Houghton Mifflin, 1950.

Complete Presidential Press Conferences of Franklin D. Roosevelt, The. Vol. 18: *1941.* New York: Da Capo Press, 1972.

Connell, John. *Wavell: Scholar and Soldier.* London: Collins Brothers and Company, 1964.

———. *Wavell: Supreme Commander.* London: Collins Brothers and Company, 1969.

Crowley, Edward L., Lebed, Andrew I., and Schulz, Dr. Heinrich E., eds. *Who's Who in the USSR, 1965.* Metuchen, N.J.: Scarecrow Press, 1965.

Cruickshank, Charles. *The German Occupation of the Channel Islands.* London: Oxford University Press, 1975.

Curzon, George N. *Persia and the Persian Question.* Vol. 1. London: Longmans, Green and Company, 1892.

Dallin, David J. *Soviet Russia's Foreign Policy, 1939–1942.* New Haven, Conn.: Yale University Press, 1942.

David, D. M. *Official History of New Zealand in the Second World War, 1939–1945: Crete.* London: Oxford University Press, 1955.

Davidich, Victor Nikolaevich. *Raizni Svoei Neshchadya* (Without Sparing One's Own Life). Moscow: Military Publishing House, 1981.

De Chair, Somerset. *The Golden Carpet.* London: Faber and Faber, 1962.

Degras, Jane, ed. *Soviet Documents on Foreign Policy.* Vol. 3. London: Oxford University Press, 1953.

Detwiler, Donald S., Burdick, Charles S., and Rowher, Jurgen, eds. *World War II: German Military Studies.* 24 volumes. New York: Garland Publishing, 1979.

Dilks, David, ed. *The Diaries of Sir Alexander Cadogan.* New York: G. P. Putnam's Sons, 1972.

Dimbleby, Richard. *The Frontiers Are Green.* London: Hodder and Stoughton, 1943.

Eden, Anthony. *The Reckoning*. Boston: Houghton Mifflin, 1965.

Edlinskii, Sergei Frantsevich. *Kapiiskii Transportnyi Flot v Velikoi Otechestvennoi Voine Sovetskogo Soiuza 1941–1945* (Caspian Transport Fleet during World War II). Moscow: Mor. Transport, 1963.

Elwell-Sutton, L. P. *Modern Iran*. London: George Rutledge and Sons, 1941.

Erickson, John. *The Road to Stalingrad*. London: Weidenfeld and Nicolson, 1975.

———. *The Soviet High Command: A Political History, 1918–1941*. New York: Macmillan, 1962.

Fabry, P. W. *Iran, Die Sowjet union und das Kriegfuehrende Deutschland im Sommer under Herbst 1940* (Iran, the Soviet Union and the Wartime Leadership of Germany in the Summer and Fall of 1940). Gottingen: Muster-Schmidt Verlag, 1980.

Fatemi, Faramarz S. *The U.S.S.R. in Iran*. London: A. S. Barnes, 1980.

Fatemi, Nasrollah S. *Oil Diplomacy: Powderkeg in Iran*. New York: Whittier Books, 1954.

Feis, Herbert. *Churchill, Roosevelt, Stalin: The War They Waged and the Peace They Sought*. Princeton, N.J.: Princeton University Press, 1957.

Ferguson, Bernard. *Wavell: Portrait of a Soldier*. London: Collins, 1961.

Grechko, Andrei. *Bitva za Kavkaz* (Battle for the Caucasus). Moscow: Military Publishing House, 1971.

Harker, Jack S. *Well Done Leander*. Auckland, N.Z.: Collins Bros., 1971.

Harriman, W. Averell, and Abel, Elie. *Special Envoy to Churchill and Stalin, 1941–1946*. New York: Random House, 1975.

Heikal, Mohammed. *Iran: The Untold Story*. New York: Pantheon Books, 1982.

Hermongle, G. *Australia in the War of 1939–1945: Royal Australian Navy, 1939–1945*. Canberra: Australian War Memorial, 1957.

Hinsley, Francis H. *British Intelligence in the Second World War*. 2 volumes. London and New York: Cambridge University Press, 1979–81.

Hull, Cordell. *The Memoirs of Cordell Hull*. Vol 2. New York: Macmillan, 1948.

Hurewitz, J. C. *Diplomacy in the Near and Middle East*. Vol. 1. Princeton, N.J.: Princeton University Press, 1956.

Irving, David. *Hitler's War*. New York: Viking Press, 1977.

Jacobsen, H. A., and Falls, Cyril, eds. *Decisive Battles of World War II: The German View*. New York: G. P. Putnam's Sons, 1965.

Jane's Fighting Ships, 1941. London: Macmillan and Company, 1942.

Jones, T. M., and Idriess, Jon L., eds. *Silent Service: Action Stories of the Anzac Navy*. 2d ed. Sydney: Angus and Robertson, 1952.

Kahn, David. *Hitler's Spies: German Military Intelligence in World War II*. New York: Macmillan, 1978.

Karanjia, R. K. *The Mind of a Monarch*. London: George Allen and Unwin, 1977.

Kazakov, Mikhail Illich. *Nad Kartoi Bylykh Svazhenii* (At the Map of Past Battles). Moscow: Military Publishing House, 1971.

Kazemzadeh, Firuz. *Russia and Britain in Persia, 1864–1914*. New Haven, Conn.: Yale University Press, 1968.

Kelly, J. B. *Britain and the Persian Gulf, 1795–1880*. Oxford: Oxford University Press, 1968.

Kennedy, Maj. Gen. Sir John. *The Business of War*. London: Hutchinson, 1957.

Khadduri, Majid. *Independent Iraq, 1932–1958: A Study in Iraqi Politics*. London: Oxford University Press, 1960.

Krasnoznamennyi Turkestanskii (Red Order Banner of Turkestan). Moscow: Military Publishing House, 1976.

Krasnoznamennyi Zakavkazskii (Red Order Banner of the Transcaucasus). Moscow: Military Publishing House, 1969.

Kuznetsov, Pavel Grigorievich. *Marshal Tolbukhin*. Moscow: Military Publishing House, 1966.

Lang, David Marshall. *The Last Years of the Georgian Monarchy, 1658–1832*. New York: Columbia University Press, 1957.

Langer, William L., and Gleason, S. Everett. *The Undeclared War, 1940–1941*. New York: Harper and Brothers Publishers, 1953.

Lash, Joseph P. *Roosevelt and Churchill, 1939–1941: The Partnership That Saved the West*. New York: W. W. Norton, 1976.

Lenczowski, George. *Iran Under the Pahlavis*. Stanford, Calif.: Stanford University Press, 1978.

———. *Russia and the West in Iran 1918–1948*. Ithaca, N.Y.: Cornell University Press, 1949.

Leverkuehn, Paul. Translated by R. H. Stevens. *German Military Intelligence*. London: Weidenfeld and Nicolson, 1954.

Lobachev, Maj. Gen. A. A. *Trudymi Dorogami* (By Difficult Roads). Moscow: Military Publishing House, 1960.

Long, Gavin. *Australia in the War of 1939–1945*. Vol. 2: *Greece, Crete, and Syria*. Canberra: Australian War Memorial, 1953.

Longrigg, Stephen Hemsley. *Iraq, 1900 to 1950*. London: Oxford University Press, 1953.

Lucas, James. *Alpine Elite: German Mountain Troops of World War II*. London: Janes, 1980.

Lukasz, Hirszowicz. *The Third Reich and the Arab East*. London: Routledge and Kegan Paul, 1966.

Makovskii, A. A., and Radchenko, B. M. *Kapiiskaia Krasnoznamennaia* (Red Order Banner of the Caspian). Moscow: Military Publishing House, 1961.

Masters, John. *The Road Past Mandalay*. New York: Harper and Brothers, 1961.

Maule, Henry. *Spearhead General: The Epic Story of General Sir Frank Messervy and His Men in Eritrea, North Africa and Burma*. London: Odhams Press, 1961.

Maxwell, Col. W. E. *Capitol Campaigners*. Aldershot, U.K.: Gale and Polden, 1948.

Mee, Charles L., Jr. *Meeting at Potsdam*. New York: Dell Publishing, 1975.

Meister, Jurg. (ed.). *Soviet Warships of the Second World War*. New York: Arco Publishing, 1977.

Mellinthin, Maj. Gen. F. W. von. Translated by H. Betzler. *Panzer Battles*. London: Cassel and Company, 1955.

Millis, Walter. *The Forrestal Diaries*. New York: Viking Press, 1951.

Millspaugh, Arthur C. *Americans in Persia*. Washington, D.C.: Brookings Institution, 1946.

Moorehead, Alan. *Don't Blame the Generals*. New York: Harper and Brothers Publishers, 1943.

Motter, T. H. Vail. *The United States Army in World War II. The Persian Corridor and Aid to Russia:* Washington, D.C.: Government Printing Office, 1956.

Pahlavi, Ashraf. *Faces in the Mirror.* Englewood Cliffs, N.J.: Prentice-Hall, 1980.

Pahlavi, Mohammed Reza Shah. *Answer to History.* New York: Stein and Day, 1980.

———. *Mission for My Country.* New York: McGraw-Hill, 1961.

PAIFORCE: The Official History of the Persia and Iraq Command, 1941–1946. London: His Majesty's Stationery Office, 1948.

Parry, A. F. *H.M.A.S. Yarra: The Story of a Gallant Ship.* Sydney: Angus and Robertson, 1944.

Platt, Brig. J. R. *The Royal Wiltshire Yeomanry (Prince of Wales Own), 1907–1967.* London: Garnstone Press, 1972.

Playfair, Maj. Gen. I. S. O. *The Mediterranean and the Middle East.* 5 volumes. London: Her Majesty's Stationery Office, 1954–73.

Prasad, Bisheshwar, ed. *Official History of the Indian Armed Forces in the Second World War, 1939–1945: The Campaign in Western Asia.* Calcutta: Sree Sarawata Press, 1957.

———. *Official History of the Indian Armed Forces in the Second World War, 1939–1945: The Royal Indian Navy.* Agra, India: Agra University Press, 1964.

Richards, Denis. *The Royal Air Force: 1939–1945.* Vol. 1: *The Fight at Odds.* London: Her Majesty's Stationery Office, 1974.

Rodger, George. *Desert Journey.* London: Cresset Press, 1946.

Sanghvi, Ramesh. *The Shah of Iran.* New York: Stein and Day Publishers, 1969.

Schulze-Holthus, (Bertold). Translated by Mervyn Savill. *Daybreak in Iran.* London: Staples Press, 1954.

Sherwood, Robert E. *Roosevelt and Hopkins: An Intimate History.* New York: Harper and Brothers Publishers, 1950.

Shirer, William L. *The Rise and Fall of the Third Reich.* New York: Simon and Schuster, 1959.

Shtemenko, Gen. Sergei M. Translated by Robert Daglish. *The Soviet General Staff at War, 1941–1945.* Moscow: Progress Publishers, 1970.

Skrine, Clairmont. *World War in Iran.* London: Constable and Company, 1962.

Slim, Fld. Mar. Sir William. *Unofficial History.* London: Cassell and Company, 1959.

Sovetskaia Voennaia Entsiklopediia (Soviet Military Encyclopedia). 7 volumes. Moscow: Military Publishing House, 1976–81.

Stark, Freya. *The Arab Island: The Middle East, 1939–1943.* New York: Alfred A. Knopf, 1945.

———. *Dust in the Lion's Paw.* New York: Harcourt, Brace and World, 1962.

Stevens, Lt. Col. G. R. *History of the 2nd King Edward VII's Own Goorkha Rifles (The Sirmoor Rifles).* Vol. 3: *1921–1948.* Aldershot, U.K.: Gale and Polden, 1952.

Sykes, Sir Percy. *A History of Persia.* Vol. 2. London: Macmillan and Company, 1951.

Thatcher, W. S. *The Tenth Baluch Regiment in the Second World War.* Abbotabad, India: Baluch Center Press, 1980.

Thayer, Charles. *Bears in the Caviar.* London: Michael Joseph, 1952.

Thetford, Owen. *Aircraft of the Royal Air Force since 1918.* New York: Funk and Wagnalls, 1968.

Truman, Harry S. *Memoirs*. Vol. 2: *Year of Trial and Hope*. Garden City, N.Y.: Doubleday and Company, 1955.

Villiers, Gérard de Translated by June P. Wilson and Walker B. Michaels. *The Imperial Shah: An Informal Biography*. Boston: Little, Brown and Company, 1976.

Warliamont, Walter. Translated by R. H. Barry. *Inside Hitler's Headquarters: 1939–1945*. New York: Praeger Publishers, 1964.

Werth, Alexander. *Moscow War Diary*. New York: Alfred A. Knopf, 1942.

Weygand, J. Translated by J. H. F. McEwen. *The Role of General Weygand*. London: Eyre and Spottiswoode, 1948.

Weygand, Gen. Maxime, Translated by E. W. Dickes. *Recalled to Service*. Garden City, N.Y.: Doubleday. 1952.

Wilber, Donald N. *Riza Shah Pahlavi*. Hicksville, N.Y.: Exposition Press, 1975.

Woodward, Sir Llewellyen. *British Foreign Policy in the Second World War*. Vol. 1 and 2. London: Her Majesty's Stationery Office, 1970.

Wyndham, Col. Humphrey. *The Household Cavalry at War: First Household Cavalry Regiment*. Aldershot, U.K.: Gale and Polden, 1952.

Yeoman, Yeoman: The Warwickshire Yeomanry: 1920–1956. Birmingham, U.K.: Silk and Terry, 1971.

Zhukov, Mar. Georgi K. *The Memoirs of Marshal Zhukov*. New York: Delacorte Press, 1971.

Index

Abadan, 37, 39–40, 47, 227; refinery built at, 7; vulnerability of refinery, 19; British plans to seize, 17, 19, 24, 64–65, 69–70, 78–79, 81; Iranian security measures, 81–82, 98, 104; attack on, 101–2, 105–6, 113, 117–18, 124, 139, 149, 154–57, 165, 172

Abdullilah, Prince, 34–36

Abwehr, 53–55, 61, 82

Adams, Captain W. L. G., 79–80, 101, 106, 109, 112

Afghanistan, 4, 6, 18, 48, 161

Afkhami, Major, 185

Afrika Korps, 50

Afshar, Lt. Col., 162–63, 168

Ahmad Shah, 8

Ahmadi, Brig. Gen. Ahmad, 184, 214

Ahvaz, 19, 41, 128, 209; British plans to capture, 70, 79, 92, 98; Iranians reinforce, 81–82; 6th Division headquarters, 81, 98, 116, 156, 160–61, 173; reconnaissance of, 81, 153–54, 169; reinforces Abadan-Khorramshahr, 104–5, 118; RAF bombs, 105, 123, 158, 171; British attack, 170, 171, 175; Germans interned through, 193–94, 200, 203, 207

Aizelwood, Brig. J. A., 148; plans advance into Iran, 64, 97, 102; leads column toward Kermanshah, 155–

56; leads column to Hamadan, 184, 186–87; meets Soviets, 190, 192–93; enters Tehran, 216

Ala, Ambassador Hussein, 224–26

Allied Supreme War Council, 21

Amery, Foreign Minister Djevad, 29, 43, 63, 76, 85, 88, 96, 99, 138, 158

Amery, Sir Leopold, 24, 57–58

Anderson, Sir John, 69–70, 72

Anglo-Iranian (Persian) Oil Company (AIOC), 23–34, 57, 69, 78, 105, 115–16, 172, 181; formed to supply Royal Navy, 7; pays higher royalties, 12; assists attack on Abadan, 65, 102, 113, 154

Anglo-Iraqi Treaty of 1939, 37

Anniston City, SS, 112

Ankara, 20, 26

Arak, 157, 204

Aras, Ambassador Teufik Rustu, 89, 96

Araxes River, 132, 134

Ardabil, 104, 136, 143, 151, 158, 167

Arfa, Brig. Gen. Hassan, 31–32, 157, 173, 184, 215–16

Arfa, Col. Ibrahim, 184

Arkwright, 2/Lt John, 164

Arthur Cavanaugh, 79

Ashkabad, 32, 84

Astara, 32, 136–37, 146–47, 152

275

20; refuses to withdraw forces from Iran, 224–25; withdraws forces from Iran, 226; motives analyzed, 228
Stalingrad, 221–22
Stampa, 159
State Department, U.S.: questions British motives toward Iran, 68, 76–77, 84–85, 88, 96, 99; Iran seeks support of, 88, 95, 141; debates reaction to invasion of Iran, 159; Dreyfus reports shah's willingness to assist Allied cause to, 202–3; coordinates policy in Iran with British, 222; warns Truman of Soviet threat in Iran, 223
Steinhardt, Ambassador Laurence A., 21, 201
Storey, Capt. William, 187
Student, Gen. Karl, 42, 44
Sturmfels, 80, 109–111
Sutton, Consul Lester, 227
Syria: role in Allied plans against Caucasus, 20–21; French forces in align with Vichy, 25, 33; Vichy leaders under pressure to support Iraqi rebels, 37; base for Luftwaffe operations in Iraq, 39–40, 45; German threat to Persian Gulf through, 42, 47–48; British plans to defend, 58, 60; British forces drawn from for operations against Iran, 64

Tabatabai, Lt. Col., 129
Tabatabai, Prime Minister Sayyid Zia al-Din, 8
Tabriz: Iranian Army maneuvers near, 26; role in Soviet invasion plan, 32; Soviet military activities north of, 50, 83; German activities in, 53–54, 61, 66, 82; role in German plans, 59; Soviets bomb, 134–35, 141, 149, 152, 158, 180; Iranian Army evacuates, 136, 141, 147, 151, 153, 186; Germans evacuate, 142–43; Soviets occupy, 138, 142, 146–47, 151, 167, 178, 182; Soviets encourage Armenian separatism in, 194; Iranian

Communists establish government in, 224–25; Iranian Army reoccupies, 226–27
Talishkive Gory Mountains, 104, 136
Tanuma, 79, 103–105, 125
Tashkent, 6, 48, 50
TASS, 49, 226
Tayfuri, Major, 116, 154, 161, 165
Tbilisi, 22, 46, 83
Tehran, 24, 26, 29, 43, 58, 60, 62, 80, 82, 87, 100, 103, 107, 122, 125, 136, 138, 140, 155, 162, 166, 168, 179–80, 182, 220; capital of Persia, 5; greets Soviet transit approval of German goods, 15; possible base for bombing Caucasus, 20; role in Soviet invasion plan, 32, 83–84; Soviet officials exaggerate incidents, 46; German activities in, 54–56, 99, 200; base for German advance south, 59; British plans to bomb, 64, 67–68; Iranian reinforcements depart from, 91; invasion notes delivered in, 103, 138, 140; Germans depart Tabriz for, 142–43; citizens learn of invasion, 144; Iranian Army deploys to defend, 145–46, 157; confusion and fear in, 149–50, 197; army commandeers vehicles in, 158; popular discontent in, 157, 166, 183–86, 190–92, 194, 197–98, 200–201, 203, 209; Soviets advance toward, 167, 180, 183; Iranian officials depart Meshed to, 170; Soviets bomb, 173, 189, 191; martial law declared in, 184–85; German efforts to remove citizens from, 187, 193, 199; Iranian conscripts released in, 189, 194, 198; occupied by Allies, 189, 194, 201–5, 209–210, 212–17; Germans arrested in, 206–7, 215–16; Allied forces withdraw from, 219; Tripartite Treaty concluded in, 220; Tehran Conference held in, 223; Soviets advance toward in 1946, 225; informed of Communist collapse in Tabriz, 227

ABOUT THE AUTHOR

RICHARD A. STEWART is a Major in the U.S. Marine Corps in which he specializes in intelligence and communications. He has published numerous articles on political-military affairs and history in such professional journals as the *Army War College Journal, U.S. Naval Institute Proceedings, Armed Forces Journal International,* and the *Marine Corps Gazette.* A 1973 graduate of the U.S. Naval Academy, he has a Master's degree in Government from Georgetown University.